SCANDAL, SENSATION AND
SOCIAL DEMOCRACY

D1542856

SCANDAL, SENSATION AND SOCIAL DEMOCRACY

THE SPD PRESS AND WILHELMINE GERMANY 1890–1914

ALEX HALL

CAMBRIDGE UNIVERSITY PRESS

CAMBRIDGE

LONDON · NEW YORK · MELBOURNE

Published by the Syndics of the Cambridge University Press
The Pitt Building, Trumpington Street, Cambridge CB2 IRP
Bentley House, 200 Euston Road, London NW1 2DB
32 East 57th Street, New York, NY 10022, USA
296 Beaconsfield Parade, Middle Park, Melbourne 3206, Australia

First published 1977

Printed in Great Britain by
Western Printing Services Ltd, Bristol

Library of Congress Cataloguing in Publication Data
Hall, Alex, 1948 –
Scandal, sensation, and social democracy.
Includes bibliographical references and index.
1. Sozialdemokratische Partei Deutschlands.
2. Press, Political party – Germany – History.
I. Title.
JN3946.S83H32   1977   329.9'43   76–46856
ISBN 0–521–21531–5

TO MY PARENTS

It happens to be the fate of German governments – forever and a day against their will – to develop an effective propaganda for Social Democracy.

Paul Singer at the 1907 party conference

CONTENTS

ACKNOWLEDGMENTS

Anyone engaged in a study of aspects of German Social Democracy between 1890 and 1914 is heavily dependent on government files and the party press for source materials. Little remains by way of private correspondence, since so much was destroyed for reasons of organisational security. There are very few diaries of leading socialists of the period which may be consulted, and in the case of that kept by Hermann Molkenbuhr – housed in the Archiv der Friedrich-Ebert-Stiftung in Bonn – only the period between 1904 and 1907 is extant. Moreover, the recollections of leading party journalists and activists, though valuable in themselves, are often marked by inaccuracies of fact and suffer from the influence of later political developments. The Social Democratic Press, however, which encompassed all shades of opinion within the movement, provides not only a useful means of orientation on the political spectrum, but also reveals much about the isolation experienced by the Wilhelmine SPD. Reactions by officialdom, especially to events in which the party was directly involved, can be gauged most easily from the reports prepared by the internal administration, as well as from the marginalia made on press cuttings by departmental heads and senior police officials.

It is to be regretted that despite recent improvements in diplomatic relations, the Government of the German Democratic Republic (DDR) still continues to deny scholars free access to its archives. Two separate applications for permission to use materials housed in the Zentralstaatsarchiv Potsdam and Merseburg, as well as a request for access to newspaper sources in the Institut für Marxismus-Leninismus in East Berlin, were rejected without explanation. This has almost inevitably led to certain deficiencies in the presentation of detailed deliberations leading to the formulation of government policy.

The research for this book, which was undertaken primarily for a doctoral dissertation of the University of Cambridge, would not have been possible without generous financial assistance from the German Academic Exchange Service (DAAD) and the Volkswagen Foundation, to whom I am deeply grateful. I owe a special debt to the staff of the

Staatsarchiv in Hamburg for their unfailing courtesy and cooperation, and I should like to express my thanks to the staff of all the archives of the German *Länder* and West Berlin which I visited, as well as to the staff of the Internationaal Instituut voor Sociale Geschiedenis in Amsterdam. My greatest debt, however, is to those teachers and friends through whose generous help I have enormously profited: Dr Jonathan Steinberg, Dr John C. G. Röhl, Prof. Fritz Fischer, Prof. Wolfgang J. Mommsen, Prof. Volker Berghahn, Dr Klaus Wernecke, Prof. Peter-Christian Witt and Herr Dietrich Ellger. I thank them all.

Hamburg, November 1975   ALEX HALL

PROLOGUE

In reality we have, therefore, 'the Bismarckian system' and as long as the state remains a *Klassenstaat* things will not change.

Vorwärts, 12 May 1891

All nations sooner or later have to come to terms with their past, but in Germany this seems – for obvious reasons – to have been a somewhat painful process, and the recent attempts at overcoming the past (*Bewältigung der Vergangenheit*) have been closely concerned with the circumstances surrounding the transition from the monarchical nation-state created in 1871 to the totalitarian dictatorship of the Third Reich. That the connections between the two are rather more broadly-based than was at first assumed emerged most dramatically in Fritz Fischer's study of German war aims in the First World War,[1] which for all its emphasis on foreign affairs clearly pointed to the intermeshing of domestic considerations. In the wake of the controversy surrounding the Fischer thesis, German historiography in the 1960s turned increasingly towards the problem of continuity in recent history, in the direction of uncovering the origins of anti-democratic thought and practice and analysing the institutional weaknesses which led to the collapse of the Weimar experiment and the steady advance of fascism. The controversy and tendentious argument to which German historical writing has often been prey[2] became reflected in the conscious shift from political and diplomatic history to studies in which social and economic considerations played a formative role. At the same time, the re-discovery of Eckart Kehr's treatise on the 'Primat der Innenpolitik'[3] pointed the way towards more detailed work on the structure and organisation of imperial society. Underpinning these efforts was a natural tendency to question previous, somewhat nostalgic, assumptions about the 'golden era' of Wilhelmine Germany, which had led a distinguished historian of the older school to describe the country of his youth as 'bathed in a kind of radiance that did not begin to darken until the outbreak of war in 1914'.[4] Above all, the approach of some historians who argued that

I

Imperial Germany was indeed making a peaceful transition to a more genuine form of democracy by 1914, was put in question by new evidence that the much-vaunted concept of the *Rechtsstaat* was rather a hollow one, in the context of the treatment of minority groups and political opponents.

Much has now been revealed about the nature of that imperial system, with its trappings of a constitutional *Rechtsstaat* yet scarcely-veiled face of monarchical absolutism, and the ideology which infused government and administration at all levels.[5] This book is in part an attempt to illuminate some of the divisions which ran through society, affecting as they did the fate and fortunes of the Social Democratic movement. It is not specifically a book about the history of the party political press, but it does aim to focus on the intricacies of the relationships between that press and a state in which Social Democrats found themselves rejected and despised by the political establishment and circumscribed by a plethora of legal restrictions. In doing so, it highlights the fact that the struggle against the SPD was the government's most difficult internal problem and, indeed, up to the first Moroccan crisis caused it more anxiety than external affairs.[6]

It is characteristic that the *Staatsideologie* which underlay the creation of the Second Reich in 1871 owed much to the absolutist tradition which had persisted in the individual states since the Thirty Years War and had conditioned people to a large amount of direction from above. The influence of Lutheranism, which denied the right of resistance against even tyrannical rulers and sanctified the principle of divine right, and Hegelian philosophy as preached in the Prussian universities from 1820, which elevated the state as opposed to the individual, and created the myth of the neutrality of the organs of state (*Überparteilichkeit*), fashioned an attitude in which sovereignty, in contrast to other European countries, rested with the monarch and not the people.[7] The acceptance of authority began in the parental home and school and continued in society at large with a respect for titles, noble birth and military rank, and particularly for those who as reserve army officers represented the country's highest social élite. Moreover, since the Reich had been practically created on the battlefields of three wars – in 1864, 1866 and 1870–1 – it was inevitable that politics would suffer from an inordinately strong military influence. And in a situation where only the state was viewed as being able to represent the whole as against the particularism of social and religious groups and political parties, liberalism remained an ineffective force.[8] That political power throughout nineteenth-century Germany was dynastic in origin and inspiration had been underlined by the failure of the 1848 reform movement in the Paulskirche.

Kaiser Wilhelm II built more consciously than any of his immediate predecessors on the received traditions of the medieval concept of *Kaisertum*.[9] He himself took every opportunity to demonstrate his unshakable belief in the historical validity of the divine right of kings (*Gottesgnadentum*). At his coronation ceremony, for example, the senior court chaplain, Oberhofprediger Kögel, was commanded to preach on the subject of 'Von Gottes Gnaden bin ich, der ich bin', and ever afterwards the Kaiser liked to repeat these words as if they applied to him and to no other being, alive or dead.[10]

Since imperial power in the Wilhelmine era had both a secular and religious justification, political dissent was often construed as both treason against the state and also blasphemy. Indeed, the Kaiser never tired of reiterating the significance of Church dogma as a cornerstone of his central political philosophy. In November 1897, he declared to a group of army recruits, 'He who is not an honest Christian cannot be an upright man nor a Prussian soldier, and cannot possibly fulfil that which is expected of a soldier in the Prussian army.'[11]

This conscious and deliberate association between loyalty to the monarchist cause and support for those agencies whose function was to provide the bulwarks of social and political stability, principally the Church, the civil service and the army, seriously weakened democratic forces in the state and merely underlined the degree of crushing autocratic rule under which Wilhelmine Germany moved into the twentieth century. The nature of this *Obrigkeitsstaat*, which was little more than a variation of popular absolutism,[12] made any kind of opposition extremely difficult and unrewarding. In 1890, for instance, the Kaiser hit out at the liberal press, declaring it to be the work of 'depraved sixthformers',[13] and two years later, at a banquet of the Brandenburg provincial diet, he attracted further attention by attacking the 'moaning minnies' of Wilhelmine society, who he hoped would remove themselves as quickly as possible from German soil.[14]

As Prussian monarch and German Emperor, Wilhelm II was endowed with a number of important prerogatives, including his right to appoint and dismiss both the Chancellor and officials of the Reich as well as his Prussian ministers. As King of Prussia his power extended over two-thirds of the territory of the Reich. As such he was supreme commander of the army, head of the civil service and diplomatic corps and also responsible for the administrative apparatus of the Reich ministries. Both here and within the fields of military and foreign policy, the

German parliament or Reichstag had no practical jurisdiction. In addition, as the result of a special arrangement between Bismarck and Wilhelm I, the military had been removed altogether from the area of competence of the Reich Chancellor, and enjoyed a relationship of special trust with and direct loyalty to the Kaiser. As a result, the army became entirely encapsulated from the rest of society.

With the accession in 1888 of Wilhelm II, a man of fixed and determined views,[15] the mutual understanding in the division of power between the Kaiser and his Chancellor, and simultaneously between the Prussian monarch and his Minister-President, was shattered, to the extent that Bismarck's view increasingly became that 'the real and factual Minister-President in Prussia is and remains His Majesty the King'.[16] The way in which the Kaiser was able to extend his personal influence over the entire bureaucracy of the Reich affecting decision-making at all levels, has itself been the subject of academic controversy.[17] His political adversaries, however, were in no doubt as to the reality of his personal power. A leading Social Democratic deputy in the Reichstag, Karl Frohme, castigated in February 1900 the 'rule of personal will' and 'pure absolutism' in Germany.[18] Moreover, the capacity of the Kaiser to govern as he wished was underlined by the growing size and influence of his three separate and autonomous, personal secretariats, the *Zivilkabinett*, *Militärkabinett* and *Marinekabinett*, which were often the only means of contact between the Kaiser and the affairs of state. Such was the level of activity that towards the end of the Kaiser's reign, the Civil Cabinet employed 17 officials (*Hofbeamte*) and was responsible for processing some 70–80,000 items a year.[19]

Despite some attempts to suggest that the position of the Prussian state was far from central to the future political development of the Reich,[20] there is no doubt that the weight of Prussian social and political traditions strongly characterised the institutions of the Reich. As Bebel remarked during the 1910 party conference,

The Prussian state is a thing of its own. Prussia is unique in the world. There is no second Prussian state. When we have conquered this Prussian state then we shall possess everything. It will entail effort and work and sweat and it may well entail much more.[21]

This realisation of Prussian dominance was felt especially keenly by those representatives of South German traditions, who viewed the decisive influence of Prussian policy-making with considerable alarm.[22] The increasing stream of legislation at the Reich level involved perforce all the individual states in new, closely-binding relationships, so that the

Prussian-dominated organisation of the Reich began to encroach more and more on the jealously-guarded rights of the states.

The responsibility for securing a harmonious equilibrium between the conflicting interests of federal unity and provincial separatism rested with the Reich Chancellor as guardian of the imperial constitution of 1871, a patchwork affair which soon began to show all its seams. Under this constitution there was in fact only one minister, the Reich Chancellor himself, who was also chairman of both the Bundesrat and the Prussian Ministry of State. Thus, the Reich tended to be effectively ruled through the Minstry of State, the more so since the absence of a Reich government as such – there was no 'Reichsregierung', only a 'Reichsleitung' – meant that the meetings of the Ministry of State developed into a regular forum for the discussion of Reich affairs.[23]

Because of the separation of responsibilities, the Chancellor was practically the only link between the various arms of the executive and had to spend considerable energy and effort in ensuring a balance between them. He was not, of course, a politician who owed his position to a rôle as leader of the strongest party in the Reichstag but, like the State Secretaries, a political servant of the Kaiser. His dependence on the Crown was not offset by the certainty of massed parliamentary support and, indeed, with one exception,[24] successive Chancellors refrained from attempting to organise coalitions. This attitude tends to accord with the view taken by a conservative parliamentarian of the period, Count Westarp,[25] that the formulation of policy was not a matter for deputies in the Reichstag, but entirely within the preserve of the allied governments under the leadership of Prussia. Indeed, the very instability of parliamentary coalitions strengthened the determination of the *Reichsleitung* wherever possible to avoid the politically awkward policy of governing through the Reichstag.

That the organisation of the Reich under Prussian leadership was not directed towards the sharing of power and responsibility had been recognised by Wilhelm Liebknecht as early as 1871, when he commented that the newly-created empire was 'an insurance against democracy'. It was self-evident in the popular description of the Reichstag as a mere 'talking-shop' (*Schwatzbude*), whose imposing building was in marked contrast to the paucity of its powers,[26] and in the attitude of the Kaiser, who declared that he could not care less whether 'red, black or yellow monkeys jumped around in the Reichstag cage'.[27] As the Prussian Minister of the Interior, von Köller, insisted in a speech to the Reichstag in 1895, though that body might decide to refuse approval to specific items of legislation, whether or not bills were submitted for discussion was entirely a matter for the allied governments.[28] At the same time, there was a constant need to come to some kind of arrangement with the Reichstag, if only to ensure the smooth passage of legislation, but the need to work with both the Reichstag and the Prussian Landtag, with their differing composition and opposing views, led to paralysing difficulties. At one stage, Chancellor Caprivi had to depend on the SPD for parliamentary approval of his trade treaties with Russia, whilst at the same time discussing measures for combating the socialist movement. The result was 'a tangled political situation'.[29]

These difficulties became increasingly apparent after the fall of Bismarck and during the politics of the 'new course' in the 1890s. It was not simply the fact that compared with Bismarck, his successors appeared like political pygmies – although the determination of the Kaiser to rule certainly did not permit the emergence of a strongly-independent Reich Chancellor – but more a reflection of the strains and stresses brought about by Bismarck's various constitutional compromises. What had seemed eminently suitable in 1871, before the full impact of industrialisation and the political challenge posed by organised labour, no longer seemed tenable twenty years later. Whereas in 1871 64% of the population had lived in villages of less than 2,000 inhabitants, by 1895 this had fallen to 36%. But the explosive impact of industrialisation on the fabric of society was not matched by any adjustments in political power and responsibility. On the contrary, the pre-industrial, largely feudal-agrarian élite, represented by the Prussian Junker class, found itself fighting a rearguard action against the increasing political demands of the rising industrial classes.[30] By the 1880s industry had already overtaken agriculture in its structural importance to the German economy, and Caprivi's trade treaties were an attempt to make the necessary transformation into a modern industrial state. They succeeded in arousing the bitter hostility of the agrarians, who set about plotting Caprivi's downfall.[31] In reacting to this crisis, the Prussian Junkers attempted to shore up their position within society by consolidating and, wherever possible, extending their political influence as a form of compensation for their weakened economic standing.

Instead of resolving this crisis, however, the Reichsleitung attempted to neutralise its political significance by diverting attention towards a new concept of 'plebiscitary politics',[32] in which monarchical charisma was combined with imperialist aims and the fashioning of a popular political base for the nationalist aspirations of the ruling élite. Thus was born the concept of *Weltpolitik*, Imperial Germany's expression of her newly-found world power status. With the creation of a

6

world-class fleet, middle-class support was to be mobilised behind the existing power structure of the Reich. Thus the *Flottenpolitik* programme was intended to serve in many respects as a lightning conductor for the failure to resolve domestic political tensions as well as an instrument for starving Social Democracy of its popular mass appeal.[33] This central strategy was designed essentially to shore up the internal security of the Reich. Such was its importance that during the Hamburg docks strike in the winter of 1896, the English syndicalist and trade union leader Tom Mann was speedily deported. Leading conservative newspapers claimed that the strike had been engineered by British commercial circles, and suggested that Mann's presence in the city was part of a concerted attempt to frustrate the construction of the new German battle-fleet and incite revolution amongst the working-class.

This constant fear of the potential threat from organised Social Democracy characterised official policy right up to 1914. It was the failure of Wilhelm II and his ministers to deal a mortal blow to the SPD, which was far from being the 'passing phenomenon' that the Kaiser thought it was in 1899, which led, on the one hand, to the incessant search for an 'external' solution to Germany's problems and, on the other hand, accounted for repeated attempts to organise an effective coalition of anti-socialist forces. Thus, *Sammlungspolitik* in all its manifestations became the domestic counterpart to the policy of *Weltpolitik*.

From the creation of the Reich onwards, Bismarck had sought to identify publicly those groups within society on whom the *Reichsleitung* could depend for support and goodwill (*Reichsfreunde*) and those who were branded as enemies of the state (*Reichsfeinde*). The Guelphs, Danes and Poles, inhabitants of Alsace-Lorraine and advocates of the '*großdeutsch*' solution all belonged to the latter category, but because of their small size and relative insignificance they could hardly be regarded as effective scapegoats for the nation's troubles. Political Catholicism and Social Democracy were of a very different order. Throughout the 1870s Bismarck pursued a relentless campaign against the Catholic Church (*Kulturkampf*), whilst simultaneously wooing the more conservative liberals, thus bringing about a permanent division of interests between political liberalism and the humanitarianism of the Centre Party. Bismarck regarded the Catholic Habsburg influence as inimical to the Reich and Prussian hegemony, but the wheel was to turn full circle before his fall from power, as he desperately sought to establish a new consensus of interests to resolve the constitutional dilemma.[34]

Bismarck's reasons for opposing socialism were strongly influenced by the history of the Paris Commune and the support given to the

Communards by leading German socialists, as well as by the activities of the Russian anarcho-nihilist movement. The last quarter of the nineteenth century witnessed an increasing challenge to concepts of traditional thought and political organisation. A gradual awareness that man was no longer a divine being, but rather a product of his heredity and environment, had been triggered off in the 1860s by Ernest Haeckel's pioneering work in the natural sciences, with its emphasis on the didactic importance of experiment and observation. These developments in analytical thinking were echoed in the political writings of Marx and Engels, as well as in the philosophy of determinism which characterised the works of German literary naturalism in the 1880s and 1890s. Such thoughts about the rôle of man in society and the organisation of the social framework in which he found himself became particularly acute at a time of rapid economic and social change. The considerable growth in population and the ensuing flight from the land into the industrial conurbations upset the traditional patterns of social behaviour, and emphasised the increasing importance of the masses and their political organisation.[35] The insistent demands for political and social emancipation from the German working class began a process of self-identification and differentiation from other traditional forms of social organisation – the nobility (*Adelstand*), the peasantry (*Bauerntum*) and the bourgeoisie (*Bürgertum*). It was this awareness, and the ensuing conflicts with the antique social and political élite which alone exercised effective power, that gave Social Democracy its chance.

In more practical terms, Bismarck's bitter struggle against the socialists owed much to their very real threat to the foundations of imperial society – to the institution of the monarchy, to traditional ethical and religious values, to the security of the Reich through the movement's overt internationalism, and not least to the continuing domination by the Junker class.[36] The result of years of stigmatisation as 'a society of bandits' left its mark on public consciousness. A leading historian, lawyer and friend of Ludwig Bamberger and Theodor Barth could write in 1891 that Social Democracy was 'the greatest enemy of parliamentarianism',[37] and the historian Friedrich Meinecke, writing in 1910, described the essence of conservative internal policy as a latent civil war against the SPD, fought with all the methods of the police state.[38] But one of the clearest expressions of the social and political divide came in May 1914 from the leading Centre Party politician, Matthias Erzberger:

The greatest internal problem with which the Reich is confronted is the smashing of the mighty power of Social Democracy; beside this problem all other questions

8

pale into insignificance. The Progressives have become an appendage of Social Democracy and now stand aloof. The Centre, National Liberals and Conservatives must collectively take up the struggle and its consequences with every determination. There is no other more necessary task than that which now confronts us and the next generation would never be able to free us from the taint of party egoism and the justified accusation of political short-sightedness and incompetence, were we to fail them now . . .[39]

The ease with which such notions were accepted as perfectly legitimate by wide sections of society casts a dark cloud not only over any pretensions to political democracy in the Wilhelmine era, but also over the nature of the Bismarckian inheritance. Writing in 1917, Max Weber attacked the widespread uncritical admiration for Bismarck, who

left behind him a nation without any form of political education . . . a nation without any kind of independent political will, accustomed to the fact that the great statesman at the helm would concern himself with political matters. Furthermore, as a result of the improper use of monarchism as a camouflage for his own power ambitions in internal party politics, he bequeathed a nation fatalistically prepared to accept unquestioningly those solutions propounded under the banner of the monarchical government, without doubting the political qualifications of those who eased themselves into Bismarck's empty chair and took up the reins of government with such astonishing ease.[40]

Far from bequeathing a socially harmonious nation, Bismarck had in fact left behind him a Germany glaring with social and economic inequalities and political disenfranchisement. The fact that in 1913 a higher official of the state still continued to earn seven times as much as an unskilled labourer added point to the *Simplicissimus* joke that 'Social Democrats are people who work and have no money.' At the other end of society, considerable wealth was concentrated in the hands of a few individuals. The President of the Reichstag, Count Ballestrem, himself had a private fortune of 56 million marks. In the circumstances it is not surprising that Walter Rathenau, in a letter to a friend in 1917, regarded the separation of individual classes (*Stände*) as so strong that he could only recall one case in the previous 30 years where the son of a worker had advanced to a position of respectability in the bourgeois world.[41]

The diplomatic corps and the upper echelons of the administration continued to remain the preserve of the aristocracy. In 1910, of the 11 members of the Prussian Ministry of State 9 were nobles, as were 11 out of the 12 heads of the provincial governments (*Oberpräsidenten*) and 271 of the 467 prefects (*Landräte*).[42] Indeed, the proportion of aristocrats amongst the trainees in civil administration (*Regierungs-referendare*) actually increased from 40% in 1890 to 55% of the total

9

in 1910.[43] By 1916, no less than 57% of all political civil servants in Prussia were of noble birth.[44] Even so, membership of all-important exclusive societies, such as the student corporations and the reserve officer corps, religious affiliations and social connections often mattered as much as mere aristocratic pedigree.[45]

At the political level, the principle of reaction in Prussia was best exemplified by the three-class voting system. In the period after 1890, 4% of the population were in the first class and 84% in the third,[46] and despite numerous efforts at reform this iniquitous franchise remained in force until 1918. Moreover, Social Democrats were often the victims of artful schemes of disenfranchisement; in many polling-stations only conservative ballot papers were 'available' and voters were subjected to various forms of intimidation and economic blackmail. There is at least one case of organised terror, when in 1890 some 500 supporters of a Social Democratic candidate, who had come to campaign on his behalf, were forcibly driven out of a village near Berlin by a group of enraged farmers and labourers.[47]

Wilhelmine Germany did not have the equivalent of §109 of the Weimar constitution, which stipulated that all Germans were equal before the law. It did, however, have a corpus of legal statutes which were increasingly used as an instrument of control. Having tried (and failed) to combat the popular dynamism of the Social Democratic movement by means of a special emergency law, the *Ausnahmegesetz*, successive governments fell back upon existing legal sanctions as a means of enforcing their legitimacy. The fact that the law tended to shroud itself in all kinds of complexities and obscurities, on the principle of *omnis definitio in jure periculosa*, enabled a subtle method of manipulation to be deployed in the institutional struggle against Social Democracy. This complex interplay between the law and the fortunes of the SPD is one of the underlying themes of this study.

It is one of the curiosities and fascinations of the Wilhelmine age that its society presents a kind of double image, of thrustful economic advance and a self-assured conduct of international affairs, and of doom-laden portents of a final cataclysm, which in 1914 did indeed sweep away the old European order. Eye-catching statistics merely hint at the vast structural changes taking place in Imperial Germany. Thus, the population increased between 1890 and 1910 from 49.5 million to 65 million, and the numbers employed in one of the new sectors of growth, the electrical industry, rose dramatically from 26,000 in 1895 to 107,000 in 1906. Similarly, the value of German exports tripled from 7.6 billion marks in 1890 to 22.5 billion marks in 1913, and such unparalleled economic achievements were reflected in the increase in the number of millionaires in Prussia alone, from 5,256 in 1895 to 9,341 in 1911.[48] At the same time, the incidence of scandal and sensation in Wilhelmine society, at many different levels and in many different forms, quite apart from literary preoccupations with decadence, strengthened the impression of an impending collapse. It was the repeated and skilful exploitation of this awareness in the Social Democratic press that represented a cornerstone of socialist propaganda.

The principal focus of this study rests on what the SPD press itself chose to regard as the shocking evidence that all was far from well with Imperial Germany, together with an account of the operational difficulties which party journalists faced in the pursuance of these aims. The development of this kind of agitatory journalism took place against the background of new-found possibilities in the field of mass communications. The increasing opportunities for rapid and effective dissemination of news and political comment created a new industry, with newspapers appearing virtually around the clock. Technical improvements increased the speed with which ordinary citizens in different parts of the Reich could be kept in touch with political developments in Berlin. The extent of these operations was such that at the turn of the century the annual newsprint requirements for the daily papers published by the Ullstein group alone was of the order of 4,164 tons. Socialist newspapers thus had to survive in a world in which competition from the bourgeois press and its powerful magnates like August Scherl was very keen, not least in the capacity to offer a potential readership a stimulating diet of popular journalism.

But as well as reflecting the characteristics of an imperial age on the edge of a disaster, the Social Democratic press simultaneously mirrored the ideological ferment which swept through the party and dictated the nature of its response to the pinpricks of absolutism. One of the most important questions which has yet satisfactorily to be answered is the reason for the continuing hold which revolutionary Marxist ideology exercised over the party right up to 1914. Despite the contradictions of theory and practice and the strains and stresses occasioned by ideological controversy, the fact remains that throughout the period of August Bebel's leadership the party remained an overtly Marxist party, averring its fundamental opposition to the Reich. This study is in part an attempt to explain that paradox.

I

SOCIAL DEMOCRACY IN IMPERIAL GERMANY

In waging our war we do not throw bombs, but instead we throw our newspapers amongst the masses of the working people. Printing ink is our explosive.

Hamburger Echo, 27 September 1910

We should never forget that we are first and foremost still a party of propaganda. Our most important practical task is at present much less the conquest of power than the conquest of the masses.

Karl Kautsky in *Die neue Zeit*, October 1903

The party

From its earliest days, the political organisations of the German working class had encompassed a wide spectrum of opinion. Some six years after the formation in 1863 of the *Allgemeiner Deutscher Arbeiterverein* by Ferdinand Lassalle, a more determined brand of radicalism led to the creation in Eisenach of the *Sozialdemokratische Arbeiterpartei*, into which was merged the *Demokratische Volkspartei* of Saxony. It was dominated from the beginning by two of the most powerful figures in the history of German socialism, Wilhelm Liebknecht and August Bebel. It was their refusal to support Bismarck's war credits in 1870, especially after the obvious collapse of Napoleon III's empire, together with their endorsements of the Communards and the resulting Leipzig court sentences for treason which clearly identified the movement with a revolutionary tradition.

Three years after the forging of unity between the rival wings with the formation in 1875 of the *Sozialistische Arbeiterpartei Deutschlands* and the drawing up of the Gotha political programme, Bismarck endeavoured to persuade the German Reichstag to pass an 'exceptional law', designed to strike at the growing popular appeal of the party. It was only after two attempts on the life of Kaiser Wilhelm I in May and June of 1878, allegedly by socialist agitators, and the mounting of a concerted campaign of hate and invective against the party, that Bismarck secured the passage of the bill.[1] §1 of the *Sozialistengesetz* provided for sweeping powers of suppression:

Political associations which, by furthering Social Democratic, socialist or communist objectives, aim at an overthrow of the existing state and social order, are to be prohibited. The same applies to associations in which Social Democratic, socialist or communist objectives, directed towards the overthrow of the existing state and social order, are manifested, in ways calculated to endanger the public peace and especially the harmony amongst differing social classes.

Other sections of this law provided for the prohibition and dissolution of meetings suspected of pursuing such aims, made illegal the collection of individual membership fees and punished those who made available public rooms for party business with prison sentences of up to twelve months. In addition, the power of an increased police surveillance (*Belagerungszustand*) was successively invoked in Berlin, Hamburg-Altona, Harburg, Leipzig, Frankfurt am Main, Hanau, Offenbach, Stettin and Spremberg, from which 893 persons were expelled, of whom 504 were married men with children. During the following twelve years until the lapse of the anti-socialist laws in September 1890, some 352 political associations were dissolved and 1,229 different publications, including 104 newspapers and periodicals, were banned.[2]

Although the party was initially compliant, hoping to avoid as much harassment and repression as possible, it gradually became clear that illegal and sometimes conspiratorial activity could not be avoided. Skeleton local party organisations remained basically intact, largely under the guise of non-political activities such as gymnastics and music-making, but they depended to a large extent on the mutual trust of small inner groups. As a result, a feeling of intense loyalty to the 'cause' was built up, which positively encouraged the development of local centres of radicalism, if only because of the many personal risks which were involved. This period in which the party was driven into clandestine activities and ingenious circumventions of the law, simply in order to retain some form of organisational structure, left a deep psychological scar on the collective group-consciousness of the movement. Right up to the outbreak of war in 1914, the SPD was able to play on the emotional legacy of these twelve years of contempt, discrimination and isolation, and to forge a special kind of 'historical memory', which manifested itself in suspicion, caution and a determination to seize maximum political advantage from those situations resulting from the misfortunes of government. As early as 1881, Eduard Bernstein indicated in an article in the *Sozialdemokrat* the future strategy which the party intended to deploy:

Our deputies are sent to the Reichstag to raise the voice of the proletariat, the voice of the suffering, the persecuted and the oppressed . . . they are the representatives of the disinherited and the outlawed.[3]

The years of public vilification, during which the party was given daily reminders of its position as an outcast from society, also succeeded in radicalising the basic ideology of the movement. The first explicit linking of party philosophy with the ideas of Karl Marx came in a statement which prefaced the published minutes of the Copenhagen party congress of March 1883. Yet Marxism was principally understood as an economic and social analysis, not as a political programme. It offered a convincing explanation for the conflict within society and the active discrimination against the working class by its oppressors, as well as providing a vision that one day such misery would vanish. At the same time, the prospect of working through the parliamentary system seemed less than enchanting. Since the German Reichstag was hardly a centre of power, there was little to be gained by using parliamentary action as an instrument for improvement and reform. Such considerations tended to produce an attitude of ambivalence and indifference, and did little to push the party towards accepting the constitutional system.[4]

When in 1890 German Social Democracy emerged from the darkness of the previous twelve years, it was convinced not only of its fundamental irreconcilability with the bourgeois system, but also of the impending collapse of the capitalist order. There was, therefore, little prospect of the party seeking a political, still less an ideological, rapprochement with the architects of the new course in the early 1890s. This was underlined by the new party programme, adopted in Erfurt in 1891, which stood for 34 years until the revisions made in 1925 and incorporated in the Heidelberg programme. The first of its two sections outlined the fundamental transformation which would follow the breakdown of capitalism but, despite its Marxist approach, it studiously avoided any reference to the word 'revolution', which might have provoked action from the authorities.[5]

Speaking at the party conference which approved both the programme and the movement's new identity as the *Sozialdemokratische Partei Deutschlands*, August Bebel declared that capitalist society was working busily towards its own collapse and the SPD need only wait for the moment when power would fall into its hands.[6] A motion proposed by Bebel, asserting that the continuing tactic of the party in the long struggle ahead was to make maximum effective use of opportunities for political propaganda, rather than hope for a sudden death-blow to the regime, was passed overwhelmingly.[7] In his 're-interpretation' of the Erfurt programme in the following year, Karl Kautsky underlined the folly in assuming too rapid a transformation:

Revolutions are prepared in economic and political struggles lasting years and decades, and take place during constant shifts and fluctuations in the power relationships between different classes and parties, often interrupted by setbacks of a long duration.[8]

No one had a more decisive influence on the continuing *Prinzipien-festigkeit* of the Wilhelmine SPD than Bebel. His was a remarkably astute form of leadership, which combined tactical shrewdness with absolute emotional commitment. It was his capacity for understanding the strains placed on the movement from without, by continuing forms of political repression, and from within, by attempts at adjusting the ideological focus, which prevented the party from collapsing into several warring factions. Such was the extent of his personal influence that a contemporary English observer could write, 'August Bebel is not only the leader of the Social Democratic Party. He is the Party.'[9] Amongst the files of the Berlin political police for July 1908 was a reference to the degree with which Bebel identified himself with the party and it with him, followed by a query, 'whether it might not be Bebel's illness which was having such an adverse effect on the party, or whether it might not be the malaise of the party which was the deeper cause of Bebel's present ill-health'.[10]

What mattered to Bebel above all else and what led the Austrian socialist leader Victor Adler to characterise the SPD as providing both 'the family home and the stuff of life',[11] was generating the dedication and idealism which alone promised the future success of the movement. Without this central concept of inspiration the party could not exist,[12] and if it were to succeed it would always need a spirit of sacrifice, pugnacity and boundless enthusiasm.[13]

It is a concomitant of the optimistic confidence that the old order would be swept away that socialist thought in the 1890s was imbued with the belief in a *Zukunftsstaat*, in an ideal republic which was within the bounds of political realisation. This became apparent in the out-pouring of socialist literature by 'idealistic' writers, who cast novels and political memoirs in a future age – in some cases actually before 1914 – when the socialist millennium had already been achieved.[14] The importance of this visionary ideology led to the development of a quite distinctive socialist sub-culture within society, nourished by the bitter rancour caused by the Sozialistengesetz and which, with its celebration of May Day and its manifold organisational activities, strengthened the feeling of separateness from bourgeois society. Sharing in this community of interests were many of the other 'outsiders' within society such as Jews, whose enthusiasm and identification with many of the ideals of the Social Democratic movement led to positions of considerable responsibility in the party organisation.[15]

In underlining the special situation in which it considered itself, the SPD succeeded in evoking an equally blunt response from those on the other side of the ideological trenches. On the occasion of further socialist electoral successes in 1894, Maximilian Harden wrote in his diary,

Herr Wilhelm Liebknecht has received a huge pile of votes so that he can ruin the state, society and all legitimate authorities as quickly and as thoroughly as possible. That is his profession.[16]

Much more forceful was the analysis of a Lutheran priest, who claimed in his war-cry[17] that there were seven factors separating the socialists from society at large: the monstrousness of the party's exaggerations, the deliberate stoking-up of dissatisfaction, the fanciful dream of a socialist Zukunftsstaat, the lack of patriotism (*Vaterlandslosigkeit*), the party's attitudes to marriage, family life and religion, and its revolutionary convictions.

It was the steadfastly radical tone of official party pronouncements which, when coupled with increasing evidence of a socialist electoral advance,[18] led to an accentuation of the ideological divide between the SPD and the establishment. Indeed, at a time when there were no 'dialogues' between government and governed and few opportunities for informal contacts,[19] public utterances were seized upon as confirmation of long-standing suspicions. Thus, Bebel's declaration at the 1903 party conference, 'I shall remain the mortal enemy of this society and social system, in order to sap its very life and, if I can, to eliminate it altogether',[20] was regarded in government circles as indicative of the continuing revolutionary intentions of the SPD.

The awareness of such potential dangers to the security of the state largely conditioned the response of the Reichsleitung to developments after the lapse of the Sozialistengesetz. In practice, there were those who favoured a more conciliatory approach and increasingly placed their hopes in a tempering of the SPD's strident and implacable hostility. However, the reception given by the party to a package of new measures in 1891, incorporating such reforms as factory inspection, the regulation of child and female labour and guaranteed Sunday rest, was decidedly cool, and after Wilhelm II tired of his pose as an '*Arbeiterkaiser*' social reform tended to remain the preserve of a small number of politicians, of whom the most prominent was Count Arthur zu Posadowsky-Wehner.[21] Where *Sozialpolitik* existed, it was pursued by governments less for its own sake than as a strategy for avoiding unnecessary conflict, and the introduction of social insurance for white-collar workers in

1911 was nothing but a tactical improvement of the position of the middle class. For the rest, official policy vacillated between increasing or relaxing the pressure which could be exerted on the Social Democratic movement through the complex system of legal statutes and police restrictions.[22]

At the same time, the intractable nature of the problems with which the Reichsleitung was confronted, led throughout the period to repeated preparations for a *Staatsstreich* or *coup d'état* from above.[23] If external dangers to the Reich were to be countered with plans for a preventive war against France, then the resolution of the Gordian knot of internal politics was to be a counter-revolutionary attack on universal suffrage and the rights of the individual, 'during which shooting could hardly be avoided'.[24] That such a course was ultimately rejected lay in the considerable dangers of unleashing a full-scale civil war against the working class and risking the secession of the southern states from the Reich.[25] These fears in no way diminished the fascination of speculating with the idea, however, as internal government correspondence and pressure from various ginger-groups indicate.[26] Moreover, it is perfectly clear that the threats of a Staatsstreich, or indeed any form of direct attack on the organised working class, were taken seriously in the leading counsels of the SPD. Wolfgang Heine expected a dissolution of the Reichstag in the autumn of 1914 and new elections to be directed against the danger of social revolution and working-class 'terrorism', and Carl Legien recalled a strong feeling, which had existed within the trade-union leadership, that in the summer of 1914 a violent clash between the forces of capitalism and the representatives of the working class was imminent.[27]

It was the common threat posed by the SPD, but also the dangers inherent in a violation of the constitution, which dictated the course of Sammlungspolitik.[28] Although its origins were evident much earlier,[29] it was only in 1897 that the intention became apparent to distract attention from pressing internal problems by the adumbration of an imperialist policy. Holstein was amongst those who argued that the Kaiser needed visible success in the external field, which would then perforce have favourable consequences on internal policy.[30] Of particular importance was the extent to which the coalition of 'steel and rye', the industrial barons and the discontented agrarians, was held together in support of the throne by an assertively nationalist, zealously patriotic ideology. It was a small step from this to enlisting the work of numerous, newly-created organisations in combating the spread of socialist influence at all levels of society.[31] These ranged from the

Alldeutscher Verband (1893) and *Flottenverein* (1898) to the *Reichs-verband gegen die Sozialdemokratie*,[32] which was created in the wake of the socialist election success of 1903.

Despite the lack of adequate financial resources, the *Reichsverband* contributed considerably to the triumph of the Bülow 'Block' in 1907, and expended vast energies in distributing leaflets and other propaganda.[33] The continued stream of 'political education' in the conservative and nationalist press often drew its source from syndicated *Reichsverband* material, and by awaking fears and anxieties it played a major part in stoking up hatred against the socialists. It is not surprising, therefore, that the Reich Chancellery viewed the Reichsverband as 'one of the most valuable internal political weapons', which deserved 'every support from the state'.[34] In the 1912 election campaign in the Spandau constituency, the Reichsverband was responsible for distributing a leaflet warning the workers in the government munitions factory that if the SPD candidate Karl Liebknecht was elected, then two-thirds of the workforce would be dismissed.[35]

The great fear within the SPD of being subjected to further additional penalties, plus the daily harassment at the hands of the law and the knowledge that advances in military science had given the government an overwhelming advantage in any direct confrontation, reduced the party's freedom to manoeuvre by a considerable amount. This often tended to intensify the caution which characterised much of the SPD's tactics, but was occasionally mistaken for some kind of fatal weakness in the party's appeal. Thus, lack of interest in and poor attendances at local party meetings were often taken as proof of the waning power of the movement and the success of government strategy.[36]

Yet Social Democratic caution was as much, if not more so, the result of a big-stick policy than of any substantial adjustments in ideological focus. Moreover, party spokesmen repeatedly pointed to the rejection of violence as a political weapon. In April 1892, for example, Bebel gave an interview to the Berlin correspondent of the *New York Herald*,[37] in which he nailed his personal colours to the mast, averring that a revolution in Germany was impossible for the foreseeable future, and insisting that the SPD would continue to make progress without recourse to violence. Similar sentiments were expressed in the party's publications, especially in the leaflets issued to celebrate May Day in 1893,[38] which reflected the view of many who fondly thought that the edifice of capitalist society would crumble before their very eyes. Even the party's chief theoretician Karl Kautsky claimed, somewhat paradoxically, that 'Social Democracy is a revolutionary party, but not a party which makes revolutions.'[39]

Nonetheless, there is a clearly discernible relationship between revolutionary terminology as a driving force and the continued growth and success of the party. Faced with the daily frustration of exclusion from real political power and influenced by its self-reinforcing concept of social and political isolation, the SPD tended to channel all its collective resentments and suppressed bitterness, occasioned by persecution under the Sozialistengesetz and the unabated discrimination and exploitation, into a kind of supercharged verbal aggression. Rhetorical radicalism thus tended to supplement and gradually supersede a belief in the imminence of the revolution as such.[40]

For this reason, opportunities to drive home the maximum effect from propaganda were seldom lost. In the wake of the party conference held at Hamburg in October 1897, an official of the local political police recorded his view that 'the terror images conjured up at party conferences, of an imminent change in the franchise, a new antisocialist law and a Staatsstreich never fail to have their effect'.[41] The central importance of this propaganda war in the overall strategy was underlined by an English newspaper correspondent in 1912, when he ascribed the party's electoral triumph of that year to the fact that Bebel and his colleagues were

the only unterrified, tooth-and-nail foes of reaction, insensate militarism and class rule, the one voice which cries out insistently, fearlessly, implacably, against the injustices which, in the opinion of many patriotic men, are retarding the moral progress and sapping the vital resources of the German nation.[42]

The importance attached to a sharp, public castigation of political malpractices and their ruthless exploitation for purposes of party propaganda, was recognised in 1906 with the creation of a party school. Its aim, as the debates at the 1907 party conference made clear, was not to act as a kind of research institute or academic seminar, but rather to put as many party members as possible through a series of specialist courses dealing with practical political agitation.[43] This primary emphasis on the work of propaganda, drawing the greatest possible advantage from examples of internal repression and government mismanagement, was to have the cumulative effect of strengthening party morale and papering-over the ideological cracks; perhaps too much so for some, since Rosa Luxemburg complained in 1910 that the party behaved 'like a nightwatchman, who only blows his horn when there is a public scandal on the streets'.[44]

These ideological differences, which had existed in embryonic form even in the period of the Sozialistengesetz, became increasingly apparent in the years of the 'new course', and as the 1890s gave way to a new century, it was painfully obvious that capitalist society was stubbornly refusing to collapse. Wilhelmine Germany, largely through the determination with which the old ruling élite clung to power, was holding together extraordinarily well. In fact, governments succeeded in retaining the upper hand right up to 1914 and at no time did the working-class movement threaten the breakdown of public order.

The emergence of a central ideological debate within the SPD has affected the interpretation of every conceivable aspect of the history of German Social Democracy. It is a vexed problem and a thoroughgoing analysis is beyond the confines of this study, but its clarification is essential to an understanding of the factors which shaped SPD attitudes generally.[45] In all too many descriptions of the practical readjustments which the party made in the period before 1914 the emphasis is placed, often exaggeratedly, on incipient tendencies towards integration within the state, as if this process can entirely be explained by reference to apparent changes in the internal biochemistry of the movement.[46] Relatively little attention has been paid to the way in which the state itself was able, through subtle varieties of economic and political blackmail, together with the effective deployment of counter-propaganda, to coerce Social Democracy into forms of acquiescence in the *status quo*. Certainly, consistency is a rare quality in political life and the SPD, for all its overt rigidity, had little claim to this distinction.

The chief figure of controversy within the party was Eduard Bernstein, who argued that if the collapse of the capitalist economy was taking much longer than Marx had predicted, it would also assume a quite different form from that envisaged by him:

Revisionism is every new truth, every new perception, and since progress does not come to a standstill and since the conditions on which we fight our battle are governed by the law of change, there will always be a kind of revisionism both in theory and practice.[47]

As a result of a series of articles in the 1890s which appeared in the party's leading intellectual journal, *Die neue Zeit*, and were later published in book form, Bernstein is usually credited with the authorship of the term 'revisionism'. In fact, the word was not actually coined by him but by Bruno Schoenlank, one of the party's foremost radical journalists.

Of critical importance for the development of Bernstein's ideas was almost certainly the fact that he had spent the formative twelve years under the Sozialistengesetz in exile, and did not return to Germany until 1910, having been decisively influenced by his contacts with the Fabian Society in London. It was the awareness that many of the revisionists had not risen from the ranks in service to the party that made them suspect in the eyes of men like Otto Wels, one of the leading Social Democrats in Berlin. Speaking at the 1903 party conference, he argued that

the campaign against those who threatened party unity could not be waged energetically enough . . . it was the revolutionary struggle which had made the party all it was and would continue to guide its fortunes.[48]

Others such as Ignaz Auer, secretary of the party since 1890 and second only to Bebel in shrewdness, were not slow to pour their scorn on revisionism as a crusading alternative. Writing to Bernstein in July 1899, Auer asked,

Do you think that it is really possible for a party which has a 50-year-old literature, an almost 40-year-old organisation and a still older tradition, to make such an about-turn? . . . What you propose would mean destroying the party, throwing the fruits of decades of work into the wind. My dear Ede, as far as your propositions are concerned, one doesn't actually say that sort of thing, one just does it.[49]

The continuing legacy of the 'heroic period' under the Sozialistengesetz was recognised by Maximilian Harden in the sharp rejection of Bernstein's revisionist programme at the 1899 party conference:

Social Democracy is no political party in the traditional sense of the word, but an Islam . . An Islam cannot exist without its beliefs . . . Bernstein's mistake was not taking this into account. He forgot that in the light of history an organism of this kind . . . has its own laws of life, which cannot be changed arbitrarily from one day to another.[50]

Not surprisingly, the short shrift given to Bernstein's arguments at the conference strengthened the government's negative reading of the general situation. The government-inspired *Berliner Correspondenz*, part of a network of indirect influence set up in the 1890s, commented that 'the Social Democrats are still aiming at an overthrow of existing society . . . the party has lost nothing of its revolutionary character'.[51] Moreover, the opportunities for collaboration with bourgeois society, certainly in Prussia, were severely limited. As the head of the Hanseatic legation in Berlin pointed out in a comment on the strength of the movement, the SPD was driven into tactics of obstruction by the existence of solid majorities against it in the Reichstag.[52] In fact, the limited political successes which the party achieved before 1914 were almost all at the grass-roots level, either by means of collaboration in individual state parliaments and on local councils, or by participation in the special industrial courts (*Gewerbegerichte*). Inevitably, this tended to strengthen the hand of trade unionists,[53] and those politicians from southern Germany where revisionism was especially strong.[54] Ludwig Frank was quite adamant in rejecting the criticism levelled at him and other Social Democrats in Baden, since the party could point with pride to a number of positive advantages gained through legislative cooperation, which nonetheless did not prevent them from sharply attacking the government whenever necessary. In fact, the dangers of seeing revisionists in one guise only are highlighted by Frank's total opposition in the Reichstag to the system of *Klassenjustiz*, and his active support for the idea of a mass strike in pursuit of the equal franchise for Prussia.[55]

Nevertheless, revisionists made little progress in their attempts to transform traditional attitudes of gladiatorial combat. As early as 1891 Auer, who later came to be identified with the party's pragmatists, had expressed strong reservations about the line adopted by the Bavarian Social Democrat, Georg von Vollmar, because the 'strict line of demarcation which has hitherto separated us from other parties . . . will be swept away'.[56] Bebel's rock-hard stand at the crucial 1903 party conference in Dresden, at which the revisionists were humiliatingly outvoted, was a testimony both to his Prinzipienfestigkeit and his almost autocratic hold over the party.[57] Such was his determination not to give one inch of ground that Bebel refused to come to the help of Auer, when he faced attempts to vote him off the party's executive committee by a radical group in Berlin. Wolfgang Heine later regarded this as 'disgraceful disloyalty to a former fellow-campaigner'.[58]

If it became abundantly clear that the SPD was unable and indeed unwilling to renounce its 'revolutionary' theory, it was equally obvious that in practice the prospect of the Zukunftsstaat was rapidly receding into the distance. Yet the need to satisfy the wishes of party activists wanting to distance themselves ideologically from the state, thereby retaining as much elan and enthusiasm as possible in the continuing growth and development of the party organisation, certainly did not diminish. It was Karl Kautsky's service to the party that he identified and drew together the apparent paradox of revolutionary theory and revisionist practice, giving it an ideological coherence.[59] He was also responsible for evolving a modern version of the strategy of attrition (*Ermattungsstrategie*), which tended to emphasise the importance of fomenting discontent as a self-generating revolutionary factor.[60]

It cannot be overlooked that the SPD in Wilhelmine Germany was a wide umbrella, sheltering left-wing Marxists, party theoreticians of the centre, as well as right-wing revisionists. It was this movement which later spawned the German Communist Party (KPD), and it was the same party which produced a Noske, a Scheidemann and an Ebert. It is not surprising, therefore, that disputes over tactics, together with personal disagreements, became increasingly common. An understandable willingness by German historians in both parts of the former Reich to lay claim to the line of political legitimacy with the Wilhelmine SPD has tended, however, to stress quite disproportionately the relative strengths of the ideological division. The SPD was neither an incipient bourgeois party, unconvinced of the validity of official Marxist orthodoxy and intent on pursuing a policy of collaboration with the state,[61] nor an overwhelmingly radical movement, whose leadership mirrored true rank-and-file feeling, but whose unity was constantly being threatened by right-wing renegades.[62] If anything, as the evidence presented later in this study will attempt to show, there was a noticeable hardening of Marxist consciousness and political intransigence within the party, since Social Democratic radicalism was largely a reflection of social relationships in the Reich. Far from witnessing a rapid, smooth and inexorable process of accommodation with the state, the years immediately before 1914 brought neither a significant reduction in conflict with the authorities,[63] nor a willingness on the part of SPD journalists to moderate their tone. The bitter rancour left by the Sozialistengesetz and the continuing ostracism by the political establishment extracted a heavy price in terms of social cohesion. All attempts to blur these lines of distinction, to wash over this important divide, fail to do justice to the true nature of the Social Democratic movement.

The party press

It is remarkable how little serious attention has been paid to the importance of the SPD press during the Wilhelmine period.[64] This neglect is all the more surprising in view of the fact that every propagandist for socialism had in the nature of things to be a propagandist for reading socialist literature. Even in the early days of the movement, it was one of the chief ways of spreading the new wisdom and both the Lassalle and Eisenach groups had their own publications. By the time of the Sozialistengesetz, the socialist press had already developed a reputation for radical journalism.[65] Within a short time after the passage of the bill, the police had suppressed nearly all of the party's publications. Not only was the voice of the movement temporarily silenced, but a whole series of individual, economic problems was created when hundreds of party workers – editors, typesetters and journalists – were without a livelihood.[66] The solution adopted to this crisis was twofold. The party

took to organising the publication of periodicals abroad, whilst en-
deavouring to maintain some additional domestic influence through the
creation of so-called 'colourless' newspapers. Of those publications
being printed outside Germany, the most important was undoubtedly
the *Sozialdemokrat*, which first appeared in Zürich in September 1879
and which had considerable influence, as well as helping to buttress
Bebel's power base in the party.[67] As a result of the skeleton basis on
which publications sympathetic to the party were kept going during the
years under the Sozialistengesetz, the movement was able to count on
no fewer than 60 newspapers in 1890.

The re-emergence of the party press after its period of official proscription coincided with a period of many new technical innovations,
such as wireless telegraphy and mechanical printing presses capable of
producing huge quantities of newspaper material, which speeded up
the process of communication within the country. What happened in
Berlin could, therefore, much more readily affect events in the provinces and vice-versa. Equally, the development of the communications media in this way had considerable repercussions on the opportunities for influencing mass opinion. Both the party and the Reichsleitung were quick to take account of the implications for their respective forms of propaganda, and if the SPD did not take to the barricades
in Wilhelmine Germany, its politicians certainly reached for their pens
and printer's ink with no lack of revolutionary fervour.

In the case of the SPD, the party press came to occupy a position of
great significance in its struggle against the state, if only because the
prospects of achieving any kind of major political success in the Reichstag were negligible. Additionally, it carried the burden of the party's
work of political education, and it was often crucially important as the
only means of sustaining contact with the party faithful. In Kassel, for
example, existing police-regulations often made speaker-programmes
and organised political activity well-nigh impossible, and the efforts of
local party activists were almost invariably channelled through the
press.[68]

Unlike the liberal press, which directed itself very clearly to those
who through their education and social standing (*Bildungsbürgertum*)
set themselves apart from the masses, the SPD press played a primary
rôle in building up a political organisation to represent the working
class. It was not in fact the party which initially provided a stable
readership for the press, rather it was the necessary groundwork of
political persuasion by party journalists that recruited the general party
membership. Such was the feeling of a genuine community of interests

as reflected in the SPD press that some workers would read a party newspaper 'three or four times and regard it as a sermon'.[69] Indeed, in the years immediately after 1890, the founding of new journals was more important to the SPD than the creation of party cells.

Hardly anyone in the party failed to endorse the powerful contribution which the press was able to make to the SPD's tactical and strategical objectives, even when they had reservations about the way in which party newspapers were fulfilling this task.[70] Adolf Braun, writing in the *Sozialpolitisches Zentralblatt* in 1892, remarked that 'the newspapers of the SPD are the most outstanding methods of agitation which the party has'.[71] Wilhelm Liebknecht argued that no member of the SPD group in the Reichstag wished to see a petrification of the party through parliamentarianism, and put on record his own view that a good treatise or pamphlet was a thousand times preferable to a speech in the Reichstag.[72]

Nonetheless, the complaints that were voiced about the press at some party conferences and elsewhere were not entirely without justification. Arguments centred around the poor quality of news-reporting and the scrimping and saving on editorial costs,[73] the convoluted terminology and general obtuseness[74] and, conversely, the absence of ideological 'instruction'.[75] There were increasing attacks on the press for its dull uniformity, and at the 1913 party conference Adolf Braun went so far as to describe 78 of the 80 daily newspapers as stereotyped.[76] However, as Auer had pointed out to critics of the press in 1891, even where the local party paper was of comparatively little value, it was still being read and that was what mattered.[77]

In fact, as is clear from the comments of its rivals and the negative respect accorded to it by the authorities, the SPD press was a force to be reckoned with. Caprivi, replying to Bebel in the Reichstag, declared that he would rather see the men in the barracks illiterate than able to read Social Democratic papers.[78] The annual reports prepared by the political police in Berlin, surveying the activities of the socialist movement, give an interesting guide to the attention which SPD editorial pronouncements commanded, as well as to their ability to trigger-off renewed bouts of agitation.

What is so remarkable is that there is no evidence of a significant tailing-off in the rhetorical radicalism in the years immediately before 1914. Thus, for example, the police report for 1909 proclaimed:

There has been a noticeably coarser tone in the SPD press than in previous years. At times it has reached boiling point. For instance, an article of the *Dortmunder Arbeiterzeitung* commenting on the visit of the Kaiser to Hohensyburg was full of pathological hatred. Sensation rules the day. Every government measure is an outrage and a slap in the face of the proletariat, every policeman is a pig and Prussia itself is a state of barbarism, inferior to all other civilised lands . . .[79]

In December 1913, the *Regierungspräsident* at Düsseldorf could write in his report to the Prussian Ministry of the Interior,

The tone of the SPD newspapers has remained the same . . . They only know how to encourage dissatisfaction amongst the working class, filling them with class hatred and stultifying every kind of monarchical, patriotic and religious feeling.[80]

In 1911, the party executive authorised the publication of a pamphlet,[81] with a wide-ranging selection of acknowledgements from bourgeois sources, all testifying to the undoubted effectiveness of the SPD press. For example, the conservative journal, *Der Türmer*, had commented in September 1905 that the SPD press exercised a virtual monopoly in the discovery and critical reporting of a whole series of public grievances. 'Apart from cases', it said, 'which could not fail to reach the public consciousness, it is the SPD which alone carries the brunt of public criticism and concern.'[82] Similarly, the Catholic Centre Party newspaper, *Rheinische Volksstimme*, had declared in May 1910 that the SPD papers were invariably the first to be read by the authorities:

Whenever claims are made, criticism levelled or doubts awakened in such papers, the instructions go out from on high and official inquiries are set in motion. It would be interesting to read the results of a survey conducted into the annual costs of these investigations.[83]

The fact is that, as far as the SPD was concerned, there was plenty to agitate about; so much was wrong with the fabric of Wilhelmine society. In this respect the effectiveness of the SPD press was unsurpassed. The method was to make use of everything which could be politically damaging to opponents of Social Democracy, employing the technique not only of allusion and personal innuendo, but a deliberate progression of ideas which took single cases as symptoms of much greater problems within society. It almost seemed at times as if the work was being done for them; Bebel declared that it was their opponents who sharpened the party's weapons.[84] Yet the determination to hammer away at the evils in society and expose all that was false and corrupt remained an abiding characteristic of many individual party newspapers. In 1896, a contemporary observer commented,

There has never been a press which has stirred up the masses in such a conscious and systematic way, and with such complete absence of scruples . . . 'All that is bad comes from above' is what Bebel said in the Reichstag during the debate on duelling in April 1896, and the SPD is governed by this principle.[85]

Indeed, it was the relentless attacking nature of the Social Democratic press which most impressed Hitler and left a lasting mark on him.[86]

Of particular concern within the confines of this study is not only the way in which the SPD was able to take advantage of the extraordinary succession of scandals in Wilhelmine public life but, more especially, the reinforcing effect this had on party attitudes to the state and to the imminence of revolution, particularly in the 1890s. Not surprisingly, perhaps, the boldest expression of the revolutionary effect of such scandals came in left-wing publications, but even middle-of-the-road papers like the *Hamburger Echo* were also sensitive to scandal, especially in other European countries, interpreting the financial scandal surrounding the former Lord Mayor of London, Sir Henry Isaacs, as part of the general theory of the moral degeneration of bourgeois society.[87]

In a letter to Adler in December 1896, drawing attention to a significant jump in the circulation of the *Hamburger Echo*, resulting from that paper's vigorous exploitation of the dockworkers' strike, Auer argued that during moments of crisis newspapers were always read more avidly.[88] It thus became almost a built-in feature of the SPD's approach to journalism to suggest a situation of permanent crisis in domestic affairs, for which the revelation of sensation stood as incontrovertible evidence that all was not well within the system. Much play was made of possible parallels with the pre-revolutionary situation in the France of the *Ancien Régime. Die neue Zeit* even went so far as to describe the scandals which preceded the revolution of 1789 as 'harmless sideshows', compared with those of contemporary society.[89] In 1892 the journal went on to declare with absolute conviction that the history of a decaying society manifested itself in scandals,[90] and four years later pronounced that the '*Götterdämmerung*' of bourgeois society was at hand.[91] Some ten years later, however, it began to entertain serious doubts as to the revolutionary impact of such revelations on Wilhelmine Germany and reluctantly suggested that capitalist society was unlikely to die of its scandals.[92] In fact, since by correcting evils and ameliorating dissatisfaction it would perforce weaken its own position, the ruling class would simply continue to view such events with the greatest indifference. There was, however, an instructive importance in the continued exploitation of scandal, since in this way the hollowness of society and the moral bankruptcy of the ruling classes could be conveyed to ordinary working people.[93]

It was not only the SPD press which seized upon the revolutionary factor of sensation and scandal. Hans von Tresckow, a member of the

Berlin police force for 33 years and well acquainted with the background to the Eulenburg–Moltke court cases of 1907–9, viewed such matters as 'the storm before the approaching tempest'.[94] Within the SPD itself, doubts were occasionally expressed as to the wisdom of indulging in scandal-mongering, especially when associated with personal failings – as opposed to those scandals which revealed the corruptness of the state in general – but Bebel went on record that it was the biggest mistake imaginable not to publish such details, 'since the opposition press then has nothing short of a field-day and our people in the country haven't a clue what they should think'.[95] Indeed, on occasions there might well have been a pandering to public taste. In 1902, for example, when the Crown Princess of Saxony eloped with her children's tutor, causing a dynastic scandal, the affair appeared to engender more interest in the socialist press than some of the current political issues.[96]

Nevertheless, it was the nature of these political issues which provided the fuel and driving energy for the party's propaganda machine. Sometimes the issues were relatively small. The Berlin political police noted, for example, the existence of an '*Arbeiter-Sanitätskommission*' which, without official links with the party leadership but enjoying its financial support, was investigating sanitary conditions in factories, industrial premises and living accommodation, with the intention of pressing for improvements and, in the case of non-cooperation by the authorities, of publishing full details of the disgraces in the *Vorwärts*.[97] At a different level came the publication by many leading SPD newspapers of numerous secret government decrees, the details of which were often politically damaging to the government and led to fury in official quarters.[98] The factor common to such differing levels of political journalism was that these and other issues were potentially explosive and were presented editorially – in terms of the rhetorical radicalism which characterised such newspapers – as political scandal and sensation.

The Social Democratic press has, of course, to be seen against the wider background of the Wilhelmine press in general. It was certainly not a prerogative of the SPD to expose scandal. On Caprivi's departure from office news appeared in several papers, especially those supporting the *Bund der Landwirte*, suggesting that he had come into the possession of 400,000 marks by rather less than honest means. This story was, however, a complete invention.[99] In a very real sense the SPD did not have a captive audience; it had to battle for its readers at a time of an enormous and unprecedented expansion in the newspaper and communications industry. According to the *Vorwärts*,[100] in 1910 there were some 3,929 newspapers and periodicals being published in Germany, compared with 2,067 in Italy and 1,350 in France. Of those in Germany, 2,306 appeared in Prussia, 438 in Bavaria, 254 in Saxony, 169 in Baden, 149 in the Thuringian states, 138 in Württemberg and 115 in Hesse. Again, of the 3,929, 1,344 described themselves as being non party-political,[101] 710 as semi-official (*Amtsblätter*), 492 were Catholic Centre Party publications, 388 Progressive, 378 Nationalist, 303 Conservative, 192 National Liberal, 100 Social Democratic and 17 Polish, Danish or Guelph in origin. According to *Schmollers Jahrbuch*, the total number of all publications and specialist journals appearing in January 1910 was as high as 9,304.[102] Certainly, every political movement and grouping of note had its own journalistic organ, and it became increasingly important to be well represented in the imperial capital.[103]

To a large extent this gargantuan publishing activity was paralleled within the Social Democratic movement. Three main enterprises carried the burden of the production of periodical and occasional publications, those founded by J. H. W. Dietz and Ignaz Auer, and the publishing concern directly associated with the central party newspaper, the *Vorwärts*-Buchhandlung. Dietz,[104] who sat for many years in the Reichstag, as did Auer, had originally founded a bookshop in Hamburg in December 1878, but after his expulsion from that city under the anti-socialist laws he moved to Stuttgart, where he was responsible, together with Bebel, Kautsky, Liebknecht and Heinrich Braun, for setting up *Die neue Zeit* in 1883 and starting the party's leading satirical publication, *Der wahre Jakob*. The administration of the Auer publishing house in Hamburg passed into the hands of a committee of management appointed by the party executive, as did that of the Dietz house in 1911. The *Vorwärts*-house was the largest of the three, publishing works of political agitation, the stenographic proceedings of the party conferences and a wide range of scientific, philosophical and socialist-theory works, as well as poetry and fiction. The Erfurt programme was distributed in nearly half a million copies and a pamphlet containing the programme and an additional commentary had an initial print of 120,000 copies.[105]

Much of the work of these three large publishing agencies was highly profitable. The total value of stock sold through the *Vorwärts*-Buchhandlung in 1910 amounted to 670,367 marks and the following year to 790,709 marks.[106] In addition, the proceedings of the party conferences sold well, averaging 40,000 copies, and the specialist publications produced for propaganda purposes, like the *März-Zeitung*, commemorating the revolutionaries of 1848 and the Communards of 1871, and the *Maifeier-Zeitung*, had annual circulations of several thousand copies.[107] There were always special distributions of printed material. Prior to May Day in 1900, for example, the Hamburg party handed out some 10,000 leaflets and 4,000 copies of *Der wahre Jakob* to the owners of over 2,500 river-craft and sea-going vessels moored in the harbour.[108] Again, the *Hamburger Echo*, in conjunction with the Auer house, produced a sharply-written leaflet directed against the Sedan celebrations on 2 September 1895.[109] This flood of literature – which reached a deluge of some 88 million leaflets in the 1912 election campaign – was backed up by local initiatives designed to stimulate interest in the SPD press and win new readers.[110]

This was particularly important in the rural areas, which the SPD found difficult to penetrate, and in 1899 the regional party conference for the Prussian province of Hesse-Nassau decided to distribute a copy of a special newspaper, entitled *Der Wegweiser*, to each of the party's agents in the field (*Vertrauensleute*). They were to be responsible for promoting *Der Wegweiser* to interested persons, distributing quarterly gratis copies and signing up new subscribers to the party press.[111] The special propaganda calendars (*Volkskalender*) were used in much the same way.[112] A further means of reaching out and intensifying the party's programme of political agitation was through the house publications of the associated organisations – the Social Democratic cycling and gymnastic clubs, choral societies and the youth movement.[113]

But the most important single factor in this network of political agitation was the local party newspaper and its staff of journalists. In 1890 the party had a total of 60 newspapers, of which 19 appeared six times weekly. Foremost amongst them was the central party organ, the *Berliner Volksblatt* which, after a decision taken at the 1890 party conference, became the *Vorwärts* as from the beginning of 1891.[114] The period immediately after the lapse of the anti-socialist laws saw the greatest number of new creations, including those which later achieved considerable prominence – the *Volksstimme* at Frankfurt am Main, Magdeburg and Mannheim, the *Bielefelder Volkswacht* and the *Elberfelder Freie Presse*.

During the early 1890s efforts were directed towards setting up new party newspapers, or to increasing the number of times a week a particular paper was published. By 1895, for example, of the 76 party journals, 39 were appearing six times weekly. At the turn of the century this applied to 69% of all party newspapers, and by the outbreak of war in 1914 this had risen to 95.7% of the total.[115] Although the SPD never achieved blanket coverage of the whole of the country, the only areas without SPD papers in 1914 were Posen, Hohenzollern, Lippe and Waldeck. The last party newspaper to be founded before the outbreak of war was in West Prussia.[116] Throughout the 1890s, however, the number of trade-union newspapers, which in any case appeared far less frequently, showed no significant increase. Socialist newspapers were, moreover, complemented by a wide-ranging selection of other journals. These included *Die Gleichheit*, the journal for women edited by Clara Zetkin, the satirical magazines directed at a mass readership such as *Der wahre Jakob* and *Süddeutscher Postillon*, as well as the more intellectual publications – *Die neue Zeit* and *Sozialistische Monatshefte*.[117]

It was Bebel who termed the editorial offices of the SPD press the high schools of the rising generation.[118] There was scarcely a Social Democratic politician of note who had not in his time been a party journalist.[119] This said much about the needs of the party. An SPD journalist was primarily a political agitator, whose main concern was with vigorous polemic and effective propaganda rather than topical reporting, and for whom events were important in terms of the agitatory material they yielded.[120] Since this army of journalists and, more often than not, the dispatch clerks (*Kolporteure*) were involved in speaking engagements on behalf of the SPD, their particular efforts could materially assist the party's total effort.[121] Indeed, editors of local papers could wield enormous influence. Thus, the political line in the local party at Bremen, as in many other cities, was laid down right up to 1914 not by the chairman or inner executive of the party, but by the editor-in-chief of the *Bremer Bürgerzeitung*.[122]

This dual responsibility as journalists and active party workers was not without its practical difficulties. Liebknecht, contrasting the working day of a bourgeois editor with that of an SPD journalist, whose work was liable to be interrupted by frequent visits from the police, court appearances and spells of imprisonment, felt that the *Vorwärts* was to be pitied for having him as its editor-in-chief:

I can hardly ever spend a complete working day in the editorial offices as I should do, let alone be there every day. I have to be responsible for the work of political agitation in general, hold meetings and be present in the Reichstag.[123]

Indeed, of the 81 SPD members of the Reichstag elected in 1903, no fewer than 39 described themselves as editors, journalists, writers or publishers.[124] Since party journalists were increasingly required to suffer long prison sentences, other disadvantages and occupational hazards, it was not surprising that they were drawn into the inner counsels of the party. At the 1912 election, 55 of the SPD candidates were journalists, representing 14% of the total, compared with the

2% in the other parties.[125] Of the 241 party journalists in 1914, 28 had received some form of university education, 10 had PhDs, 76 were printers, bookbinders or lithographers, 16 locksmiths, 13 carpenters and 10 painters. Significantly, four-fifths of all party journalists were working-class in origin.[126]

Each editorial staff consisted of a number of journalists, often with separate responsibilities, who occasionally alternated as the nominal editor-in-chief (*verantwortlicher Chefredakteur*), whose technical and legal status made him criminally liable for anything printed in his name. This is why several of the smaller party papers, with correspondingly fewer staff, often employed what was known as a '*Sitzredakteur*', a nonentity who was prepared to carry the consequences of libel and other legal actions, to enable his colleagues to continue their creative work. The existence of this practice was often vigorously denied by the SPD, but with the barrage of penal restrictions hurled at the party press,[127] this was both sensible and indeed necessary from a practical point of view.

It is largely thanks to the expert system of police surveillance that one is able to piece together the careers of so many leading party journalists.[128] No copies were made of outgoing letters and incoming mail and the manuscripts of original articles were invariably burned, to prevent them from falling into the hands of the police. Such was the continuing legacy of persecution under the Sozialistengesetz that when Ebert arrived at the party's administrative offices in Berlin in 1905 and asked for a typewriter and telephone, he was told that there were none, since 'one could not deliver the secrets of the party into the hands of the opposition'.[129]

As might be expected, many of the party's journalists came from humble surroundings. Hermann Molkenbuhr, who later held a key position as one of the party secretaries in Berlin, worked both as a child and young man in chicory and cigarette factories; Karl Frohme, a member of the Reichstag and on the editorial staff of the *Hamburger Echo* from 1890, started his career in machine-building; others, like the chemist Emanuel Wurm and the lawyer Max Quarck, were privileged to receive some form of higher education.

Many were figurers of considerable intellectual standing within the movement, like Bruno Schoenlank for example, who forsook the promise of a brilliant academic career as a protégé of Gustav Schmoller to take on badly-paid journalistic work for the SPD and the prospects of endless prison sentences. By way of the *Sozialpolitisches Zentralblatt* and the *Vorwärts*, he took over the newly-created *Leipziger Volkszeitung* in October 1894, whose editor he remained until his nervous breakdown and premature death in 1901.[130] During this time the paper had become one of the handful of outstanding SPD publications, unrivalled on the party's left wing, and praised for its enlightened approach to the arts, which included the serialisation of contemporary works by leading European writers. Similarly, Alexander Helphand (Parvus) in the few years that he was permitted by the authorities to edit the *Sächsische Arbeiterzeitung*, was responsible for a series of major contributions to Marxist theory. These were so highly regarded that Lenin, who at the time was spending several years of exile in Siberia, implored his mother to obtain the paper for him.[131] Throughout the period there was considerable mobility on the part of individual journalists, who rapidly gained experience of different local conditions and, depending on their respective personalities, were often able to mould local political life. Scheidemann, for instance, speaks in his memoirs[132] of a very humble beginning, when he acted not only as editor but also as despatch clerk, advertising manager, treasurer and secretary to the local party. In 1900, however, he joined the editorial staff of the *Fränkische Tagespost*[133] in Nuremberg, before moving to the *Offenbacher Abendblatt* in 1902 and to a position as editor-in-chief of the *Kasseler Volksblatt* in 1905.

In general, an editor and his staff had considerable freedom over content and interpretation. The central party executive naturally made use of the press whenever it had cause to issue a call-to-arms or a full policy statement, since this was the quickest and, in most cases, the only way of reaching the party faithful. Direct interference was much less common although, as Adolf Braun informed the 1902 party conference,[134] Auer used his position as party secretary to put pressure on individual editors, and it was never clear whether he was writing in a private capacity or on behalf of the party executive.[135] The importance attached to the editorship of the *Vorwärts* was such that the Brunswick party proposed a motion at the 1897 conference that he should be elected annually by the whole party assembly.[136]

As a result of such pressures, the party leadership agreed to set up a kind of watchdog committee for the paper, called the *Presse-Commission*,[137] whose membership was drawn from each of the constituency parties in Berlin. This committee had, in common with the party executive, equal voting rights in the appointment of staff.[138] In other areas similar committees had existed under different names from the early 1890s onwards.[139] They were often closely involved in questions affecting the financial security of the paper. In 1894, for example, after the Hamburg party had held a number of well-attended meetings dealing with press affairs, the local committee (*Neuner-Commission*) was asked to report on the possibility of turning the *Hamburger Echo* into an evening paper. Its findings referred to the needs of smaller party papers, dependent on the *Echo* for their news, which might best be served by an afternoon edition. It could not positively recommend a change-over, however, because of the likelihood of increased costs, coupled with technical difficulties.[140] At a meeting of all the Hamburg constituency parties, who retained ultimate responsibility for a change of this kind, members voted in favour of adhering to the *status quo*. The commission's influence was similarly felt in 1897, when it frustrated an attempt to increase the salaries of the *Echo* editorial staff by ten per cent; and in Leipzig, in a dispute between Franz Mehring and Friedrich Stampfer, over the former's insistence on employing Rosa Luxemburg to write for the *Leipziger Volkszeitung*, the local committee decided against Stampfer, who resigned from the paper in 1902.[141] This kind of local participatory democracy worked surprisingly well, as a survey conducted by the *Verein Arbeiterpresse*[142] in 1906 showed, when it sent out a questionnaire to each party paper requesting information on the nature and frequency of the work of these watchdog committees.[143]

Finance was a continuing problem for the party press. Journalists needed to be paid and enterprises which ran at a loss had to be supported. Editors were certainly not overpaid. The editor-in-chief of the *Vorwärts* in the Liebknecht era received an annual salary of 7,200 marks, his deputy a mere 500, and three other members of the editorial staff were paid between 200 and 300 marks. By way of contrast, the chief editors of conservative papers received 24,000 marks and those of liberal journals almost as much.[144] Even allowing for the low level of salaries, most of the smaller party newspapers required constant support, and even the *Leipziger Volkszeitung* was heavily dependent in the first nine years of its existence on subsidies, which came mostly from the profits of the associated bookshop and printing-works.[145]

When money was not available from the profits of local social events, including May Day rallies, it came from central party funds. In 1893 this amounted to 50,000 marks, which Auer insisted could not be regarded as money down the drain.[146] In 1907, the highest single subsidy of 16,000 marks went to the *Königsberger Volkszeitung*, but the party also made available 17,000 marks to the Polish language newspaper *Gazeta Robotnicza* and 20,000 marks to *L'Humanité* in Paris.[147] In 1897, the total income from subscriptions and advertising in the whole of the party press was a little over three million marks,[148] and by 1905 this had more than doubled. From both sources the *Vorwärts* had an income in 1911 of almost two million marks. Costs were also high, but even so the paper still made an overall profit of 165,000 marks. This meant that with the profits from the leading party newspapers and their associated bookshops, a sum of 300,000 marks was paid over into central party funds.[149]

A major problem continued to be income from advertising. Most employers and businesses declined, for obvious political reasons, to place advertisements in the Social Democratic press and the out-of-work were often compelled to take other papers simply in order to find employment. Since a working man was usually unable to afford two daily newspapers – the price of the party press was often above the average – this had enormous repercussions on potential circulation figures. The stark fact was that the proportion of income derived from advertising by the *Vorwärts* in 1892 was only a quarter, in 1900 not quite a third and by 1914 still only one-half of the income it derived from subscriptions.[150] In the bourgeois press the reverse was the case. Sympathetic advertisers were, in any case, likely to be frightened off by direct or indirect pressure from the authorities.[151] At the 1913 party conference proposals were advanced to equip the party press with a central advertising agency, but not until 1919 was this established in Leipzig.[152]

An important characteristic of the German press has always been its regional structure. Few newspapers, then as now, had claims to nationwide importance. Indeed, in 1885 there were only 97 papers in the whole of the Reich with a circulation between 10,000 and 40,000 and only five of these regularly sold more than 40,000 copies.[153] Of all German newspapers published in 1900, only 3.5% reached a circulation of more than 15,000 and this figure includes the widely-successful *General-Anzeiger* group.[154] The press was organised on the basis of individual subscriptions,[155] so that circulation figures do not take account of the wider readership reached through the family circle and groups of workmates. Social Democratic newspapers were also available in certain public houses and in this way came to the attention of those too poor to purchase their own copies. This financial consideration almost certainly accounts for the stagnation and, in some cases, actual decline in circulation figures in the years 1907–9 and after 1913. Nonetheless, by any relative standards, the Social Democratic press continued to prosper. The *Hamburger Echo* increased its circulation from 8,000 in 1890 to almost 80,000 in 1912[156] and the *Vorwärts*, which counted 25,000 subscribers in 1891 had increased this figure almost sevenfold by 1912. The total circulation of the party press stood at 254,000 in 1890 and had reached almost a million and a half by the outbreak of war.[157] Vigorous campaigns were conducted by each local paper in order to increase circulation, and advances were proudly recorded on the title page.[158]

The bulk of the criticism within the party centred on the relationship between the number of subscribers and the votes polled in Reichstag elections.[159] It is perfectly true that at no time during the period did these two statistics begin to coincide – unlike the relationship between trade-union membership and subscriptions to the trade-union press – but then it would have been a strange, not to say disappointing, state of affairs if the SPD had actually mustered more subscribers than voters. The party certainly had an immense uphill struggle in rural areas, and the bailiffs on the East Elbian and Mecklenburg estates frustrated matters by maintaining a ban on the sale and circulation of all SPD literature, including its display in local public houses.[160] In numerical terms, too, it was much more likely that with the growth of the Social Democratic movement the increases in votes polled at elections would outstrip advances in circulation figures. The Halle delegate to the 1898 party conference even went so far as to suggest that the number of subscribers was a safer criterion for the basic strength of the movement than the level of the Reichstag vote.[161] There remained an even more glaring discrepancy in the numbers of the politically organised, that is, those who were official party members. In 1905, of some 600,000 industrial workers in the Kingdom of Saxony, 440,000 were registered as having voted for the SPD and 134,000 were listed as subscribers, but only 48,000 actually belonged to the party.[162]

Efforts continued to improve the attractiveness of a Social Democratic newspaper. Apart from cosmetic changes – typography, layout and simplification of terminology – it devoted more attention to the presentation of hard news. Demands for the creation of a central press bureau for the dissemination of news had been voiced especially loudly at the party conferences in 1894, 1895, 1898 and 1899. There were some, including Mehring for instance, who believed that it was no business of the SPD press to compete on the same terms as the bourgeois press,[163] but it was becoming increasingly apparent that the readership expected as good a news service as that provided by other papers. From 1896 onwards, the *Vorwärts* began to act as a clearing-house for news reports and transcripts of proceedings in the Reichstag,[164] and following an arrangement made with the newly-opened Kiel branch of the Wolff telegraphic agency, the *Schleswig-Holsteinische Volkszeitung* scored an immediate improvement in its news service.[165]

It was not until March 1907 that a conference of all SPD editors met in Berlin to finalise details of a central news and telegraphic agency, which would supply the entire SPD press with items of general and specific party political interest. In the years after its establishment in July 1908, it provided a regular news service to all members of the press syndicate, and in April 1909 set up a special department to service the needs of the trade-union press. Matters of personnel were to be decided by the party executive and an advisory committee of five annually-elected journalists, and the costs of the enterprise were to be carried by central party funds.[166] In the pre-election year of 1911 the bureau's budget was no less than 85,000 marks, requiring an effective subvention of 30,000 marks.[167]

At a more personal level, Friedrich Stampfer had for some time been running a daily news-diary from Berlin, syndicated to most of the leading SPD papers. His aim[168] was to concentrate on the formulation of coherent party politics, at a time when the SPD seemed to be losing its way in theoretical disputation. Rosa Luxemburg characteristically and somewhat unkindly referred to Stampfer's efforts as the 'Groß-Lichterfeld [Berlin] opinion-factory for gluing up the brains of the proletariat'.[169] This approach was emulated at the opposite end of the political spectrum by the radical left wing. In 1908 Anton Pannekoek started his own correspondence and from 1910 Karl Radek began sending out a weekly news-sheet to fifteen different papers. The influence of the *Sozialdemokratische Partei-Correspondenz*[170] which, from 1906 onwards, began sending out fortnightly digests of material for agitation purposes to all SPD speakers, members of the Reichstag and other parliamentary bodies, as well as to the party press, led Luxemburg, Mehring and Karski to establish the rival *Sozialdemokratische Korrespondenz* in December 1913. Despite the extreme left-wing bias of this publication, many of Luxemburg's articles, especially on militarism, the Zabern affair and the Prussian electoral system, were reprinted in the *Vorwärts* and other party newspapers.[171]

It was in the Rhineland that the central press bureau's lack of effectiveness in the field of party propaganda was most keenly felt, and this example of regional radicalism brought a remedy in its own separate news bureau. The party leadership in the huge industrial complex of the Ruhr had repeatedly made known to the central executive that it felt that the specific requirements of socialist agitation in the region – the struggle against industrial magnates and the SPD's political opponents, especially the enormously strong Centre Party – were not being sufficiently met by the work of the bureau in Berlin.[172]

The initial aims of the Rhineland bureau were considerable, since they envisaged a level of operations comparable to and competitive with the resources deployed by the *Volksverein für das katholische Deutschland* in Mönchengladbach. It commenced its work in February 1911, aided by massive support from local trade unions, including the association of mineworkers in Bochum, and a grant of 30,000 marks from central party funds. The first director of the bureau, which had a staff of six and was located in Düsseldorf, was a former editor of the *Essener Arbeiterzeitung*, Heinrich Limbertz. A police report on the progress of operations,[173] based on copies of correspondence sheets which police officials had secretly been able to obtain, together with other information which had come into their hands, revealed that the bureau was enjoying close links with party newspapers well outside the region. In addition to supplying purely political news, the weekly correspondence-sheet had special rubrics devoted to scandals which it had managed to unearth in the lives of political opponents. Despite the initial fervour, this does not seem to have been a case of wilful separatism and grumbles were soon voiced that the money would have been better spent elsewhere.[174]

Although by and large the party leadership kept a firm grip on the running of its press, there were two editorial scandals which ruffled the surface of outward party unity. The first of these, and by far the most important, affected the composition of the editorial staff of the *Vorwärts* in 1905. It is here that the policy-shaping influence of the party leadership can be most clearly felt. For some time in the early 1900s there had been growing disaffection between the *Vorwärts* and *Leipziger Volkszeitung* over matters of a common editorial line. Six of the eleven members of the *Vorwärts* staff, including Liebknecht's successor as editor-in-chief, Kurt Eisner, found themselves increasingly isolated, especially from the views of the Berlin Presse-Commission under Otto Wels.

The intention had been to ease out some of the more obstinate individuals, but all six – Büttner, Kaliski, Gradnauer, Wilhelm Schröder, who later edited the *Sozialdemokratische Partei-Correspondenz*, and Eisner himself – had seized the initiative by resigning *en masse*.[175] The head of the Prussian legation in Dresden, Count Dönhoff, suggested in a letter to Bülow[176] that the threads of the crisis ran into the hands of Franz Mehring at the *Leipziger Volkszeitung*, which had described the action of the six men as 'treason against the party'. Dönhoff saw the affair and the uncompromisingly radical attitude of the party leadership as symptomatic of the increasing influence which left-wingers were beginning to exercise within the party. The somewhat excited tone of Dönhoff's letter also revealed much about preoccupations in government circles with the effect on the SPD of the revolutionary example in Russia. Sharply-worded editorial statements, such as appeared in papers like the *Leipziger Volkszeitung*, were taken as evidence of the party's fundamental threat to the established order, and were compared with articles in the socialist press in Russia, which had been able to push its readership into a frenzy of political action. Dönhoff's views were typical of the sort of advice which the Reichsleitung received from its political antennae in the provinces, but such assessments tended to overlook the extent to which the party was concealing its own inactivity behind a bluster of revolutionary rhetoric.

The SPD, however, was quite clearly convulsed with the effects of the internal dispute amongst party journalists and recriminations followed from both sides. The *Vorwärts*[177] published the decision of the joint meeting of the party executive, the Berlin Presse-Commission, the party's agents in the city and the chairmen and treasurers of all eight Berlin constituency parties, which accepted the resignations of the six men. Bebel himself published a personal statement in the paper,[178] denying that he had attempted to influence the outcome of the meeting. Three days later the six responded with a joint statement,[179] and proceeded to organise the publication of a pamphlet justifying their case.[180] Although the views of men like Dönhoff, that the dispute was not indicative of a serious split in the party, were undoubtedly correct, nonetheless the affair left behind it a sour taste in many of the other editorial offices.[181]

The second editorial crisis, which was symptomatic of the increasing exclusion of the revolutionary left from control of the press, occurred in Württemberg in 1912.[182] August Thalheimer had been responsible for setting up the *Freie Volkszeitung* at Göppingen in 1911, and in the period immediately before the 1912 Reichstag elections had alarmed the advocates of party unity by publishing a number of highly provocative articles.[183] Since the paper very soon got in financial difficulties, the regional and central party executives seized the opportunity to state their demands for their continuing support – the dismissal of Thalheimer.[184] These incidents, however, were the exception rather than the rule and did not materially affect the surprising degree of cohesiveness which the party press as a whole manifested.

2

THE LAW AND SOCIAL JUSTICE

If as in the Bismarck era a deliberately corrupting influence of the government makes itself felt, and an all-powerful minister signals to the courts one day with a whip and the next with a carrot, if he puts a gun to their head with his cyclostyled demands for prosecution and a day later complains before the assembled parliament about the malevolence which the courts show towards him, then the danger may well indeed be imminent, of which Helvetius spoke, when he claimed that lawyers were always the ready servants of despotism.

Die neue Zeit, 28 December 1892

The apparatus of the law

The SPD press and indeed the Social Democratic movement as a whole were only as radical and effective as the authorities allowed them to be. Deprived of statutory powers under the Sozialistengesetz to restrict socialist activity to an absolute minimum, successful governments fell back, in the increasingly turbulent uncertainties of the 1890s, on reinforcing the bulwarks of social and political order.[1] In practice this meant leaning, rather heavily in most cases, on the army, the churches and, most ominously, on the full apparatus of Wilhelmine law. This new dimension in the control of organised political opposition was, however, both the regime's most effectual means of support as well as its most exposed weakness. Even when carried on behind closed doors, justice was a matter of everyday concern, and hardly anything stirred the collective consciousness of the SPD more or made for such telling journalism than the manipulative use of the law, whether against the party organisation or the press.

That both sides were aware of the existence of a system of 'political justice' made it not so much a scandal as a charade. When in 1906 Hugo Haase, a leading Social Democratic lawyer, quoted the remarks of a member of the *Reichsgericht*,[2] he was not unearthing a new piece of political outrage, he was merely stating the obvious:

Since the wicked Social Democrats can no longer be contained within the straitjacket of a draconian emergency law, the common law must provide the necessary means to shackle them. Since the criminal law in general has not been devised with the intention of providing a weapon against Social Democracy, such yardsticks will just have to be made to fit the bill by a careful and exact process of legal stretching and squeezing.[3]

How far the law could be stretched and squeezed in this way occupied the attention of leading ministers in the summer of 1890. The Minister of the Interior, Herrfurth, writing to Caprivi,[4] was convinced that the state faced its greatest problem in the realm of the press. Under the Sozialistengesetz, the fear of suppression had at least prevented the emergence of much radical journalism but now, under the new conditions prevailing, it would fall to police departments throughout the country to carry out continuous checks on the publication of socialist material. Herrfurth went on,

If it should prove feasible, in all cases where a conviction is reasonably certain, for the state prosecuting offices to press ahead with charges and for the courts to be influenced in their sentencing policy by the dangerous nature of socialist publications, it would be possible to prevent a return to the situation of complete dissoluteness such as existed before the Sozialistengesetz.

A similar sense of dedication was required in the control of the party's political organisations. All meetings were to be placed under the strictest surveillance and halted as soon as adequate reasons would allow, and any transgression of the law was to be dealt with as speedily as possible. In addition, Herrfurth intended to give precise instructions to all Regierungspräsidenten that they were to make the fullest use of local police regulations and bye-laws when acting against the movement.[5] Even so, he was not convinced that such a rigorous application of the existing law to individual cases would ensure long-term success, but he held out the possibility of bringing in new legislation at the Reich level to provide necessary reserve powers.

Caprivi, for his part, was unable to see a parliamentary majority for any new measures of legislative control,[6] believing that such a step might well sow disunity amongst pro-government forces and hand the Social Democrats further material for agitation. In such a situation it became more important than ever to make use of all existing opportunities for political control through the courts, and he considered further that the security of the state should be invoked by state prosecutors as a matter of course. Instructions to all senior prosecuting attorneys (*Oberstaatsanwälte*), detailing the government's general strategy and incorporating guide-lines for judicial policy, were sent out by Schelling, the Minister of Justice, on 6 September.[7] The galvanising effect of this circular is instanced by the action taken by the Oberstaatsanwalt at Breslau, who took it into his hands to order his department to subscribe to, and thoroughly read, all socialist papers in the area. He had to be reminded by Schelling that this was really the task of the police, who might well feel that their toes were being trodden on.[8]

Directives from government departments right up to 1914 never failed to draw attention to the need for close-knit cooperation between the executive and the judicature, which was deemed essential to the government's hopes for long-term internal stability. Herrfurth's successor, Count Botho Eulenburg, whilst stressing the importance of the law in controlling excesses in the press and in the field of political organisation, was one of the first to develop the idea of coordinating all the efforts of wide sections of the population in this and other related areas of activity, thus supplementing and extending the nominal powers of the state. This was reflected in the decision to authorise military intervention during civil disturbances, as well as in pointing the way towards the evolution of a long-term strategy of ideological warfare.[9] A considerable furore was created by the publication of this highly confidential document by the *Vorwärts* on 29 November 1893. The ability of leading SPD papers to obtain copies of such highly-explosive items of government correspondence was to become one of the most remarkable features of the Social Democratic press during the period. The exact manner of means was always shrouded in mystery and such successes were usually explained by recourse to a standard editorial formula, 'through a lucky coincidence', but it is not inconceivable that the contents of these and other documents were communicated to the SPD by the politically disaffected in the leading government ministries. Often when a minor official felt personally slighted or thwarted, he would turn to a socialist newspaper, since no one could bang the drum quite so loudly as the SPD press.

There were, of course, innumerable instances where the SPD was able to orchestrate an effective campaign of protest against the manipulation of the law. The case of Leo Arons in the 1890s[10] showed the extent to which the universities in particular could be subjected to political control, in the interests of the official attack on socialist influence. Arons, an SPD activist and a Jew who had married into the wealthy banking family of Bleichröder, had been teaching physics as a Privatdozent at Berlin University since 1890. The general code of 1794 had defined the precise relationships between the state, whose rights over the conduct of internal policy in the universities were therein recognised, and individual members of the teaching staff, who as salaried civil servants (*Beamte*) were regarded as owing complete loyalty to the government.[11] This did not apply, however, to those academics holding the title of Privatdozent, who under the terms of their *venia legendi* were entitled to give lectures and conduct seminars, and who were directly responsible to the individual faculties concerned on all matters of discipline.

Arons' qualities had been sufficiently recognised for the faculty to apply to the Ministry for permission to appoint him as a professor without tenure; this was refused in May 1892.[12] By that time his socialist sympathies and generous financial contributions to party funds were becoming widely known, and in the summer of 1893 the Polizeipräsident, in a letter to the university senate, referred to the extent of Arons' political activities. Over the next four years, the Ministry of Cults proceeded to apply mounting pressure in order to secure the dismissal of Arons. Reluctant at first to comply with outside demands for a disciplinary court of inquiry, the university at length consented in February 1896, but reported that it could find no evidence against Arons.[13] After the passage of a special bill, the 'lex Arons' in 1898,[14] the Ministry was able to order a new disciplinary inquiry and, by appealing against the verdict of that court to – somewhat conveniently – the Ministry of State, to rescind Arons' appointment in January 1900.

The identification of the objectives of the police with the interests of the state, at least in Prussia, had a long history of respectability. Since the task of the police force was to protect the state from those dangers which would seem to threaten its existence, there developed a necessary inner relationship between the political police and the system of political justice.[15] Courts were required to bring to account those individuals against whom no other charge could be levelled than that they did not share the views of the existing political consensus. The roots of this association can be traced to the policy of Karl von Hinckeldey, Polizeipräsident in Berlin between 1846 and 1856, who managed to secure the agreement of his monarch that the police headquarters in Berlin should henceforth assume responsibilities for the political police in the whole of Prussia. Its central position in safeguarding the interests of the Prussian state led it to assume similar functions of constitutional protection (*Staatsschutz*) for the entire Reich.[16] From 1821, the Polizeipräsident in Berlin had been the de facto Regierungspräsident, a marriage of two entirely separate administrative functions, representing a considerable concentration of power and political influence.[17] It was not surprising that the powers and responsibilities of the political police increased enormously under the Sozialistengesetz. In 1880, the Berlin police department already employed 5,286 persons; by 1908 this had risen to 9,414, and the police building was the third largest in the city, after the royal palace and the Reichstag.[18]

Perhaps even more significant than the links between the police and

44

local government was the close association between the law and public administration. In no other country, with the possible exception of Austria, was such a thorough legal training a necessary precondition of service, not merely for members of the judicature, but for all those in higher administration. A French *préfet* did not have to be a qualified lawyer in the way that a Regierungspräsident or Landrat did in Prussia. Lawyers and public servants had exactly the same form of legal training: three years study in jurisprudence at university level, followed by a four-year period of apprenticeship attached to the courts and two qualifying examinations.[19] The consequences were considerable. In 1916, W. Franz, professor at one of the leading technical high schools, could write:

Germany has become a land of lawyers, a country in which, apart from the Minister of War and the State Secretary of the Navy Office, all men in authority from the Chancellor down to the secretaries of local associations and those in the ramifications of private industry, are men of law.[20]

Bethmann Hollweg is an excellent example of the processes of internal Prussian administration. In 1886, when aged 30, he was appointed a Landrat, later received promotion to Oberpräsident of Brandenburg and, under Bülow's Chancellorship, became Minister of the Interior. Two other qualities characterised the system of public administration: its conservatism and its openness to the military ethic. By 1914, nearly three out of every five trainees for public administration (Regierungsreferendare) belonged to the nobility. In addition, 92% of all Oberpräsidenten, 64% of Regierungspräsidenten, 68% of Polizeipräsidenten and 57% of Landräte were of similar noble descent.[21] At a lower level, those non-commissioned officers who had completed their military service were entitled to government employment (*Militäranwärter*). This curious system owed its origin to the eighteenth century, when the Prussian army swallowed up 4% of the total population; it remained in force since it was virtually the only way of guaranteeing a sufficiently high level of recruitment.[22]

Those who moved into judicial administration in the service of the Reich were, therefore, well-equipped in terms of ideological training and social background to act in the interests of political conservatism. The corpus of German law itself provided a further insurance against concepts of political equity. The constitution of the Prussian state, which remained in force until 1918, dated from the period of counter-revolution in the aftermath of the upheavals of 1848. Ostensibly it gave expression to four basic rights, those of personal freedom and the inviolability of the home, and the freedoms of speech and political association. However, none of these rights could be considered unconditional, since each was expressed in terms of limitations provided by other laws.

Moreover, the influence of Prussian legal philosophy had been felt in neighbouring parts of the German Confederation. The Prussian criminal code or *Strafgesetzbuch* of April 1851 was copied in a large number of North German states in the ensuing decade, so that long before the Reich was unified there was a considerable degree of legal uniformity. It is not surprising, therefore, that the *Reichsstrafgesetzbuch* of May 1871 was closely modelled on the Prussian pattern, and it was only in the legal grey areas not covered by that document that individual state laws were invoked.[23] The *Reichsstrafgesetzbuch* ranged over the whole field of human relations, governing those between private individuals no less than those between an individual and the state. Specific sections related to incitement to civil disobedience, class hatred and intimidation – which proved especially responsive to political interpretation – as well as drawing legal distinctions between actions which threatened internal order and those which affected the security of the state. Thus, §85, dealing with sedition (*Hochverrat*), referred to the overthrow of political stability from within, whereas §86 (*Landesverrat*) was more concerned with activities which were calculated to expose the state to dangers from without. Clearly, a very great deal depended on the ability of the courts to take account of political considerations in the interpretation of such laws.

Each Prussian province had a single *Oberlandesgericht*, except that in the case of Hesse-Nassau there were two, at Frankfurt am Main and at Kassel. Directly responsible to these thirteen courts were the 94 *Landgerichte*, separated into civil and criminal bench divisions, which also acted as courts of appeal for the *Amtsgerichte*, the equivalent of the petty sessions, of which there were over 1,100 in Prussia alone.[24] The powers of these Amtsgerichte were narrowly defined and restricted to the imposition of fines of up to 300 marks. The hierarchical nature of this legal framework meant that cases could be referred from a lower to a higher court, as far as the final court of appeal, the *Reichsgericht* in Leipzig.[25] However, in those instances where a case was first heard at the Landgericht level, no appeal was possible at all, except in quite obvious examples or irregularities in the interpretation of the law. For that reason, the Landgerichte tended to produce long and weightily written judgments, in which the possibility of challenging any aspects of legal interpretation was carefully excluded.

On the other hand, judgments in the *Schwurgerichte*, the jury-courts, were delivered orally. Here and in the *Schöffengerichte*, where the composition of the bench included lay-judges, existed the only opportunities for lay participation in the processes of the law. Even so, the extremely narrow and restricted social and political basis on which jurors and lay-judges were chosen militated against any genuine popular representation.[26] The selection procedure was highly complex: the commissions set up to choose lay judges consisted of nine people, including the chairman of the local Amtsgericht, an official appointed by the state government (in Prussia nearly always the Landrat), and seven other members elected by special selection committees set up by the local district councils, which in turn owed their origins to the three-class voting system. Only petty officers were brought before the Schöffengerichte and a state prosecutor was always empowered to challenge a decision with which he disagreed at the Landgericht level. The appointment commissions for the lay judges also met to prepare a short list of vetted candidates for the Schwurgerichte, except that in this case they had to refer their suggestions to a panel of state judges, who alone exercised responsibility for the final choice.[27]

Moreover, it was always possible for the presiding judge of a Schöffengericht to exert pressure on his less experienced colleagues, and for the jurors of a Schwurgericht to be confronted with a directive from the chairman of the court, as happened on at least one notable occasion.[28] In addition to sanctions applied by the courts, the absence of an equivalent to the Habeas Corpus Act provided a further weapon against political recalcitrants. As Ludwig Frank pointed out,[29] it was not such a rare thing for custody (*Untersuchungshaft*) to be as much as ten times the length of the actual prison sentence. One judge in Berlin was alone responsible for some 5,000 annual orders for custody.[30]

The ultra-conservative nature of the judicature had to a large extent been the outcome of deliberate government policy. Eckart Kehr, in a major piece of analysis on the Puttkamer ministry of 1881–8,[31] identified the practical and ideological need of the Bismarckian Reich not only to deal with the new and consuming problems created by the emergent industrial state, but to defend it against the growing menace of political dissent, especially from Social Democracy. It became abundantly clear, especially in the late 1870s, that public administration, the judicature and the universities, staffed in most cases by idealistic, reforming liberals of the 1840s, were unequal to the demands of holding Bismarck's highly-tenuous constitutional structures and political compromises together.

The solution adopted for the judicature was threefold. By pushing through a reduction in the number of the courts – these and other administrative changes were accomplished by the new *Gerichtsverfassungsgesetz* of 1879 – very many of the older judges who had qualified in the 1840s became redundant. At the same time, any remaining restrictions on advance through the ranks of defending counsel (*Avancementssperre*) were removed, so that most of the rump of judges of a liberal persuasion decided to move back into private practice, in order to escape the influence of political direction from above. The third element in this transformation was that throughout the 1880s scarcely any new judicial posts were created,[32] and since the liberal old guard had been eased out of power, this meant that for a decade no positions became vacant as a result of retirement. Kehr seeks to explain the increases in posts within the judicature dating from 1889 as a kind of government thank-you-present to the waiting generation, for their patience and proven political dependability.

The whole corps of judges in the Wilhelmine period was drawn from those who had been court assessors in the 1880s and, moreover, only those who had been through the additional sifting processes of the state prosecutor's office had a hope of being appointed to higher judicial positions. This system of reaction under Puttkamer was, in a direct parallel drawn by Kehr with the single-minded ruthlessness of Alexander the Great's military campaigns, 'a systematic segregation of bureaucracy and the officer corps . . . against the proletariat'.[33] Nor was it the case that this system of discrimination fell into disrepute in the 1890s. Since it was the prerogative of the crown to confirm all appointments to the judicature, it was possible for the Prussian Minister of Justice to declare in the Landtag in March 1896,[34] that there was no legal requirement to accept a graduate as a *Referendar* (apprentice or junior lawyer) or *Assessor* (legal assistant in the courts), merely because he had passed all his examinations. In any case, the acceptance of a Referendar depended on the decision of the presiding judge of the Oberlandesgericht to whom the candidate had applied, and a rejection was binding on all other presiding judges. Indeed, the sons of Wilhelm Liebknecht, Karl and Theodor, had a considerable struggle in the 1890s before their appointments were eventually confirmed.[35]

The four years spent as a Referendar were widely regarded as an excellent opportunity for testing a candidate's ideological reliability (*Gesinnungsschnüffelei*), and he was liable to be dismissed unconditionally at any time. Even as a qualified lawyer there were difficulties to be faced. Arthur Stadthagen, one of the most vehement opponents of revisionism within the SPD, had been excluded from legal practice by the *Ehrengericht* in Leipzig, because of his caustic comments on the quality and political bias of Prussian judges. A fellow Social Democratic lawyer, Hugo Haase, had to suffer several attempts to bring him before disciplinary inquiries. He was also called before the Ehrengericht, to answer a charge-sheet which ran to 61 pages and instanced the incompatibility of his political activities with membership of the legal profession.[36] Further difficulties which had to be surmounted were those of a financial nature. A private income was indispensable to the long period of training before appointment to a permanent post,[37] and the highest posts in the judicature were in any case the preserve of that special class in society – the reserve army officer.[38] A further bias operated against the appointment of Catholics. Of the top 24 civil servants in the Ministry of Justice in 1910, 21 were Protestant and only 3 Catholic, and of all higher judicial civil servants at this time over 72% were Protestant and only 24% Catholic. This compared with a total Protestant population of 61% and a total Catholic population of 36%.[39]

Other victims of this system of calculated bias were Jewish lawyers who attempted to move out of private practice. Only 3–4% of all the judges in Prussia were Jews and these never advanced beyond the Amtsgericht level. In Saxony, Hesse, Brunswick and Württemberg, states where anti-semitic feeling was strong, all Jews were excluded, and the Bavarian government, which had initially confirmed Jews as state prosecutors, introduced from 1901 onwards a *numerus clausus* regulation for all Jewish judges and state prosecutors.[40]

Since the state prosecutor represented the state, it was not surprising that his powers were especially formidable, even extending to the right to sit at the same physical level in the court as the judge. Not only did he occupy the same office building as the judge, but he was also required to liaise with court officials to ensure the speedy conduct of business. In addition to his responsibilities for preferring charges, conducting the prosecution and proposing sentences, he had an almost complete control over the preliminary inquiry stage (*Vorverfahren*), and all files of evidence accumulated by the police and the court of the first hearing were regarded as his property. The entire correspondence of the court, including requests for witnesses to be present, had to run via the state prosecutor's office, as did any application for an appeal against conviction and sentence. It was often possible for a state prosecutor to select the higher court of his choice for the hearing of an appeal – Oberlandesgericht or Reichsgericht – according to the likelihood of achieving the desired result.[41] Such men gained easy access to positions of great influence. The chief of police in Hamburg, Gustav Roscher, who for the sake of simplicity called his children by numbers, from one to six, spent five years as a state prosecutor in Essen,[42] and Karl von Schönstedt, the Prussian Minister of Justice from 1894 to 1905, had a distinguished career of legal service, including the presidency of the Oberlandesgericht at Celle. When he retired from office, Bülow recommended that he be awarded the coveted Order of the Black Eagle, because 'he has at all times been a steadfast and courageous defender of the monarchical idea and consequently the *bête noire* of the Social Democrats'.[43]

The major question is: did this system succeed in its intentions? There was certainly an increasing temptation to fall back on the law as a permanent solution, especially since the introduction of new legal statutes seemed to be fraught with difficulty.[44] As Albert Südekum remarked of the judiciary in 1913, 'There are not many criminally-minded perverters of justice, but those who do so unconsciously are very many.'[45] On the other hand, those responsible for the execution of justice were far from convinced that they were sufficiently well equipped, and governments frequently inclined to the view that the courts were not carrying out the full burden of the policy. The desperate wringing of hands indulged in by both sides was symptomatic of the vast strains created within the judicature by the imposition of a policy which went beyond the purely legal requirements of the *Strafgesetzbuch*. The Kaiser and General Waldersee were amongst those who accused the courts of insufficient zeal in operating against the SPD,[46] but it would be a mistake to assume that the courts were unwilling to cooperate, even when they realised the difficulty of dealing with abstract political ideas in a court of law.[47] Moreover, lapses in acting for the interests of the state at all times were not tolerated. When Maximilian Harden first faced a charge of *lèse-majesté* in April 1893, he was rather surprisingly found innocent and acquitted. This 'judicial carelessness' cost the judge concerned his position and he was prematurely retired.[48]

Occasionally, it was the police who came in for strictures from the judicature. Thus, the Oberstaatsanwalt at Kiel complained that policemen were often unable to quote in court the exact words used by a socialist agitator – often essential to secure a conviction – because their level of education was usually inferior to that of the speaker. There was a tendency to ascribe such failures to the general cleverness and verbal dexterity of party agitators, who were thought capable of suggesting ideas and associations without recourse to incriminating detail.[49] During the period of internal discussion prior to the drafting of the anti-subversion bill (*Umsturzvorlage*) in December 1894, the Ministry of Justice received a stream of lengthy submissions from all the Prussian Ober-staatsanwälte, bemoaning the inadequacy of the existing law and calling for the introduction of sharper provisions in the *Strafgesetzbuch*.[50]

The real danger to the state was much less the absence of institution-alised terror through the courts, much more the ebbing away of public confidence in justice and impartiality. This was a theme regularly taken up by liberal commentators such as Hans Delbrück, and it also occupied the attention of some of those involved in administration. Thus, the chief of police in Hamburg was convinced that there was nothing more conducive to successful political agitation by the SPD than an over-zealous application of all existing penal provisions. Far from arguing in favour of a policy of *'laisser faire, laisser aller'*, he nonetheless re-garded the counter-pressure exerted by the SPD against the state as a direct consequence of the pressure applied by the courts.[51]

The failure of successive governments to recognise the moral force of SPD charges against what came to be known as *'Klassenjustiz'* says much about the absence of a political consensus in the Wilhelmine period, and accounts to some degree for the continuing electoral suc-cesses of the party. Governmental intransigence to the idea of a general relaxation continued to remain a feature of official policy. What tended to reinforce this kind of rigidity was the gradual realisation that the SPD was proving increasingly adept at evading the laws and escaping prosecution or heavy sentencing by a more circumspect, not to say clever, attitude to what could be done with impunity. Party newspapers, for example, were especially successful at stopping just short of the mark.[52]

Social Democracy in conflict with the law

The attitude of mind to which governments had become conditioned during the Sozialistengesetz was that Social Democracy was an illegal organisation which deliberately set itself outside the law, and which could only be combated by applying every instrument of legal repres-sion at their command. It was not surprising, therefore, that the period between August 1886 and January 1889 saw no less than 55 trials in which individuals were charged with violating sections of the Sozial-istengesetz. One of the largest and most spectacular of these 'show' trials was held at Elberfeld in November 1889, when 90 socialists, in-cluding Bebel, were accused of contravening the law as members of a secret political society.[53] Preparations for the trial lasted over a year, files ran to some 18,000 sides and no fewer than 470 witnesses were called.[54] In practical terms, however, it was a catastrophe for the state, since 43 of the defendants had to be acquitted for lack of suitable evidence. Yet it was from this trial that state prosecutors up and down the country drew a most important lesson, which was that the state had always to provide both substantial political and legal arguments when pursuing Social Democrats in the courts.

Fourteen years later, in November 1903, a number of party members in Königsberg and Memel were arrested on charges of 'Geheimbündelei', of indulging in secret activities contrary to the security of the state. The case opened up not only the considerable links between the SPD and its Russian counterpart, but also the hand-in-glove co-operation between the Prussian and Russian political police. Socialist literature had been supplied to Russian revolutionaries for a number of years by the Vorwärts bookshop in Berlin, and the party at Königsberg was alleged to have been involved in smuggling pamphlets across the border.[55] For their part, the Prussian authorities had enlisted the help of the Russian border police in detaining – for considerable periods in custody – those suspected of aiding the organisation on German soil.[56]

The trial of nine Social Democrats, including Otto Braun, opened in July 1904 before a presiding judge who had been specially transferred from duty in Erfurt, and lasted for eleven days. The actual charges related to sedition and libel on the Tsar. It quickly transpired that Germany was the only country which had concluded the sort of agreement with Russia which enabled her to proceed against those suspected of helping foreign revolutionaries.[57] In fact, the state prosecutor argued as part of his evidence that by supporting revolutionary activity in Russia the accused were, by implication, guilty of plotting against the security of the German state. The defence was in the hands of Karl Liebknecht and Hugo Haase, whose detailed legal arguments and rhetorical tour de force resulted in the charges of insulting the Tsar (Zarenbeleidigung) being dropped.[58] The outcome was that three of the accused were acquitted; the remaining six, however, were convicted of organising a secret society and sentenced to short terms of imprisonment. Bebel called the episode 'a débâcle for all things Prussian and the Reich'.[59]

Since it was possible to detect signs of conspiratorial intent in the party's associated activities, such organisations came under particularly close scrutiny and were often subjected to increased police restrictions. In Saxony, for instance, all working-men's cycling and gymnastic clubs, choral and further education societies, were repeatedly dissolved from 1894 onwards, whilst their bourgeois equivalents, as well as the army veterans' associations (*Kriegervereine*) and church social organisations, continued to flourish unmolested.[60] The *Oberverwaltungsgericht*, the Prussian constitutional court, obliged in January 1896 by pronouncing on the political nature of the party's leisure activities.[61]

Of especial concern was SPD activity amongst the young and the success of the ideological struggle for the rising generation. The action taken against Karl Liebknecht in 1907, for publishing a tract on the evils of militarism in Germany, owed much to the fact that it was originally delivered as a speech to the first conference of the German socialist youth movement in Mannheim.[62] Even parental guardianship was at risk: a father was deprived of the rights over his 16-year-old son, because he had failed to prevent the boy's continuing membership of the local SPD gymnastic club.[63] Such incidents came to form the backbone of the '*Nadelstichpolitik*', a policy of persistent guerilla warfare waged against the party by the authorities.[64] The Sabbath ordinances were frequently invoked: two party members in Breslau were sentenced in August 1910 for distributing leaflets on a Sunday, whereas the local state prosecutor refused to act upon party complaints that a local landowner had been responsible for organising a distribution at the same time, which had been carried out by his employees, using a small army of bicycles and horse-and-carriages.[65] As late as April 1914, the Regierungspräsident in Danzig was still forbidding the use of red ribbons on funeral wreaths and, on the occasion of Auer's funeral in April 1907, the *Vorwärts* had to remind its readers that no valedictory speeches were permitted at the graveside.[66] Public houses faced other forms of official pressure, notably from the military, who placed boycotts on all those establishments which offered hospitality to Social Democrats.[67] In much the same way, all soldiers in Halle were forbidden in February 1911 to attend public cinematographic shows, since these were currently featuring newsreels of the funeral of Paul Singer.[68]

There were undoubtedly some parts of the country which seemed to suffer disproportionately from the interest of the local prosecuting offices. One of these was unquestionably Magdeburg, where the early 1890s came to be called the 'Maizier era', after the name of the local state prosecutor. The situation there deteriorated so rapidly that at one stage, in April 1893, as a result of the large number of cases brought against local SPD journalists, the party paper was completely without an editor.[69] The local police spared no pains in order to ensure maximum vigilance. Alarmed by the display of socialist literature in the window of the bookshop run by the local paper, a two-man guard was mounted in front of the shop window in November 1897. The guard was changed every three hours and stood during shop hours throughout the working week. A total of 336 policemen mounted guard for 504 hours until January 1898, when it was considered sufficient to post only one man on guard duty. Three months later the whole exercise was abandoned. As a result of this police attention, the bookshop became something of a tourist attraction and the sales turnover and numbers of subscribers to the party paper increased to such an extent that a new rotary printing machine had to be hurriedly purchased and pressed into service.[70] Other tactics of harassment by the local police included daily 'visits', the confiscation of picture post-cards and photographs of SPD politicians for failing to display the names of the printers and publishers, and a summons relating to the height of the sunblinds outside the window of the bookshop.

Berlin, of course, had more than its share of court cases which reflected varying degrees of brutal police efficiency and absurd comicality. Thus, in order to disperse a crowd which had shown some reluctance to accept the police dissolution of a political meeting, some hundred policemen, disguised as tramps, proceeded to draw their rubber truncheons. The whole incident received a very bad press and not only from the SPD papers, since it had rapidly become apparent that the ensuing violence had been the work of police *agents provocateurs*. This critical press comment resulted in nine editors appearing on charges of libelling the police, before a presiding judge whose remarks, 'Oh balderdash, public opinion does not exist', earned him a lasting place in SPD editorials.[71]

If governments regularly demonstrated their fear of the possibility of a violent revolution, the Social Democrats were equally aware that imprudence on their part might well trigger off measures of even greater severity. Both the knowledge that came from the publication of secret government documents and the daily evidence of further repressive action by the authorities, tended to produce an attitude of considerable caution from the party leadership. As early as February 1890, Engels had warned Wilhelm Liebknecht against giving any excuses for the Kaiser and the army to intervene militarily,[72] and during the protest demonstrations of the early 1900s, aimed at a reform of the Prussian three-class voting system, the party watchword was summed up in the slogan, '*Laßt Euch nicht provozieren, die Reaktion will schießen.*'[73] Occasionally, moments of confrontation would take on a comical aspect, as in the incident of the '*Treptower Wahlrechtsspaziergang*',[74] but the risks which party activists were prepared to take were often affected by direct threats to their economic livelihood. Thus, every state employee lost his job if he joined a trade union or was identified as a socialist,[75] and workers were frequently dismissed if they took unpaid leave to observe May Day. Similarly, a number of schoolteachers in Bremen, who had taken the initiative in sending a telegram to Bebel on the occasion of his seventieth birthday in 1910, were dismissed by the city senate.[76] Indeed, such was the extent of repression through the courts that between 1890 and 1912, Social Democrats were sentenced to a total of 164 years hard labour, 1,244 years imprisonment and 557,481 marks of fines for purely political offences.[77]

Yet however fruitful the pursuit of the SPD through existing law seemed, the temptation to bring in new legislation, aimed specifically at undermining the very foundations of the movement, was always strong, especially in the 1890s. The first of these attempts at concocting a sequel to the Sozialistengesetz and at the same time encouraging a situation where a Staatsstreich would appear inevitable, was initiated by Botho Eulenburg, the Prussian Minister of the Interior, in May 1894.[78] He proposed introducing a bill against internal subversion (*Umsturzvorlage*), not in the Prussian Landtag where it would have had a greater measure of support, but in the Reichstag. Caprivi, against whom Eulenburg was secretly intriguing, foresaw the considerable difficulties involved in steering the measure through, but the assassination of the French President Carnot the following month substantially increased the pressure for a comprehensive bill for the whole Reich. According to Hohenlohe, the bill took shape as a result of the 'anger, indignation and disquiet in all circles, especially in National Liberal quarters, after the murder of Carnot'.[79]

The inability of Caprivi and Eulenburg to work harmoniously together led to their respective dismissals in the autumn, and it was left to Hohenlohe, whose Chancellorship had several advantages as far as the Kaiser was concerned,[80] to pick up the threads of the planned bill. Despite his concern to avoid the impression of introducing a renewed Sozialistengesetz,[81] Hohenlohe accepted that the proposals, which involved a sharpening of several sections of the *Strafgesetzbuch*, 'had been necessary for some years'. Moreover, notwithstanding the fact that the measure had been received critically, even by parties sympathetic to the establishment, he believed 'it would be fatal for the government to withdraw or amend its proposals as a consequence of the agitation stirred up by liberal circles'.[82]

Those principally concerned in combating the SPD had, of course, been approached for their suggestions prior to the drafting of the bill. The submissions of the chief state prosecutor (*Oberstaatsanwalt*) at

Frankfurt am Main, in particular, left no doubt as to the dire nature of socialist agitation in general, which fomented dissatisfaction, envy and hate amongst the 'dispossessed', and used the columns of the SPD press to launch every conceivable attack on the German Reich and its institutions.[83] In his appreciation of the situation, the governing mayor of Hamburg underlined the need for the police to intervene preventatively, especially where socialist newspapers had been responsible for stirring up the masses.[84] Writing to Engels in February 1895, Bebel referred to recent events as

links in a chain, which is being fashioned in order to make our lives as miserable as possible . . . Military administration and the judicature are joined hand in hand. If one listens to them, one is to believe that we are on the edge of a precipice, that everything is being undermined.[85]

In its final form, the Umsturzvorlage was presented to the Reichstag on 25 April 1895. In an attempt to secure the backing of the Centre Party for the measure, it had acquired a number of clauses relating to blasphemy, the display of 'indecent' literature and attacks on Church doctrines. At the same time, liberals became convinced that the Umsturzvorlage would seriously curtail freedom of speech and conservatives felt that the proposals simply did not go far enough. In the course of a speech to the Reichstag, for example, Freiherr von Stumm suggested a short but effective bill whose two clauses would have deprived Social Democrats of their franchise and introduced the expulsion or internment of agitators.[86] In the circumstances, it was not surprising that the Umsturzvorlage was decisively rejected the following month. Commenting on the affair, Hans Delbrück observed that the campaign had 'made the government look ridiculous and has robbed the parties of the centre of the last ounce of their reputation. The only party to have profited is the SPD.'[87]

The next attempt to undermine the strength of the movement by recourse to existing law also ended in defeat for the Reichsleitung. Acting on instructions from the then Minister of the Interior, von Köller, the Berlin Polizeipräsident dissolved the entire local party organisation in the city, including the network of agents, the Presse-Commission, the propaganda and general management committees, as well as the six constituency parties. The outcome was a show trial in May 1896, at which the charge-sheet included the names of 47 prominent Social Democrats, among them Bebel, Auer and Singer.[88] During the period of legal argument in the courts, involving the Oberverwaltungsgericht and, ultimately the Reichsgericht, which ruled in November 1896 that von Köller's action had been technically invalid, the party executive and administrative machine were forced to move to Hamburg, where they remained until 1897.

The humiliation of the Reichsleitung in this way highlighted the amazing tangle of regulations affecting the operation of the laws of political association. Each state had its own individual statutes, mostly dating back to the 1850s which, in the case of Prussia, Bavaria, Saxony, Hesse, Oldenburg and Brunswick, prohibited the linking of local political clubs with any central organisation. In order to secure the passage of the code of civil law (*Bürgerliches Gesetzbuch*) through the Reichstag, Hohenlohe had agreed in June 1896 to a compromise which foresaw the repeal of all restrictions on political associations. Unfortunately, the Kaiser refused to agree to such an apparent capitulation and it was not until December 1899 that the '*Verbindungsverbot*' was eventually lifted.[89]

The Kaiser's uncompromisingly negative attitude has to be seen in relation to the demoralising effect caused by the defeat of the Umsturz-vorlage and the boost this had given to socialist agitation. In addition, a sustained campaign had been mounted by the SPD throughout the summer months of 1895 against the proposed celebrations marking the twenty-fifth anniversary of the Prussian victory at the battle of Sedan. Incensed at the unchecked flow of editorial criticism directed against the commemoration and the Prussian military heritage from which it derived, he telegraphed instructions to von Köller that no effort was to be spared in bringing all culprits to account.[90] In a letter to Hohenlohe he wrote,

I have seen with indignation and deeply injured sentiment the socialist newspapers, whose knavish abuse of the sacred memory of the great Kaiser surpasses all that has gone before. That has been perpetrated with the utmost calm, in full awareness of the failure of our law and with absolute impunity in the face of our justice, dominated as it is by Jewish liberalism . . . Something must be done in Prussia, however, then the Reich will follow.[91]

Consequently, the Kaiser ordered a bill to be prepared for the Prussian Landtag, prohibiting the SPD from holding public meetings, and another for the Reichstag, which threatened those convicted of slandering the memory of his imperial ancestors with severe penalties. At the end of August he telegraphed further instructions to Hohenlohe that a full-scale campaign of support for the government, coupled with an ideological offensive against the socialists, was to be mounted via the establishment press.[92] His own 'official' reaction took the form of a speech on Sedan Day itself, 2 September, when he called the SPD 'a rabble . . . not worthy of being called German'.

As a result of the manipulation of public opinion, Hohenlohe was able to record his hopes that a majority might be found in the Prussian Landtag to support the proposed new penal measure, and it was an indication of the importance the Kaiser attached to its success that he was prepared, if necessary, to change his Chancellor.[93] Moreover, his hard-headed determination was reflected in von Köller's view that 'the howls of protest that it is a law of proscription [*Ausnahmegesetz*] do not add up to much, since in the last analysis every penal law is a law of proscription'.[94] On 19 September, however, Hohenlohe pointed to the illusion in assuming that a new bill would necessarily bring about an improvement in the situation:

> The way Social Democracy is organised, it will be able to pursue its aims even without branch associations and meetings. Its press should be suppressed. That would bring success. However, this is impossible. What we need is another Reichstag . . . The fear of Social Democracy must be stronger and must count for more than the fear of a Staatsstreich.[95]

In effect, it was some 18 months before the bill, the 'lex von der Recke' as it came to be called after the incumbent Minister of the Interior, was laid before the Prussian Landtag.[96] Previously, public meetings could only be dissolved if they contravened sections of the *Strafgesetzbuch*, but the new bill proposed giving the police powers to ban meetings whenever a danger to public order was evident. This wide-ranging interpretative freedom led the *Vorwärts*, in a comment on the proposals, to describe the government's intentions as 'setting up an unbounded system of police despotism'.[97] In an effort to alert public consciousness to the dangers, the party organised numerous demonstrations, including 14 mass meetings in Berlin alone. The opportunities thus presented to the SPD for further agitation occupied the attention of the vast number of speakers in the debates in the Landtag, many of whom were alarmed at the obvious intention of the government to allow socialists to appear as martyrs in the eyes of the people. One deputy from Königsberg warned that 'history teaches . . . that out of police measures and police tyranny have emerged those violent movements which lead to revolution'.[98] Another pointed out that the SPD's most valuable propaganda was not through associations or meetings, but from hand to hand, mouth to mouth, at the workplace, in the factory, at home, in the public houses or on the street, and that all this would be untouched by the planned new measures.[99] Significantly, the view of von der Recke remained that the SPD was not 'a reformist party . . . but a revolutionary party, whose aim is the destruction of the existing state and social system'.[100] Despite strenuous government efforts, the bill failed to secure a majority – albeit by only four votes – and it was the narrowness of this success that contributed in good measure to the SPD's decision to contest future elections to the Landtag.

Party bitterness and nervousness increased with the publication by the *Vorwärts*[101] of a secret, internal memorandum drawn up by Count Posadowsky, which had invited comments from employers on further possible restrictions in the political rights of the trade-union movement. This was by way of a prelude to what was the last attempt at forcing through a substantial piece of discriminatory legislation against the working class – the hard-labour bill or *Zuchthausvorlage* of 1899. This again derived from an initiative of the Kaiser, who had announced details in a speech at Bad Oeynhausen on 6 September 1898. Only four days later, Empress Elisabeth of Austria was murdered in Geneva by an Italian anarchist and, as with the assassination of Carnot in 1894, this fuelled the fires of official concern. Considerable support for major changes in the existing law had come from numerous employers' as-sociations, which had frequently protested at the use of 'socialist terror' during labour disputes and strikes, and had organised petitions to the Reichstag and Bundesrat, expressing the hope that an initiative would soon be undertaken.[102]

As drafted, the bill aimed to strengthen §153 of the industrial code (*Reichsgewerbeordnung*), by proposing deterrent sentences in a state penitentiary (*Zuchthaus*) for those guilty of intimidating blacklegs during strikes.[103] Despite Hohenlohe's doubts about the efficacy of the measure, the Kaiser was determined on forcing it through and, indeed, sharpened all draft clauses sent to him.[104] The *Zuchthausvorlage* was subsequently presented to the Bundesrat in April 1899 and introduced in the Reichstag two months later. Hohenlohe put up a spirited defence of the proposals,[105] but it was soon apparent that opposition was mount-ing, and in a memorandum in October the Grand Duke of Baden urged the Kaiser to withdraw the bill:

There is no prospect of pushing the measure through, it only induces dangerous horse-trading, strengthens Social Democracy, divides the establishment parties and weakens the authority of government.[106]

In fact, the Zuchthausvorlage had to be postponed because of the more pressing claims of Tirpitz' navy law, but this did not alter the decisive parliamentary defeat it suffered in November.

With the failure of this bill, it is tempting to see a watershed in government policy. The hopes of controlling the growth of the socialist movement by new pieces of repressive legislation – and the Umsturz-vorlage, lex von der Recke and Zuchthausvorlage were designed as the instruments of such a policy – had been dashed by the forces of parliamentary opposition. To some extent this marked the degree of stalemate which had been reached between the Reichsleitung and the parliamentary parties, since however hard governments tried they could not always count on rubber-stamping operations, especially from the Reichstag. Nonetheless, this parliamentary impasse merely highlighted the pressing need to stem the advance of Social Democracy by institutional means. Significantly, there was no real softening in the application of existing law after 1900, and the repeated rebuffs which had occurred in the Reichstag and Prussian Landtag in the 1890s led governments firmly away from the inconvenience and political riskiness involved in creating new law through the legislature. Instead, government strategy relied increasingly on enforcing those sections of existing law which held out the greatest hopes of a discriminating control of political dissent.

Indeed, from the turn of the century on the courts succeeded in achieving in practice the political aims of the Zuchthausvorlage, by a more extensive application of §153 of the industrial code.[107] To some extent, there was even a change in attitude by employers' associations who regarded this method of control, of 'Rechtsbildung durch Rechtssprechung', as a much smoother and more preferable way of re-interpreting the law in their favour.[108] Like the SPD, trade-unionists had long suffered from the practice of the courts. As early as 1873 Lujo Brentano had written, 'The German worker has the right of combination [Koalitionsrecht], but if he makes use of it he is punished.'[109] Similarly, successive governments seemed to be guided by Puttkamer's view, expressed in the Reichstag in May 1886 that 'Behind every large labour movement . . . lurks the hydra of violence and anarchy.'[110]

Some five years after the failure of the Zuchthausvorlage, in August 1904, a conference of employers' associations at Magdeburg actually demanded measures which went beyond the proposals of the original bill.[111] Under the renewed pressure from some quarters for repressive legislation, it was not surprising that the *Vorwärts* claimed in December 1904 that the succession of recent cases involving alleged breaches of the peace had been occasioned by a general order from the Prussian Ministry of Justice, which had pointed to the possibility of using this law against strike pickets.[112] Nor was it only Prussia which felt the effects of such legal interpretations. Nuremberg, for example, experienced a series of very bitter labour struggles in 1906, involving strikes and lockouts, which led to 205 separate charges under §153 of the industrial code.[113]

Yet it was in Prussia itself that the most violent clashes between organised labour and the authorities took place. Of these, the riots in the Berlin suburb of Moabit in the autumn of 1910 deserve particular attention, because they represent in microcosm the deep-seated divisions in Wilhelmine society. The disturbances had grown out of wage demands by workers in a coal business, anxious to compensate for increases in the cost of living,[114] and rapidly developed into a violent confrontation with the police, who had been given precise instructions to act 'with extreme severity'.[115] In all, some 30,000 people were involved, many of whom were goaded into acts of violence by *agents provocateurs*.[116] Two workers were killed, and 104 policemen and 150 demonstrators seriously injured. The award of 95 medals to policemen for their heroic action in suppressing the riots was complemented by a campaign in the establishment press, conjuring up the red spectre of revolutionary terror.[117] The events in Moabit were widely regarded as evidence of a continuing radical trend within the SPD, and Bethmann Hollweg informed the Prussian Ministry of State on 21 October that the Kaiser had telegraphed instructions for a new bill, intended to afford protection to all non-strikers.

For its part, the SPD viewed the propaganda campaign in the establishment press as part of the necessary preparation for a new repressive bill, and for this reason the party executive took the unusual step of dissociating itself from the riots.[118] However, to alert the general population to the seriousness of possible counter-revolutionary attacks, demonstrations were held in many cities, including Berlin, where no fewer than 21 meetings took place. Bethmann, in speeches to the Reichstag in December 1910, was concerned to pin the whole blame for the incident on the SPD, and began investigating the possibilities of using the proposed reform of the *Strafgesetzbuch* as an additional means of waging war against the movement. The Prussian Minister of Justice, speaking in the Landtag, declared that within the terms of the proposed revision, the government would consider depriving defence counsel of the right to call their own witnesses.[119]

In the trials which followed in the wake of the disturbances, long sentences of imprisonment were passed on the ringleaders for breaches of the peace and resistance against the power of the state.[120] Typical of the interference which came from the Ministry of Justice was the order that all cases involving insults to police officers would have to come before the Landgericht and not the Schöffengericht, which would normally have been responsible.[121] A particularly appalling case of official tyranny was the treatment of a widow whose husband, fearing for the safety of their son, had gone out to search the streets during the riots and had been struck dead by blows from mounted policemen. The authorities refused an inquiry into the incident and in March 1911 the SPD executive issued a statement, offering a reward of 2,000 marks for information leading to the identification or arrest of those responsible for the man's death.[122]

The 1912 miners' strike in the Ruhr was the occasion for a similarly firm response from the authorities. Officials of the Ministry of Justice opined that the SPD press had played a major part in fomenting the industrial action, and special arrangements were set in force to ensure the speedy progress of all court proceedings.[123] In order to cope satisfactorily with more than 2,000 individual charges,[124] the Ministry had arranged for all cases, as with Moabit, to come before the Landgericht, as well as taking on extra legal staff to cope with the situation. One of the junior lawyers involved, himself working on some 40 cases a day, aptly termed the whole episode 'Sonderjustiz im Schnellverfahren'.[125]

The use of strikes as a political weapon had in fact been partially sanctioned in the party's struggle against the Prussian three-class voting system, and the attempts to introduce other regressive franchises. Several of the state governments had reacted to SPD electoral successes by recourse to new franchise laws. In Saxony, the old electoral law of 1868 was replaced in 1896 by the three-class system and thirteen years later by a four-class arrangement. Brunswick (1899) and Lübeck (1903) had also adopted changes and in Hamburg, where the first socialist had been elected to the city parliament in 1901, the senate passed a similar bill in 1905.[126] A general strike was subsequently called for 17 January 1906, which coincided with other protest movements in different parts of the country. The demonstration in Hamburg rapidly degenerated into violent clashes with the police, however, and two people were killed.[127]

The over-zealous reaction by the authorities was due in large measure to the concern aroused by the abortive Russian revolution of 1905, which had set alarm-bells ringing in official departments throughout the Reich. Thus, demonstrators in Saxony who had been arrested in December 1905 were sentenced within a short space of time to a combined total of 20 years imprisonment, in order to forestall the possibility of further demonstrations originally planned for the following month.[128] Indeed, the round of inter-ministerial discussions which took place at this time revealed not only the extent of official anxiety, but also the realisation that in many cases the struggle against the SPD was a continuous holding operation.[129] Such nervousness was reflected, for ex-

ample, in the refusal to permit the French socialist leader Jean Jaurès
to enter the country and address a public meeting in Berlin, whereupon
the *Vorwärts* and other leading SPD newspapers simply printed in full
the text of the speech Jaurès was to have delivered.[130]

The *Reichsvereinsgesetz* of 1908, a uniform set of combination laws
for the whole Reich,[131] was in part an attempt to overcome the dangers
of such foreign revolutionary 'infiltration'. As a result of the '*Sprachen-
paragraph*', all public meetings had henceforth to be conducted in the
German language. This hit particularly hard at the Polish minority –
of whom there were almost 4 million in 1908, representing 10% of the
total population in Prussia – and, indeed, Polish workers in the Ruhr
took the step in 1913 of holding their annual conference in the Dutch
town of Winterswyk, in order to escape this provision.[132] Although the
right of women and minors to belong to a political association was guaranteed under the new law and the extent of police surveillance somewhat
reduced key reserve powers, involving the ability to ban or dissolve
meetings because of danger to the public order, were still retained. In
March 1910, for example, instructions were issued from Berlin that all
meetings originally planned to discuss the three-class voting system were
to be prohibited,[133] and later that year a member of the SPD Reichstag
group was forced to abandon his speech to a gathering near Wiesbaden.[134]

Such attempts to curtail the freedom of SPD parliamentarians were
by no means limited to public meetings. In 1910, the lower house of
the Prussian Landtag, which by then included six Social Democratic
deputies, had rushed through a change in the rules of its procedure
(*Hausknechtsparagraph*), thus effectively limiting freedom of expression. During a debate in May 1912, the Speaker of the house, von
Erffa, ordered one of the SPD group, Julian Borchardt, to be forcibly
removed from the sitting by a small police detachment. Borchardt's
offence had been to heckle continuously a highly provocative speech
by a National Liberal deputy. As the *Hamburger Echo*[135] pointed out,
this action by von Erffa was itself illegal, as well as being an unwelcome
reminder of the intervention of the military in 1848, resulting in the
dissolution of the Prussian parliament. This incident succeeded in
momentarily stirring middle-of-the-road opinion, whilst the SPD made
every effort to exploit the potential of the situation. In Cologne, for
example, the party press was responsible for organising five mass demonstrations and others took place in von Erffa's own constituency.[136]

By this time, von Erffa had issued writs against Borchardt and a
colleague, Robert Leinert, who had come to Borchardt's assistance in

the Landtag, although the Oberstaatsanwalt in Berlin rejected attempts by the two men to institute action against the police officer commanding the detachment. An added twist to the situation developed on 10 June, when von Erffa suffered a stroke and died. Liberal papers which had at first come to the rescue of the SPD, now began insinuating that the six members of the parliamentary group were somehow responsible for the Speaker's death. When the case eventually came before the courts in the autumn, tempers had somewhat cooled, but both men were given fines for resisting the police in the execution of their duty.[137] When their appeals were predictably rejected by the Reichsgericht in May 1913, the *Vorwärts* devoted a stinging editorial to the arbitrary use of such police power.

It was, of course, the party press which took the lead in reporting and exploiting such instances of continuing political harassment during the period – the newspaper was, after all, the only effective means of rapid communication – and it was the party press which, in doing so, took the greatest risks and most regularly ran the gauntlet of official repression.

The party press in conflict with the law

In theory, the *Reichspressegesetz* of 1874 enshrined the principle of freedom of the press. It was a theoretical freedom as much bound by the limiting effects of other laws as the nominal absence of censorship. Sensitivity to the political effects of stage drama resulted, for example, in the prohibition of public performances of, amongst others, Hauptmann's *Die Weber* and Sudermann's *Morituri*; and the editor of the *Magdeburger Volksstimme* twice received prison sentences for quoting from Büchner's *Dantons Tod* and for printing the text of Heine's 'Weberlied'.[138] Students at Munich University were expressly forbidden to read the *Vorwärts*,[139] and similar restrictions affecting socialist literature also applied to the military. If a newspaper became involved in a libel suit, no matter how often it might plead that it was acting in the public interest, it was not entitled to the protection afforded by §193 of the *Strafgesetzbuch*, which made allowance for fair comment. Its ability to escape critical detection by the law was considerably restricted by the requirement that a copy of each publication had to be delivered free of charge on the day of issue to the local police authority (*Pflichtexemplar*). The Hamburg police, for example, received in 1900 a total of 183 different newspapers in 17,520 copies, and committed some 54,000 cuttings to their files.[140]

At no time could it be said that the authorities exercised any beneficial regard for the right to express views of political dissent.[141] All those
connected with the production of a newspaper were considered criminally liable. This affected the printing staff and compositors no less than
the members of the editorial department – those responsible for writing
individual articles (*Verfasser*), for collecting and editing them (*Her-
ausgeber*) and for publishing them (*Verleger*).[142] Each newspaper employing several journalists (*Redakteure*) was required to have an editor
(*verantwortlicher Redakteur*), with whom rested the final decision on
whether or not to publish a particular article. Even the existence of
Sitzredakteure did not prevent many of the SPD's front-rank agitators
from spending many months in prison, however, and it remains remarkable, in view of the regularity with which journalists were required to
attend court hearings and serve their sentences, that party newspapers
were published at all.

Both the police and the local state prosecutor's office had the power
to order the confiscation of printed material, arising from the failure to
print the name of the publisher or chief editor on the copy, or resulting
from the publication of details of army manoeuvres,[143] or items considered likely to arouse class-hatred, to intend *lèse-majesté*, or those
which constituted a treasonable offence.[144] The procedure governing
such confiscations was exceedingly complicated. If the confiscation was
ordered by the local state prosecutor, he was required to apply to the
nearest court within 24 hours for confirmation of his action, and it was
incumbent upon the court to ratify his decision within a further 24
hours. If the confiscation was undertaken by the police, the matter had
then to be referred to the state prosecutor within 12 hours, and he was
then required to make a court application within the following 12
hours, except that in such situations the court was granted a period of
grace extending to five days, before announcing its decision. In both
cases the court order confirming the confiscation was limited to two
weeks, and criminal proceedings had to be instituted before the expiry
of this limit.[145]

Naturally enough, this required the closest of cooperation between
the police and the local *Staatsanwalt* and a readiness to act decisively,
qualities which were not always in evidence. The Minister of Justice,
Schelling, had cause to complain to all senior state prosecutors in December 1893 that there were still considerable breaks in time between
the confiscation of material and the ensuing court hearings, and that
some prosecutors were under the impression that a confiscation was
sufficient in itself.[146] A year later he ordered still greater cooperation

and more effective coordination between the local authorities.[147] With regard to newspapers, it was essential to the deterrent effect of the confiscation that action should follow almost immediately,[148] but in the case of periodicals and single publications the police were assisted in their work by a directory of all confiscated material, which was sent out from Berlin and revised at quarterly intervals right up to 1914.[149]

Difficulties in ensuring the success of official action of this kind could always be circumvented by recourse to what was known as the principle of 'fliegender Gerichtsstand'.[150] This made it possible for all those connected with the editorial and production aspects of a journal to be prosecuted in any other locality where that publication happened to be distributed. This resulted, for example, in a case of libel, for which the Bavarian authorities could not guarantee certain conviction under their system of jury-courts, being heard by a court in Saxony which duly obliged.[151] The official armoury of inconvenience was supplemented by two other requirements: the 'Zeugniszwang' and the 'Berichtigungszwang'. The former enabled the courts to compel a journalist to give evidence, even when professional rules of conduct were involved,[152] and the latter asserted the official right to 'correct' any information as printed.

By far the greatest restriction on the freedom of the Social Democratic press came with the application of the laws relating to defamation of character. There had been considerable sensitivity in public life even before 1890 – Bismarck, for example, was responsible in his time for almost 10,000 writs for libel and slander – but the situation of increased socialist press activity in the 1890s led to a more systematic use of the whole range of legal possibilities. The German offence of 'Beleidigung' was derived from the Roman law concept of *iniuria*, and had developed in the seventeenth and eighteenth centuries as a kind of legal portmanteau term, which could be made to embrace any remarks considered to annoy or displease a fellow being.[153] Thus, the use by the SPD press of the terms '*Kriecherverein*' for the army veterans' associations (*Kriegervereine*) – involving a neat pun on the two German words '*Krieger*' meaning warrior and '*Kriecher*' meaning crawler – and '*Reichslügenverband*' for the *Reichsverband gegen die Sozialdemokratie* resulted in numerous charges and convictions for libel. The tendency to indulge in personalised attacks on individuals was noted by Schelling in a circular to senior state prosecutors in July 1891.[154] Since the nature of such attacks had much wider repercussions, for the institutions of state which such individuals happened to represent or the social classes to which they belonged, it was the duty of all prosecutors

66

to act on their behalf by initiating prompt legal proceedings. A corresponding awareness of all such implications by the local Schöffengericht, resulting in a number of heavy prison sentences, led the Landrat at Hersfeld[155] to report that SPD comment vis-à-vis the local police had been noticeably more restrained in recent months. Similarly, two leading articles on the Zuchthausvorlage, written by the editor of the *Schleswig-Holsteinische Volkszeitung*, were interpreted by the local Landgericht as a libel on the Chancellor and the State Secretary of the Interior, and resulted in a two-month prison sentence. The hothouse atmosphere and easy irritability which characterised social relationships in public, was aptly conveyed by Wilhelm Liebknecht in a Reichstag speech in 1897, when he remarked,

We still have no proper system of public life in Germany; just as in our private lives we fear the fresh air and, in order to avoid a draught, shut all the windows, so we also have a dread of the political fresh air which comes from speaking freely. . .[156]

More far-reaching in its application was the notorious §95 of the *Strafgesetzbuch*, which related to *lèse-majesté* or, more correctly, *Majestätsbeleidigung*.[157] Its very importance rested in the identification of the ruling head of state with the political interests and security of the state, so that, potentially, all critical comment could be construed as a direct attack not only on the personal honour of the monarch, but also on the constitutional foundations of the state. Since the nature of absolute power in Wilhelmine Germany was regarded as drawing its legitimacy from the religious traditions of the Middle Ages – power was God-ordained and vested in a secular representative – the allegedly atheistic Social Democrats, '*die gottlosen Sozialdemokraten*', represented a direct threat to the system by their refusal to accept the religious justification of such power.[158] An exposition of this law was rendered all the more difficult by its deliberate vagueness and, indeed, there seemed no possibility of avoiding this state of affairs, since no court of law was held competent to judge the actions of the supreme ruler. This led to all kinds of absurdities: a woman in the Ruhr was sentenced to three months imprisonment in June 1894 for *lèse-majesté* committed by 'movements of the hand',[159] and a conservative paper argued that since the *Vorwärts* referred to 'Wilhelm II' and not to 'S. M. der Kaiser', this amounted to a hidden form of *Majestätsbeleidigung*.[160]

Other sections of the *Strafgesetzbuch* were based on the assumption that all other princes of ruling houses, together with their dependants, should be accorded the same protection as the Kaiser.[161] An unsigned postcard, addressed to Schelling,[162] complained bitterly that a citizen of Berlin had been sentenced to eight months imprisonment for libelling the crown prince – then a child of nine years – and in 1897 the editor of the *Hamburger Echo*, Reinhold Stenzel, received a similar sentence for libelling the Belgian king.[163] It is largely through the chronicles of such cases, published by the SPD press,[164] that the arbitrary use of this law percolated through to general consciousness.

Not surprisingly, the SPD had the dubious honour of supplying most of the martyrs. One of the worst, and by no means untypical, cases in the early 1890s befell the then editor of the *Magdeburger Volksstimme*, Heinrich Peus. Following a speech to local party workers in October 1891, he was arrested on a charge of *lèse-majesté* and was repeatedly refused bail to visit his wife, who was dying after a confinement. Originally sentenced to a term of two years imprisonment and five years loss of citizenship[165] by the local Landgericht, the Reichsgericht ordered a re-trial, because the lower court had acted illegally in depriving Peus of his civic rights. At the new hearing in September 1892 he was sent to prison for twelve months.[166] Engels, in a comment to Bebel after the first hearing,[167] saw in the 'outrageous Peus verdict' a symptom of the harsher administrative and judicial policy already being pursued. In fact, the cases of *lèse-majesté* continued to increase steadily in the first half of the 1890s, rising from 509 in 1890 to 621 in 1894.[168]

Amongst those affected in this way was Wilhelm Liebknecht, whose remarks made at a gathering on the eve of the 1895 party conference in Breslau were regarded as contravening §95. Liebknecht had already been singled out for special favour when, together with his colleagues in the SPD Reichstag group, he had remained seated during the '*Kaiserhoch*' on the occasion of the inauguration of the new parliamentary building in December 1894. Despite considerable efforts, the local state prosecutor had been unable to persuade the Reichstag to rescind the parliamentary immunity from prosecution, to which Liebknecht was entitled under §30 of the imperial constitution.

On this occasion, however, the charge of *lèse-majesté* brought against Liebknecht was aided by the 're-discovery' of an ancient legal principle – the *dolus eventualis*, which allowed a court to discern the intent to commit an offence, even where this could not be directly inferred from the words of a speech or printed article. When questioned in the Reichstag about the validity of this judicial doctrine, the Minister of Justice, von Schönstedt, declared that its application rested on a further legal observation: *si duo faciunt, idem non est idem*.[169] In fact, in the years that followed, the Reichsgericht, taking its precedent from the Liebknecht case, often ordered a re-trial in cases of acquittal, simply because the court in question had not taken account of the *dolus* principle.[170] Attempts by Liebknecht to appeal against his conviction and sentence all came to naught, and in December 1897, at the age of 72, he began a term of imprisonment lasting four months.[171]

Judging by the undiminished vigour with which cases of *lèse-majesté* were pursued in the courts and the harshness of the sentencing policy – in January 1899, for example, the editor of the party paper in Magdeburg was given a sentence of four years, for publishing an anecdotal story set in distant Baghdad – there is no reason to suppose that the theoretical freedom of the press had much validity in substance. Indeed, it was not only the Social Democrats who fell foul of the law in this way: Ludwig Quidde, who achieved prominence as the result of his study of the Roman emperor Caligula,[172] was himself convicted for pointing out in a speech that there was no justification in calling William I 'William the Great' unless one wished to distinguish between him and 'William the Little'. Others who also suffered such legal retribution were the editors of the satirical magazine *Simplicissimus*, and Maximilian Harden, editor of *Die Zukunft*, except that in these cases the inconvenience of conviction was very often mitigated by the imposition of periods of *custodia honesta (Festungshaft)*, which bore no relation to the prison sentences passed on Social Democrats. When the *Frankfurter Volksstimme* published in September 1903 what purported to be a circular from the Ministry of Justice, instructing state prosecutors to pursue all offences of *lèse-majesté* committed by Social Democrats with unrelenting determination, it merely seemed to confirm acknowledged legal practice.

However, in the first few years of the new century, there were signs of considerable unease in government circles as to the wisdom of legal action resulting from petty denunciations and instances of an essentially trifling nature, which in recent years had led to an increasingly high rate of acquittal.[173] In January 1907 an actual relaxation in the law was promised in a decree issued on the Kaiser's birthday. It took some time for the fact to emerge that the substance of the imperial decree and the bill that it had foreshadowed,[174] altered little as far as the Social Democrats were concerned. The Kaiser had specifically asked that legal action should only be initiated in cases of 'malevolent' intent. As the *Vorwärts* remarked,[175] the entire result of the 'reform' was the ludicrous state of affairs that a *lèse-majesté*, when committed by a monarchist, would in future go unpunished. A memorandum prepared by the State Secretary at the Reich Office of Justice, Nieberding,[176] actually pointed to the increased importance of 'political considerations' in the application of the revised laws. Inevitably, this would lead a court to consider the political opinions and possible motives of anyone brought before it on a charge under §95 and, although there was a welcome drop to an all-time low of 39 cases in 1908, the instances of prosecutions arising from political convictions (*politische Tendenzprozesse*) again showed an alarming upward trend in the years before 1914.[177]

Quite apart from the nebulousness of such laws, there were other legal trip-wires calculated to cause equal uncertainty and confusion; nowhere more so than in the exposition of a small section of the *Strafgesetzbuch* – §360xi – under which were collected all those offences likely to be committed by Social Democrats and not covered by sections of existing law. The offence of '*grober Unfug*' (gross misdemeanour) was originally intended to cover minor breaches of the public order, but its theoretical elasticity, its susceptibility to different forms of legal interpretation, led to the SPD terming it the '*Kautschukparagraph*'. Thus, for example, the Reichsgericht decided in 1894 that the wearing of a red buttonhole emblem was itself a disturbance of the peace,[178] and attempts by the SPD to proclaim a boycott of public houses unsympathetic to the socialist cause were similarly treated.[179] Even the mere distribution of leaflets and election addresses led to convictions under this law and, in order to take advantage of its comprehensiveness, the Bavarian authorities often succeeded in doctoring charge-sheets with this view specifically in mind.[180]

Whereas virtually every party newspaper faced official harassment on all sides – the *Hannoverscher Volkswille*, for instance, had to endure attempts by the local state prosecutor in the years 1902–4 to persuade individuals and firms to issue writs against the paper[181] – the SPD press in the *Reichsland* of Alsace-Lorraine had to contend with a situation in which even its theoretical freedom was not guaranteed.[182] In the first few months of the existence of the *Elsaß-Lothringer Volkszeitung*, its subscribers were brought individually to the police headquarters in Straßburg and interrogated.[183] Despite the enormous difficulties it faced, the paper continued to rail against the pinpricks of administrative measures against the party,[184] and an article which appeared on 21 March 1894 caused the then Under-Secretary for Internal Affairs, von Köller, to order the suppression of the paper under the '*Diktaturparagraph*'.[185] Every attempt to re-found the paper under a different name in the following four years was frustrated by the authorities in Straßburg, nor was any Social Democratic speaker from the Reich permitted to address meetings in Alsace-Lorraine.[186] The discovery of copies of the

Offenburger Volksfreund, one of the party papers in Baden, in the home of a worker accused of the murder of a factory-owner, led to that paper being banned in 1895. Not until November 1898 did a successor publication emerge, in the form of the *Freie Presse für Elsaß-Lothringen*.

Some individual party papers were always prone to suffer eternal vigilance at the hands of the authorities. Hugo Haase himself defended different editors of the *Königsberger Volkszeitung* on no less than 64 separate occasions over a period of 17 years, and his diary for 4 April 1906 consisted of four cases against the paper, all for some form of libel and all ending in conviction.[187] Revolutionary rhetoric continued to be regarded as proof of revolutionary intentions; as the *Rheinische Zeitung*[188] remarked, the merest reference to historical examples of insurrection was sufficient to ensure a conviction under §130 of the *Strafgesetzbuch*, which forebade incitement to class-hatred. The *Leipziger Volkszeitung* was singled out for special attention in this way: in February 1906 the paper's editor faced charges arising from 25 recent articles, which had dealt with the historical origins of the suffrage movement. He was sentenced to 21 months imprisonment.[189] On the basis of all existing law, the *Vorwärts*[190] calculated that in the period 1890–1910 members of the working-class movement had received 1,188 years of imprisonment, 111 years of hard labour (*Zuchthaus*) and over half a million marks in fines. Perhaps it was not surprising, therefore, that the rate of recidivism leapt from 25% in 1882 to 45% in 1908.[191]

The continued firmness shown by the authorities was reflected in the period immediately before 1914. In February 1912, for instance, there were 15 cases against party editors and 18 in February of the following year. Again, in the first six months of 1913 there were no fewer than 104 convictions against SPD journalists, resulting in prison sentences totalling 40 years and fines of almost 11,000 marks.[192] This excessive use of repression through the courts had its corollary in the steadily increasing amount of litigation. In the years 1881–5 there were 232 cases and in the period 1906–10 391 cases for every 10,000 inhabitants.[193] According to the *Statistisches Jahrbuch für das Deutsche Reich*, 1914 witnessed the incredible number of 6,776,727 court cases – not taking into account an additional three-and-a-half million cases heard in the commercial and labour courts – which meant, assuming two parties to each hearing, that approximately one person in five was involved in a court case each year.[194]

This appalling situation had given rise to concern on all sides, not least from those, like Hans Delbrück, who saw in the signs of a collapse of public confidence in the administration of justice, the direct results of socialist propaganda brought about by a policy of officially-inspired political discrimination.[195] As far as *Die neue Zeit* was concerned, the failure of bourgeois society to uphold the impartiality of the courts was but a symptom of its own rapid degeneration.[196] Despite the fluctuations in approach by local authorities and some inexplicable absurdities in the sentencing policy, what stands out in the period between 1890 and 1914 is the central importance occupied by the law as a major bulwark of society.

Even though the government set in motion the machinery for an overhaul of the *Strafgesetzbuch* – whose legal anomalies unquestionably pressed Germany back into medieval times – it seemed reluctant to relinquish the considerable powers of political persuasion through the courts and, indeed, was concerned to supplement them wherever possible.[197] In December 1902, a 21-man commission of jurists began meeting in the Reich Office of Justice to examine questions of legal reform. Its unanimous recommendation was that the jury-courts (*Schwurgerichte*) should be abolished and that participation should be confined to the Schöffengerichte. In exchange for the proposal to make all verdicts in the lower courts subject to appeal, the commission suggested that the state prosecutor should be empowered to demand a higher sentence at the appeal stage.[198] Not until April 1911 did a drafting commission meet to prepare a revision of the *Strafgesetzbuch*, and the outbreak of war in 1914 put an end to its work.

The failure to be cowed into complete submissiveness says much about the independent spirit of the SPD press. Since there was, however, a limit to the amount of physical discomfort that party journalists were prepared to suffer at the hands of the law, it was only to be expected that repression through the courts would result in a slight moderation in the tone of editorial comment. Yet judged by their reaction to events within society, the verbal radicalism of Social Democratic newspapers seemed to have lost nothing of its characteristic sting. Party journalists continued an uphill struggle, almost forlornly at times, against the abuses of a political system, in which 'Weltpolitik' and 'Flottenbau' remained the watchwords, and not those of equality before the law and social justice.

The SPD and 'Klassenjustiz'

Social Democratic accusations of a built-in bias in the operation of justice in Wilhelmine Germany had come to be gathered under the generalised rallying-cry of 'Klassenjustiz'. More than any other party slogan, it had the effect of stirring up popular emotion and releasing pent-up reserves of resentment and fury, but the claims made in its name were by no means examples of misplaced judicial intentions. There was a substantial argument of fact which supported even the wildest of propaganda articles on the subject; a realisation that was aptly expressed by Hans Delbrück in 1903, when he wrote,

One of the sources from which the tremendous power of Social Democracy draws its strength . . . is the sense that we in Germany do not live in a system of equality before the law. It is the concept of 'Klassenjustiz' which awakens a most passionate form of hate.[199]

It was not simply a question of the burden of proof of innocence resting on the defendant, so much as the accepted practice of denying to all political dissidents the benefit of the doubt in cases of conflicting or circumstantial evidence and unsubstantiated prosecution submissions. Those who belonged to the professional classes were always deemed to have acted with good intentions, especially when the victims of their offences happened to be Social Democratic activists. Doubts about the impartiality of justice, together with concern over the absence of fair play, were felt even at the simplest level of civil action. Whenever a working-man had occasion to make a complaint against a public servant or official body, it was a wonder if the local state prosecutor did not proceed to turn the tables on the unfortunate plaintiff and bring him before the court on a charge of defamation of character.[200] The sad truth was that purely extraneous considerations – the clothes a man happened to wear or the political convictions he held – continued to impress the courts of law much more than concrete legal evidence.

At a public meeting in Stuttgart in August 1907, Karl Liebknecht referred to the four principal manifestations of 'Klassenjustiz': the way in which physical appearance influenced character assessment, always to the detriment of the working class; the one-sided evaluation of legal material and evidence; the application and use of specific laws; and the severity of the sentencing policy against known political dissidents.[201] Such practices were actively endorsed by wide sections of bourgeois society and repeatedly given prominence in editorial comment. Thus, for example, the conservative *Kreuzzeitung*, noted for its tone of high moral rectitude, ended a leading article in 1891 with the request that 'God may grant us an intellectual Sedan, a victory over these enemies within.'[202] At the same time, the SPD was acutely aware of the propagandistic effect of its sustained campaign against the operation of 'Klassenjustiz',[203] whilst careful to avoid the perils of particularised comment. In 1905, during the inter-ministerial discussions on further measures to control the Social Democratic movement, a leading civil servant in the Ministry of Justice complained that only rarely was it proving possible for the oft-repeated attacks on 'Klassenjustiz' to be pursued as libel, since the SPD tended to refer not to specific courts and individual verdicts, but in generalities affecting the system as such.[204] In terms of the party's belief in the impending collapse of bourgeois society, the growing economic strength of the working class was bound to lead to a thinly-disguised counter-attack of this kind, to what the *Vorwärts*[205] described as 'a policy of brutalised white terror'.

Of the more generalised assaults on the absence of social and legal equity, none was calculated to damage institutional pride more than mocking criticism of the '*Rechtsstaat*'.[206] There is some doubt as to the exact origin of this term, as it came to be applied in Prussia and then in the other leading German states. It was long associated with Robert von Mohl, a constitutional lawyer at Tübingen, who used the concept in the 1820s to distinguish new forms of nineteenth-century state organisation from those semi-feudal absolutist states in which rulers exercised supreme personal power.[207] However, the word 'Rechtsstaat' was also used in 1808 by Adam Müller, a philosopher of reactionary conservatism, and there is some reason to suppose that the concept was never linked solely with the forces of liberalism.[208] Indeed, the extent to which the judiciary were really independent of the executive and the guarantee of basic human rights was actual and not merely notional, were precisely the issues on which the Wilhelmine SPD concentrated so much critical venom.

Nowhere is the continuing influence of semi-absolutist personal rule more apparent than in the instances of interference in the judicial process by Wilhelm II. In August 1896, for example, the Kaiser addressed a telegram to the chairman of a disciplinary court, which had instituted proceedings against the mayor of Kolberg for making available to the SPD a meeting-hall in his locality. It read,

May the clear decision of the court help to remove all traces of doubt amongst my subjects as to how they should react to the unscrupulous rabble, which negates everything, aims at the overthrow of all order and which therefore places itself completely outside the law; which only recently helped to drag through the mud the exalted name of the German people abroad and whose influence will only end when all Germans to a man rally together to ensure its destruction.[209]

Seen in those terms, it might well have been the rule of law which governed the organisation of the Prussian state, as Otto Hintze has argued,[210] but it was not a rule which would stand the light of day. Schönstedt's view of the applicability of differing legal standards[211] and a state prosecutor's confidential remark to Hugo Haase that §153 of the industrial code was directed in its whole conception against the working class,[212] were but two sides of the same coin, in which law as formulated and administered by the representatives of a ruling class was used as an instrument of perpetuating the narrow base of existing political power. This involved not only the operation of the criminal law, but also attempts to abrogate those natural rights (*Naturrechte*) which were regarded by the SPD as part of man's innate personal dignity.[213] Thus, a leading conservative argued in the early 1890s[214] that all Social Democrats should be deprived of their civic rights (*bürgerliche Ehrenrechte*) and declared unsuitable to hold any public office.

This was more or less the fate that befell those already convicted of contravening the perjury laws.[215] Quite apart from disqualification from voting in elections or standing as a candidate, for periods to be determined by the individual courts, those who had perjured themselves faced an additional social stigma: they were denied the right to give evidence on oath in any future court of law. The taking of the oath had a symbolic importance over and above its purely judicial function. Just as critical comment amounting to *lèse-majesté* was interpreted as threatening the religious justification of the Kaiser's supreme power, so the refusal to swear the full oath or the intention to mock its significance by giving false evidence assumed an additional, wholly political, importance. A negation of the religious basis of the oath in this way amounted to a negation of the temporal and spiritual power on which the authority of the state rested.[216] There was, of course, no alternative for religious dissidents, who were not permitted to affirm, and since the state regarded the oath as a means of extracting the full truth in a court of law, it punished by sentences of up to six months imprisonment those who refused to repeat the oath in its entirety.[217]

The suggestion that political opponents of the establishment resorted to the practice of swearing false oaths, in order to facilitate the acquittal of companions accused of civil or criminal offences, was not a new one. It had gained a wide acceptance through the notoriety enjoyed by some of the propaganda tracts directed against Social Democracy in the early 1890s.[218] There had also been a succession of minor instances where members of the judicature had called into question the innate truthfulness of certain witnesses, especially when their political sympathies had been established beyond doubt. Thus, a court in Magdeburg sentenced eight Social Democrats in May 1892 to a total of eleven years hard labour, for denying that an SPD activist had uttered words attributed to him at a public meeting.[219]

Such attempts to reflect unfavourably on the credibility and character-worthiness of Social Democrats were given a new and more compelling inspiration in the summer of 1892. One of the state prosecutors at Hamburg, Antonius Romen, whose previous career had been characterised by notably successful prosecutions against Social Democrats,[220] had taken the step of questioning each of several defence witnesses on the details of their personal political convictions. He later used this evidence, combined with his assertion that it was part of SPD policy not to regard the taking of an oath as binding in any way, in order to argue against the admissibility of all defence submissions. These charges were immediately rejected by the *Hamburger Echo*,[221] but some two weeks later, on 28 July, they were repeated during the course of a trial involving the editor of a trade-union paper, accused of libelling the harbour authorities. The chief defence witness had at first been unwilling to answer Romen's question relating to membership of the SPD and, after the court had agreed to allow the right of Romen to put such a question, the witness was warned that failure to answer would result in a charge of contempt of court.

Once more, political sympathies for the SPD were used as evidence of general unreliability; in this particular case, the editor concerned was convicted and sentenced to four months imprisonment. There followed a series of highly inflammatory editorials in the *Hamburger Echo*, the first of which resulted in police raids on the offices of the paper, confiscations and a charge of libelling Romen.[222] From the substance and style of the leading articles which the paper published during the first week of August, there is no doubt that the *Echo* regarded itself as being in the front line of attack, and that it felt obliged to protect the party from unjust accusations levelled against the general membership. One editorial in particular,[223] distinguished by the tone of high moral rectitude which informed so much of the party's official comment, referred to Social Democracy as 'the conscience of society'.

Repercussions from the affair were soon felt at the national level and began attracting detailed comment in a large number of newspapers of a liberal persuasion; thus, the *Frankfurter Zeitung*[224] remarked rather tartly that 'the law of proscription against Social Democracy had not been eliminated in order for state prosecutors, on their own authority, to concoct a new law of proscription against Social Democratic witnesses'. In collaboration with the local party leadership, the *Hamburger Echo* very quickly organised a series of six mass protest meetings, to deal specifically with the accusations made by Romen in recent court hearings. These meetings, which were held on 9 August and at which some of the leading figures in the movement had been invited to speak, attracted attendances of almost 20,000 people and caused the local police considerable headache.[225]

Arising from the speeches made at one of these meetings, Arthur Stadthagen and the *Echo*'s chief editor, Emil Fischer, were accused of slandering Romen. At the subsequent court hearing in July 1893, postponed from December of the previous year because the prosecution did not wish to forfeit its announced intention of calling three of the leading members of the SPD Reichstag group as witnesses,[226] the state prosecutor demanded a sentence of eight months imprisonment for Fischer and one of four months for Stadthagen. In his final submission, he declared that the Social Democrats were carrying out 'a form of [sic] terrorism directed at the right of free expression of opinion', that the party was in the habit of responding to unfavourable comment with systematic character defamation, and that civil servants, state prosecutors and judges in particular had 'the right to vigorous protection from such terrorism'.[227]

The initial trigger-effect of the incident at Hamburg unleashed a series of meetings organised by local Social Democratic parties throughout the country, at which prominent speakers continued to discuss the accusations made against the SPD and the nature of the party's response to them. Similarly, the implications of this further twist in what appeared to be an officially-inspired campaign of insinuation and discrimination received copious comment in the columns of the party press. This led, predictably enough, to several court cases arising from charges of libel on Romen. At one of these, in July 1893, at which the editor of the *Halberstädter Sonntagszeitung* was fined 500 marks, Romen himself, called as a prosecution witness, was forced to admit his authorship of an anonymously published pamphlet, which he had used as part of his court evidence in Hamburg.[228]

For years afterwards, the SPD press needed little excuse to unearth the details of the Romen affair and draw the necessary lessons. Since party papers, in their chronicle approach to news-reporting, never lost touch with either their martyred heroes or those regarded as having visited outrages upon the party, it was no surprise to find details of Romen's political career – for his symbolic importance transcended his purely legal function – faithfully recorded. In particular, his excursions

77

into journalistic counter-propaganda, most notably in August Scherl's influential paper *Der Tag*, received assiduous attention.[229]

Romen's message, as might have been expected, was taken up by many others in the years that followed. In 1893, a judge in a case at Minden uttered the view that the SPD actively encouraged perjury in the party interest,[230] and in 1911 a judge at Altona declared that it was well known that strikers were not so particular about their oath-taking when giving evidence in a court of law.[231] The direct effects of the Romen doctrine, the judicial assumption that if a man belonged to the SPD he could not be regarded as a reliable witness, were felt especially keenly in the 1890s, in the rash of perjury trials which at one stage almost threatened to vie with instances of *lèse-majesté* for editorial importance.

Yet there were also frequent cases of judges and prosecutors making denigratory remarks about Social Democrats and pursuing a line of calculated insinuation, to the extent of openly questioning the credibility of anyone associated with the party. This happened, for example, in September 1892, when the presiding judge at the Landgericht in Breslau gave further evidence of judicial bias against the SPD, when he declared during a court case that the party leadership had actually instructed its membership to perjure themselves. These remarks caused such an outbreak of fury amongst the party press that the comparatively moderate *Münchener Post*[232] was moved to brand him openly as a liar. In Breslau itself, the editor of the Social Democratic *Volkswacht*, Karl Thiel, spoke at a mass protest meeting, at which a somewhat over-optimistic resolution was passed, calling on the Minister of Justice to suspend the judge from his duties.[233] The radical tenor of Thiel's remarks resulted in a charge of slander, for which he was sentenced to eight months imprisonment.[234]

All cases of perjury were heard by the jury-courts (*Schwurgerichte*), from which there could, of course, be no appeal to a higher authority; and for virtually all of the listed offences within this category the *Strafgesetzbuch* required a sentence not of imprisonment, but of penal servitude or hard labour (*Zuchthaus*), universally feared because of the unusual degree of severity involved. The *Vorwärts*, for instance, published in 1895[235] details of the harsh treatment accorded to those in state penitentiaries, including pointed references to some of the more ridiculous absurdities, such as a spell of fourteen days solitary confinement in a darkened cell for a case of coughing during the sermon in the prison chapel.

For this reason, the extraordinary developments at Essen early in

1895, which led to the sentencing of seven men for perjury, attracted an unusual degree of editorial attention in the columns of the SPD press.[236] As so often, the case in question arose from a comparatively minor incident, but it had as its root cause an underlying antagonism, between the Gewerkverein christlicher Bergarbeiter, a miners' association formed in 1894 under the spiritual direction of the Catholic Centre Party, and the SPD miners' union, whose leader, Ludwig Schröder, had played a major rôle in two industrial disputes in the Ruhr.[237] Since it proved increasingly difficult for the miners' union to find meeting-places and the police had the habit of dissolving those meetings which did take place, the organisational unity of the miners tended to be preserved for the meetings of the Christian miners' association which they often attended, with the specific intention of defending themselves from the attacks made there on the trade-union movement. At one such meeting, held at Baukau near Herne in February 1895, Schröder and his six colleagues found the hall well-posted with members of the local constabulary, ordered there at the request of the chairman of the Christian miners' association.[228] Before the meeting began, they were told to leave and when they refused – having paid their entrance money and believing themselves legitimately entitled to stay – they were forcibly ejected by members of the constabulary.

It was the account of these proceedings, as published in the newspaper of the miners' union, the *Deutsche Berg- und Hüttenarbeiter Zeitung*, which resulted in the editor facing a charge of libelling the constable concerned, a man named Münter. At the trial held in June, Münter swore on oath that he had not touched Schröder and could only assume that the miners' leader had fallen to the floor 'in shock or fright'.[239] Schröder and his companions all gave corroborating evidence that Münter had indeed used force whereas, curiously enough, witnesses called from the Catholic miners' association could neither remember the exact course of events on the night in question, nor recall the part played by Münter in ejecting Schröder. The editor of the miners' paper, Johann Margraf, was duly convicted of libel, and the state prosecutor thereupon ordered the immediate arrest of the seven defence witnesses on charges of suspected perjury.

The resulting trial in August 1895 revealed not only an incredible pettiness of circumstance and triviality of detail, but also the astonishing way in which court procedure was manipulated in favour of the prosecution – the defence counsel was prevented from continuing with the case, after he had been previously given permission to appear as a witness, and Münter was allowed to change his account of events, to the extent of admitting that he might have been responsible for bringing Schröder to the ground by 'certain bodily movements'.[240] What these were was never made clear, and Münter continued to deny that he had pushed or knocked Schröder to the floor. Only one of the seven accused was acquitted of perjury, but by way of compensation was found guilty of swearing a false oath – a further example of Wilhelmine legal niceties – and the other six all received sentences of hard labour averaging three years.

The outcry was predictable. The *Hannoverscher Volkswille*,[241] for example, claimed that the revelation of one law for the haves and another for the have-nots, as evidenced in the case at Essen, together with the publication by the SPD press of secret government documents in which the authorities were 'instructed' to treat the Social Democrats according to certain precepts, represented a more effective form of political leverage than a dozen party agitators working flat-out for the rest of their lives. Franz Mehring, in an editorial for *Die neue Zeit*,[242] wrote contemptuously of 'the empty litany of the German Rechtsstaat', declaring that one would need to search with a lantern for the people in Germany who did not find the verdict wrong and unjust, and that the judgment was 'the mark of a brilliant flash of lightning, opening up the yawning abyss towards which society is racing at tremendous speed'.

Similar sentiments were echoed by all the leading SPD newspapers except one – the *Frankfurter Volksstimme* – and the attitude of the party press to the somewhat ambivalent editorial stance adopted by the Frankfurt paper says a lot about the intense feeling of group solidarity, and the sense of soldierly defiance in the face of official repression. At a meeting of the local party in Frankfurt, the *Volksstimme* was censured for its 'tactless and unwarranted' editorial line, and both the *Vorwärts* and *Hamburger Echo* carried scarcely-veiled criticism of their colleagues' action. The editorial staff of the *Volksstimme* responded with a full statement, in which they dwelt heavily on the fact that they had to write every sentence under the eyes of the local state prosecutor, and that hardly a week passed by without legal proceedings of one kind or another being instituted against the paper. Any outspoken comment on the judgment at Essen would merely have precipitated further action. The *Vorwärts* was quite incensed at what it regarded as a weak-kneed and contemptible self-justification by the Frankfurt paper, in which respect for the power of the state prosecutor had apparently become the overriding consideration. For its part, it reminded the party at large that hardly any other paper had had to suffer more than it in terms of restrictions on its effective freedom, but in spite of this it strongly deplored any tendency to sacrifice party interests or abandon the defence of individuals caught up in the struggle against the state, for the sake of avoiding unpleasant confrontations with the law. There was no place in party ranks for those who felt obliged to accommodate editorial policy to extraneous considerations, and those unwilling to suffer adversity in the struggle with authority should move out of the firing-line.[243]

Amongst other SPD press comment, considerable attention was focused on the occupations and social standing of the twelve jurors responsible for the verdict at Essen – a farmer, a building-manager, an architect, a wine-merchant, two landowners, two contractors and three businessmen – but a great deal of criticism was also directed at the individual who had contributed most to the fate of the seven. This resulted in innumerable cases of libel, so much so that the *Hamburger Echo*[244] coined a new word, '*Münterbeleidigung*', to describe the phenomenon. As was standard practice, those convicted of the offence were required to carry the costs of printing details of the court judgment in all the local papers.

To the right-wing conservative press, the socialist howls of protest against 'Klassenjustiz' deserved only the firmest official response. In the wake of the defeat of the Umsturzvorlage and the evidence of deliberate socialist unlawfulness, the *Hamburger Nachrichten*[245] could write of 'a life-and-death struggle . . . between the state and Social Democracy'. A victory for the SPD would result in the liquidation of the Kaiser and Reich, the state, the family unit and all property. 'Is it therefore not natural', the paper argued,

whenever Social Democracy attempts to deceive and endanger the administration of justice by wilful acts of perjury, for the state to draw the consequences . . . In the end, it must be led to exclude Social Democrats from the protection offered by its agencies of justice, and to refuse to punish offences committed against Social Democrats, since they obviously regard themselves as standing outside the law. . .[246]

Each of the seven men was to serve his sentence in full. Soon after the trial, the SPD began organising collections throughout Germany for the dependants, including the proceeds of specially arranged variety shows and donations from abroad, such as the sum of 240 marks received from Melbourne. The editor of the *Münchener Post* was himself fined for inviting contributions from his readers,[247] but only a year after the trial had taken place the fund already stood at 60,000 marks. Numerous attempts were made, mostly by those of the liberal centre who had been shocked by the Essen verdict, to organise petitions and appeals for clemency.[248] The local party at Essen continued to show a symbolic defiance by re-nominating Schröder as its Reichstag candidate, even though this violated the rules governing election procedure. It no doubt helped to offset the further humiliation to which Schröder was subjected, of being brought in chains and with a shaven head, to face an additional charge, of having illegally organised a miners' union in Upper Silesia two years previously.[249]

In the fifteen years or so following the original trial, repeated efforts were made to re-open the case and submit new evidence. The difficulties of persuading the authorities that a mistake had been made were compounded by a special provision of the code of court procedure, which referred all applications for a new hearing to the court of first conviction. The appeal court, the Oberlandesgericht at Hamm, merely confirmed the rulings of the Schwurgericht at Essen that there were no grounds for questioning the convictions and sentences. In the meantime, most of the leading figures in the trial had graduated to higher positions, including the state prosecutor, who had been rewarded with the position of Oberstaatsanwalt in Kiel,[250] as well as Münter himself, who in addition to his new job with a municipal council in Berlin, was also involved in a highly dubious hedge-lawyer's practice.[251] It took the initiation of disciplinary proceedings against Münter in 1908, on suspicion of conspiring with others to make false statements, together with the evidence of two former members of the Christian miners' association, who had emigrated soon after the incident at Baukau and had only recently returned to the country, to persuade the appeal court at Hamm to hold an investigation into the case.[252]

After a further delay of almost a year, the re-trial took place at Essen in January 1911. Of the seven accused, two were no longer alive and Münter had died during the course of the disciplinary proceedings against him. For the first time former colleagues and superiors gave evidence of his own record, of his misappropriation of regimental funds whilst in the army, of his alcoholism and his frequent bouts of brutality in the course of duty. This evidence was almost certainly deliberately suppressed by the prosecution at the trial in 1895,[253] and the unwillingness of those qualified to do so to speak out against the assertions made by Münter, reveals much about the extent of official tyranny at the time. Even so, the establishment attempted to extricate itself from the mess with remarkable panache: the state prosecutor at the second hearing complained that the affair had been brandmarked as a political trial,[254] and the conservative *Deutsche Tageszeitung*[255] even went so far as to accuse the SPD of being morally guilty for all that had happened.

The only grudging acceptance by officialdom that it had been wrong, apart from reversing the original judgment, was to pay out sums of compensation to Schröder and his surviving four colleagues.[256]

In the interim, the stream of perjury cases against members of the party had continued unabated. In December 1898, a Hannover court sentenced a man to three years hard labour for perjury,[257] and a similar sentence was passed on two men in Lower Silesia in July 1913.[258] Here, the discriminatory harsh judgments were contrasted in press comment with examples of mitigating circumstances as 'discovered' in cases involving those from the professional classes. A doctor in Kiel, for instance, received a mere fifteen months imprisonment for conviction on a large number of separate charges,[259] and in a series of trials at Konitz in 1900 additional, anti-semitic considerations worked to the advantage of the accused in securing their acquittals.[260]

An especially hard line seemed to be taken against the SPD in Mecklenburg. There, a deep-seated antagonism between the police and the party had resulted in a severe curtailment of Social Democratic activities and in innumerable court actions against the party organisation, a good proportion of which, however, the police failed to win because of the almost complete lack of evidence. In August 1899, two policemen were sent to observe the proceedings at a social evening organised by the bricklayers' union in Wismar. They later claimed that two well-known party activists, Steinbrügger and Wollenberg, had insulted them during the course of the evening. At the ensuing trial, the evidence of a bystander named Holst was considered crucial, since he stated that he had heard only Steinbrügger utter remarks attributed to both men. This resulted in a small fine for Steinbrügger and an acquittal for Wollenberg, whereupon the state prosecutor appealed against both verdicts, and at the re-trial the two men were sentenced to terms of imprisonment. These were sufficient grounds to proceed against Holst on a charge of perjury, and at his trial at Güstrow in March 1900 the prosecution claimed that Holst had acted out of 'the most sordid party political interests'. The defence failed to make any impression in referring to the fact that Holst's original testimony had actually resulted in his friend Steinbrügger being convicted. After the jury had retired for a mere seven minutes before pronouncing their verdict of guilty, the presiding judge passed a sentence of three years hard labour on Holst. Shortly afterwards, the *Mecklenburger Volkszeitung* carried a report that on the evening following the trial, one of the jurymen had been heard to declare that the motive for Holst's perjury had been more than obvious in the bitter hostility between police and SPD.[261] Only in later years did it become known that the police-sergeant who had given evidence against Holst frequently suffered from delusions.[262]

Another perjury trial in Mecklenburg in 1902 illustrated the extra-ordinary lengths to which the authorities were prepared to go in punishing what were regarded as deliberate attempts to evade the course of justice. The police in a small village, described in the court action that followed as 'a hot-bed of socialist activity', instituted proceedings against the landlord of a public house, who had made available one of his rooms to the local SPD Reichstag candidate for the purpose of conducting constituency business. This activity had allegedly taken place on a Sunday before noon (*Kirchenzeit*), thus violating the local Sabbath ordinance. The evidence given by one of the constituents that he had eaten a bowl of soup *before* going to call on the SPD candidate, thus implying that business had not commenced until after lunch, was challenged by others who insisted that the soup had been consumed *after* his return from the meeting. At the ensuing perjury trial, all the police evidence revolved around the time that the bowl of soup had or had not been consumed, since it was felt that the testimony as given under oath would have cleared the landlord of the original charge. In the event, the constituent, whose own Social Demo-cratic allegiance had been established during the case, was found guilty and sentenced to two years hard labour.[263]

There was only a moderate decline in cases of perjury during the period, from 1,552 in 1892 to 1,308 in 1903,[264] and in 1905 the liberal *Hamburger Fremdenblatt*[265] could report that perjury still accounted for some 15% of all annual sentences of penal servitude. In vain did the SPD try to point out, with reference to the high percentage of incidences of perjury in predominantly rural areas of Prussia, where socialist representation was not strong, that the party could not legiti-mately be accused of deliberate untruthfulness.[266]

The application of differing legal standards in disputes involving the SPD had already been noted elsewhere. Whenever members of the party attempted to defend themselves or to secure legal satisfaction for some wrong committed against them, members of the judicature became noticeably blind to the weight of evidence or were usually quick to find extenuating circumstances. Like Kleist's Michael Kohl-haas, Social Democrats gained little in the way of recognition by the courts of just grievances.[267] Equally, especially whenever they had contravened the criminal law, they could expect no form of clemency, as was typified by the trial in Dresden of nine building-labourers in

February 1899, on charges of serious breaches of the peace and attempted murder. The nine, who had been celebrating a roof-topping ceremony (*Richtfest*) the previous July, had got themselves into a brawl on a neighbouring site, after discovering that despite the ten-hour rule, fellow workmates were still being forced to work in the evening. When they refused to disperse, the site-manager drew his revolver and fired a number of shots at them. The nine men then proceeded to set about the manager and were only stopped by the intervention of the police.

At the three-day trial, from which the public was excluded, all nine men were found guilty and given sentences totalling 53 years hard labour, 8 years imprisonment and 70 years loss of civil rights. The SPD executive took the unprecedented step of issuing a statement, published in the *Vorwärts*[268] and other leading party newspapers which began, 'Workers of Germany! An outrage has taken place. . .' It went on to make clear that whereas it neither condoned the behaviour of the nine nor objected to the right of the criminal law to take its due course, it viewed the severity of the sentences as a deliberate act of class-warfare and, given conditions in the penitentiaries, as tantamount to death-warrants. As with the Essen perjury trial, it immediately set in train arrangements for nationwide collections for the dependants.[269]

The trial provided the SPD press not only with further proof of the existence of 'Klassenjustiz', but also with welcome agitation against the Zuchthausvorlage. Editorial comment was exceedingly caustic. The *Volksblatt für Hessen und Waldeck*[270] spoke of a form of class absolutism and terrorism no less brutal than that exercised by the feudal aristocracy, and referred to the Dresden judgment as 'a gigantic fruit hanging from the poisonous tree of capitalist power, a gigantic plague-boil on the body of this reactionary and corrupt society'. *Die neue Zeit*, which devoted three full editorials to the matter, declared that the verdict exemplified the principle not of *fiat justitia* but of *vae victis*.[271] It, in common with others, criticised the bourgeois press for failing to bat so much as an eyelid, when it had previously raised the roof over the Dreyfus affair, although the *Frankfurter Zeitung*[272] recalled Disraeli's phrase of the 'two nations' in its own comment, and the Brussels paper *La Réforme* described the outcome of the trial as 'un jugement monstrueux'.[273]

Comparisons abounded with other instances of discriminatory sentencing: the *Vorwärts* recalled a brawl at Eisleben in 1891 when a number of Social Democrats had been attacked by members of a patriotic miners' association, who had all been acquitted at the subsequent trial.[274] Not surprisingly, the rashness of much of the comment in the SPD was rewarded with a number of court actions for libel. Some positive effects were felt, however: the *Sächsische Arbeiterzeitung*, for example, reported that as a result of its stand against the Dresden judgment, it had increased its subscribers by more than a thousand.[275] In addition, protest meetings were held in different parts of the country,[276] the local party arranged the distribution of 160,000 copies of a special propaganda leaflet,[277] and Georg Gradnauer, one of the 'revisionist' six on the staff of the *Vorwärts*, succeeded in raising the issue in the Reichstag.[278]

The uproar, which was sustained by the SPD for several weeks, had two constrasted effects. A good many conservative papers had argued that the incident at Dresden was a necessary and direct consequence of socialist agitation in general. This disturbing development in counter-propagandistic thinking, coupled with the enormous amount of pending litigation, persuaded the SPD executive to issue instructions to the party press to moderate in tone all further comment on the trial and reduce references to it to a minimum. This directive was not well received by the *Vorwärts* and other leading papers, and *Die neue Zeit*[279] in particular criticised the executive for adopting an unjustifiably defensive position. This action did emphasise, however, that the party leadership was ever-mindful of the possible consequences of providing the authorities with too many hostages to fortune. For its part, the judicature had come to regret the appalling severity of the sentences. Indeed, nine of the twelve members of the jury took part in petitioning the authorities for clemency,[280] and over the next six years each of the nine convicted in 1899 was either pardoned or released before time, usually to coincide with the birthday of the King of Saxony.

If the Dresden trial was an example of the active discrimination of the courts against members of the working class, there were others which manifested a kind of passive discrimination. One such was the trial in 1905 of four young men, all from families of high social standing, on a charge of raping a fifteen-year-old serving-girl. The defence case rested entirely on the suggestion that the girl's character was not entirely blameless; in fact, as only emerged after the trial, one of the four had succeeded in seducing the girl only a few days previously.[281] Nonetheless, all four were acquitted of the charge by a jury which consisted of three estate agents, four businessmen, an industrialist, a building-inspector, a musician, a property dealer and a master chimney-sweep.[282]

Since the four youths hailed from what was the most fashionable and desirable suburb of Hamburg, the *Hamburger Echo* took especial delight in asking whether the same jurors would have reached a similar verdict, if the victim had been the daughter of an industrialist or businessman and the accused four working-men.[283] It virtually answered its own question in subsequent weeks by reporting, from many different parts of the country, instances of biased sentencing in cases of rape. Thus, a court in Stuttgart sentenced a butcher to 16 months hard labour,[284] and a hairdresser in Fürth received no less than seven years penal servitude.[285] As so often, the SPD's enthusiasm for exploiting the potential from the situation led to demonstrations of popular protest – one such in Hamburg was addressed by the women's rights leader Dr Anita Augspurg[286] – but also to official action against those party newspapers which had fanned the flames of popular emotion. Those affected in this way were the editors of the *Hamburger Echo*, the *Harburger Volksblatt*, who initially received a sentence of six months imprisonment for criticising the verdict,[287] and the *Schleswig-Holsteinische Volkszeitung* in Kiel, whose editor was fined 400 marks for reprinting extracts from an editorial which had originally appeared in the *Hamburger Echo*.

It was part of Social Democratic propaganda that the spirit of 'Klassenjustiz' manifested itself in all aspects of the administration of justice, including the treatment of detainees and the measure of freedom accorded to prisoners. Thus, a despatch clerk with the *Magdeburger Volksstimme*, awaiting trial on a charge of distributing prohibited literature, was placed in chains for twenty days, after refusing to disclose how he had received an extra food ration.[288] Similarly, in contravention of a Bundesrat ruling of 1897, a party journalist imprisoned at Lingen was not given an opportunity for private study, but was forced to spend all day manufacturing cartridge cases.[289]

The contrasted handling of socialist and non-socialist offenders by the courts was a constant theme in daily news comment: a woman who stole a bundle of firewood from a neighbour's cellar in order to heat some milk for her new-born child, was sentenced to a year's imprisonment, whereas a building-manager who had broken his walking-stick over the head of a woman in the street escaped with a fine of 300 marks.[290] *Die neue Zeit*[291] complained in 1905 that the first action of the new Minister of Justice, Beseler, had been to commute a sentence of imprisonment passed on Count Pückler for persistent anti-semitic agitation and incitement to racial hatred, into one of *custodia honesta*.

Students were amongst those whose excesses were treated with exceptional tolerance: an undergraduate at Cologne, who had seriously wounded two women after becoming drunk, was acquitted after the court had received a testimonial signed by his university professor, attesting to (sic) his mother's migraine and his own tendency to lose self-control when under the influence of alcohol.[292] A further disturbing feature was the tendency of several courts, as well as some government circles, to confuse anarchist aims with SPD propaganda: during the trial of a Social Democrat for theft at Lübeck in 1897, the judge remarked that the question of personal ownership was unlikely to be understood by a party whose motto was 'Property is theft.'[293]

That Wilhelmine justice had indeed become transformed into 'an institution for the struggle against the socialists'[294] was painfully apparent, and new evidence of the undiminished harsh repression through the courts continued to emerge right up to 1914. One particular appalling instance was the murder in cold blood of a picket, who was stabbed to death by a factory-worker in June 1913. The crime had been observed at a distance of 150 metres by two policemen, who were later said to have aided the escape of the culprit. As a result of the strong feeling aroused, an angry mob proceeded to storm the factory. The following spring, seven of the ringleaders were given sentences totalling 33 months imprisonment for disturbing the peace. The culprit himself, who had some six previous convictions, was acquitted at his trial in October 1913 on the basis of justifiable self-defence.[295]

In the light of accumulated evidence of this kind, it is not surprising that Social Democratic confidence in the just processes of the law had completely evaporated. It had been a feature of party policy since the Erfurt programme of 1891 that the existing method of judicial appointments was to be replaced by a system of secretly and directly elected judges.[296] It remained an inescapable conclusion of public life in Wilhelmine Germany that those who possessed the financial means were able to indulge in pettifogging litigation and play the system for all it was worth. Since no form of legal aid was available to the under-privileged and since judicial procedures were characterised by extreme sophistry, there were many who were forced to accept injustice rather than bring a court action; and when the same individuals were on the receiving end of Wilhelmine justice they were often deprived of their earning power by the imposition of long sentences of imprisonment or were compelled to face the burden of paying stiff fines. It was the triumph of a system of dual values, in which the scales of justice were replaced by a double-faced Janus-mask, thus enabling, in Franz Mehring's words,[297] 'the German patriot to warm his hands at the fire of "Klassenjustiz"'.

3

THE CONFLICT WITH
THE ESTABLISHMENT

In Germany there exists not the rule of law, but the power of the police . . . The police in Germany are not all-powerful, but they are the most powerful of all the authorities.

Der Stukkateur, Hamburg, 13 July 1907

The police

Writing in the early 1830s, Alexis de Tocqueville declared that 'there are no revolutions in Germany, because the police would not permit it'. This *bon mot* had a peculiar relevance for the Wilhelmine period, since the police became in a very real sense the eyes and ears of the government and shared, together with the army, the task of providing a secure and effective form of internal stability. An enormous extension of the range of actual police responsibilities, including direct responsibility for the security of the state, was a particular feature of the internal administrative development of the absolutist-monarchical state of the nineteenth century. In Tsarist Russia, for example, the establishment in 1826 of the 'third section' under Nicholas I represented a significant step towards subjecting intellectual thought and political heterodoxy to the increasingly critical scrutiny of the police, even though its later failure to afford the most elementary protection – of life and limb – casts some doubt on the effectiveness of its new powers.[1]

Similar trends, involving the addition of a full apparatus of arbitrary powers to existing responsibilities for the maintenance of public order, began to emerge almost simultaneously in the Hohenzollern Prussian state. As early as 1809, the first signs can be detected of a deliberate policy designed to set in train a clear separation between local authority administration and its nominal responsibility for police functions. Such functions were henceforth regarded not as directly subordinate to a municipal authority, but rather as a legitimate extension of absolute state sovereignty (*Staatshoheit*).[2]

That the activities of the police in this respect should be seen demonstrably to underpin the basis of the government's political authority, is typified by the comment of the Berlin Polizeipräsident, von Jagow, on the behaviour of the local force in suppressing the 1910 Moabit riots, when he declared, 'The police have strengthened the prestige of the state.'[3] Nowhere was the joint concern of the two most powerful absolutist systems in Central Europe at the fundamental threat to the established order better illustrated, than in the collaboration between the political police of Tsarist Russia and Wilhelmine Germany, in uncovering the network of subversive activity which led to the Königsberg sedition trial in 1904.

The functions of the police in combating movements with subversive aims and providing the government with an accurate intelligence service in the Bismarckian Reich, were institutionalised in the creation – following the enactment of the anti-socialist laws in 1878 – of the departments of political police, attached to each major police authority in the country.[4] The very concept of such a special department, concerning itself with the political allegiance of individual citizens and the potential strength and importance of dissent from established orthodoxy, seriously put in question the validity of the Rechtsstaat principle. No one could feel himself safe from the threat of possible prosecution arising from the statement or practice of personal political convictions. It became of paramount necessity to make the fullest possible use of all such powers of official surveillance, so much so that the Minister of the Interior, von Puttkamer, was moved to say in the Reichstag in 1888 that without the political police the security of the state could not be maintained for 24 hours.[5] In recalling these words in 1897, *Die neue Zeit* retorted that a state which could not exist for 24 hours without the political police did not deserve to exist at all.[6]

During the years 1878–90 the political police had contributed greatly to the government's appreciation of the long-term objectives of the outlawed socialist movement. The picture which emerged tended to emphasise, perhaps unduly, the anarcho-revolutionary nature of these objectives so that, over a period of time, a kind of conditioning took place occasioned by the drip-feed effect of continuous daily reports from all over Germany. This accounted not only for the rigid and inflexible positions taken up by government ministers and advisers in the 1890s, but was also a primary reason for the retention of the system of political surveillance, even after the lapse of the Ausnahmegesetz.[7]

The crucial part to be played by the municipal heads of police was emphasised by Holstein in a letter to Hohenlohe in November 1894:

An energetic and dependable Polizeipräsident can do a lot in order to minimise the nuisance of the press. His power is an elastic one, whereas the Minister of

Justice can only work slowly and by degrees through changes in personnel – which are difficult – and through new bills.[8]

As a result, the close links between individual police authorities, state prosecuting offices and central government departments were developed further in the 1890s. It was not uncommon, for example, for the officials of one department to send particular articles from the local SPD press for reaction and comment to another department in a quite different part of the country. The regular exchange of personal and confidential information on individual citizens was facilitated by the German practice requiring each person to register locally at his nearest police-station (*Anmeldung*), and to complete essential formalities before moving into a different area (*Abmeldung*). No part of the country was spared such rigours of police supervision: the *Hamburger Echo*, for instance, claimed in 1909 that the Prussian political police carried out a systematic form of surveillance of political activity in the southern German states from the vantage point of the city of Frankfurt am Main.[9]

The surveillance of political meetings was usually of a highly detailed kind, and the reports prepared by official stenographers often included the precise nature of interruptions from the floor, often ludicrously irrelevant at that. This painstaking approach was all the more remark-able in view of the fact that the course of Social Democratic and trade union meetings was frequently reported verbatim in the local party press. When the annual party conference was held in Hamburg in 1897, local officials prepared their own comprehensive report – which ran to 1,284 sides – of conference proceedings. A few weeks later, when the party's own official stenographic proceedings were published by the *Vorwärts* bookshop, the Hamburg police department sent a copy to each police authority, advising them that should a fuller and more authentic version be required, duplicates of the Hamburg police report could be made available on request.[10]

According to official departmental regulations, representatives of the political police engaged in the surveillance of meetings were not actually considered present and were therefore instructed, for example, to take no part in official toasts.[11] The legendary omnipresence of officialdom in this form is neatly conveyed by the front cover of the SPD's satirical journal *Der wahre Jakob*, in its edition for 26 September 1899. This showed a group of men dressed in deep-sea diving-suits, seated on the sea-bed in apparently animated conversation, with 'an old man of the sea' (*Aegir*),[12] complete with *Pickelhaube* and notebook and pencil in hand, standing in attendance. The inscription read:

Since it had come to the attention of the police department in What's-its-name [*Dingsda*] that the union of deep-sea divers was conducting its meetings on the sea-bed, it turned in its hour of need to old Aegir, who promised to provide the department with the necessary reports.

Some indication of the extent of police responsibilities can be gauged from tasks which ranged from the enforcement of local curfews (*Polizeistunde*), to the deportation of undesirable foreigners (*Reichsfremde*). In the three years 1903–5, expulsions totalled 1,694 persons, and the *Bremer Bürgerzeitung*[13] commented sadly that only Tsarist Russia exceeded Germany in the number of deportations considered necessary in the interests of the state. With the increasingly important rôle which citizens' action groups, such as the *Reichsverband gegen die Sozialdemokratie*, formed in 1904,[14] and established pillars of support like the army veterans' associations (Kriegervereine) came to play in the struggle against Social Democracy, the political police became particularly involved in the problems of organisational liaison and in assisting groups loyal to the establishment (*staatserhaltende Parteien*) wherever possible. It was no surprise, therefore, to find the department at Bochum providing local colliery-owners with full details of the political involvements of pit foremen and no surprise, either, to find the SPD press making maximum capital out of the disclosure of such practices.[15]

Similarly, the *Vorwärts* took great delight in referring to the attempts by the Berlin department to bribe a member of its editorial staff into passing on confidential party information. It prominently displayed on its front page a request for the official concerned to collect the bribe of 60 marks from its offices. Understandably enough, no one from the police department arrived to claim the money.[16] On the other hand, paid police spies from the Berlin headquarters managed to infiltrate local parties and gain access to the highest counsels.[17] An indication of the close relations which the Berlin department enjoyed with leading conservative newspapers was the publication by *Die Post* in November 1911 of a highly confidential report on the activities of the SPD in arranging protest meetings against the Turkish–Italian war. This report was only drawn up on 12 November and appeared virtually verbatim in the following day's edition of the paper.[18]

At times of internal crisis, such as the planned demonstrations against the Prussian three-class franchise in January 1906, the police reserved all national telegraph and communications links for official use. Nonetheless, police submissions throughout the period pointed to the severe strain which the continued campaign against Social Democracy – at all levels of national life – was placing on its resources. The Regierungs-präsident at Wiesbaden, for example, painted a particularly distressing picture in 1900 of the difficulties which his staff of 120 men in the city's police department were having to face. It was partly a question of coping with the problems arising from the greater ease with which people could travel the country – the guest-books for 1899 showed that a total of 123,513 strangers had passed through the city – and all that that implied for the known political character of individual communities, and partly also the need to ensure the Kaiser's personal security on his frequent visits to Wiesbaden and other local spas.[19] In the major cities the work of the plain-clothes squads, entrusted with the preservation of public decency (*Sittenpolizei*), was an additional burden. Prostitution was considered by the Frankfurt police to be a major problem,[20] and amongst the two million inhabitants of the capital of the Reich there were said to be no fewer than 50,000 *Straßenmädchen*.

The net effect of this system of internal administration was to extend the official arm of government into the homes and lives of nearly every citizen in the country. An additional form of indirect control was the received tradition of what was regarded as socially and politically acceptable. As the *Hamburger Echo*[21] pointed out, 'There is much in Prussianised Germany which, though not expressly forbidden, is still not officially permitted.' In this respect Wilhelmine governments went a long way towards the ideal, ironically characterised by Ludwig Börne, of implanting a policeman within every loyal citizen's breast.

It was precisely this kind of invasion of personal liberty, especially as it affected the right to political dissent, against which the SPD rebelled. The heavy-handed and often totally autocratic actions of the police were a perpetual source of renewed inspiration for the leader-writers. In terms of editorial energy and topical importance, the campaign of the party press against the baneful influence of the *Polizei-staat* yielded only to its vigorous assault on the militarist ethic. Even bourgeois circles began to be affected by the constant stream of propaganda. A debate in the lower house of the Prussian parliament in February 1903 revealed the widespread feeling – which was eagerly echoed by the SPD press – that the public existed for the sake of the police and not vice-versa.[22] In much the same sort of way, the conservative *Altona Nachrichten*[23] argued that since members of the general public could not always be guaranteed their rights when in conflict with the police, it was no surprise to find them giving such credence to the doctrines of Social Democracy. The results of such concerted propaganda were often reflected in an increasing tendency to offer resistance to the police and even to indulge in acts of civil disobedience. Many of the younger party agitators, as the Polizeipräsident at Kassel noted in March 1894, actually stressed the value of a head-on struggle with the authorities as a means of sharpening the party's intellectual teeth.[24]

The nature of such struggles against the administration in general took many forms. Although police departments took the most stringent precautions to ensure secrecy of operations – all contacts with the press in Hamburg, for instance, had to be conducted via the political police (*Abteilung IV*) and no police employee was permitted to discuss internal matters with any journalist – there were substantial and often highly damaging leaks of information. In a secret memorandum to all officials, the *Polizeidirektor* at Hamburg remarked in May 1897,[25] that some stories which had circulated in the press could only be traced back to indiscretions on the part of individual employees, and he felt compelled to point to the direst consequences for those involved. Such leakages were also felt to prejudice inquiries into criminal cases, and a further memorandum in 1906 – the contents of which were disclosed by the *Hamburger Echo*[26] – underlined the necessity of preserving a strict wall of silence.

If the publication of confidential information could occasionally be traced back to sympathies which individual employees held for the aims of the Social Democratic movement, this does not always explain the frequency or suggest convincing reasons for the ingenuity, with which the SPD press was able to print in full the texts of secret central and local government directives. In fact, the Berlin correspondent of the *Kölnische Zeitung* was appalled that even with the huge apparatus deployed by the political police against the SPD, it consistently failed to uncover the most perplexing of matters – precisely how the *Vorwärts* came into possession of such splendid anti-government propaganda.[27]

Such successes were by no means confined to the central party newspaper. In November 1895, the *Freie Presse* at Elberfeld-Barmen[28] printed the full text of a circular from the Regierungspräsident at Düsseldorf, von der Recke, to all area police authorities, requesting regular and detailed reports on all matters affecting the life and health of the whole Social Democratic movement. For its part, the *Bergische Arbeiterstimme* at Solingen was able to obtain particulars of the first of these confidential reports, which ran to fifteen sides of foolscap.[29]

The value of such sensational disclosures by the party press lay in bringing home to the working masses the extent of deliberate antisocialist discrimination, and in providing the party leadership with a unique understanding of the methods being employed against the movement as a whole. All this tended to give the propaganda battle an extra piquancy, although there was much that the SPD did not, and could not possibly, know about government thinking on matters affecting internal repression.

The fact that an element of good fortune was involved in obtaining such documents was often overlooked by the conservative press. The *Schlesische Zeitung*, for example, refused to believe that a conspiracy was not involved and argued that, if all else failed, socialist editors should be prosecuted under §259 of the *Strafgesetzbuch* for receiving stolen goods.[30] Since government spies were known to be at work within the party's organisation, the SPD saw no reason why it should not use the same weapons with which it was being beaten. Thus, in 1906 the *Vorwärts* was able to publish a certain amount of confidential *Reichsverband* correspondence, copies of which were made available to the paper by an employee with socialist sympathies. When he resigned his position, with the aim of allowing a full-time party agent to take his place, the ruse was discovered and taken as evidence of a concerted socialist campaign of bribery and corruption.[31]

Party newspapers in the Ruhr enjoyed a particular success in making governments feel uncomfortable. To some extent, this was a reflection of the concentrated strength of Social Democratic support in the region and the bitterness of the political struggles. On 13 September 1905, when the nation's leaders were still in the process of reacting cautiously to the revolutionary aftermath in Tsarist Russia, the *Freie Presse* at Elberfeld published not one, but several, top-secret documents relating to the activities of the political police. These included further details of internal surveillance operations, together with a circular from the Polizeipräsident at Berlin, which indicated that particular attention was being paid to those *Reichsausländer*, such as Kautsky, Helphand and Aldolf Braun, who were closely connected with the work of the SPD.

As so often with disclosures of this kind, the details were syndicated to other party newspapers. On this particular occasion, however, the state of acute watchfulness was more apparent at the centre of internal coordination in Berlin than at points of the regional compass. It was obvious that duplicates of the original documents had somehow come into the possession of SPD journalists working on the *Freie Presse*. On 14 September, and before papers outside the Ruhr had published the text of the government documents, the Minister of the Interior sent an irate letter to the Regierungspräsident at Arnsberg, in whose administrative area the *Freie Presse* was published, demanding immediate full-scale inquiries and ordering a speedy and successful outcome to the affair.[32]

In the week that followed extensive inquiries did in fact take place throughout the region, in an attempt to establish whether government employees had been responsible in any way for passing on details of the documents. On 19 September, 21 employees of the town administration at Gevelsberg were interviewed and their statements taken. Three days later, the Regierungspräsident reported to the Minister in Berlin that the suspects had been narrowed down to two, but that there was still no conclusive evidence. As a direct result of this incident, the Regierungspräsident ordered a drastic revision of all methods of internal security. There had been other instances in which disaster had only narrowly been averted. In February 1902, for example, the mayor of Bochum informed the local Landrat that he had discovered two secret documents lying on the street, which he assumed had been dropped by a messenger entrusted with their despatch.[33] In the directive issued from Arnsberg on 23 September[34] to all prefects and mayors in the region, the Regierungspräsident ordered that the binding of every administrative file should be the responsibility of those persons who had been carefully screened for their absolute political reliability, and that the binding, moreover, should be carried out only in the presence of a senior official, who would be required to ensure that at all other times the files were kept safely under lock and key.

In this particular case, the action taken amounted to closing the stable door after the horse had bolted. As the result of the evidence of three of his fellow-lodgers, the originator of the *Freie Presse*'s *coup de théâtre* was discovered to be a junior bookbinder named Robert Reh, who had been employed in the council offices at Gevelsberg. Reh had in fact removed copies of the relevant documents to his lodgings, where he proceeded to make a number of transcripts, before passing them on to the general secretary of the metalworkers' union, who happened to be a local correspondent for the *Freie Presse*. The whole episode turned out to be a singularly unhappy one for the authorities. Although he had escaped arrest by fleeing from Gevelsberg, Reh later gave himself up to the police in Ölsnitz in Saxony. However, under Saxon law there were no charges which could be brought against Reh and since the incriminating evidence had vanished – or had presumably been destroyed by the editors of the *Freie Presse* – there remained only a possible deportation, since Reh was a native of the Habsburg province of Moravia.[35]

One of the most obvious ways in which the SPD press came into direct conflict with the administration, as has already been shown, was in the publication of critical comment, either on some aspect of current policy, or on the actions of a named individual or group of people. Official response to unwelcome publicity frequently took the form of a vendetta. Thus, the editor of the *Volksblatt für Hessen und Waldeck*, Paul John, was fined 300 marks in September 1895, for libelling a local judge. In a subsequent case on the same day, he was given three weeks imprisonment for libelling the police in Kiel, and two months later a term of four weeks for libelling the local mayor. In January 1896 he received two further convictions, for character defamation and for libelling the police in Kassel, for which he was given an additional sentence of three weeks.[36]

In April 1911, when the editor of the *Hamburger Echo* had suggested that the police authority in neighbouring Altona was concerned to polish up its tarnished public image, he was fined a total of 600 marks.[37] During the trial of a man at Recklinghausen, on a charge of insulting the local police, the state prosecutor declared that there could be no question of treating a Social Democrat equally and fairly.[38] When the SPD devoted particular energy in the autumn of 1910 to attacking the behaviour of the police in dealing with the Moabit riots, the Minister of the Interior sent instructions to all Regierungspräsidenten, emphasising that the aim of the party was deliberately to stir up popular feeling against the police, and calling for the sternest possible treatment of every actionable offence.[39]

Such measures were complemented by official chicanery at various levels. In September 1906, for example, the district party organiser at Stolp, Adolf Herrmann, was shot and killed on his way home by a trigger-happy policeman. Despite a storm of local protest, the court refused to convict the policeman because of difficulty in establishing the exact course of events, and in fury the local party erected a commemorative plaque in memory of Herrmann. The local mayor thereupon ordered all references to Herrmann's name to be erased, on the grounds that mention of individuals represented a danger to public order.[40]

Much worse was the almost daily flood of evidence that the police were consistently exceeding their legal powers and indulging in quite unwarranted acts of physical brutality and maltreatment. The systematic exploitation of such cases – the *Hamburger Echo* sententiously entitled its series, 'Chronik der Polizeimißgriffe' – frequently uncovered quite horrifying tales of human limbs being hacked off by policemen armed with swords. Nor were Social Democrats the only victims of such arbitrary power. During a brawl in Wilhelmshaven, for example, the nose of an English sailor was sliced clean away. In addition, there were continuous reports that suspects arrested by the police and taken in for questioning were being ill-treated.[41] The *Vorwärts* made a particular distinction between the extra brutality of the country police when compared with the Berlin city police, although it argued that the behaviour of the latter differed little from that of the Russian Cossack troops, with their thin whips made from hippopotamus hide (*Nagaika*). Indeed, in referring to the response occasioned by SPD demonstrations against the three-class voting system in March 1910, it colourfully described 'the feverish fury with which hundreds of mounted policemen stabbed wildly into human flesh'.[42]

It was often quite impossible to ignore the existence of official police brutality, although the courts tended to overlook it or else find extenuating circumstances. The *Vorwärts* recorded 131 different cases involving court appearances by policemen in 1898 alone, and was unable to show much surprise at the number of recorded excesses, in view of the authorisation for the use of firearms in civil disturbances.[43] In March 1900, in the city of Frankfurt alone, there were no fewer than eight cases in which policemen were involved, and the outcome was invariably an acquittal or a ridiculously low fine. In several instances, the court actually declared that arrest had been totally unnecessary.[44]

Some of the reasons for such wild excesses can be explained by the fact that very many of the lower echelons of the police force were drawn from the army. Members of the general public tended to be treated in much the same way that fresh recruits were tyrannised by their army superiors. Since the lower classes were most often at the receiving end of police ill-treatment, it was no surprise to find members of the SPD Reichstag group drawing on the repeated evidence as presented by the party press, and using it in attempts to force admissions of responsibility from government ministers, who were more than adept at the art of stone-walling.

Mounting discontent at official toleration of police tyranny found its expression in the formation of a number of citizens' action groups. The SPD was closely involved in the progress of one such group in Hamburg, which bore the illustrious name of the 'Verein zum Schutz gegen Schutzleute'. At its inaugural meeting in September 1895, at which the political police, as might have been expected, were also present, one of the editors of the *Hamburger Echo* was elected secretary of the organisation.[45] It pledged itself to give protection and legal assistance to all those who regarded themselves as victims of police tyranny, and to take up all cases of the misuse of police authority.

Public response, in the form of large attendances, was initially very strong, but after the first flush of enthusiasm the enterprise almost ran aground. To some extent the wind had been taken out of the organisation's sails, by a series of disciplinary proceedings initiated in the remaining months of 1895 against members of the local police force. Moreover, since the 'Rechtsschutzverein' as it later came to be called, developed into the mouthpiece of its bourgeois chairman, the SPD took up an increasingly cool position.[46] It was quite content to take a back seat and allow middle-class energies to be directed towards exposing police malpractices, especially when it saw the prospect not only of reaping the benefit in terms of added propaganda, but also of appealing successfully to junior police employees to join the party organisation. In any case, it was a characteristic of SPD tactics to make the maximum possible use of its press and not to involve itself in the formation of ad hoc groups, whose activities were likely to be severely restricted by the existing law.[47] The legacy of this particular affair, which petered out during the course of 1896, was the increasing use by the party press of the polemical slogan '*Schutz gegen Schutzleute*'.

Hamburg had good reason to recall the phrase little more than a year later. On the outskirts of the city, in the township of Wandsbeck, which at that time came under Prussian administration, the local police chief, a man called Schow glorying in the titles of '*Stadtrat, Polizeichef, Amtsanwalt und Premierleutnant der Reserve der Artillerie*', was at the centre of a scandal with rather more than purely local significance. Schow had agreed to drop the charges which a 23-year-old postal employee faced for assaulting a young woman, in return for which he ordered the young man to remove his trousers and lean over a sofa, whereupon he administered seven strokes of a leather whip.

One of the curious features of the *Gesindeordnung*, which regulated the relationships between employers and their domestic servants, was the right of corporal punishment (*Züchtigungsrecht*). This only disappeared from the statutes with the introduction in 1900 of the code of civil rights (*Bürgerliches Gesetzbuch*). It was quite clear, however, that no such right of corporal punishment extended to police officials in the conduct of their inquiries. Had it not been for the fact that the seven strokes of the whip occasioned severe swellings, which forced Schow's 'victim' to seek medical attention, the matter might probably never have come out into the open. In fact, during the course of the storm that followed, fuelled by highly critical editorials in the

Hamburger Echo,[48] it emerged that dozens of local inhabitants had agreed to submit themselves in similar fashion, rather than face the near certainty of conviction and sentence by a court of law. At a mass protest-meeting, attended by several thousand people, a motion condemning Schow's arbitrary power was passed, and copies were sent to various municipal authorities.

Officialdom was slow to respond to the uncovering of the affair. It took much critical comment in the local press, plus an article in a French newspaper, recording with astonishment that Wandsbeck was not to be found in a remote part of East Prussia but on the outskirts of Germany's second largest city,[49] before a decision was taken to suspend Schow from his duties. Since by this time each official move was being closely scrutinised, in particular by the SPD press, it did not come as any great surprise when, in mid-June, the mayor of Wandsbeck announced that Schow had 'agreed' to leave office, for which act of self-denial he was to be compensated with full pay until the end of the year. At a hastily concocted and speedily despatched trial the following month, Schow escaped with a fine of 100 marks for assault.

As with the case of the state prosecutor Romen, notoriety of this kind seemed to act as a positive boost to a personal career. In September of the same year, Schow took up a position as a lawyer in Plön, and little more than a year later he was promoted to become notary to the Oberlandesgericht at Kiel.[50] The wider political and constitutional issues of this case – leaving aside reflections on the sado-masochistic interest of senior police officials – were ignored by all except the Social Democratic and liberal press. There appeared to be little in the way of official concern at the power which an individual administrator seemed able to exercise over the just processes of the law, or any real awareness that the much-vaunted reference to Prussia as a '*Rechts- und Kultur-staat*' had a very hollow ring to it.

The discovery in the years that followed of further irregularities and malpractices in police affairs merely seemed to underline the relevance of the issues which the SPD continued to raise. That the consequence of such disclosures was bound to be a serious drop in public confidence in the impartiality and integrity of the police – if not in the morale of the police force in general – escaped all but the wisest counsellors. It required a court case in Lübeck, for example, to uncover the existence of a special fund, the '*S-Kasse*', which was financed by a kind of tax on the immoral earnings of the city's prostitutes. The proceeds from this fund, to which each prostitute was expected to contribute a weekly sum of two marks, were ostensibly earmarked for their own medical treatment. However, not only was the accumulated sum of money – of the order of 20,000 marks – used to provide gratuities and financial assistance to police employees, but the chief of police himself also made use of the fund in order to stage social events for his men and provide them with holiday travelling expenses.[51]

What produced much wider ripples of concern and consternation was the discovery in 1913 of widespread bribery and corruption in the Cologne police force. On 3 October 1913, the party newspaper in the city, the *Rheinische Zeitung*, published an article in which it made a number of charges against senior policemen. These related to the acceptance of gifts during the investigation of certain criminal cases. It was inevitable that the Cologne police should raid not only the paper's offices, but also the editor's private home. Evidence in corroboration of these charges, however, had already come the previous month in the form of a court case, in which a police inspector had admitted responsibility for accepting a bribe.[52] The decision to serve the editor with a writ for libelling the local police force was – seen from the official point of view – almost certainly a mistake, since it gave the paper an unparalleled forum for proving the basis of its specific allegations. Indeed, what emerged from the course of the trial was that only the tip of a much larger iceberg had been exposed in the original article of the *Rheinische Zeitung*.

Apart from the almost common practice of accepting gifts and presents, especially after successful completion of inquiries into cases of theft, a number of people had been involved in arranging for large sums of money to be paid regularly to members of the police force. In addition, officials had accepted presents, given with the express intention of influencing applications for licences and other concessions. Moreover, individual landlords had felt themselves obliged to make cash payments or provide goods in kind in return for official favours. Thus, for example, a large city restauranteur had provided over a period of four years 160 bottles of wine and spirits, innumerable boxes of cigars and 600 marks in cash. Similarly, the officials of the city racecourse – one of the largest establishments in the country – had arranged for 500 marks to be sent to the Polizeipräsident, with the aim of directing the energies of his staff towards curbing the activities of unofficial bookmakers. They were not to know that the bookmakers themselves had organised collections and had paid over to the police a considerably larger sum, in order to allow them to continue their highly lucrative operations in peace.

Clearly, a violation of the law had been involved, since §331 of the *Strafgesetzbuch* forbade paid officials of the state (Beamte) to accept any form of gratuity. Individual complaints about such practices had been made over a number of years to the authorities in Cologne. Where complaints originated from within the police department, they were dealt with either by arranging a transfer or even dismissal on one pretext or other, and where they came directly from members of the general public, pressure to forget particular incidents took the form of threats to issue writs for character defamation.[53]

The fact that not simply a handful, but large numbers of the Cologne force had been a party to this form of corruption, led the *Leipziger Volkszeitung* and other SPD papers to refer to the scandal as '*ein ganzes Polizeipanama*'. What was particularly alarming, as emerged in the evidence of one witness during the trial,[54] was that the police, as a matter of course, gave preferential treatment to clearing up those cases for which they had received 'advance payment', whilst neglecting their duties in others for which they had received no financial remuneration. As the SPD press was quick to point out, this militated heavily against the interests of working people, who could not afford to join such a gravy-train of bribery and corruption.

The trial of the editor of the *Rheinische Zeitung*, Sollmann, was held in January 1914 and took up the best part of two weeks. Some 150 witnesses were called, including some members of the general public who had indulged in, or been forced to acquiesce in, cash payments and gifts of this kind. Nearly all those employed by the police department made use of their *Zeugnisverweigerungsrecht*, the right to withhold information relating to the conduct of their affairs as state officials. The outcome of the case was that Sollmann received a fine of 500 marks for libelling the Cologne police, although the judgment of the court made specific reference to the fact that his accusations had been borne out in large measure by the weight of evidence.

This almost inevitable condemnation at the hands of the law was offset by the successes scored by the *Rheinische Zeitung* in terms of popular agitation. In the period of a fortnight, the number of its subscribers jumped by over a thousand, and the publication in the form of a special propaganda pamphlet of the full trial proceedings sold 10,000 copies, and public demand was so heavy that a second printing had to be ordered. A further bombshell to official pride was the action of a group of policemen from the Cologne force in supplying the *Rheinische Zeitung* with details of their own departmental rules and regulations. These extended as far as defining what was to be permitted during off-duty periods, the out-of-hours activities which it was considered right and proper for a policeman to attend, and the clear instruction that a member of the force was to embarrass and inconvenience an officer in the king's army as little as possible, even where the latter might have broken the law.[55] Bourgeois circles were stunned not only by the way in which the SPD had once again scored a major propaganda triumph, but by the depths of unmistakable corruption revealed within one of the pillars of the state. The *Berliner Volkszeitung*[56] commented sadly, 'The Prussian three-class state is mortally ill.'

At the conclusion of the trial, the Cologne Polizeipräsident ordered immediate disciplinary proceedings to be instituted against three staff inspectors but, together with the Regierungspräsident, he was himself summoned to Berlin for a personal audience with the Minister of the Interior, von Dallwitz. As the *Vorwärts* reported,[57] he was given a period of extended leave, and the paper assumed he would not return to his desk. The failure to draw any long-lasting lesson from the affair was castigated by the *Vorwärts* in March,[58] when it attacked the Centre Party for supporting and helping to pass a new annual police budget for the city of more than a million marks, a figure which was further supplemented by special subsidies from central state funds. Only a month later, the case opened in Berlin against three police-sergeants on charges of bribery and corruption.[59]

Intrigue and opportunities for corruption tend to flourish most successfully in systems of government freed from the scrutiny of democratic parliamentary control. Bismarck in his time had availed himself of the arts of conspiracy and deception; he had been instrumental in organising the press campaign against the mortally-ill Kaiser Friedrich III and his English wife, and had intrigued against colleagues in government. In 1890, after his fall from power and his withdrawal to Friedrichsruh, his position as a national figure was somewhat weakened. His influence remained, however, enhanced by the fact that many of his loyal lieutenants were still in positions of responsibility within government. The revolution of the 'new course' of the early 1890s was therefore less than complete, and Bismarck soon began to pose a threat by attracting disgruntled and ambitious opponents of the regime.

Above all the 'mistakes', such as the failure to renew the Reinsurance treaty with Russia and the abandonment of a protectionist trade policy subjected the Reichsleitung to persistent attacks from an increasingly vocal group around Bismarck, to the extent that the SPD press in particular spoke mockingly of a 'government in parallel' (*Nebenregierung*). These tensions amongst differing key factions were symptomatic of the struggle for power which was being waged within the oligarchy

of the Reich, and which ended in the triumph of the Kaiser's 'persönliches Regiment' in the late 1890s. It was characteristic of the times
that these conflicts rarely emerged into the open, but were hidden
behind a succession of anonymous press campaigns, in which veiled
references and ciphers often assumed an extraordinary importance.
Every now and again a window would be opened on a bizarre world
of private and public intrigue, in which guilt was by association and
honour often determined by recourse to the ancient practice of duelling.

Throughout the first half of the 1890s a flood of newspaper articles
had appeared in the establishment press, as well as in foreign journals,
which were sharply critical of leading ministers and the Kaiser himself.
Some of these included fanciful suggestions, such as the claim that
Wilhelm II was already suffering from the disease to which his father
had succumbed and that, moreover, there was a tendency towards
insanity in the Hohenzollern family line. Increasing concern at the
failure to discover the source of these press articles contributed in 1894
to the setting-up of the government's own special news and information
department, the *Pressereferat des Auswärtigen Amts*.[60] Amongst the
murkier episodes dredged up at this time was a personal scandal affecting the State Secretary in the Reich Office of the Interior, von Boetticher.[61] In order to help Boetticher's father-in-law, who had been
responsible for the fraudulent conversion of banking funds totalling one
million marks, Bismarck had secretly arranged in 1886 for a consortium, including Bleichröder, Hansemann and Mendelssohn, to cancel
the debt. A corresponding sum of equalisation was then paid to the
consortium from secret Guelph funds. Boetticher was later to claim
that Bismarck had authorised publication of the story in a fit of
malice.[62]

With the fall from office of Caprivi in the autumn of 1894, the
object of the mysterious press attacks increasingly became the German
Foreign Office and the man who had succeeded Herbert Bismarck as
State Secretary there, Freiherr Marschall von Bieberstein. Suspecting
the involvement of the Bismarck group in this campaign, Marschall
instructed the Berlin Polizeipräsident, von Richthofen, to spy on
Herbert Bismarck whenever he was in Berlin.[63] Richthofen, who
happened to be a fervent admirer of the ex-Chancellor, pleaded that
he was unable to entrust the work to a suitable agent, whereupon
Marschall simply ordered Herbert's activities in the capital to be
shadowed by officials of the Foreign Office. It is quite clear that
Herbert was forewarned by the police department and Marschall
gained little by this manoeuvre.

Attempts by Otto Hammann, the head of the newly-created press section in the Foreign Office, to obtain help from the political police in tracking down those responsible for the continuing flood of hostile articles met – as later emerged[64] – either with a complete failure to cooperate or the claim that the campaign was being directed by agents working for the socialist press. In a letter to the Kaiser in January 1895,[65] Marschall was able to report, however, that as a result of his own departmental inquiries, the identity of a suspect had already been established, and that he himself would spare no effort to uncover the source of the dissaffection. These details were duly passed on to the political police.

Writing to Hohenlohe the following month,[66] Richthofen declared that his department was in possession of information which clearly incriminated a journalist named Normann-Schumann, and that he would undertake appropriate action. Normann-Schumann had been inter alia the Berlin correspondent of the *Saalezeitung*, which was a staunch advocate of Count Waldersee's claims to the Chancellorship. His activities in this field were already known to the SPD, and the *Vorwärts* had referred to them – although not disclosing Normann-Schumann's identity – early in 1893. Julius Motteler, the head of the party's secret organisational network during the years of the Sozialisten-gesetz, had uncovered some of the threads of the affair in Paris, where articles critical of the new course had appeared in the *Mémorial Diplomatique*.[67]

A further eccentric twist to the affair came in September 1896. At a banquet in Breslau, Tsar Nicholas II concluded his reply to a toast proposed by his host with the words, 'Je puis vous assurer, sire, que je suis animé des mêmes sentiments traditionelles que Votre Majesté.' In the official version released by Wolff's news bureau, the words 'Votre Majesté' had been replaced with 'mon père'. Since Alexander III had been noted for the strength of his anti-German feeling, this version of the text implied a continuation of the old Tsarist policy. Two articles which appeared in the *Welt am Montag*, on 28 September and 5 October, first voiced the suggestion that the text had been purposely doctored, and that this had been deliberately carried out on the orders of the Foreign Office.[68] The clear implication was that current German foreign policy was being directed towards renewing hostility with Russia and seeking a rapprochement with Britain. Since it was common knowledge that Marschall was seeking to achieve more cordial relations with Britain, this version of events seemed credible enough.

However, the suggestion that the Foreign Office had doctored the text was a complete fabrication. After extensive inquiries, the source was traced to two journalists, Heinrich Leckert, a mere stripling of 20, and Karl von Lützow, a former officer in the Bavarian army. They were both charged with libelling the Lord Chamberlain (*Oberhof-marschall*), August Eulenburg, who had been identified with the pro-Marschall circle in the two articles. During the preliminary hearings before the trial opened in December, evidence was taken from Hohenlohe father and son, Marschall, Holstein and Philipp Eulenburg. What emerged during the court proceedings was not only the fact that Leckert and Lützow had both been paid agents of the political police,[69] but that their immediate superior, Polizeikommissar Eugen von Tausch, was at the centre of a vast network of intrigue and corruption.

It was this aspect of the affair which revealed most clearly to the SPD the extent to which the political police had been prepared to compromise its own position by becoming the tool of a naked struggle for power. The evidence of the corruptibility of one of the key institutions in the state thus provided the party with renewed confirmation of the disintegration of bourgeois moral values. Of equal concern, however, was the way in which an individual of dubious personal qualifications like Tausch had been able to create a position of considerable influence for himself, so that in a letter to his son Hohenlohe was able to describe him as 'persona gratissima' with the Kaiser.[70]

Initially concerned with investigations into press affairs, from which period dated his contacts with innumerable journalists, Tausch had obtained personal loans from leading press magnates such as August Scherl and had, in return, passed on items of confidential information. Lavish and extravagant by nature, he quickly got into financial difficulties and became particularly susceptible to outside proposals.[71] Despite the fact that he had been dismissed from the army in 1885 for embezzling regimental funds, Tausch was appointed head of three departments after the reorganisation of the Berlin headquarters. Richthofen described him as especially hard-working and reliable. After the deaths in 1895 of the administrative head of the Berlin political police, von Mauderode, and Richthofen himself, Tausch became to all intents and purposes the best-informed man in the entire department, and it had even been rumoured that he was to succeed Mauderode.[72]

At their trial in December 1896, Leckert and Lützow were both convicted and each received a sentence of eighteen months imprisonment. Although their connections with Tausch had clearly been established, and Tausch's own responsibility for intra-governmental intrigue had been partially uncovered, an enormous number of questions had remained unanswered and the press buzzed for several weeks with wild, but often surprisingly accurate rumours. The failure to exonerate those who had been tarred with the brush of guilt by association led to a most extraordinary incident immediately after the trial. This was Marschall's own personal attack on the machinations of the political police, in what came to be known as his '*Flucht in die Öffentlichkeit*', which he had published in the *Reichsanzeiger*.[73] It was a desperate attempt to prevent himself becoming enveloped in what Kurt Eisner described as 'a typhoon of filth from a scheming opposition'.[74] This action occasioned a great deal of adverse criticism, especially from conservative circles, and Bülow regarded it as unheard of for a Prussian minister to attack a Prussian authority in this way. For his part, the leader of the Reichspartei, Wilhelm von Kardorff, was convinced that revelations of this kind could only assist the SPD.[75]

There was indeed much official consternation, and not only because of Marschall's unprecedented statement. The Kaiser telegraphed to Hohenlohe on 6 December, 'What dreadful muck is being stirred up in the Lützow trial',[76] and the following day he recorded his displeasure at the bad impression that the scandal had made at a banquet the previous evening, given in honour of representatives from all over the Reich.[77] He was particularly furious at Marschall's flouting of convention and his manner of arranging what could only be described as a '*Zirkusvorstellung*'.[78] It was a rich harvest for any press and von Jagow reported from the Prussian legation in Munich that the local press had succeeded in portraying the political police as the only real villain of the piece.[79] News of the affair had by this time spread across the frontiers, and on 8 December *The Times* commented,

For the first time for many years we have a strong light thrown upon the relations of the German inspired press, the German political police and the German State Departments to each other. The result is not edifying, and suggests strong doubts as to the utility of the first two of those institutions.

Not unnaturally, the entire spectacle seemed to rebound most to the advantage of the SPD. On 4 December, Bebel had written to Adler, 'The Leckert–Lützow trial is grist to our mill; I intend to make the most of this episode in the third reading of the bill on criminal procedure',[80] and a week later he commented, 'The trial was capital . . . We really have been lucky . . . '[81] It was the sort of occasion which placed no further demands on the party other than intelligent reporting and enabled them, moreover, to stand back and cheer on both sides from the touchlines. To the *Vorwärts*,[82] the scandal had been a stormy petrel announcing the forthcoming tempest, and it took especial delight in recalling the diamond necklace affair of 1787 and the Teste-Cubières and Praslin cases which led up to the revolution of February 1848. *Die neue Zeit*,[83] in a reference to the real men behind the scenes (*die wahren Hintermänner*), regarded Tausch as little more than a pawn in the pay of the *Hofkamarilla* and high military circles. The part played by the SPD press in piecing together disparate scraps of information and constructing a network of conspiratorial relationships was a considerable one; and the state prosecutor at the Leckert–Lützow trial, in an obvious reference to recent press comment, declared that henceforth anyone who dared to speak of a '*Nebenregierung*' would be charged with *lèse-majesté*.

The mounting embarrassment which the affair was causing in leading government circles was reflected in the renewed speculation of a possible Staatsstreich. On 22 January 1897, in the aftermath of the dockworkers' strike in Hamburg, which had threatened the execution of the Kaiser's naval-building programme,[84] Waldersee sent a personal memorandum to the Kaiser.[85] In it, he emphasised that it should not be left to the SPD to determine the moment of reckoning with the state, and urged the Kaiser to authorise an internal pre-emptive strike.

It was with the hope of flushing out the figure of Waldersee behind Normann-Schumann – who had himself gained a social entrée to the highest court and government circles through Waldersee – that Marschall undertook his 'Flucht in die Öffentlichkeit'.[86] In fact, as Bruno Schoenlank recorded in his diary in March 1897,[87] following a conversation with Maximilian Harden, the Normann-Schumann business had ruined Waldersee's political prospects, and he was no longer 'the coming man'. The nature of the close links between Waldersee and Normann-Schumann did not, however, become public knowledge until the party's *Münchener Post* broke the story on 17 December 1902.

Nevertheless, the scandal had not ended with the conviction of Leckert and Lützow. Almost immediately, the Berlin Oberstaatsanwalt ordered a search of Tausch's home and his arrest on suspicion of having committed perjury. It became increasingly clear during the early months of 1897 that Tausch would face some form of criminal proceedings. A series of events suggested that official concern was directed towards ensuring that a minimum amount of further incriminating detail should be revealed. Normann-Schumann had been safely out of the country before the actions brought against Leckert and Lützow, but Max Gingold-Stärck, a journalist on the staff of the respected

Berliner Tageblatt, which had given evidence that Tausch had tried to persuade him to open up links with the Foreign Office, where his contact was to be none other than Holstein,[88] fled to London in February. He was followed by Metzsch-Schilbach, a former Saxon army officer, who had also been in the employ of Tausch.[89]

More significantly, shortly before the trial opened of Tausch in May 1897, Waldersee had a long talk with the Berlin Polizeipräsident, von Windheim, with the intention of avoiding all mention of his name in court.[90] Two former ministers, Köller and Bronsart von Schellendorf, amongst whom Tausch had helped to sow the seeds of political discord, both agreed to synchronise their evidence, so that neither would compromise the other.[91] Hohenlohe, locked in a struggle with the Kaiser over the drafting of two important bills, even approached Holstein in the hope of arranging a compromise, in which matters could conveniently be hushed up.[92] Increasing official nervousness as the trial approached was reflected by Baroness Spitzemberg in her diary, when she pointed to the danger that Tausch, in a spirit of revenge, might blow everybody sky-high.[93]

Marschall had already underlined the possibility that the Social Democrats might be in possession of additional incriminating evidence, when he made a personal statement during the course of a debate in the Reichstag. It was quite obvious to him that the SPD leadership already possessed information which might prove highly damaging to the political police. Had the trials not taken place and had Marschall preserved a diplomatic silence over the affair, it would have been left to the Social Democrats to explode the bombshell.[94] Indeed, a conversation between Julius Motteler and Wilhelm Liebknecht in July 1897 suggested that this was in fact the case, and almost certainly accounted for the decision not to call Liebknecht as a witness in the trial against Tausch.[95] The trial of Leckert and Lützow had, however, provided more than enough political sensation, and the SPD was once again able to publish a highly-successful pamphlet which included a transcript of the entire proceedings.

In the course of his statement to the Reichstag Marschall had further suggested that the responsibility for the court scandal involving a series of anonymous, obscene letters – attributed at first quite erroneously to the *Zeremonienmeister* Kotze – could also be laid at the door of the political police. That this episode, which had cost the life of Kotze's opponent in a duelling encounter, should continue to remain shrouded in mystery, was emphasised by the swift action taken by the courts in confiscating literature on the subject.[96]

To forestall the possibility of further damaging accusations and counter-accusations, Lützow was arraigned with Tausch as a fellow-accused in May 1897, which meant that he could not be called as a witness against his former chief. The code of criminal procedure gave additional help to those operating the strings behind the prosecution, since §53 laid down that all employees of the state, including those who were no longer in active service, or who had retired, could only give evidence in a court of law with the express permission of their superiors and that this permission, moreover, could be refused whenever and wherever the interests of the state were involved.[97] This 'Pflicht der Amtsverschwiegenheit' thus acted as a further wall of protection and insulation from unwelcome exposure. Even Bebel's appearance, as the sole Social Democratic witness, was used by the Oberstaatsanwalt as a means of launching a personal attack on the SPD leader's public utterances on the scandal. This remarkable use of a court of law as a means of avoiding the direct issues involved and attacking non-participants in the affair was without parallel, and led Bebel to publish a personal statement in the SPD press sharply criticising the complete capitulation of the law to political interests.[98]

Several days before the verdict was officially announced, Philipp Eulenburg had already informed the Kaiser that Tausch would be acquitted.[99] When judgment was announced, proclaiming the innocence of Tausch and sentencing the hapless Lützow to an additional two months imprisonment for fraud and falsification of documents, the public gallery broke out into loud ovations. The *Hamburger Echo*[100] took great delight in recording the presence in court of a large number of society women who, fondly imagining they had been witnessing a theatrical event of some importance, had not omitted to bring along their opera-glasses. *Die neue Zeit*[101] commented pithily, 'The incomprehensible . . . here becomes an event.' In a letter to Adler,[102] Bebel could hardly contain himself.

The Tausch trial has ended in the best possible way for us; once again a splendid episode like that succeeds in shaking the credibility of the state and government. We are such lucky fellows. All that our opponents do works simply to our own advantage. And the tragic nature of it. The only man who has the courage to campaign openly for an honest form of government [Marschall] has to capitulate, and one of the representatives of the most abominable corruption triumphs. Long live corruption!

Amongst the political consequences of the whole affair was the departure of Marschall. He had already incurred the displeasure of the Kaiser for his 'circus performance', and there were further grounds for antipathy.[103] As early as October of the previous year, the Kaiser had remarked to Philipp Eulenburg that he would not tolerate Marschall any longer and that he did not care 'if twenty Lützows came to be convicted'.[104] After the Tausch trial, Marschall was given leave and officially resigned his Foreign Office position in October when, on the recommendation of Philipp Eulenburg, he became ambassador in Constantinople.[105]

Not until November 1897 was Tausch suspended from his duties, and disciplinary proceedings against him did not begin until the following January. By this time Normann-Schumann, who had continued to write a number of articles in the French press under a variety of pseudonyms,[106] had sent a 30-page document of personal accusations to all the leading German editorial offices. In it he spoke contemptuously of 'the big dung-heap in the Wilhelmstraße', charged Holstein with responsibility for the fall of Bismarck and admitted having contacts with leading foreign newspapers, including the *New York Herald* and *Osservatore Romano*.[107] Tausch himself was prematurely retired in December 1898 on nearly full pension, and almost immediately accepted a job as inspector with an insurance firm.[108] The SPD press continued to follow with interest both the career of Tausch and those of the other two defendants, reporting for example the principal stations along Leckert's descent into the world of crime,[109] and it never failed to exploit the background to the scandal at every given opportunity.

For the first time, the seedier aspects of the country's system of a political police had been illuminated from within. The affair had strengthened SPD suspicions of the corruptness of government and its various agencies,[110] but it also revealed how dangerously close had been the prospect of a Staatsstreich. Henceforth, Social Democratic tactics were influenced by considerations of greater caution. Party agitators continued to make the most of opportunities, however, and during the third reading of the budget bill in March 1901 Richard Fischer instanced two further cases of intrigue conducted by the Berlin political police, as well as repeating SPD charges that such secret activities were financed from Reich funds. Bülow successfully parried awkward questions by referring his would-be inquisitors to the Prussian Minister of the Interior and the Prussian parliament – in which, of course, no Social Democrats were represented.[111]

Although the affair severely depressed government morale and gave a considerable uplift and added justification to SPD propaganda, it had little or no effect on the distribution of political power or on the influence which the political police continued to wield. In fact, the information service of the political police whose annual budget, provided from secret government funds, had been increased from 120,000 to 200,000 marks in 1895, received a further increase in 1900 to the tune of 300,000 marks.[112] Wilhelmine Germany's own 'third section' continued to remain, in Bebel's words, 'a bunch of knaves and blackguards'.[113]

The municipal authorities

Affairs such as those involving leading police officials, which noticeably ruffled the surface of political life, provided opportunities for huge propaganda feasts, but in between the editorial diet of the Social Democratic press retained more modest proportions. The struggle between the SPD and officialdom at the local level took the form of a continuous warfare, with perpetual sniping at institutions and agencies of government. There were, of course, regular attacks on Prussian ministries and the Offices of the Reich. In October 1899, for example, the Prussian Ministry of Railways was goaded by a series of articles in the *Vorwärts* into publishing a rebuttal of the charges in the official *Berliner Correspondenz*. It particularly objected to the socialist re-naming of its ministry – in an obvious reference to the spate of recent major railway accidents – as the 'Ministry of Misadventures'.[114] The railway authorities at Altona, too, came under heavy fire from the *Hamburger Echo* in 1911 for allegedly causing the death of an elderly employee through crass negligence. They had at first denied that the man had been entrusted with the dangerous task of cleaning the rails and claimed, moreover, that safety precautions had been perfectly adequate. At the trial of the paper's editor in September 1911, the state prosecutor demanded a prison sentence, since the offending article had been typical of the system which the socialist press chose to adopt of scarifying the authorities and causing dissatisfaction amongst the working classes. In the event, the editor escaped with a fine of 600 marks.[115]

Similarly, the SPD press attempted to make capital out of the Hamburg senate's handling of a cholera epidemic in August 1892, especially since the authorities refused to place foreign ships under quarantine regulations, because of the commercial losses that would be involved. Even when comparatively minor issues were at stake, it is significant that people turned to their local party paper in the hope of securing a forum for justice. Thus, in August 1894, the SPD agent in the small town of Schwanheim published a personal statement in the *Frankfurter Volksstimme*, in which he referred to an incident at the local school. A little girl had been caned by her teacher for covering a school-book with a page from the *Volksstimme*. The agent declared that he would immediately report all such incidents to the editorial offices of the paper.[116]

A common feature of such attacks on officialdom was the insistence on upholding the natural dignity of man and demanding the guarantee of elementary human rights for all those who felt themselves in any way oppressed. So, for example, in industrial areas the party press gave prominence to reporting accidents and injuries at work, especially where these resulted from inadequate safety measures. In 1898, the *Frankfurter Volksstimme* waged a major campaign against Farbwerke Hoechst, not simply in terms of the company's exploitation of workers for huge profits, but also for the failure of management to provide swift medical attention for acid burns.[117] Two years later the paper reported that, in order to relieve themselves, employees in the naphtol and nitrate workshops were forced to make use of portable lavatories within the work-area, and were also made responsible for emptying them.[118]

Far more serious were the quite reprehensible conditions which existed in some of the country's mental institutions and workhouses. These were highlighted by a case in the Rhineland in 1895, which virtually took on the qualities of a medieval horror-story. The previous year a journalist named Mellage had published a pamphlet in which he described the forcible incarceration of a Scottish Catholic priest in an asylum for the mentally disturbed near Aachen.[119] As the result of earlier efforts and the submission of affidavits from expert medical opinion, the unfortunate man was released in the summer of 1894, and Mellage used the evidence he had accumulated to suggest publicly that the asylum was being run inter alia as a penal institution for refractory Catholic clergy. Its administration was in the hands of a monastic order, the Gesellschaft der Alexianer, founded in the fourteenth century at the time of the Black Death in order to care for the sick and bury the dead. Although it received financial help from them, it was only indirectly responsible to the church authorities in the Rhineland. Nonetheless, the anti-clerical implications of the affair were seized upon by the SPD press, which gave the ensuing trial – at which Mellage faced a number of libel charges – the widest possible coverage.[120]

What emerged during the course of the trial was that the inmates had been systematically ill-treated over a number of years. A public health officer described how patients were subjected to various forms of water torture; other witnesses either reported from personal experience, or testified to the existence of, straitjackets, stranglings with leather straps, bad food and indescribable sanitary conditions. Recalcitrant patients were hit over the head, hurled down flights of stairs or chained up by their hands and feet. Doctors at the asylum, who were paid according to a system of percentages and bonuses, had apparently been unaware of, or unwilling to take account of, frequent instances of brutality leading to death.[121] What was especially alarming was that the existence of these appalling conditions would never have come out into the open if Mellage's pamphlet had not sparked off a trial for libel. Mellage had himself tried to alert the *Generalvikare* in Cologne and Paderborn, as well as the Cardinal's office in Cologne, to the misuse of authority at the Mariaberg asylum, but without success.

Following on from the furore in the press, the matter came before the Prussian parliament, but not before it had been postponed in order to allow deputies to take part in the celebrations marking the completion of the Kiel canal. As *Die neue Zeit*[122] put it, 'First pleasure, then business!' The Minister responsible for health matters, Dr Bosse, announced that he had ordered the closure of the Mariaberg asylum, and proposed to set up some two dozen commissions, whose responsibility it would be to control the licensing of all such institutions.[123]

This affair had, of course, raised the wider question of the treatment of the mentally sick. It was perhaps not so surprising that conditions existed similar to those at Mariaberg, in view of the fact that men like Pastor von Bodelschwingh – a Protestant cleric who ran a number of such institutions – were on record as claiming that nervous disorders were clear cases of demoniac possession. To *Die neue Zeit*,[124] the increasing evidence of mental sickness, coupled with rising unemployment, were directly attributable to the evils of capitalist society. What little statistics there are on this subject do confirm an upward trend: in 1888 there were 257 lunatic asylums in the country, with 67,444 patients in care, and by 1901 some 332 institutions, with responsibility for 120,872 patients. After 1902 the term 'asylum' was extended to take in several other categories, so that there is no direct correlation with earlier figures. Even so, in 1907 there were no fewer than 505 institutions caring, if that is the word, for 198,412 patients.[125] Certainly, the SPD press never gave up reporting details of the miserable fate which awaited many of the inmates.[126] The *Bergische Arbeiterstimme*, for example, printed extracts from a letter which the husband of a woman epileptic, confined to a sanitorium in Bielefeld, had received from her, in which she spoke of regular beatings, overfilled dormitories, the absence of proper medical attention and the deliberate exploitation of patients' labour.[127] In October 1895, the Regierungspräsident at

Cologne bemoaned not only the fact that recent cases of this kind had given the SPD considerable material for agitation, but also that press coverage had cleverly stopped just short of giving the authorities adequate cause to intervene.[128]

Conditions in the workhouses of Wilhelmine Germany were scarcely better. In March 1895, the *Rheinische Zeitung* published a letter which contained a number of accusations against the administrators of a poorhouse in Brauweiler, which housed over a thousand men and women, nearly all from the lowest levels of society. Earlier that month, the director and his house doctor had faced charges of causing the death of one of the inmates through negligence, but both had been acquitted, since the court remained unconvinced of any criminal intent. The letter to the *Rheinische Zeitung* drew attention to a veritable arsenal of instruments of torture, and spoke of elderly people being kept deliberately on a starvation diet. Many, already suffering from the lack of heating and the widespread use of corporal punishment, had been driven into a premature death. Both the director of the institution and the regional administration for the Rhineland felt themselves to have been libelled and the editor, Adolf Hofrichter, was duly brought before the courts in December 1895.[129]

Although a large number of witnesses corroborated in detail the essence of the published accusations, the state prosecutor demanded a sentence of eight months imprisonment, because Hofrichter's alleged intention had been 'to blow up the affair into a major scandal'. The prosecutor's argument was that the *Rheinische Zeitung* was read predominantly by the poorest sections of society, who would be stirred into feelings of hatred against the institutions, which would entirely frustrate the intentions of the state in setting them up. This submission was accepted by the court, and the presiding judge declared that Hofrichter's aim had been not to criticize the operation of the system, but to attack the integrity of the institution's director and his immediate superiors. Hofrichter was duly convicted and given a sentence of three months imprisonment.[130]

The fact that such barbaric methods of treatment were considered necessary at all was further evidence, according to the SPD press, that the capitalist system was reaching the end of its tether. Further disclosures – in 1898 at Delmenhorst, for instance[131] – of appalling conditions in state institutions, revealed the widespread abuse and misuse of authority. Often, the resulting trials for character defamation provided the SPD with the only means of substantiating the basis of editorial claims. Even so, the penalty that journalists paid suggests that the authorities were concerned to stifle all unwelcome criticism rather than to tackle the problem at its source.

The war against militarism

The spirit of militarism hangs rather heavily over the German past. It is a commonplace that the Prussian army had played a decisive rôle in the unification of the modern German nation-state. It continued to remain a dominant feature in national affairs. The failure to dis-tinguish clearly between political authority and military competence – the relationship, as defined by Gerhard Ritter, between *Staatskunst* and *Kriegshandwerk*[132] – marked the anti-democratic character of the Wilhelmine period. When the Kaiser declared in April 1891 at a ban-quet held in Berlin that 'The soldier and the army, not parliamentary majorities and decisions, have welded the German Reich together. My confidence rests with the army', he was merely underlining the army's position of undisputed social and political pre-eminence in the state.[133] Indeed, the irrelevance of parliamentary institutions and their necessary subordination to traditional concepts of state power, was a view which held high favour with establishment circles, as the ultra-conservative Prussian Junker Oldenburg-Januschau demonstrated in a speech to the Reichstag in January 1910, when he asserted that at any time the Kaiser should be able to order a lieutenant to take ten men and close the building.[134] Moreover, the attitude of mind which could confuse the offices of state with a parade-ground was sharply revealed in a comment by Caprivi as Chancellor:

I don't know, when I was commanding officer and ordered my corps to stand still, they did so; whenever I issue an order here, all the *Geheimräte* fidget around. . .[135]

The democratic accountability of the army to the elected representa-tives was made virtually impossible by the existence of the royal pre-rogative and right of disposal (*Verfügungsrecht*) in army matters, grounded in Article 45 of the Prussian constitution and Article 63 of the Reich constitution. It was accepted that no minister could intervene in the close and personal relationship between the King and his army, or seek to limit the extent of the royal *Kommandogewalt*. Consequently, the Prussian Minister of War was given neither full authority over military matters nor countersigned regulations, but was reduced to overseeing the funding of the army and other administrative matters, whilst still having to defend the concept of the Kommandogewalt before the Reichstag. Moreover, attempts at political interference simply led the Kaiser to transfer further responsibility from the War Minister to the Military Cabinet and General Staff. Indeed, the independence of the army was reflected in all kinds of ways, not least in the setting up of a separate military diplomatic corps, which reported directly to the Kaiser and Chief of Staff.[136]

Not surprisingly, therefore, the Kaiser lived in an overwhelmingly military environment, surrounded by adjutants who formed his special military entourage (*maison militaire*). This tended to push military considerations into the foreground, to the detriment of purely political factors in internal politics. Above all, the Kaiser never failed to stress the uniqueness of the relationship between him and the army, proclaiming at a passing-out ceremony in 1893:

The soldier is not to have *his* will, rather you should all have *one* will; there is only *one* law and that is *my* law.[137]

The superior influence enjoyed by the militarist ethic in German society – in which the army was seen as a kind of training ground for adult citizenship – had profound and unfortunate consequences on social behaviour. For example, the exaggerated importance attached to the position in society of the reserve-army officer produced a synthetic and illusory sense of social superiority, and there were many who craved such distinctions above all else. The case of the finance minister von Scholz who, at the age of 56, was promoted to lieutenant *à la suite*, because in his period of active service he had only reached the rank of sergeant (*Vizefeldwebel*), was not an isolated occurrence. Equally characteristic was the fact that Bethmann Hollweg, who on his appointment as Chancellor had been given the rank of major and, like his predecessors, wore his uniform in the Reichstag, had to be content with a seat at the Kaiser's banqueting-table which was below those of more senior officers. Moreover, the Kaiser's assertion in November 1891 that the most fitting company for a soldier was other soldiers and not civilians,[138] simply tended to reinforce the idea of the army as a state within the state, responsible only to its own received traditions. Yet far more important were the conditioning effects on the human psyche. Those qualities which army life seemed to encourage, namely the blind subjugation of individuals to the will of their superiors and the complete disregard for human sensitivity – a process of '*Abstumpfung*' – were precisely those which caused an anonymous historian to publish in 1893 a polemic against the suffocating rôle of the militarist ethic in German society.[139]

It was almost impossible to escape either the army's constant physical presence or its subtle influence on many different aspects of national life. In Berlin alone, for example, there were five infantry and five field-artillery regiments, a corps of engineers, a life guard corps, a mounted military-police corps, as well as an army services battalion and the sovereign's own regiment. Of these, the Kaiser's *Garde-du-Corps* was the *ne-plus-ultra* and represented the acme of the social pyramid in Germany,[140] Moreover, Prussian influence on the character and composition of army units remained pre-eminent; of the 21 army corps in the Reich, no fewer than 18 were Prussian.[141]

Specifically Prussian, too, was the alliance between the military and the civilian bureaucracy through the institution of the *Militäranwärter*, which ensured a stable and respected position in the employ of the state after completion of military service.[142] There were frequent proposals for extending the range of suitable employment; in 1893, for example, the *Militärisches Wochenblatt*, widely regarded as the official organ of the Ministry of War, suggested that in order to solve the problem of the under-recruitment of sub-lieutenants, they should be allowed to take up positions as part-time elementary school-teachers.[143]

The Wilhelmine state was not without its pomp and ceremony. No illustrated magazine or journal was considered complete without regular details and pictures of military processions, court pageants and other festivities, and the annual celebration of the Kaiser's birthday, on 27 January, was a preponderantly military affair. The craze for memorials and statues of monarchist-militarist idols, what the SPD press tersely dismissed as '*Denkmalsunfug*', reached a fever-pitch in 1894, with a government bill to provide 4 million marks for a monument to Kaiser Wilhelm I. Only the Social Democrats voted against the proposal, although the budget had in fact been cut from an initial demand for 8 million marks. This set off a chain-reaction throughout the country, and the *Hamburger Echo*[144] referred to the efforts of a Protestant pastor in a village in Southern Germany to erect a commemorative obelisk in front of his own small church. Even a veteran republican from the 1848 revolutions, the poet and theorist Ludwig Pfau, had offered to help in the construction of *Kaiserdenkmäler* in Stuttgart and Heilbronn. Such bourgeois preoccupations were a rich source of satire and occasioned the SPD to produce in 1904 a propaganda sheet in the form of a specialist publication, *Hau-Mich-Aus. Zentralorgan für Denkmalweihen und Heimatschmuck*.[145]

Far more serious was the continuing practice amongst army officers of the duel, which Schopenhauer had once described as 'the most serious bit of buffoonery in the world'. By proclaiming the officer's sense of professional honour (*Standesehre*) and his right to defend it, the duel was still one more way of underlining the social differences between the military and civilian population.[146] As such, it provided the SPD press with further evidence of the deep-seated class divisions within society.[147] Although the Catholic Centre Party frequently expressed its opposition to the practice, duelling as a form of settling disputes had a wide social acceptance even outside the army. Former army officers, such as the two Zeremonienmeister, Kotze and Schrader, who resorted to a duel in 1894, found it perfectly acceptable to retrieve their honour in this fashion, and the victor had little to fear in the way of serious retribution from the state, even when the outcome was death.[148] Members of student societies who rejected the duel were considered unsuitable as officer material, and even the annual conference of the Anti-Duell-Liga at Munich in October 1907 found it perfectly logical to reject the duel in theory, whilst refusing to condemn it in practice.[149] Despite an order in council issued in 1897,[150] which was intended to limit the practice, the tradition survived intact right up to the outbreak of war in 1914.

The essence of the army's internal function was to act as a bulwark of social order. To this end a series of stringent provisions existed in order to protect soldiers from exposure to socialist influence. In particular, all junior ranks were denied the freedom to attend any sort of political meeting without the express permission of an officer, were forbidden to possess or circulate any form of socialist literature and were required to denounce fellow-soldiers if they suspected them of any connections with the SPD. So that ignorance of these regulations should not frustrate the government's long-term ideological objectives, the Minister of War, von Gossler, insisted against the advice of the Minister of Justice that they should be printed annually in the *Reichsanzeiger*. Not until 1908 did von Einem entertain doubts as to the wisdom of providing the SPD with so much free propaganda.[151] In 1894 Count Botho Eulenburg informed all Regierungspräsidenten that as a direct result of a personal initiative from the Kaiser, hostels were to be built in a large number of towns, which in addition to providing a social and recreational centre for the troops, were intended to screen junior ranks from all possible contact with Social Democrats.[152] Nor were the army authorities above intercepting mail, in order to check whether the recipients were socialist sympathisers.[153]

Despite this, the SPD was extraordinarily successful in coping with the situation. As Bebel remarked in a letter to Engels in June 1893,[154]

Socialist literature is circulating in the army to a greater extent than one could hope for; there is an excellent sense of keeping the stuff hidden. The Kaiser, so I heard from a well-informed source in Straßburg, has decreed that no Social Democrat is to be given a stripe, let alone aspire to become an NCO, not even those doing just a year's service. The result is that those regiments which draw their recruits from socialist areas, have a serious shortage of suitable junior ranks . . .

Official views of the '*Staatsfeindlichkeit*' of the SPD, given renewed confirmation with each vote in the Reichstag against a military bill, were naturally reflected in the attitude towards individual cases of conscription. Thus, the *Rheinische Zeitung* could report less than a year before the outbreak of war in 1914 that a man in Cologne, who had originally been given a special dispensation to allow him to complete one year's reduced military service, was later informed that he would be required to serve two or more years, since his activities on behalf of the SPD were incompatible with the 'moral qualities' required of one-year military service applicants.[155] Characteristically, local notices detailing the existence of military boycotts against certain public houses, carried the explanation 'Out of bounds to military personnel, since frequented by prostitutes, pimps and Social Democrats.'[156]

Nowhere was the anti-democratic nature of the army more evident than in its intended use as an instrument of internal repression,[157] and in its readiness to participate in schemes for a coup from above. Indeed, only two days after the Reichstag elections of February 1890, General Waldersee declared his support for a Staatsstreich, and throughout the 1890s he remained in the front rank of those pressing for a pre-emptive strike against 'the enemy within'.[158]

At one stage the conflict engendered with the Reichstag over the army bill of 1892 threatened to provide a suitable excuse for such a move.[159] In a direct parallel with a similar crisis in 1887, when Bismarck had tried to secure parliamentary approval for a long-term military budget (Septennat), Caprivi proposed expanding military conscription in order to meet the need for an increased army.[160] He even went to the lengths of arranging for a propaganda campaign to be waged in the press by a specially appointed member of the Reich Chancellery, whose responsibility extended to tapping sources of private finance and who – without the knowledge of Caprivi – prepared contingency plans in the event of a dissolution of the Reichstag.[161] This dissolution duly took place in June 1893 since, although a number of concessions had been made, no majority could be found for the bill, and its successor was eventually passed by a more amenable Reichstag the following month.

Knowledge of the arrangements made by military and civil authorities, in order to ensure effective cooperation in suppressing undesirable political activity, provided the SPD with ample material for political exploitation. As early as October 1892, the *Fränkische Tagespost* was able to reveal details of such contingencies,[162] but the biggest stir was created when Heinrich Limbertz (of the Rhineland press bureau) made public at the 1910 party conference what came to be known as the 'Bissing-Erlaß'. This circular, from the GOC of the 7th Army Corps, Freiherr von Bissing, and dated 30 April 1907, was notable for its decidedly extremist tone, in which it made reference to 'the suppression of all seditious newspapers and the immediate imprisonment of journalists as well as leading agitators and other ringleaders, regardless of parliamentary immunity'.[163] What characterised this and other similar documents was not simply the prospect of military rule during a crisis, but the scarcely restrained readiness of the troops to engage in an immediate violent confrontation with the forces of subversion.[164] Indeed, the Minister of War sent out a directive to all chief commands in February 1912, emphasising once again the importance of decisive action in the suppression of civil disorders,[165] and some two years later precise instructions were issued on the use of weaponry during disturbances.[166]

Military commands had in fact been authorised to supply police forces with arms on a number of occasions, and the intention was that they should be used wherever appropriate. In 1898 the *Vorwärts* created a further sensation, when it published a letter from the Minister of the Interior, von der Recke, to the Regierungspräsident at Erfurt, noting with some distaste that the police had failed to quell a series of local disturbances through hesitancy over the use of their weapons, thereby damaging the political credibility of the state and causing it serious loss of face.[167] Similarly, the high command in Breslau was ordered in 1906 to make available to the local police 150 army revolvers for the purposes of riot control.[168] The importance of setting aside sensitivity to personal considerations had already been emphasised by the Kaiser in a celebrated comment to recruits in Potsdam, when he declared,

During the present subversive activities of the socialists, it can happen that I will order you to shoot at your own relatives, brothers, even parents – which may God forbid – but nonetheless you will have to obey my command without demur.[169]

By way of reciprocal help the army authorities expected, and regularly received, from the local police full details of socialist and trade-union publications,[170] as well as other information which bordered on areas of military competence,[171] and there is little real evidence, as some have argued,[172] to suggest that the police were increasingly reluctant to cooperate in the witch-hunt against the SPD.

Ensuring the long-term absolute reliability and dependability of the army was reflected in the concern for consolidating the educative function of the period of military training, and in warding off attempts at ideological subversion by the SPD. This strategy was in itself some-what counter-productive, since the party press was well aware of the hand-in-glove cooperation between the military and civil authorities, and regularly managed to furnish its readers with conclusive evidence to this effect. In October 1906, for instance, the *Mannheimer Volks-stimme* published a circular from the Baden Minister of the Interior, referring to the need for the closest possible surveillance of the new army intake, in the light of the decision taken at the 1905 party con-ference to inform all new recruits of their legal rights.[173] The source for the *Volksstimme*'s disclosure was almost certainly responsible for the additional publication in the *Karlsruher Volksfreund* of a memor-andum from the Minister, calling for immediate investigations into the reasons for this highly embarrassing leak.[174]

The union of army and state found its clearest expression in civilian life in the activities of the army veterans' associations (Kriegervereine), which were seen as upholding military traditions and patriotic fervour beyond the period of active service. The Kaiser himself regarded them as 'the army in civilian dress', and the choice of name for the national federation of associations – the *Kyffhäuserbund* – was more than a conscious reference to the mountain in Thuringia inside which, as legend had it, the grandson of Friedrich Barbarossa was lying asleep and watching over the nation's destiny.[175] Since these organisations had an important social rôle in the community, especially in rural areas, their influence in preserving the militarist ethic in society was very marked. Their existence can be traced back to an order in council made in 1842 by Friedrich Wilhelm IV, although their enormous ideological potential to the government's anti-socialist strategy was only recognised in the early 1890s. In a joint circular from the Prussian Ministers of War and of the Interior, all Kriegervereine were denied permission to dedicate and carry flags – which were ceremoniously donated by the Kaiser – until they had included in their regulations the absolute right to exclude all those whose political sympathies were considered unpatriotic.[176] It proved difficult, however, to exclude all Social Democrats from such organisations and, following the 1903

Reichstag elections, the chairman of the Prussian Landeskriegerver-band, General von Spitz, had to threaten recalcitrant associations with expulsion.[177] By 1912 there were 31,000 Kriegervereine in Germany, with some 2,800,000 members, and in Prussia alone 500 new associations were being formed annually.[178] Their ideological work was characterised by a constant stream of leaflets, pamphlets and other publications,[179] and was often supplemented by similar organisations such as the Kaiser-Wilhelm-Dank, Verein der Soldatenfreunde, which in the decade 1897–1907 had been responsible for the gratis distribution of almost 600,000 books and magazines.[180]

As the Prussian garrison-spirit infected so much of national life, it would have been remarkable if it had failed to make some sort of impression on SPD thinking. Drawn as conscripts into an army whose organisation and function were directed against their own political movement, Social Democrats were not slow to evolve ideas of reform. Chief amongst these was the demand that an army which owed its *raison d'être* to the personal autocratic power of the monarch, should be replaced by a national people's army (*Volkswehr*), organised on democratic lines with, for example, promotion according to ability, the abolition of batmen for officers and an end to tedious and repetitive barrack-room and parade-ground routines. These proposals were amplified in a pamphlet which Bebel published in 1898, *Nicht stehendes Heer, sondern Volkswehr.*

The crucial point is that the SPD was as conscious as any other group within Wilhelmine society of the need for external defence, and was prepared to make a contribution towards that end. For this reason party speakers reiterated their willingness to fight, if necessary, in order to preserve the existing boundaries of the German Reich.[181] But this attitude did not reflect approval of military objectives, still less was it an acceptance of the political and social organisation of the state. It was the clearest expression of the fact that Social Democrats still regarded themselves as Germans and entitled to play a part in shaping their country's future. This was underlined by Bebel in the Reichstag, when he declared that the SPD would fight to defend Germany 'not for your sakes, but for ours, for all I care in order to spite you'.[182] Failure to appreciate this distinction was the reason why von Vollmar's view that 'international' did not necessarily mean 'anti-national', expressed at the 1907 congress of the Socialist International, occasioned such a sense of outraged bewilderment amongst foreign delegates.[183] Indeed, in a curious way the prospect of war could not be regarded as unwelcome to the SPD, which frequently argued that the escalation and intensification of internal conflicts would inevitably lead to a state of war. It is quite clear that the party expected to gain from the ensuing collapse, and construct on the ashes of old imperial Germany a new democratic ideal of social organisation.[184]

Attempts have often been made to read back from the events of 1914 and the attitude of the SPD to the approval of war credits, evidence of the party's fundamental acceptance of the status quo. Such views tend to overlook both the expectation that the SPD would profit from the new situation, as well as the overwhelming tide of euphoria and public enthusiasm, fuelled by government propaganda, which would have steamrollered in its path the entire party organisation, had it resisted the national mood. It was in the light of this irresistible momentum that Noske later coined the phrase of the SPD voting for the credits, 'in order not to be trampled to death in front of the Brandenburg Gate'.[185]

Preoccupation with an apparent SPD volte-face in 1914 has also tended to obscure the party's unrelenting opposition to measures which seemed to bolster the ambitions and power of the military, or its derision at the diversification of the militarist ethic into what the SPD press termed 'militarism of the high seas'. It was Paul Singer who laid down the official party policy in a speech to the 1892 conference.

The attitude of Social Democracy to militarism is self-evident from our programme. Everybody knows what our position is: we are the enemies of militarism and will continue to struggle against it until the system lies smashed to pieces on the ground. As far as the military budgets are concerned, we do not share common ground with the Progressives [Freisinnige], who once uttered the slogan, 'Not a penny and not a man for this ministry' but, in keeping with our principles, we say 'Not a penny and not a man for militarism, for the prevailing militaristic system'.[186]

Nor did rank-and-file members hesitate to give expression to their own sentiments in this respect; between October 1892 and March 1893, for example, more than 750 mass meetings were held in different parts of the country to protest at Caprivi's new army bill.[187] Again, the SPD was the only party to vote against the expenditure of 1,700,000 marks for the celebrations marking the opening of the Kiel Canal in 1895.[188] Above all, it was the futility of expecting any measure of reform from within which emerged in the view of one delegate to the 1893 party conference, when he argued that

Militarism belongs to those species of blood-sucking insects which do not undergo any form of metamorphosis, but which have to be crushed to death and destroyed if you want to get rid of them.[189]

Although continuing attacks on the militarist system in the party press represented a constant source of irritation to the authorities, it was the new danger to their long-term ideological struggle against internal subversion, represented by Karl Liebknecht's appeal to the proletarian youth movement, which threatened to tip the advantage against the state. In November 1906, some two years after the appearance of the first socialist youth organisations in the Rhineland-Palatinate and in Berlin, a conference was held in Mannheim which was attended by representatives of the movement.[190] The occasion was notable for an attack by Liebknecht on the prevailing militarist ethic, in which he summed up the recipe for long-term ideological success in the slogan, '*Wer die Jugend hat, hat die Armee!*' Drawing on the metaphorical associations of decadence and decay, which ran like a *Leitmotiv* through socialist attacks on the Wilhelmine Reich, Liebknecht described the aim of anti-militarist propaganda as 'the wearing down and disintegration of the militarist ethic, in order to accelerate the organic decomposition of nationalism'.[191]

When the text of his speech was printed the following year, as a propaganda pamphlet aimed at a mass market,[192] official action was ordered – albeit after a hesitant delay – from within the Ministry of War.[193] All remaining copies of the pamphlet were confiscated and Liebknecht was brought before the full panoply of the Reichsgericht in October 1907 on charges of sedition, with the Supreme State Prosecutor (Oberreichsanwalt) leading the case against him. On hearing the news of Liebknecht's conviction and sentence of eighteen months *custodia honesta*, Bülow commented maliciously, 'This judgment is very pleasing, especially in view of the unanimous condemnation which anti-militarist agitation in France is experiencing.'[194] However, increasing concern at the government's failure to control the spread of socialist ideas amongst the young led in 1914 to a secret proposal from the Minister of War, which envisaged compulsory gymnastics courses and open-air recreational activities for all males from the age of 14 until entry into military service. The intention was thus to stimulate and develop a deep-rooted sense of 'fear of God, feeling for one's homeland and love of the Fatherland'.[195]

By far the strongest condemnation in the party press was reserved for the mounting evidence of dehumanisation within the army itself – the sad and shocking stream of cases of ill-treatment. Every revelation by SPD journalists of the fundamental rottenness of the existing state pales into insignificance by comparison with the atrocities uncovered in the treatment of recruits and junior ranks. Publications by former active soldiers bear eloquent testimony to barrack-square tyranny:

one soldier, who was unable to march perfectly in step with his platoon, was forced to jump backwards and forwards for several hours over a deep ditch until, exhausted, he lost his footing, fell into the ditch and broke a leg.[196] Brutality was often pursued to the point where the victim sought release in death. The party paper at Bochum reported four cases of suicide in March 1914, by soldiers whose bodies showed extensive signs of physical ill-treatment,[197] and a court-martial at Metz in July of the same year heard that two soldiers had been so severely beaten that one victim hanged himself and another died from multiple internal injuries.[198] Indeed, the suicide rate amongst soldiers remained alarmingly high throughout the period; on average between 220 and 240 soldiers took their own lives in desperation every year.[199]

It was by no means easy to seek redress for ill-treatment. There was a complex procedure (*Beschwerderecht*) under regulation standing orders, as a result of which a soldier had to submit an official complaint not earlier than the morning after the incident had occurred and not later than three days following.[200] Since every soldier upon leaving the army required a testimonial from his commanding officer to hand to a prospective civilian employer, few were prepared to risk becoming labelled an official nuisance. There were added difficulties and dangers: in December 1905 a court-martial at Dersau sentenced a soldier to six months imprisonment (*Frivolitätsstrafe*), for 'falsely' accusing an NCO of having beaten him. For these reasons, those statistics which do exist probably mask a much higher incidence of ill-treatment. In Württemberg, no fewer than 3,247 cases brought before the military courts in the period 1902–13 dealt with ill-treatment,[201] and in the decades before 1914 there was an annual average of 800 such cases,[202] with a staggering total of 2,394 instances in Prussia alone in 1899.[203]

The first evidence of the widespread nature of cruelty of this kind came with the publication by the *Vorwärts* on 31 January 1892 of a secret decree from Prince Georg, Duke of Saxony and supreme commander of the 12th Army Corps. This document had been forwarded to all commanding officers the previous June and concerned itself entirely with the ill-treatment of soldiers and other unchecked military excesses:

A large number of the considerable cases of physical ill-treatment . . . can only be described as artful torture, as the result of brutality and degeneracy, which one would hardly have imagined possible in the men from whom our NCOs are drawn, nor likely to happen, given the control and supervision which characterise our military service . . . The files show that recruits, as well as those of long-standing service, have been beaten or whipped for weeks, even months on end, with a systematic regularity. . .[204]

The contents of this document thus gave SPD propaganda a new cutting edge, sanctioned by what amounted to official admissions of army brutality. Engels wrote to Bebel on 2 February,

I was so beside myself with joy at reading the decree that I almost jumped into the air. This will unleash a proper fury in higher circles. That something like this should get into the godless Social Democratic press – have our chaps really got such connections with 'My magnificent army'?[205]

Details of a similar circular, which had been issued by the GOC of the 2nd Bavarian Army Corps in October 1890, and which was sent out again in December 1891, also appeared in the party press. Count Dönhoff's report to Caprivi from Dresden,[206] commenting on recent disclosures of this kind, suggested that the SPD obviously enjoyed close relations with individual army subalterns.

Instances of cruelty and brutality persisted alarmingly. In 1903, an NCO at Rendsburg who, on the recommendation of his commanding officer, had already been accepted for the police force in Hamburg, was convicted of 1,500 individual cases of ill-treatment, of which 300 were classed as serious.[207] The Catholic Centre Party newspaper *Germania* complained that this continuing flood of evidence was providing the SPD with twofold gain: young people were flocking in droves to the red flag, and the party itself was being blessed with ample material for agitation.[208] The SPD's determination to continue its all-out war on the evils of militarism was proclaimed by Auer in a speech to the Reichstag in 1895:

We shall deal with you, but not by stepping with empty hands in front of armed troops and providing them with a target. No, we shall deal with you by exposing again and again, and under all conditions, the abuses within the system, by organising the proletariat and – because we represent a just cause – by bringing all humane and right-thinking people onto our side.[209]

That some soldiers continued to be crippled for life and others were forced to suffer perpetual humiliation at the hands of their superiors was a sad commentary on the conditioning which took place within army units. The outcome was increasingly a lack of respect for the personal dignity of human life, as underlined in the words of a former army captain,

What emerges in the ill-treatment of soldiers is not virility and still less gallantry, much more a form of pathological craving, in the last resort cruelty characterised by degenerate sensuality, which revels in the pain of the victim.[210]

It was not only within the barrack-rooms that the worst excesses of militarism became apparent. In April 1892, for example, a worker in

Berlin who, while drunk, had made threatening remarks to a sentry on duty, was shot dead in the process of attempting to run away. Shortly after the incident, in which an innocent bystander had also been injured, the grenadier concerned was promoted and given a personal audience by the Kaiser, who presented him with a personally signed picture.[211] In the same year, a lieutenant killed a shopkeeper in Koblenz after a violent argument. Again, in October 1896 another army lieutenant, von Brüsewitz, drew his sword in a restaurant and hacked to death an unarmed mechanic with whom he had quarrelled. The matter was raised in the Reichstag the following month, but the War Minister, von Gossler, refused to accede to demands for a full government statement.[212] Official sensitivity to the wider implications of this particular affair was reflected in the decision to ban performances in Karlsruhe of three one-act plays, collectively entitled *Morituri*, by the naturalist playwright Hermann Sudermann, in which military brutalism was subjected to pointed satire.[213]

The authorities reacted with the same kind of vigour to SPD criticism of military intemperance as they did to attacks on the civil administration. There was not much that could be done about the deliberate naming in the SPD press of all officers convicted of ill-treating subordinates, but whenever the basic facts were embroidered with comment, the law proved much more helpful. In August 1900, for instance, Hermann Molkenbuhr was fined 300 marks for insulting the entire German officer corps, by allowing a satirical piece on the Brüsewitz episode to be published in the *Hamburger Echo*. When the *Danziger Volkswacht* published extracts in March 1913 from a book by a leading trade-union journalist,[214] the paper's editor as well as the author were brought before the courts to face similar charges of libelling the officer corps. The author escaped sentence, because the work had originally appeared in 1910 and the period of legal entitlement to prosecute (*Verjährungsfrist*) had expired, but the editor was fined 300 marks. Nor is there much evidence to suppose that SPD attacks of this kind weakened, or that official response lessened in the years before 1914. In June 1913, for example, the *Hamburger Echo* published a hard-hitting editorial, entitled 'Germany's Disgrace', recording further appalling details of excesses and widespread brutality, and concluding, 'In no other army in the world . . . does there exist anything even remotely comparable with the abominations in the Prusso-German army.'[215] Six months later, the editor concerned was convicted and fined 600 marks.

Amongst party agitators, Rosa Luxemburg faced a number of court proceedings arising from her repeated attacks on the evils of militarism, most spectacularly in the spring of 1914, when she was charged with slandering the officer corps at a public meeting. She thereupon announced her determination to prove her case in court and, following an appeal in the SPD press, over a thousand readers responded with willingness to provide evidence of bullying and ill-treatment. When the trial opened, her defence counsel was able to announce material covering more than 30,000 instances of brutality. The prospect of answering such a mammoth indictment obviously occasioned severe official doubts as to the efficacy of pursuing the charges against Luxemburg, and after three days the hearing was adjourned, never to be resumed.[216]

Judgments from the military courts were distinguished at once by a severity towards those who had demonstrated their disloyalty to their fellow-soldiers, and by a noticeable leniency in a high proportion of convictions for ill-treatment and misuse of authority. Thus, in November 1903 a court-martial at Metz sentenced a young lieutenant to six months imprisonment and dismissal from the service, for publishing a novel which dealt all too obviously with the increasing degeneracy of the army officer corps.[217] During a Reichstag debate, Karl Frohme quoted the example of an NCO who had been given a sentence of six years, together with a dishonourable discharge, for taking a number of SPD newspapers into the barracks and showing them to fellow-soldiers.[218] Similarly, several army reservists at Dresden who had sent a letter of complaint to the *Sächsische Arbeiterzeitung* in the course of completing their period of annual training, were court-martialled and given heavy sentences.[219] On the other hand, the SPD press lost no time in pointing to the underlying bias in the sentencing policy as applied to officers and NCOs facing charges of ill-treatment. An NCO convicted of 77 cases in 1902 was given three months, from which one month was deducted for the period spent in custody, and 22 soldiers who ill-treated a recruit to the extent of permanently disabling him, were given sentences ranging from 14 days to two months.

The actual number of examples of ill-treatment cited in individual cases appeared to have little effect on the outcome of the hearing, so that a Berlin court-martial thought a sentence of 15 months perfectly adequate for an NCO convicted of having exceeded his powers on no fewer than 600 separate occasions.[220] Often, the worst excesses were simply excused on the grounds of internal 'disciplinary measures'. When the Minister of War, von Falkenhayn, sent out a general circular on the ill-treatment of subordinates in May 1914, he thought it appropriate to refer to the fact that the minimum sentence had nearly always been imposed, and that this could not fail to weaken confidence in military justice and lower respect for military courts in general.[221]

It was frequently argued by Social Democratic politicians that the strongest influence on civil justice was precisely the operation of military law.[222] This is hardly surprising, in view of the fact that in eighteenth-century Prussia the local squire was both the company commander and the district judge. Indeed, the dangerous possibility of military influence stretching its tentacles increasingly into the domain of civil jurisdiction was highlighted by the arrest in October 1893 of the editor of the *Sächsische Arbeiterzeitung*, Georg Gradnauer. The military authorities in Dresden, incensed by the paper's unceasing criticism of the officer corps, planned to bring Gradnauer before a court-martial, but there was widespread condemnation in the Saxon press of this arrogation of responsibility, and the case was eventually dropped.[223] The deliberate vagueness which marked out the parameters of military jurisdiction (*Militärgerichtsbarkeit*) was itself a reflection of the failure to restrict the operation and theoretical competence of military law specifically to those serving with the armed forces, since all those employed by military authorities in whatever capacity – engineers and clerical staff, for example – were similarly affected. Not surprisingly, the SPD had little success when it tabled a motion in the Reichstag in 1898, which would have had the effect of placing military personnel who had committed criminal offences under the jurisdiction of the civil courts.[224]

Nowhere is the gargantuan struggle against entrenched military traditions in Prussia more evident than in the controversy surrounding the powers of the court-martial, which to some extent built on the tradition of the secret nocturnal sessions conducted by the irregular tribunals or vehmic courts of the Middle Ages (*Vehmgerichte*). Attempts had been made throughout the 1870s to introduce a revised code of military legal procedure in the Reichstag, but these were frustrated by the firm opposition of Bismarck and Kaiser Wilhelm I. Uniformity of procedure in the Reich was made more difficult by the existence of three different codes in Prussia, Bavaria and Württemberg. In Prussia, the proceedings of the courts were almost inquisitorial and the entitlement to be defended was nominal and not actual.[225] Although the right of appeal was not conceded, the possibility of some form of revision existed in the right of confirmation (*Bestätigungsrecht*) by the presiding officer or, in more serious cases, by the Kaiser as the supreme military authority. This either gave validity to the original judgment or opened up the possibility of clemency through a reduction in sentence.

There were close parallels between the codes in Prussia and Württemberg, whereas in Bavaria military law had been more directly influenced by civil procedures. Thus, for example, the principle of the jury was accepted and, in contrast to Prussia where there was usually only one, there were several officers with a measure of legal training (*Auditeure*) who were responsible for the conduct of the proceedings. Moreover, the defence was given greater manoeuvrability, even extending to the right of appeal. Again, unlike Prussia, where courts-martial could be held in the field, the locus of the Bavarian courts was strictly laid down.

In 1892 Caprivi authorised a series of government deliberations, with the purpose of preparing a revision of the Prussian code.[226] The draft which eventually emerged revealed the considerable limitations of the proposed reforms, since there were to be no restrictions on the ability to convene a court-martial anywhere in the field, and the presiding officer (*Gerichtsherr*) was still to be empowered to determine the conditions under which the proceedings were held. These often varied considerably from court to court. In addition, the public was still to be excluded, only oral submissions were to be permitted and the right of upholding the verdict rested as before, with the presiding officer. This insistence, both on the Bestätigungsrecht and the secrecy of the proceedings, was to become a major stumbling-block to reform, and several hundred petitions submitted to the Reichstag in the spring of 1893 urged the revision of the Prussian code on the lines of the Bavarian model.

However, ministers faced not only the implacable opposition of the Kaiser,[227] but also that of the Chief of his Military Cabinet, General von Hahnke, who saw in the demands for open courts a weakening in the position of the allied governments and a dangerous compliance with democratic tendencies.[228] Indeed, Hohenlohe's diary entry for 2 November 1895[229] records Hahnke's determination that the Prussian army should remain a separate body, into which nobody could peer with critical eyes.[230] The Kaiser's continuing opposition was strengthened by an anonymous newspaper campaign in April 1896, protesting at the dilatory progress of a new military code, and which Wilhelm II regarded as a personal conspiracy directed at him by Marschall von Bieberstein. As a result of a situation in which the Kaiser saw the Reichstag as planning to encroach on his powers, there were further persistent rumours of a Staatsstreich.[231]

A further key issue in the argument surrounding the proposed reforms was the refusal of the Bavarians to accept the principle of a single military court for the whole Reich, under Wilhelm II. Hitherto there had existed three separate courts, the *Oberkriegsgericht* in Dresden for Saxony, the *Generalauditoriat* in Schwerin for the two Mecklenburg states, and the Generalauditoriat in Berlin for Prussia and the remainder of the Reich. The Kaiser, who had been involved in a long dispute with his Minister of War, Bronsart von Schellendorf, over the contents of a new courts-martial bill,[232] agreed to a compromise in which he conceded public trials in return for a central *Reichsmilitärgerichtshof* in Berlin.[233] This was vigorously opposed by the Bavarians until a further compromise was reached in 1898, when the Prince Regent agreed to the establishment of a central supreme court in Berlin, on the understanding that he would be able to appoint the officers of a separate Bavarian division.

After considerable delays and difficulties, the new military code for the Reich, with a total of 471 sections affecting the codification of all military legal matters,[234] passed through its various stages in the Bundesrat and Reichstag in March 1899 and came into force the following October. It is significant that during the internal deliberations on the proposed bill, a dominant rôle was played by the Prussian Ministry of Justice and not by the Reich Office of Justice,[235] and that the appointment and dismissal of the president of the new Reichsmilitärgerichtshof rested entirely with the Kaiser.

It had taken a considerable length of time and several government crises to achieve only a moderate advance in the liberalisation of archaic military legal procedures, and was thus a clear indication of the many old, deeply-entrenched traditions and the considerable obstacles with which any reformers were faced. Moreover, many of the old iniquities of military law remained, and the *Vorwärts* referred in 1907 to several of the barbaric absurdities against which Social Democrats had struggled in vain. Thus, if a soldier in a public house became involved in a dispute with an officer over a girl and made any threatening gesture towards his superior, this would be sufficient to guarantee him a sentence of ten years imprisonment.[236]

It was only in 1901 that the Bundesrat agreed to the publication of military statistics. The figures for 1901–5 show a comparatively low rate of acquittal; 10.77% in the army and 10.58% in the navy. compared with 18.8% in the civil courts. Over the same period, there were no fewer than 4,762 cases of misuse of official power.[237] Of the 77,629 soldiers convicted by courts-martial between 1901 and 1905, 429 were given the severest sentence of all – hard labour – and of these, 139 received five years or more, 173 between two and five years, and 117 between one and two years.[238]

The intervention of the military in local affairs often lit up its special position in the state to a remarkable degree. It was the struggle of the woodcutting community in the Bavarian village of Fuchsmühl, with its peculiarly Wilhelmine dimensions – complex disputes over legal interpretation and the yawning chasm between natural justice and the precise letter of the law, coupled with the unchecked action of the local military – which gave this affair its special significance.[239]

Under a special provision of the 1852 forestry-law, the rights of a local community to cut wood could be revoked by copyhold landlords. Such cases were extremely rare, if only because both parties to the agreement were content to underline the semi-feudal nature of the relationship. In the spring of 1892, however, an absentee landlord in Fuchsmühl and alderman (*Landgerichtsrat*) in Munich, Freiherr von Zoller, decided to apply for a rescission of the traditional woodcutting rights on his land. This decision was challenged by the small community of 200 people, on whose right to cut wood their entire livelihood depended. There was in any case considerable confusion over the legality of Zoller's application, since in an earlier judgment the constitutional court (Oberverwaltungsgericht) had decided that the land in question, the forest of Lehenswald, was in fact state land.[240] Attempts to mediate in the dispute failed and in 1893 Zoller took up litigation. There followed a series of interminable legal arguments in various different courts. In October, the Landgericht decided in favour of Zoller, whereupon the woodcutters appealed to the Oberlandesgericht in Nuremberg, which in April of the following year dismissed Zoller's case on a legal technicality, whilst simultaneously denying the rights of the community at Fuchsmühl. The inhabitants then turned to the highest Bavarian court, the *Oberstes Landgericht* in Munich (paralleling the Prussian *Kammergericht*), whose judgment in October 1894 declared that the woodcutters possessed no legal rights over the forest land.

The previous winter, the inhabitants had been prevented from exercising what they regarded as their legal entitlement to cut wood (*Rechtholz*). At the same time, Zoller had authorised his bailiffs to cut wood from the forest, which was then sold through the estate offices. The position of the woodcutters worsened with the approach of winter because, quite apart from the lack of fuel, creditors began calling in their loans, on which the right to cut wood had been an important security. On 29 October 1894, the woodcutting community took the law into its own hands and moved into the Lehenswald. The sub-prefect (*Bezirksamtmann*) of the district, Johann Wall, immediately ordered the arrest of the village mayor, Josef Stock, and two other alleged ringleaders, and telegraphed to the nearest infantry regiment for military assistance.

The following day at 10 a.m., a 50-man military detachment arrived and proceeded to 'clear the forest'. This action resulted in the death through bayoneting of two elderly men, the serious wounding of four men and the wounding of thirteen others, of whom two were women. One young man was chased for over a quarter of an hour by two soldiers, and received 17 gashes in his back, which were so serious that, according to the local medical officer, he would remain a cripple for life.[241] No member of the military detachment sustained any form of injury, and this was immediately interpreted in the SPD press as evidence that the supposed 'resistance' of the woodcutters had existed purely in the minds of the soldiers.

There was an incensed and predictable outcry from the leading SPD paper in Bavaria, the *Münchener Post*,[242] but unreserved criticism also came from certain sections of the non-socialist press. To the Social Democratic press in general, however, this incident had a much wider, indeed national, significance, and could only result from the inevitable contradictions within the existing social and political order. Alone amongst the Bavarian papers, the *Münchener Post* sent one of its leading journalists and later editor-in-chief, Adolf Müller, to Fuchsmühl, in order to assess the situation locally. In addition to sending back regular reports, Müller also prepared a monograph – to date the only one – on this sad episode, which duly appeared at the end of November. At the instigation of the police headquarters in Munich, preliminary proceedings were started against Müller on the grounds of misrepresentation of fact, but the case foundered for lack of evidence.

In order to keep up the momentum of public condemnation, the small group of Social Democrats in the Bavarian state parliament requested the Minister-President on 13 November to ask the Prince Regent for a recall of the Landtag. Owing to the highly idiosyncratic system of parliamentary sessions and two-year budgetary periods, the next session was not due until the following autumn. The rejection of this request without explanation on 18 November produced a stream of editorial protests from the SPD press, not only against the Bavarian state government, but also against the other parties represented in the Landtag, notably the Catholic Centre Party and the Liberals, who had not given their support to the proposal.

The affair continued to make local – and in the case of the SPD press, national – headlines for some considerable time. In February 1895, the sub-prefect for the area went into premature retirement and although it is likely that he was subjected to internal pressure, the failure of the Bavarian Minister of the Interior to act decisively at the time of the original incident did little to inspire public confidence. Indeed, disciplinary proceedings were only instituted against Wall in May 1896, when he was sentenced to the ludicrous fine of 15 marks, for failing to notify his superiors of the action he had taken.[243]

Meanwhile, the authorities had proceeded with charges against 146 inhabitants of Fuchsmühl, for breaches of the public peace and infringement of the forestry laws (*Forstfrevel*). By the time these cases came before the courts in April 1895, action had already been taken against the editors of six Munich papers for their coverage of the incident. Amongst those sentenced to a small fine and then – after the successful appeal of the prosecution to a higher court – to a somewhat stiffer fine, was Eduard Schmid of the *Münchener Post*, who later became the SPD's first chief governing mayor in the Bavarian capital. Of the 146 woodcutters who faced charges in the monster trial that took place, only two were acquitted and the rest all received prison sentences varying in length from a few weeks to several months. Four of the alleged ringleaders, including the village mayor, were given sentences of four and a half months. In November their appeals were rejected by the Reichsgericht, but in January 1896, in a display of official compassion, they were pardoned by the Prince Regent.

Throughout the year, the SPD had succeeded in sustaining interest in the wider issues raised by the Fuchsmühl affair, and when the matter was eventually debated by the Bavarian parliament in October 1895, on an SPD censure motion, Centre Party politicians in particular were prepared to accept the validity of socialist strictures on the pitfalls of an overly rigid and narrow interpretation of the law. One prominent Centrist and university professor Freiherr Georg von Hertling, actually claimed – in a direct comparison with the *Ancien Régime* – that whereas the formal law had clearly been on the side of the propertied classes, it was the neglect of their social responsibilities to the community as a whole which had acted as one of the levers of the Revolution.[244] The ominous implications of these remarks were not lost on the Bavarian government, which in June 1896 introduced a new forestry law, which laid down that the right to cut wood could not be terminated arbitrarily by the owner of the copyhold.

However, it was impossible to forget the events of October 1894.

Whenever the military next intervened in civilian affairs, it invariably occasioned the cry, 'Fuchsmühl!'. The *Münchener Post*, for example, reported an incident on New Year's Eve 1895, when a military patrol arrested two civilians for complaining about the right of an officer to secure preferential treatment in a public house (*Beachtung der Gruß-pflicht*).[245] The behaviour of military personnel on these and other occasions revealed precisely how far, despite a system of universal conscription, the armed forces remained separate and encapsulated from the rest of the population. In particular, the Fuchsmühl episode demonstrated that the influence of Prussian militarism had succeeded in engulfing the Bavarian army, to the extent that it no longer thought of its function exclusively in terms of external protection, but accepted responsibility for the preservation of internal political order.

Not surprisingly, there were wider repercussions of the affair for the course of internal Bavarian politics. Fuchsmühl had demonstrated to the SPD the inherent weakness of Bavarian liberalism, which had been unable to free itself from a very strong pro-establishment attitude throughout the affair. To some extent this may have reflected the conservative views of the high proportion of lawyers in the 'Liberale Vereinigung', but it also showed a marked incapacity for forward-thinking political judgment. Increasingly, Social Democrats looked upon the Liberals as their principal electoral opponents, and in 1899 created local sensations by concluding pacts with the Catholic Centre Party in Munich and in the Bavarian Palatinate.

The failures of liberalism at the national level were also evident in the stand which the SPD almost alone took against the ignominious behaviour of German troops in China at the turn of the century. In May 1900, an attack on foreign labourers working on the Peking–Hankow railway sparked off the anti-Western Boxer rebellion, and the assassination the following month of von Ketteler, the German minister in Peking, culminated in a siege of the Western legations. On 27 July, Wilhelm II inspected at Bremerhaven the German element of a combined international relief force, which was to be commanded by General Waldersee. The occasion was notable for the widely-reported speech of the Kaiser, whose capacity for conjuring up dire visions of the 'Yellow Peril' was virtually unsurpassed, in which – uttering the fateful words, 'No quarter will be given' – he exalted his troops to give cause for the name of Germany to be remembered in China for a thousand years. There is no doubt that these remarks were ill-considered and likely to cause widespread disapproval, and it was symptomatic of the growing sensitivity of official sources to the opportunities presented for criticism of the government, that the official text of the 'Hunnen-rede' was heavily doctored.[246]

There was no possibility, however, of doctoring the letters which German troops in China sent back home. It was the publication of these documents, described by the SPD press as 'Hunnenbriefe', which opened up yet another unhappy chapter of military excesses. The first of them began appearing in print in the late autumn. For the most part, they concentrated on details of the military campaigns, but many betrayed to an alarming extent the way in which the troops had become undisciplined and rapacious. A soldier from Magdeburg reported,

> We treated them [the Chinese] like so much cattle . . . all that came before us was shot down mercilessly. We gave no quarter. We completely burned down the town of Tientsin, together with everything inside – women, children, cripples, invalids and livestock.[247]

Similar impressions of the situation ouside Tientsin were recorded by the author of a letter which the *Vorwärts* published in 1901.[248]

> What I have seen here today has made my hair stand on end. What didn't catch fire of its own accord was set fire to with malice. The coffins were ripped open and the silk shrouds torn from the corpses or set on fire. Even the bodies of the women were laid bare and mishandled in obscene ways.

Further evidence of unheroic deeds was published by the *Vorwärts* to coincide with the second reading of the budget, and depicted a veri-table orgy of looting, pillaging, murder and rape.[249] One detachment which took 76 Chinese prisoner subjected its victims to physical torture, before lining them up on the edge of a mass grave and executing them.[250]

There was a noticeable absence of legal proceedings against editors who published these '*Hunnenbriefe*', but whenever comment on the campaign in China was more generalised, SPD journalists in particular ran considerable risks. Two editors of the *Vorwärts*, for example, were given sentences of six and seven months respectively in December 1901, for insulting the East Asian expeditionary corps, and the court judg-ment accused the SPD of deliberately falsifying the texts of certain letters.[251] Similarly, police in Altona raided the homes of several local party organisers and confiscated thousands of copies of a propaganda leaflet protesting at the conduct of the government's China campaign. As a result, two prominent local Social Democrats were convicted of *lèse-majesté* and sentenced to several months imprisonment.[252]

Practically the only light relief in the rapidly accumulating evidence of the crushing weight of German military influence on civilian life came in October 1906, with the exploits of a certain Wilhelm

Voigt, a veteran of 27 years Zuchthaus, and better known by his only claim to fame – as the 'Hauptmann von Köpenick'. Dressed in the uniform of an army captain, Voigt assumed command of a twelve-man detachment and ordered it to march to the town hall at Köpenick, just outside Berlin. Here he proceeded to authorise the arrest of the local mayor and a clerk, before helping himself to 400 marks from the petty cash.[253] It was some ten days after his '*Heldentat*' that Voigt was eventually arrested and, after a summary trial, sentenced in early December to four months imprisonment.

To the *Vorwärts*, which claimed that the events at Köpenick could only have taken place within the German Reich, this episode seemed a biting satire on the so-called cultural achievements of the Prussian state in the one hundred years since the battle of Jena.[254] It is true that the nineteenth century had seen no real diminution in the powers of military competence within the state. The ability of a country vagabond to transform his humble position in society by putting on a captain's uniform – even the Kaiser, when shown a photograph of Voigt in uniform, was said to have remarked that he displayed an officer's demeanour – was in itself quite farcical. What underlined the potential gravity of the situation was the virtual impossibility of offering any form of resistance, whether by the members of the detachment, who risked a sentence of many years imprisonment or hard labour by failing to honour their blind obedience (*Kadavergehorsam*), or by the unfortunate mayor, who as an army reserve officer himself was not likely to question the authority of a superior. It was the combination of the magic power of the uniform and the words 'On the orders of the All-Highest', which led Friedrich Naumann to describe the pseudo-captain as 'Machiavelli in the waistcoat pocket'.[255] That the Köpenick affair was no isolated example of the talisman effect of a military uniform was underlined by an item which appeared in the *Leipziger Volkszeitung* in 1913: a man masquerading as an army paymaster at Straßburg informed the garrison of the impending arrival of the Kaiser, and ordered the troops to the parade-ground to await the arrival of the All-Highest.[256]

If the centenary celebrations marking the revival of the Prussian state in 1906 had been clouded by the Köpenick affair, what the SPD press insisted on calling the 'scandal' of Zabern (Saverne) marred the double anniversary year of 1913, which witnessed not only the revival of the victorious battle spirit of 1813, but also the 25th anniversary celebrations of the Kaiser's accession.[257]

Alsace-Lorraine, perhaps more than any other state in the Reich, was firmly under Prussian influence. Not until May 1911 was it granted a constitution and parliament, and even then every legislative proposal required the personal approval of the Kaiser. The higher echelons of the bureaucracy were almost exclusively Prussian. Now the pursuit of a policy of 'Germanification', whether of the Danes in Schleswig-Holstein or the Polish minority in the Rhineland, depended for its success on a large military presence, and here Alsace-Lorraine was no exception. Indeed, the rate of conscription was four times higher than in any other part of the country, so that out of a population of 1,791,738 in 1910, those on active military service numbered no fewer than 82,276.[258] The view that the army was the best school for '*das Deutschtum*' was bolstered by the endless number of army manoeuvres and showing-the-flag rituals throughout the state.

It was the use of a term of abuse for the local population – '*Wackes*' – that sparked off the events of November 1913. The word had actually been forbidden by a regimental order, in an effort to avoid unnecessary provocation, but during a barrack-room class the instructor, Lieutenant von Forstner, added injury to insult by offering a reward of ten marks for each 'Wackes' his audience cared to knife. These remarks were leaked and appeared in the *Zaberner Anzeiger* for 6 November. Some two weeks later, Forstner impugned the dignity of the French flag and poured scorn on the Foreign Legion. A statement incorporating the substance of his comments, witnessed by those who were present there at the time, again found its way into the local press. The expectation of serious trouble from the inhabitants of Zabern led the Governor or *Statthalter*, Count Wedel, to request the immediate suspension or transfer of Forstner. This request was refused by the Kaiser.[259] Significantly, the commanding officer of the regiment, Colonel von Reuter, regarded a message of approval from the Kaiser as a complete vindication of his general policy.

Shortly afterwards, Reuter addressed his junior ranks and described the public disclosure of remarks made within the garrison as a breach of the soldier's oath of loyalty. Ten soldiers were thereupon arrested on charges of having leaked confidential information, and almost immediately all other Alsatians serving in Forstner's company were transferred to different regiments. On Reuter's direct instructions, the offices of the *Zaberner Anzeiger* were raided – occasioning a sharp protest to command headquarters from the government in Straßburg – and there next followed the 'Wackesjagd', a campaign of official intimidation of the local population. Unfortunately, the knowledge that Forstner regularly sullied his bed-sheets at night, which had duly made the rounds of the local inhabitants, led to considerable ridicule whenever he appeared on the streets. As a result, Forstner was accompanied by a personal guard of four men on those occasions when he ventured outside the barracks. The silent belligerence of the population, as interpreted by the military, gave way to public levity and derision at the appearance of Forstner and other troops on the streets. On 28 November, some thirty people who had incurred the displeasure of the military by openly displaying their mirth, were hauled off to spend 24 hours in the coal cellar of the barracks (*Pandurenkeller*).[260]

In the midst of the local unrest at Zabern, the Crown Prince, Friedrich Wilhelm, sent two telegrams to Reuter. The pithiness of their texts – '*Bravo*' and '*Immer feste druff!*' – could not have done more to provoke further ill-feeling amongst the inhabitants, nor more clearly extend the official seal of approval to the actions of Reuter's troops. When the texts of the Crown Prince's telegrams suddenly became public, all employees of the postal and telecommunications departments at Zabern and Straßburg who were deemed likely to commit similar indiscretions were immediately transferred to other positions.[261] Only a few days later, during army manoeuvres at Dettweiler, a detachment commanded by Forstner rampaged through the village, and Forstner himself struck down a half-lame shoemaker who was unable to reach safety.

Meanwhile, the full implications of the latest military outrages had been noted by the SPD press.[262] A speech in defence of Forstner by the Minister of War on 28 November and Bethmann Hollweg's insistence that the king's uniform had to be respected at all times, led the SPD executive to issue a statement which appeared on the front pages of all Social Democratic newspapers on 4 December. It spoke with contempt and scorn of the attempts by government spokesmen in the Reichstag to vindicate the military dictatorship in Alsace-Lorraine, and sent out to all local parties a call to organise mass protest meetings as soon as possible. This was part of a deliberate strategy designed to counter Bethmann Hollweg's claim that the Zabern affair was of local significance only.[263] It was the Chancellor's failure to dissociate himself from the military command in Zabern which led the SPD to propose a vote of no confidence in the Reichstag. The extent to which the party had succeeded in evoking widespread public concern at what the *Hamburger Echo* termed 'the dictatorship of the bayonet',[264] was reflected in the voting figures. Of 351 deputies present, 293 – including National Liberals, Progressives and the Centre Party – voted for the motion, 4 abstained and only 54 voted against the motion.

Following his poor showing in the debate, Bethmann Hollweg was summoned to join Count Wedel and Reuter's superior, the GOC of the 15th Army Corps in Straßurg, General von Deimling, and the Kaiser's military entourage at Donaueschingen. The outcome of the deliberations was some attempt to mollify public opinion. The Crown Prince was transferred from his position as C-in-C of the Danzig regiment of hussars to the General Staff in Berlin, where it was felt that he would be more under the eyes of his father.[265] In addition, two battalions which were stationed in Zabern were moved to Hagenau, and an announcement was made that military judicial proceedings would begin at once against all those who had exceeded their statutory powers.

The first court-martial involved the trial of three soldiers who had been responsible for leaking information to the local press. Together they received 14 weeks detention. Forstner himself was brought before the court on 19 December to face charges of assault and the misuse of a firearm. He was given the minimum possible sentence of 43 days imprisonment.[266] At the news of this verdict there was an immediate outburst from Junker circles, and the Berlin Polizeipräsident, von Jagow, took the unusual step of publishing a signed article in the *Kreuzzeitung* for 22 December, in which he argued that since military exercises were derivative of absolute state sovereignty (*Staatshoheit*), they could not be regarded as infringements of any law. A conviction, as in the case of Forstner, was therefore plainly a miscarriage of justice. This intervention by a leading civil servant in a case which, until the hearing of an appeal, was still officially *sub judice*, received a great deal of adverse criticism, principally from the SPD press. The *Rheinische Zeitung*, in an extension of logic commented,

Every butt stroke, every thrust of a sword, every shot from a police Browning or military equivalent, is an act of absolute state sovereignty ... A chief of police who puts forward such views is a public danger.[267]

In the light of such reaction from the establishment, it came as no very great surprise when, at the hearing of his appeal in January 1914, Forstner was acquitted: the military appeal court accepted the right of an officer to protect himself from the possibility of assault (*Putativnotwehr*). At the same time, Colonel von Reuter and his adjutant were facing charges of misuse of authority. Reuter's attitude was that because of the alleged insults against his officers and the failure of the civil authorities to act accordingly, he had been obliged to take the law into his own hands. The basis on which he later claimed entitlement to act was an order in council dating back to 1820, which gave the military a statutory right of intervention in civilian affairs, whenever the ability of the civil administration to uphold the public order was put in doubt.[268] The charade of the hearing, at which submissions from representatives of the local administration were brushed aside, was underlined when, even before all the evidence had been heard, the presiding military judge sent off congratulatory telegrams to Jagow and Oldenburg-Januschau, announcing the acquittal of the two men.[269] Wickham Steed, the correspondent of *The Times* reported simply, 'In Prussia the army is supreme and through Prussia the army rules Germany.'[270]

Government propaganda throughout the crisis had been at pains to stress that there was no basic antagonism between the army and the population at large, and that army officers were in no sense enemies of the people. Large sections of the establishment press were agreed that there had been shameful provocation from the local residents of Zabern, and there were even suggestions that the affair had been deliberately stirred up by French agents. The inescapable fact, however, is that events at Zabern had done nothing to assuage SPD attacks on 'die Militär-Diktatur in Permanenz'.[271] At no time during the crisis was the authority of the Reichstag asserted over the military apparatus. Indeed, for much of the time the Reichstag was kept wholly in the dark, since the flow of vital information was between Straßburg and Donaueschingen. The vote of no confidence in Bethmann Hollweg was little more than a symbolic gesture; the Chancellor's wholehearted support of the military strengthened his own precarious position with the Kaiser, and at the same time denied the right of the Reichstag to exercise any effective power.[272]

The lines of definition between military and civil authority, and the relationship between administrative responsibility and the rule of law remained totally blurred. Moreover, the right of a leading public servant to interfere with the judicial process had not been questioned. When von Deimling's promotion to the rank of full general was announced in March 1914, there were few amongst establishment circles who doubted that he had received his rightful reward. And although a select committee was set up by the Reichstag to investigate the Zabern affair in detail, the weaknesses of the bourgeois parties quickly became apparent, and when the committee dissolved itself at the end of February, once again the SPD was left alone.

4

THE SPD, SCANDAL AND SOCIETY

The history of a decaying society has a habit of revealing itself in scandals; its archives are the court files of cases of scandal.

Die neue Zeit, June 1892

The age of decadence

In May 1872, in an astonishing piece of premonition, Bismarck confided to Lucius von Ballhausen, later to become his Minister of Agriculture,

My sleep is no form of rest; my dreams are the continuation of my conscious thoughts, if I ever manage to sleep at all. The other day I saw the map of Germany in front of me: one rotten blotch after another appeared and flaked off.[1]

Even allowing for French preoccupations with Panama and 'L'Affaire Dreyfus', which dominated the 1890s, and the social and cultural shock produced in England in 1895 by the trial and conviction of Oscar Wilde for acts of gross indecency, it is remarkable to what extent the daily events of political life in Wilhelmine Germany were filled out with spicy revelations of one sort or another. At the same time, the literature and culture of the period reflect an uneasy awareness of traditional values in disintegration, affecting the whole of Central Europe.[2] The unmistakable impression of a doomladen society was conveyed most vividly in Max Nordau's widely-discussed work 'Degeneration', which appeared in 1893. The cultural pessimism of the poet Rainer Maria Rilke, a self-styled 'Schüler des Todes', was matched in countless works by Thomas Mann, Stefan George and Friedrich Nietzsche. Oswald Spengler began work on his *Untergang des Abendlandes* even before the outbreak of war in 1914, and the related themes of decadence and decay which characterised that pre-war epoch were drawn together in 1930 in Herman Broch's monumental epic, *Die Schlafwandlertrilogie*.

The curious juxtaposition between appearance and reality, between the dynamic, bustling exterior of Wilhelmine Germany and the gnawing, corrosive forces at work behind the façade of unshakable confidence, between the concepts of 'Sein' and 'Schein', played an extremely important thematic rôle in the development of German literature and politics during the period. This was revealed, for instance, in a comment made in October 1900 by the *Hamburger Echo*.[3] On the very same day that Bülow replaced Hohenlohe as Chancellor, on 17 October 1900, the first successful flight of a Zeppelin took place at Friedrichshafen. The paper averred that no 'political Zeppelin', not even the talents of a smooth and accomplished statesman like Bülow, would be able to pilot the ship of state through the social and political storms engendered by the *Zeitgeist*.

This prevailing sense of *fin-de-siècle* had a deep significance for the Social Democrats, especially during the 1890s, when each day seemed to bring renewed confirmation of the corruptibility of individuals in high places. The symptomatic importance of such events was always recorded by the party press; it was conclusive proof that the establishment was rotten to the core and would cave in of its own accord, given time and a degree of patience. A central linking factor in all the attacks made by SPD newspapers on the establishment was the element of scandal, which simultaneously had the advantage of awaking public interest and creating propagandistic object-lessons. In particular, party journalists regarded it as their duty to expose the hollowness of bourgeois claims to be the guardians of public morality.

A feature of the general development of the German press in the 1890s was its central importance in the making and breaking of the reputations of public men. Very often it was a newspaper article which brought to public consciousness details of a personal failing, and a general technique employed by socialist and non-socialist journals alike was the sustained campaign of attack on an individual and the organisation or set of principles with which he was publicly identified. The use of scandal in this way often had a twofold success; it sold newspapers and it discredited political opponents. Similarly, the exaggeration of particular circumstances, coupled with a sensationalised presentation of detail, usually succeeded in stirring up popular emotion. In the summer of 1891, for example, anti-semitic feeling ran especially high after the tendentious exploitation in certain sections of the establishment press of the murder of a four-year-old boy, in the Rhineland town of Xanten. The child had been found with his throat cut and his body completely drained of blood, and the finger of suspicion was soon pointed at a local Jewish butcher, who was accused by Ahlwardt and other anti-semitic demagogues of practising Jewish slaughter rites.

Despite several extensive police inquiries, however, the evidence remained inconclusive.[4]

At the other end of the spectrum, popular fascination with stories of life at court, and the singular capacity of court circles to provide compelling newspaper material, such as the decision of the Crown Princess of Saxony to elope with her children's tutor in 1902, combined to produce a special mystique surrounding the affairs of royalty. In general, the SPD refrained from following the lead set by such overtly commercial *Skandalblätter* as *Das kleine Journal* of Frankfurt, and the persistence of even the bourgeois political press in reporting the latest royal *Klatschgeschichten* was not appreciated by the Kaiser, who took the step of banning the *Kölnische Zeitung* from all royal residences for this very reason. The stir created by the publication of part of Hohenlohe's memoirs in 1906, revealing as they did intimate details of court affairs, was a further indication of public susceptibility to titillation of this kind.

The SPD was itself often the target of attempts by the establishment press, hoping to stir up scandal in the socialist ranks. The *Kreuzzeitung*, with whom the SPD press had a mutually hostile relationship, put about a story in 1894 that the party was becoming increasingly dependent on Jewish funds, citing as evidence an alleged contribution of 300,000 marks to party funds by Leo Arons. It was only when the story began appearing, in one form or another, in most of the other leading establishment papers, that the *Vorwärts*[5] felt obliged to abandon its aristocratic silence and counter this form of skulduggery. Feigning surprise that anyone could have chosen to believe such a story, it announced that the entire party audit-books were open to inspection on this matter.

The conservative *Die Post* indulged in similar stories; in May 1904 it gleefully reported that a former lady-friend of Paul Singer, Gustava Schettler, had been sentenced on charges arising out of immoral earnings, and even went so far as to suggest that Singer, as a bachelor, had made use of the facilities offered by her house of ill-repute.[6] Some two years later the same paper, in company with much of the establishment press, became obsessed with Bebel's holiday-home on the shores of Lake Zürich. In fact, an unknown admirer had left Bebel his entire fortune and although the will was contested, Bebel's share was so considerable that even after donating half of it to central party funds, there remained enough money to purchase a villa for use during his increasing periods of convalescence.[7] Nonetheless, anti-socialist delight at the news that Bebel was a full-blooded capitalist in the making goaded the *Vorwärts* into making a furious reply, in which it pointed out that the SPD leader occupied only three rooms and a kitchen in the 15-room villa.[8]

More general shock methods, designed to alarm public opinion, were undertaken by the Reichsverband gegen die Sozialdemokratie which claimed, in a leaflet aimed at all German women, that marriage in the Social Democratic 'Zukunftsstaat' would be little more than glorified prostitution, with the inescapable prospect of educational communes and a complete destruction of traditional family life.[9] Typical of the SPD's response to attacks of this kind was an element of puritanical self-righteousness, which often underlined the self-preferred isolation of the party leadership from contamination with the mire of capitalist society. It was for precisely these sentiments, uttered at a pre-conference rally, when he claimed that the SPD stood so high that muck thrown at it – from whatever quarter – would always fall short of its target, that Wilhelm Liebknecht was convicted of *lèse-majesté* in 1895.

Nor did the SPD come anywhere near exercising a monopoly over the disclosure of highly embarrassing material. It was a leading Centre Party politician, Matthias Erzberger, for instance, who uncovered most of the scandals in the colonial administration,[10] as well as taking a leaf out of the SPD's book by pointing to the close relationship which existed between politics and industry. This was most clearly manifest in the Tippelskirch affair.[11]

The Prussian Minister of Agriculture, Podbielski, had acquired through his wife a 40% share interest in the firm of Tippelskirch, which organised the purchase and shipment of supplies for the colonies. Not only had officers in the army and highly-placed officials in the colonial administration been bribed to make requests for specific deliveries from Tippelskirch, but during Podbielski's tenure of office long-term contracts had been signed with the firm, thus practically guaranteeing a monopolistic position. However, to forestall the idea that pressure of public opinion could actually bring about the dismissal of a minister, the Kaiser at first refused to accept Podbielski's resignation. It was another three months before the minister, on whom the Kaiser ostentatiously bestowed a high decoration, was allowed to depart. As if to underline the comparative triviality of the affair in official eyes, Podbielski became a director with the AEG concern and retired in relative luxury and splendour to a castle near Lake Constance.

But it was the SPD which had a particular, vested interest in benefiting from the virtually continuous presentation of institutional weaknesses and personal failings. Embarrassment in high places was welcome political capital to a party which found itself constantly reminded of its pariah position within society. As a result, editorial comment in the Social Democratic press tended to dwell on the fact that scandals in public life were but links in a common chain. Thus, the downfall of a hated adversary was but a symptom of a deeper malaise within society. Such reflections were increasingly bound up with an analysis of bourgeois morality as distinct from proletarian morality.[12] So, for example, the *Hamburger Echo*[13] regarded marriage for reasons of financial improvement or social advancement, together with the popularisation of adultery in some leading circles and the establishment's hypocritical attitude to prostitution, as typical of the self-interest which characterised upper-class morality. To this end the party press did not baulk at publishing details of *Sittlichkeitsverbrechen*, which involved members of the 'better' sections of society, particularly when they held positions of responsibility in the community.

Discussion of sexual matters in Wilhelmine Germany was by no means confined to the private domain. Indeed, on both sides there seemed an uninhibited desire to relate sexual morals to the fundamental well-being of the state. In 1913, for instance, a Professor Blaschko published a major work with the intriguing title of *Syphilis als Staatsgefahr*, and some years earlier the annual conference of the Deutsche Sittlichkeitsvereine had heard a Prussian *Sanitätsrat* explain that the 'materialistisch-naturalistische Weltanschauung' was responsible for the spread of venereal disease. Since this phrase was a scarcely disguised metaphor for Social Democracy, the *Hamburger Echo* felt obliged to point out that the earliest recorded case of syphilis in Germany was in 1493, and that the merchant-trading fleets which had brought the disease to the country were unlikely to have been the harbingers of Marxism.[14]

Much fun was had at the expense of these Sittlichkeitsvereine or morality leagues. In Neuß the city council was prevailed upon not to give financial support to the local swimming association, on the grounds that the sight of young boys dressed only in bathing-trunks was not conducive to public decency. The activities of the 'Verein deutscher Fürstinnen zur Hebung der Sittlichkeit', which boasted two queens and 35 princesses from ruling houses, also came in for satirical comment.[15] It was for irreverent criticism of these morality leagues, transgressing the Bavarian blasphemy laws, that the writer Ludwig Thoma was imprisoned for six weeks in 1904, a time which he used to good effect by completing his satire on bourgeois morality entitled *Moral*.

On the other hand, there is considerable evidence that these Sittlich-keitsvereine expressed a real and growing bourgeois concern at the widespread incidence of immorality. At their annual conference in 1904, a Protestant pastor declared that the state of present morality reminded him of the decline of Greece and of Sodom and Gomorrha. Not even the army was spared from criticism of this kind, since there was a common belief that far from being a *'Schule der Zucht'*, it was much more a *'Schule der Unzucht'*.[16] In similar vein, the *Hamburger Echo* pointed out that during the celebrations marking the opening of the Kiel canal, a number of additional brothels had been opened in the city, in order to cope with the large influx of visitors.[17] Official conni-vance in the practice of the oldest profession seemed to be underlined by a ludicrous decision of the Prussian Kammergericht in July 1906, that brothel-house keepers did not have to pay taxes since their business was not strictly permitted by the authorities.

The criminal underworld had already received an unwelcome glare of publicity after the murder of a Berlin nightwatchman by a pimp named Heinze, whose trial in 1891 opened up a vast catalogue of prostitution, pornography and vice.[18] *Die neue Zeit* commented,

The marshy ground on which the towering structure of so-called modern civilisa-tion stands, has suffered a severe earthquake, and the structure itself is tottering in an alarming way from the foundation-stone to the roof.[19]

Such was the Kaiser's concern that he issued an ordinance to the Ministry of State on 22 October, recording his profound dismay at the material dredged up in court, and declaring that prostitution and the practice of procuring had become 'a common danger for state and society'.[20] The outcome was the introduction of a bill, the *lex Heinze*, designed to tighten up existing laws on obscenity and public indecency. It received the strong support of the Conservatives as well as the Centre Party, which was keen to extend the scope of the bill in order to take account of its own ideas on the relationship between law and morality. However, all other parties and artists generally were opposed to the measure, since it envisaged even tighter controls on creative and artistic independence than already existed. Although it was defeated in the Reichstag, several attempts were made throughout the 1890s to re-introduce the bill and an emasculated version was eventually adopted in May 1900.

At about the same time, upper-class morality received a further shock with the much-publicised court proceedings against an eminent banker and multi-millionaire named Sternberg, on charges of criminal seduction and rape.[21] At his first trial in April 1900, Sternberg was acquitted on two counts and sentenced to two years imprisonment on a third, but as a result of this hearing so much additional evidence came to light that a second trial took place in October of the same year. This was a monster affair which lasted very nearly two months, and such was the official anxiety at the nature of the charges that the public was excluded from the proceedings. In the event, Sternberg was given a sentence of two and a half years hard labour.[22] What this particular case revealed was the disturbingly easy alliance between the world of high finance and criminal prostitution, together with further evidence of the corruptibility of several police officers who had been incriminated in the affair. To *Die neue Zeit*,[23] the Sternberg business in all its ramifications was 'a most edifying testimony to the moral health of bourgeois society' and some years later, when it had occasion to refer to a succession of similar scandals involving public morality, it remarked that 'it will soon be easier to count the grains of sand on the sea-shore than the symptoms of putrescence of this kind'.[24]

The Hammerstein affair

It goes without saying that the higher the social and political standing an individual enjoyed in the community, the more interest the SPD showed in exploiting the propaganda potential inherent in a personal scandal. It had good cause and ample opportunity to do so in 1895, when the outer façade of utter respectability collapsed around a representative figure of the Prussian nobility and editor-in-chief of the *Kreuzzeitung*, Wilhelm Freiherr von Hammerstein.[25]

Die neue Preußische Kreuzzeitung, which took the Iron Cross as its emblem, first appeared as a representative of the extreme Protestant Conservatives, the old Prussian aristocracy and Church orthodoxy during the early stages of the counter-revolution in June 1848. It prospered considerably as the leading voice of the establishment in Bismarck's day, when his personal nominee, Hermann Wagener, was firmly in charge, and Hammerstein owed his own elevation to the editorial chair in November 1881 in no small part to the good relations he enjoyed with the Iron Chancellor. After the fall of Bismarck, Hammerstein was able to extend his personal authority considerably, and as a member of the Conservative leadership in the Reichstag and Prussian Landtag he exercised a decisive influence amongst party counsels. When he bought up the only other Conservative daily newspaper of note, the *Deutsches Tageblatt* in 1891, he became the most powerful establishment journalist. Together with the idiosyncratic ex-*Hofprediger* Adolf Stoecker, Hammerstein was responsible for the formulation of a new Conservative policy statement at the Tivoli Conference of December 1892.

Apart from marshalling a united phalanx of Prussian Junkers against the trade policies of Caprivi, Hammerstein had devoted particular attention to a campaign for the re-introduction of a Sozialistengesetz. His attitude in this respect was neatly summed up in a remark to his confidant Hans Leuß, '. . . there is no other method to be employed against Social Democracy except to provoke workers and have them shot.'[26] His own ambitions were not inconsiderable, and after the fall of Caprivi he attempted to promote the candidature of Botho Eulenberg, with a view to succeeding him eventually as Chancellor. This plan was frustrated, however, by a group of younger Conservatives in the Reichstag, who were unwilling to join Eulenberg in his demand for a complete suspension of universal suffrage.[27]

What characterised Hammerstein's leading articles in the *Kreuzzeitung* was their ringing tone of moral puritanism, as well as the quality of a personal crusade for traditional ethical values, which were summed up in the phrase '*Sitte, Religion und Ordnung*'. Such was Hammerstein's fervour in this respect that he took a leading part in the work of the parliamentary commission entrusted with the work of drafting the Umsturzvorlage.

News of a personal scandal had been brewing for some time. Rumours had been current in parliamentary circles throughout the winter months of 1894–5, and according to the *Hamburger Echo*,[28] the SPD press had been well briefed in advance and had only held back from making the first disclosures, so that Hammerstein should become clearly identified in the public eye as the standard-bearer of establishment views on morality. In the event it was two Frankfurt papers, the *Kleine Presse* and the respected *Frankfurter Zeitung*, which broke the first news of Hammerstein's personal insolvency and his impending resignation as chief editor of the *Kreuzzeitung*. The charges levelled against Hammerstein related to the misuse of several hundreds of thousands of marks belonging to the paper, the misappropriation of a pension fund and the concluding of deals with suppliers of newsprint at vastly inflated prices. During April 1895, when these details became public, there was an understandable amount of bewilderment and confusion occasioned by repeated denials from Hammerstein that these stories bore any relation to the truth. Indeed, he took the somewhat rash step of issuing writs for libel against the editors of a number of papers.

Much of the interest centred around his refusal to resign his position, despite repeated leaks that the editorial board of the *Kreuzzeitung* had insisted upon his dismissal. The fact that a desperate struggle for power was taking place behind the scenes was emphasised by the Paris paper *Le Temps*, which reported on 4 July that the board had withdrawn its original dismissal notice, after Hammerstein had threatened to leave for Switzerland and publish material highly damaging to the Conservative leadership. In particular, he was said to be ready to make public a number of letters from Freiherr von Manteuffel, which purported to reflect unfavourably on the Kaiser. From the beginning of July, however, Hammerstein's name suddenly disappeared from the front page of the *Kreuzzeitung*. By this time a series of charges and counter-charges was coursing quite regularly through the columns of the press, and Hammerstein was placed under increasing pressure to allow the courts to proceed with the cases of libel. Pressure was most probably forthcoming from other quarters too, for on 8 July, in a somewhat uncharacteristic gesture, he announced that he had resigned his membership of the Conservative groups in the Reichstag and Prussian Landtag.[29] A week later, party officials in his Reichstag constituency of Halle-Herford declared their opposition to him, and shortly afterwards the electors in his Landtag constituency of Stolp (Pomerania) passed a unanimous resolution against Hammerstein's continued representation of their interests in Berlin.[30] In fact, Hammerstein did not formally resign his mandates until September.

The same month the *Vorwärts* published what came to be known as the 'Funeral Pyre Letter' (*Scheiterhaufenbrief*).[31] This was a letter which Stoecker had written to Hammerstein a year after the formation of the 1887 cartel, which revealed how far Conservatives were prepared to indulge in intrigue for the furtherance of party ends and how successful Bismarck had been in hoodwinking Kaiser Friedrich III into supporting the continuation of the cartel.[32] The mystery as to why Hammerstein should want to embarrass his friend Stoecker in this way was not resolved until some time afterwards, when it became apparent that in order to provide himself with some urgently-needed cash, Hammerstein had offered the *Vorwärts* through an agent the sale of a number of politically 'valuable' items of private correspondence.[33] There was not the slightest doubt that the paper would be accommodating to Hammerstein's financial demands, and in the same month the *Vorwärts* was able to score a further journalistic coup with the publication of several other letters from the collection.

Disturbing details of Hammerstein's accumulated debts had become known by the late summer. As a direct result of mounting criticism in wide sections of the press that the weight of circumstantial evidence more than justified immediate action by the state prosecutor's office, the editorial board of the *Kreuzzeitung* at length entrusted the Berlin Staatsanwaltschaft with official inquiries into the case. By the time the authorities were notified by the board in mid-September, Hammerstein had already fled the country.

It is significant that despite extensive public discussion of the case and the criminal nature of much of Hammerstein's business affairs, no initiative had come from the state in the form of an official investigation. Criticism of this conscious abrogation of responsibility was especially bitter in the SPD press, which was still simmering with the injustice of the Essen perjury trial, and which contrasted the inactivity against Hammerstein – for whose arrest a warrant was not issued until 18 September – with the treatment accorded to the editor of the *Vorwärts*, who was kept in custody whilst awaiting trial for a minor press offence, on the specious grounds of *Fluchtverdacht*.

For their part, the members of the editorial board of the *Kreuzzeitung* had been concerned to minimise the consequences of the scandal and avoid any serious political repercussions. The Königlicher Kammerherr and Regierungspräsident von Colmar, for example, had done everything possible to persuade Hammerstein to resign his position quickly and quietly, and the chairman of the board until the summer of 1895, the Königlicher Zeremonienmeister, Count Kanitz, had repeatedly sought to protect Hammerstein from the possibility of public exposure. This conspiracy of silence was attacked not only by papers such as the *Hamburger Echo*,[34] which specifically accused a prominent member of the board, Count Finckenstein, of failing to inform the state prosecutor's office until after 'the bird had flown', but also, curiously enough, by the Oberstaatsanwalt in Berlin. He used a case against the editor of the SPD paper in Hannover, in which he himself appeared as a leading witness, as a public platform for complaining that members of the editorial board had hindered prompt investigations by a form of passive opposition, and had actually suppressed vital evidence relating to the forging of documents.

Further embarrassment was caused in late October with the announcement of criminal proceedings against a former journalist on the *Kreuzzeitung* and Conservative deputy, von Rathusius-Ludom, on charges of deceit, embezzlement and forgery of documents. The SPD press could have had few complaints about the stage-management of the spectacle, coming as it did in the midst of the disarray occasioned by the defeat of the Umsturzvorlage and the Kaiser's invective against 'the socialist rabble'. *Die neue Zeit* found the affair 'an excellent apple of discord to be thrown into the army of loyal patriots, assembling for the heroic struggle against the rabble'.[35] Although the liberals in general sought to derive maximum profit from their own exploitation of the scandal, the Conservatives hit back in kind when a prominent liberal lawyer, Friedmann, was accused of misappropriating 6,000 marks of trust-fund money.[36] Nonetheless, the Conservatives suffered electorally. In the bye-election for Hammerstein's seat in the Reichstag, held at the end of November, their candidate failed to win a clear majority in the first ballot and was defeated by the National Liberal candidate, with the support of the Progressives, in the second ballot. The Social Democratic candidate also managed to increase his share of the vote.[37]

In the meantime, extensive inquiries had been made into the whereabouts of Hammerstein overseas. Since October 1895 he had been living in Athens under an assumed name, working as a newspaper correspondent. He had made the fatal mistake of visiting the German consul-general in the city, who recognised him from a photograph circulated by the Berlin police. Despite the fact that there was no extradition treaty between the two countries, a number of articles written by Hammerstein in which he had attacked Greek policy were taken as sufficient evidence of 'unfriendly acts', and he was handed over to the German authorities in January 1896. The same month, the managing clerk of the firm which had supplied the *Kreuzzeitung* with newsprint suddenly disappeared, leaving behind him debts of 50,000 marks, and shortly afterwards another prominent Conservative, Freiherr von Schorlemer-Alst, was arrested on charges of forgery and excluded from the reserve officer corps by a military court of honour.[38]

Hammerstein's trial did not take place until April 1896. Only then did full details of his financial profligacy become public. As editor-in-chief of the *Kreuzzeitung* he had been paid an annual salary of 36,000 marks, with an additional housing allowance of 4,000 marks. Together with the directorship of two insurance companies and the expenses he was entitled to claim as a deputy in the Landtag, his annual income was well in excess of 50,000 marks. When he took up his position with the paper, Hammerstein already had debts of 127,000 marks. As a result of mounting financial difficulties, he entered into a special arrangement with a Berlin paper firm in December 1889, which guaranteed him personal loans totalling 200,000 marks at a high rate of interest. The guarantor for this deal was supposedly Count Finckenstein, whose signature, together with that of a witness, had been forged by Hammerstein. In addition, Hammerstein had signed a long-term contract for regular supplies of newsprint, and as a direct consequence the *Kreuzzeitung* had paid out – over a period of five years – some 100,000 marks above the current market price. Between 1885 and 1895 he had borrowed from friends, acquaintances and subordinates well in excess of 500,000 marks, and his most distinguished creditor was undoubtedly Countess Waldersee, who lent him a sum of 100,000 marks.[39] The *Berliner Volkszeitung* quoted Hammerstein's total debts as of the order of 800,000 marks. These were largely accumulated as the result of riotous living and extravagant entertaining, and not the least of the lurid sidelights of the affair was the knowledge that Hammerstein had kept an expensive mistress, the actress Flora Gaß, whom he was also accused of having helped to procure an abortion.[40] In the circumstances, Hammerstein could not hope for much in the way of official clemency, and he was sentenced to three years hard labour and a fine of 1,500 marks, as well as being deprived of his civic rights for five years.

The *Kreuzzeitung* never quite recovered from this mortal blow to its reputation as a bastion of moral integrity. It became the object of a whole series of satirical and polemical articles mostly, but not exclusively, in the *Witzblätter* of the period.[41] The SPD had already drawn its own symptomatic conclusions from the affair. It later took particular delight in reporting the case of a 'provincial Hammerstein' in the town of Emmerich, where the editor of the clerical *Niederrheinische Zeitung*, who had continuously preached unbending Catholic morality from the columns of his paper, was arrested on charges of misappropriating large sums of money from working people.[42] The parliamentary Conservatives, for their part, did the utmost to extricate themselves from an unhappy situation, to the extent that the party's official organ, the *Konservative Korrespondenz*, repeatedly disclaimed the view – somewhat unconvincingly – that Hammerstein had exercised any leading influence over policy.

The Kaiser

It is impossible to conceive of the Wilhelmine age without thinking of its fountain-head and guiding-spirit, Kaiser Wilhelm II. Though he vacillated in matters of public policy and struck up an image as one of the most remarkable poseurs of the period, the Kaiser was motivated essentially by a sense of mission, characterised by his unfaltering commitment to uphold the religious and secular traditions of his divine inheritance. His almost deliberate self-identification with the deity found its most vivid expression in May 1897 at the ceremony of consecration for the new garrison church in Potsdam. The flyleaf of the altar bible bore the Kaiser's handwritten inscription. 'Obey my voice, and I will be your God, and ye shall be my people', and in the chancel bible, which he had also presented, stood a signed quotation from the New Testament, 'For without me ye can do nothing'.[43] But if on the one hand he envisaged himself leading a spiritual coalition of his chosen people on earth, the Kaiser clearly had no illusions about excluding the Social Democrats from his patriarchal benevolence, for as early as May 1889 he had declared that for him every Social Democrat was both an enemy of the Fatherland and of the Reich.[44]

Hardly anyone made as many official and quasi-official pronouncements as the Kaiser. There has occasionally been a tendency to view his speeches as little more than the 'oratorical derailments' to which Hohenlohe referred. Certainly, there were too many of them to be explained as a kind of intellectual *lapsus linguae*, and the SPD press received the texts with the same seriousness with which they were undoubtedly delivered. Although Bruno Schoenlank of the *Leipziger Volkszeitung* believed that the Kaiser's rhetorical flights of fancy were occasioned by his low tolerance level of alcohol,[45] the German head of state was far from being viewed as a buffoon figure by his political adversaries. Indeed, every speech against the party received the fullest possible coverage in the SPD press, which took great trouble to answer allegations with specific counter-arguments of its own.[46]

Unquestionably, there was a genuine fear of revolution which ran as a *Leitmotiv* through such speeches,[47] and little can be discerned of a truly conciliatory approach towards establishing social harmony within the state. In return, no Social Democratic journalist was prepared to yield one inch of ground from its territorial isolation. As *Die neue Zeit* put it,[48]

The Kaiser seems to set great store by declaring before the whole world how unbridgeable the gulf is which separates him from the largest party of the German people, and it is superfluous to say that we neither want nor are able to prevent him from making this deduction.

In any case, the SPD felt it had little to lose from repeated attacks of this kind. In a comment to the Reichstag in 1902 Bebel declared,

Who knows if we should have increased our strength by as much as we have, had it not been for the 'Kaiserreden'. I estimate every 'Kaiserrede' against us at about 100,000 votes gain. If this sort of agitation is to be directed against us in future, well, we have nothing against it.[49]

The question remains whether such outright opposition reflected rank-and-file opinion in the party and in the country at large. Undoubtedly, the ordinary working-man was often caught up in the elaborate pageantry of state ceremonial and the excitement of a visit from the 'Reisekaiser'. Every display of apparent working-class affection for the monarchy was noted with great approval by police departments, and even a kind of passive neutrality on the part of SPD agitators was regarded as a minor triumph. Thus, when in 1908 the head of the Hanseatic legation in Berlin detected a groundswell of popular support for the Kaiser, he wrote that 'it is a clear and characteristic sign of the monarchist sympathies of the majority of the people in the country that the SPD does not dare to shake at the foundations of this institution'.[50] The Berlin political police thought it highly significant that the *Vorwärts* reported the assassination of the Empress of Austro-Hungary in 1898 with 'tact and sympathy'.[51] Certainly, there were many Social Democrats who would have welcomed a constitutional monarchy along English lines, but for every expression of royalist sentiment there were immeasurably more declarations of republican allegiance. Thus, at the 1898 party conference Richard Fischer asserted,

We have the fortitude to tell workers everywhere, at every given opportunity, that they have nothing to hope for from the monarchist government and everything to fear, and that the necessary prerequisite for the eventual triumph of the working class as organised in the SPD is the fight against, and the defeat of, the monarchist spirit.[52]

At the 1904 meeting of the Socialist International in Amsterdam, Bebel described himself, in common with all other Social Democrats, as a dyed-in-the-wool republican and, in the words of the Berlin police report,[53] 'went so far as to make the treasonable claim that it would not be the greatest of disasters for the Fatherland if it ended up as a republic by way of its own Sedan'. Even one of the most opportunist of leading Social Democrats, Karl Frohme, published a sharply anti-monarchical book in 1904,[54] thereby incurring the wrath of the *Kreuzzeitung*, which called it 'an assassination of the monarchy and existing constitution'.[55] For his part, Bülow sought to argue in the Reichstag in 1903 that efforts in the direction of the social and political improvement of the working masses were being made more difficult by the SPD habit of mixing up socialist endeavours with anti-monarchical objectives.[56] The extent of the anti-royalist drift was such that the Reichsverband gegen die Sozialdemokratie organised vast distributions of propaganda leaflets in 1910, which simultaneously attacked SPD republicanism and attempted to rekindle a loyal monarchist spirit.[57] Less than a decade later, the candle of institutional monarchism was snuffed out with hardly a murmur.

Surrounding the trappings of the Wilhelmine monarchist state was the almost neurotic obsession with titles and decorations. Amongst the 28 new decorative orders which the Kaiser instituted was the 'Wilhelmsorden', given for 'social services'. Its first recipients in January 1896 included, significantly, Bismarck, Pastor von Bodelschwingh and Frau von Stumm. The 'Roter Adlerorden' in all its manifold and precise gradations was awarded to several thousand loyal subjects every year.[58] The Berlin Polizeipräsident von Borries, in particular, had an insatiable mania for awards and decorations and, to great amusement, would appear at every official function festooned from head to toe.[59]

Such natural vanity gave rise to a veritable trade, often to mutual benefit. Thus, for example, a *Kommerzienrat* negotiated with Bülow for the conferment of an aristocratic title. He had originally promised a sum of 500,000 marks to a charitable cause to be nominated by the Kaiser, but Bülow held out for more and eventually obtained no less than a million marks.[60] Whenever the Kaiser had some special project in mind, such as his proposal in 1907 to create a fleet of airships (*Luftflotte*), he would organise a banquet to which leading bankers and industrialists were invited, and circulate a subscription list. Since those present felt that they could not possibly contribute less than their host, the sums raised in this way were often considerable.[61]

Similar practices could be seen at work, in one form or another, in the manipulations surrounding the church-building scandal of the 1890s. The origins of this unique church-building programme in and around Berlin and other parts of the Reich owed much to the personal initiative of the Empress Auguste Viktoria. She had become convinced that the total of 37 churches in Berlin could not satisfy the complete spiritual needs of a population of one-and-a-half million. Moreover, certain suburbs in the city were becoming increasingly Social Democratic in character and were clearly in need of institutionalised pastoral care. Accordingly, she entrusted her personal *Oberhofmeister*, Freiherr von Mirbach, with the organisation and funding of a massive church-building programme, and almost immediately the Evangelischer-Kirchlicher Hilfsverein came into existence.[62] In the period up to 1900 alone, some 55 new churches were built in Greater Berlin, and for this purpose over 30 million marks of capital was raised either by public subscription or private donation.[63] Most of the individual contributors parted with large sums of money on the firm promise of awards, titles or the coveted royal warrant (*Hoflieferantenprädikat*), and Mirbach played a vital part in arranging the financial equation of private charitable benevolence with public distinction. The whole business was viewed with considerable disdain by the SPD press, which resorted to its standard formula, 'Religion ist Privatsache'. On the other hand, it did not fail to point out the extent of official pressure: thus, a Landrat in Saxony was 'instructed' to transfer capital from municipal funds to the account of the Kirchenbauverein.[64]

However, the SPD press was quite unaware of the deeper ramifications of the affair until the failure of the Pommersche Hypothekenbank in 1904. It then emerged that in addition to his own private account with the bank, Mirbach had opened up a special account, 'Konto K', specifically for the church-building programme. He succeeded in persuading the bank to donate a million marks to the project, for which it was suitably rewarded in 1900 with the title of 'Hofbank'. When Mirbach's journalistic mouthpiece, *Das kleine Journal*, ran into serious financial difficulties, it seemed perfectly natural for him to transfer 50,000 marks to the paper's account from banking funds.[65] Unfortunately for him, Mirbach's ledger-book manipulations had the effect of squeezing the lemon dry. As a result, considerable irregularities in the affairs of the bank came to light and proceedings were started against two of the directors. The whole investigation had to be conducted with extreme delicacy and lasted almost two years, at the end of which the two men were convicted and sent to prison. The real culprit, however, escaped with impunity, and since Mirbach continued to enjoy the confidence of the Empress there was little prospect of bringing him to account.

Predictably enough, SPD coverage of the building-programme affair ran up against the law. It had become known that the Kaiser had donated the royalties from his 'Song to Aegir' to the building-fund, and when the Kaiser-Wilhelm-Gedächtniskirche was consecrated in 1895, an incautious reference to the 'Aegirkirche' brought the editor of the *Vorwärts* a sentence of six months imprisonment for *lèse-majesté*.[66] The Kaiser's obsession with the name of the Nordic sea god to whose memory he had christened or dedicated all manner of objects, received a curious compliment in the very same year. The authorities at Hamburg had been informed that the Kaiser had expressed a wish to drink coffee 'on one of the islands on the Alster'. Since there were no islands on the artificial lake in the heart of the city, but equally, being unwilling to create possible ill-feeling and irritation with the All-Highest, the city senate decided after weeks of deliberation to construct at enormous cost an artificial island in the centre of the lake. This island, which had a surface area of 5,800 square metres and rested on 750 piles, was named 'Aegir-Insel', and on his arrival the Kaiser was greeted by a performance of his 'Song to Aegir'.[67]

Another island was at the centre of perhaps the most celebrated case of *lèse-majesté* in which SPD journalists were involved. Unlike many other cases of this kind, it was quite obvious from the start that the Kaiser was the direct object of the article in question, although scrupulous care had been employed in avoiding all reference to him. It was a case, moreover, in which the Kaiser's own influence in initiating criminal proceedings was clearly felt.

For a long time the *Vorwärts* had been supplied with secret information from court and government circles, which had always proved to be authentic. In August 1903, the paper received a document which bore the letter-head of the equerry to the crown prince. The equerry's title had been struck out and replaced with 'Adjutant' and the amended letter-head had been pasted onto a separate sheet of paper, on which details of an elaborate building project were set out. The scheme revolved around an apparent decision to proceed with the construction of a fortified castle on the island of Pichelswerder in the River Havel near Spandau. Its purpose was to serve as a refuge for the Kaiser, in the event of his forced withdrawal from the city during an insurrection.[68] Ostensibly, the plan seemed plausible enough and formed the basis of an article which appeared on 16 October under the heading of 'Die Kaiserinsel'. Although the semi-official *Norddeutsche Allgemeine Zeitung* imediately issued a denial, the *Vorwärts* continued to give credence to the story.

On 20 August, the Kaiser telegraphed to Bülow at Norderney:

Since the *Vorwärts*, despite all official denials, continues brazen-facedly to repeat its fairy-tale, even going so far as to declare yesterday that it was in possession of written proof for its accusations and claiming, moreover, that 'the highest level' had lied to the *N.A.Z.*, it is necessary to proceed against this piggery with all possible force. Should the *Hofmarschall* act on the basis of *grober Unfug* or should the Crown issue a charge for defamation? This nonsense has almost completely taken in *Die Post* and a stop must be put on it. If I can't get satisfaction through the courts, I'll use my revolver in the editorial offices.[69]

In his reply, Bülow confirmed that he had ordered immediate action against the paper.

A direct campaign against the journalists of the *Vorwärts* would doubtless be welcomed by them. They are trying to stir up a scandal. We ought not to do them this favour, but instead pillory them publicly by revealing the complete fabrication of their insolent calumny.[70]

There was some uncertainty as to the most appropriate course of action, since the *Vorwärts* had ascribed responsibility for the scheme to Hofmarschall von Trotha and Hofarchitekt Ebhardt. In a telegram to Bülow, the State Secretary at the Reich Office of Justice, Nieberding, pointed to the difficulties of providing the prosecution with adequate grounds to proceed under §95. However, the problem was solved by 31 August, when the completed charge-sheet, indicting the editor and staff journalist with both *lèse-majesté* and *grober Unfug*, and running to no less than 57 sides, was delivered to the appropriate court office. The speed with which the legal machinery could be made to work was underlined a month later when the defence, in the course of preparing its case, lodged an official protest with the authorities. Within 24 hours a ruling had been given by the Kammergericht, signed, authenticated and delivered to defence counsel.[71]

The hearing itself was held on 16 October and both journalists were represented by the combined talents of Hugo Haase and Karl Liebknecht.[72] The prosecution had summoned an impressive array of witnesses, including the heads of the Zivilkabinett (von Lucanus) and Militärkabinett (Count von Hülsen-Haeseler), as well as the equerry and adjutant to the Crown Prince. Moments before the police had broken into the editorial offices of the *Vorwärts*, a member of the staff had burned – in traditional SPD fashion – the only piece of evidence which might have supported the defence case. As it was, the state insisted that the story was a complete invention and since prosecution witnesses refused to answer pertinent questions put to them by Liebknecht, the proceedings were largely a formality. The editor of the *Vorwärts* was sentenced to nine months imprisonment and his assistant received four months. Kurt Eisner, who had been called as a witness but had declined to name the paper's informant, never doubted that the document was genuine and that all the court witnesses had perjured themselves. The theory put forward by Friedrich Stampfer was rather more subtle and seems highly plausible; that the 'Kaiserinsel' story was a deliberate trap, concocted by someone with access to court writing-paper, into which the *Vorwärts* had so neatly fallen.[73]

Some five years later, the Kaiser once again became the object of a major press affair. The article which appeared in the edition of the *Daily Telegraph* for 28 October 1908 and which was quickly labelled 'The *Daily Telegraph* Interview',[74] was not an interview in the proper sense of the word, but rather a resumé of the comments expressed by the Kaiser at a gathering of English friends and acquaintances during the autumn of the previous year. The owner of the guest-house on the Isle of Wight at which the Kaiser had been staying, Colonel Stuart Wortley, prepared the text of a newspaper article incorporating Wilhelm's stated views, in the mistaken hope that it would contribute to improved relations between Britain and Germany. He then sent the completed draft to the Kaiser for final corrections.

When the article duly appeared and the contents were made known in Germany, there was an immediate storm of controversy. This was occasioned not so much by the Kaiser's undoubted right to make official pronouncements on foreign policy, or even, as in the case of the 1896 Kruger telegram, to undertake his own diplomatic initiatives, but by the patently absurd character of his statements in the article. According to the Kaiser, for example, he had rejected overtures during the Boer War to join an alliance against Britain and had made available to his grandmother, Queen Victoria, details of a war strategy worked out by the German General Staff. Furthermore, he claimed that the German battle-fleet was being built not against Britain, but against Japan.[75] The uncompromising tone of some of his views, that the English were 'mad as March hares', for instance, was destined to worsen rather than improve diplomatic relations between the two countries. It also caused particular alarm amongst those government circles which, because of the immense financial strains imposed by the naval arms-race, were seeking some form of accommodation with Britain.

The central question is why the outrageous character of these statements had not been modified or erased altogether from the draft of the article before publication. It is a daunting and complicated task reading and unravelling the memoirs and recollections of this episode by leading contemporaries, since what emerges is the degree to which personal relationships were regularly affected by considerations of jealousy, professional envy and often bitter acrimony. Such factors can easily obscure the truth behind a particular incident and make motivation more difficult to understand. In the case of Bülow, who as Chancellor was nominally responsible for the clearance of the article, his own highly-tendentious account merely provoked equally one-sided attempts at rectification.[76]

What cannot be proved conclusively is that Bülow actually read the fatal manuscript, which had been forwarded to him at Norderney. At the time he was preoccupied not only with external matters, such as the Casablanca episode, but also with the exceptionally complicated finance reforms planned for 1909. Despite Bülow's assertions that he had given precise instructions to the Foreign Office for checking the contents of the draft, those who were entrusted with this task were given no guidance in the revision of the text. The two men who might have been able to avert the ensuing hullabaloo were both absent from their desks on holiday at the time; the State Secretary, von Schoen, and the chief press officer, Otto Hammann.[77]

The result was that the article was checked for errors of fact and stylistic niceties, but no attempt was made to comprehend the possible effect which publication might have. It is itself a reflection on the blinkered attitudes of officials at the time that no one seriously questioned the advisability of allowing the text to remain unaltered. Bülow's personal responsibility for the débâcle that followed was, however, quite incontrovertible, since on four separate occasions after receipt of the article at Norderney he had had an opportunity of raising with the Kaiser, either in person or in writing, the substance of the manuscript.[78] Moreover, the suspicion that, having seen the text, Bülow had somehow calculated the certain public humiliation of the Kaiser, was strengthened after his speech in the Reichstag on 10 November. The need for some clarifying statement followed in the wake of the storm of public disapproval, especially embarrassing to loyal monarchists, who nonetheless joined the liberals and Social Democrats in condemning the meddlesome nature of the 'persönliches Regiment'.[79] Bülow, as much concerned with protecting his own reputation as with defending the right of the Kaiser to conduct foreign policy in whichever fashion he thought appropriate, arranged for a personal statement to be published in *Der Tag*, in addition to the 'official' version of events as put out by the *Reichsanzeiger*.[80]

For his part, Wilhelm II was visibly affronted by the general public reaction to the 'interview' and retired for some weeks to a country seat in the Black Forest. On 4 December, the head of the Hanseatic legation in Berlin reported that the Kaiser's 'state of mind is continually very depressed. He is in the constant company of several Hofprediger, who speak of a complete derangement of personality'.[81] Attempts were made in the Hamburg city parliament to propose a joint initiative with other state legislatures, with the intention of expressing strong disapproval at any further imperial interference in official affairs. The Hamburg senate was seriously concerned about the effect of this action on the Kaiser, ordering its representative in Berlin to keep the news from him at all costs, and was heartily relieved when the initiative collapsed.[82]

But the damage had already been done, and although the SPD 'made a killing out of the affair',[83] it was the establishment press which bared its teeth for the first time in a wholly uncompromising way. Not the least of those who drew important consequences for the future was the Kaiser himself. Convinced that he had been 'betrayed' by his civilian ministers, he relied even more than before on the support and advice of his *Geheimkabinette* and military counsellors.[84] This newly strengthened relationship was to bear its inevitable fruit during the Zabern affair some five years later. Bülow's days as Chancellor, too, were clearly numbered. When speculation as to his imminent dismissal increased in July 1909, the *Hamburger Echo*[85] recalled that the Kaiser had quite unexpectedly made the Hussar general Podbielski his Minister of Posts, and concluded that it would occasion no real surprise if he were to appoint as his next Chancellor a lord of the bedchamber. In the event, it was to be Bethmann Hollweg.

The Hofkamarilla

The general atmosphere of suspicion in public life in Wilhelmine Germany owed much to the widespread existence of political intrigue and extra-parliamentary influence, themselves a natural concomitant of the semi-absolutist form of government. Although Bismarck had already set an inglorious precedent in his time, skilfully discrediting a major political rival for the Chancellorship in the 1870s, it was only after the accession of Wilhelm II that personal ambitions and antagonisms began to play such an important part in the shaping of policy. Thus, the *éminence grise* of the Foreign Office, Holstein, had a hand in the replacement of Waldersee as Chief of the Imperial General Staff by Schlieffen in 1891. Miquel secretly conspired against Caprivi, and Posadowsky was elbowed out of power in 1907 when he had outlived his political usefulness. According to the Centre Party newspaper *Germania*,[86] Bülow was himself the object of intrigue in the autumn of 1906. He managed, however, to obtain advance information of a plan which provided for the appointment of General Hellmut von Moltke as his successor, and cleverly leaked the details to the *Berliner Tageblatt*. Seen in this light, his sudden decision to call an election in December 1906 owed less to the inauguration of the 'Block' alliance than to the need to consolidate his own position and dish his opponents. It was a calculated gamble that paid off, and Bülow's suspicions that the instigator of the plot against him was Philipp Eulenburg, by far the most influential member of the Wilhelmine 'Hofkamarilla'[87] resulted in his own scarcely concealed *Schadenfreude* at the latter's eventual public disgrace.

The existence of camarillas[88] had long been a consistent feature of Prussian political life. Only during the reigns of Friedrich Wilhelm I and Friedrich II was their influence negligible, and by far the most celebrated in the nineteenth century was the group around Friedrich Wilhelm IV.[89] Public comprehension of this state of affairs was not helped by the extreme facility with which individual members of the camarilla would appear and then disappear from view, like figurines on a revolving clock; nor by the many different combinations of personalities which would momentarily throw up one alliance of interests, to be succeeded in turn by yet another.

Leading figures of the Wilhelmine camarilla were the object of attacks made by the satirical magazine *Kladderadatsch*, beginning in December 1893.[90] Although they were not actually named in the succession of humorous verses, dialogues and anecdotes, the choice of characters – 'Troubadour' and 'Insinuans' (Botho Eulenburg), 'Spätzle' and 'Intrigans' (Kiderlen) and 'Austernfreund' and 'Calumnians (Holstein) – left little room for doubt as to their identity. These attacks illuminated the continuing conflict between the architects and opponents of the new course, since their origin was to be found in the unwillingness of a number of publicists and officials in the Foreign Office to forsake traditional Bismarckian orthodoxy. Above all, the substance of the articles, for which two *Geheimräte* in the Foreign Office – with the connivance of Maximilian Harden – were responsible, reflected some of the tensions in government circles arising from increasing evidence of the Kaiser's personal rule. It is quite obvious that feelings ran particularly high in this affair,[91] but the Kaiser was determined to prevent a major scandal which would publicly expose a divided ministry within the Foreign Office. Characteristically, *Die neue Zeit*[92] saw the whole business as 'a little local difficulty' within the ruling élite.

Much more serious was the personal scandal affecting the Kaiser's closest friend, Philipp Eulenburg. The responsibility for uncovering it rested with Maximilian Harden, who had long been amassing his own dossiers on Eulenburg's sexual idiosyncrasies. Harden's first attack on Eulenburg had been made in *Die Zukunft* as early as 8 October 1892 and he received further information on Eulenburg's sexual inclinations during the Tausch trial.[93] In 1902 he became additionally aware of the close relationship between Eulenburg and a senior French diplomat, Raymond Lecomte.[94] The name of Eulenburg was also contained in a secret register of known homosexuals which the Berlin police under von Tresckow had been responsible for compiling at the turn of the century. The list further included the *Stadtkommandant* of Berlin, Count Kuno von Moltke, the private secretary to the Empress, Bodo von Knesebeck, *aide-de-camp* Count Hohenau, the GOC of the *Garde-du-Corps*, von Kessel, Prince Friedrich Heinrich of Brunswick and countless others.[95] It was only through chance that the Kaiser failed to read this list.[96]

Harden also received additional material from Holstein, who held Eulenburg responsible for his own dismissal in 1906 and proceeded to make the first of several approaches to Harden, with a view to securing some form of retribution.[97] Harden had been alerted to the possibility of a close relationship between Eulenburg and Moltke during the latter's divorce proceedings, and in an attempt to accomplish his primary objective – the political destruction of Eulenburg and the camarilla – he had even gone so far as to mend his fences with Bülow. Harden's hopes of being able to persuade Eulenburg to withdraw gracefully from court circles, by means of skilful innuendo in earlier articles, were frustrated, however, by Eulenburg's obduracy. As a result, Harden felt he was left with no other option than to lift the veil from the full scandal.

The sensational disclosures, which appeared in *Die Zukunft* in November 1906, unleashed not only a series of trials which occupied the attention of the courts for the best part of two years, but had immediate consequences for all the participants in the affair.[98] Eulenburg was excluded from the court. Moltke was forced to resign as Stadtkommandant and Prince Friedrich Heinrich of Brunswick had his appointment as a Knight of the Order of St John rescinded. The backwash of the scandal seemed to affect nearly all those in public life; Bülow himself, for example, was accused of homosexual practices and was compelled to sue for libel.[99]

The court proceedings involving Harden, Moltke and later Eulenburg, whose steadily worsening medical condition precluded any conclusive verdict, present a wholly unedifying picture. Wilhelmine Germany had been rocked by a major social scandal in the highest circles, affecting the Kaiser's personal advisers and trusted friends, and the constant moralising exhortations of the ruling élite suddenly reeked of hypocrisy and cant. For a time, it seemed as though the whole social order of morality had been overthrown. The *Hamburger Nachrichten*[100] spoke of all the filth imaginable being dredged up and put on public display, and there were uncomfortable strains within the 'Block': the head of the Hanseatic legation in Berlin commented that the parties of the 'Block' might well fall apart 'but, out of regard for opinion abroad, the impression must be avoided at all cost that the reason for this rests with the Moltke trial'.[101]

Irony had it that the very party which had been consistently under attack from its bourgeois opponents as anti-religious, immoral and dissolute, now proclaimed itself to be the conscience of society. In October 1907 the *Hamburger Echo* asked,

How much longer must the historians of the political and cultural history of Germany seek their documentary evidence in court-files, in the reports of scandal trials? Is this the glory and grandeur of the Reich, the splendour of speeches, of banquets and monuments? Have we gone as far as Imperial Rome?[102]

Its own editorial treatment of the court proceedings left no doubt as to the strength of its moral puritanism. The fact that Count Lynar of the *Garde-du-Corps* had invited young officers back to his villa to participate in group orgies, was not only seized upon as evidence likely to alarm the parents of all young soldiers, it was also valuable grist to the SPD's anti-militarist mill. Again, the party which had itself been accused of opposing the institution of marriage observed with *Schadenfreude* the uproar created by the comments on marriage attributed to Count Kuno von Moltke by the court testimony of his ex-wife.[103] A society which had prided itself on impeccable manners and immaculate social bearing had been discovered, as the *Rheinische Zeitung* put it, 'in situations one might only expect to find in the ape-house of a zoo'.[104]

According to the *Bremer Bürgerzeitung*,[105] the Moltke–Eulenburg scandal was but the distress-signal of a decaying society.

And we are supposed to be shaking at the foundations of this state? Those who accuse us of doing so are perfectly right: let us give it up! A building which rests on such splendid supports will collapse of its own accord. Let us content ourselves with pulling out a rotting prop from the timber-work, or pointing obligingly to an insecure part of the structure, and let us leave it to the incorrigible optimists to do some patching up here and some buttressing there. When it crashes to the ground, they'll soon run.

This image of bourgeois society as a tumbledown mansion built on marshy ground was a favourite one with leader-writers and exercised their copious imagination throughout the period.

Amidst the tumult caused by the whole affair, the question of unequal treatment before the courts again raised its head. The sentencing of Karl Liebknecht for sedition and the editor of the party paper in Königsberg, who had been denounced by a bourgeois competitor of *lèse-majesté* in the autumn of 1907, was contrasted with the comparatively lenient treatment accorded to Harden.[106] Moreover, it was perfectly clear to the SPD that the state had fought shy of a perjury charge against Eulenburg until the last possible moment, in marked contrast to the penalties which Social Democrats had suffered in lesser cases. There was considerable disquiet, too, over Eulenburg's psychosomatic sickness which, with the connivance of his personal physician, resulted in specially favourable treatment from the authorities, and led to an indefinite adjournment of the case against him.[107]

Of great significance was the apparent capitulation of the chief protagonist in the scandal to the old order. Harden, whose view of the Kaiser as 'a great chap' was not forgiven him by the SPD press,[108] allowed himself to be persuaded against proceeding with further evidence. In June 1909 he accepted from Albert Ballin, acting on Bülow's instructions, a sum of 40,000 marks and agreed to withdraw his appeal to the Reichsgericht.[109]

The scandal did little to change the distribution of effective power within the Reich. There had been little in the way of collaboration amongst the political parties, in defence of parliamentary freedom and democratic rights against the trappings of personal absolutism. The 'saviour incarnate', as the *Rheinische Zeitung* dubbed Harden,[110] had not in fact proclaimed the dawning of a new age. In truth, once the fuss had died down and the Eulenburg–Moltke affair had given way to the next preoccupation – the *Daily Telegraph* interview – the political landscape appeared much as before. The general view amongst party journalists was that one kind of camarilla had simply been replaced by another, but the conviction that the old order had been fundamentally weakened emerged stronger than ever before. As *Die neue Zeit* put it,[111] 'May they continue to bring their barrowfuls of courtly filth into the market-place: they are doing our work for us.'

The 12,000 marks affair

Since industry and, in particular, large industrial concerns were chiefly responsible for providing Imperial Germany with her remarkable economic strength, it is not surprising that they gradually emerged as the most favoured estate in the land. Wilhelm II, more than any predecessor, drew industrialists, businessmen and leading bankers to court. Those favoured in this way included Friedrich (Fritz) Krupp, 'König' Stumm, Albert Ballin, Max von Schinkel, Carl Fürstenberg and Gwinner and Helfferich of the Deutsche Bank.[112] For the Social Democrats, Bebel made a number of pointed attacks on the Wilhelmine plutocracy, and thought it noteworthy that a successful entrepreneur or magnate received greater attention and favour at court than many an aristocrat whose lineage stretched back beyond that of the Hohenzollerns.[113] This new alliance of interests was reflected not only in the close relationships between the Kaiser and his leading industrial managers, but also within government and bureaucracy, to the extent that spokesmen for the landed estates felt their privileged position increasingly under threat from economic and political rivals.

Since these new business interests owed no allegiance to any democratic institutions nor acknowledged the sovereign power of elected legislatures, their influence proved difficult to counteract. The Social Democrats, in particular, felt themselves to be directly affected by the exercise of such hidden, extra-parliamentary influences, the more so since the employment prospects and economic livelihood of the bulk of the party membership and socialist electorate were determined by a handful of powerful industrialists. The *Hamburger Echo*[114] for its part, detected the existence of a double camarilla at the apex of political power; of feudal barons and agrarian demagogues on the one hand, and of reactionaries (*Scharfmacher*) intent on pressing governments into acts of punitive repression against the working class on the other.

No one goaded the government more flamboyantly than the leading magnate of the Saar, Karl Ferdinand Freiherr von Stumm-Halberg. Born in 1836, elected to the Prussian Landtag in 1867, a member of the select coterie of the Herrenhaus in 1882 and the Staatsrat (Privy Council) in 1890, he was possessed of a fanatical hatred for Social Democracy, which he described as '*lèse-majesté* incarnate'. As far as he was concerned, the SPD was nothing but 'a collection of all those elements imbued with hate, poison and envy against their better-situated fellow citizens'.[115] In answer to the exposition of republican, utopian sentiments from the Social Democrats in the Reichstag in 1893 he replied, 'Your Zukunftsstaat is nothing more than a large penitentiary, coupled with a common rabbit-hutch.'[116]

Unlike Social Democracy such colourful rhetoric did not conceal the absence of real power; it was an expression of it. Stumm demanded a military-type discipline from his work-force, regarding them more as soldiers of the national economy than as individual human beings,[117] and instantly dismissed an employee suspected of socialist sympathies. His firm view was that no one who pursued 'revolutionary' tendencies had the right to expect employment in the public sector or in private industry,[118] and whenever it came under his jurisdiction he banned the sale of all socialist literature. Such methods of 'Unternehmer-Terroris-mus', of arbitrary industrial power, survived him. Following attempts late in 1904 to found an SPD paper for the Saar, proclamations were posted on the walls of the local factories threatening with dismissal any worker who took out a subscription.[119] Perhaps because of these ogre-like qualities, Stumm was scarcely ever absent from the columns of the SPD press in his lifetime, and on his death in 1901 the *Bremer Bürger-zeitung*[120] commented with mock regret, 'One of the most effective agitators for the SPD has been taken from us.'

Throughout the period workers struggled unsuccessfully to win for themselves a right to work which was not dependent on political con-formism. Nowhere was the determination of employers' organisations to exclude potential malcontents and socialist sympathisers from their work-forces more evident than in the compilation and circulation of black-lists.[121] Once again, the SPD found welcome propaganda in the existence of such lists, details of which were publicised regularly. In 1907, for example, the *Vorwärts* published a register drawn up by the employers' federation of house-painters and decorators in the Duisburg area,[122] and the *Hamburger Echo* referred to a list of workers in the building-trade in use in Aachen.[123] The same paper published in the following year a directive from the executive of the colliery-owners association of the Ruhr, whose signatories included Hugo Stinnes, with the names of 3,876 miners who were to be refused work.[124] Such methods of operation were helped enormously by the connivance of the courts; when a group of workers sued an enamel firm in Düsseldorf which, following a recent strike, had sent their names to all other enamel factories in the country, the Oberverwaltungsgericht in Cologne judged that such lists were perfectly legal.[125] This decision was upheld by the Reichsgericht in May 1902.

The close association between politics and industry, especially between governments and the Zentralverband deutscher Industrieller (ZdI), formed in January 1876 to champion the interests of heavy industry, had been apparent throughout the 1890s. In July 1890, for example, the Verband deutscher Metallindustrieller, with the full support of a general meeting, had voted a sum of 3,000 marks to be distributed via the Berlin police headquarters to all policemen who had been on duty outside the 83 factories of the metal employers' association, in order to enforce lockouts following widespread absen-teeism on May Day.[126] In the autumn of 1900, the *Leipziger Volks-zeitung* reported that as early as 1894 the Reich Chancellery, the Foreign Office and the Ministries for Internal Affairs and Trade &

Industry had received financial contributions from the ZdI, and that since May 1895 the same organisation had helped to finance the publication of the semi-official *Neue Reichskorrespondenz*, designed by the government to supplement its ideological struggle against socialists.[127] Its annual contribution for this project alone was of the order of 16,000 marks.[128] It was understandable enough that such 'cooperation' would be rewarded in kind. Thus it was only the politically astigmatic who expressed surprise when in 1900 the ZdI received details of government proposals considerably in advance of the municipal trade councils and representatives of commerce.

Such was the power of the ZdI that it did not scruple to employ methods of intrigue whenever it felt that its interests were at stake. So, for example, it clearly had a hand in the course of events which led to the resignation of the Minister of Commerce, von Berlepsch, in 1896. The way in which the general secretary of the ZdI, Henry Axel Bueck, had schemed against von Berlepsch with the intention of ousting him from power, was brought to light when the *Vorwärts* published a private letter from Bueck to a South German cotton manufacturer. In it Bueck expressed his satisfaction at 'having got rid of Berlepsch',[129] whose advocacy of a system of local boards of trade had aroused strong opposition from within the ZdI.

There are considerable grounds for supposing that the State Secretary at the Ministry of the Interior, Count Arthur Posadowsky-Wehner, who succeeded Boetticher in 1897, was the ZdI's next principal target. Posadowsky had been a Landrat in Posen and had spent eight years as *Landeshauptmann* of that province; his agrarian sympathies were noted in a diary entry by Hohenlohe, who had been regaled with apocalyptic visions of an industrialised German state, whose inexplorable development could only end either in a collapse into a republic or, as in Britain, into a '*Schattenmonarchie*'.[130] Rightly or wrongly, Posadowsky had come to be clearly identified in the public eye with attempts at producing ameliorative social legislation, although to an already embittered SPD the publication of a circular issued by him in December 1897 merely stoked up the fires of class resentment.[131] This document proceeded to invite comments and suggestions from all levels of regional and local administration, on a series of proposals designed to counter the operation of SPD 'terrorism' against blackleg labour. These proposals, the outcome of which led to the drafting of the Zuchthausvorlage, would have introduced further restrictions on the effective power of trade unions, including the prohibition of picketing.

It is against this background that one of the most sensational disclosures ever made by the SPD press must be seen. On 22 October 1900, the *Leipziger Volkszeitung* published a memorandum from Bueck to all affiliated members of the ZdI. It read,

> I have received a personal request from the Reich Office of the Interior for the sum of 12,000 marks, to be made available for the purpose of financing the public campaign in support of a bill designed to ensure the protection of industrial working conditions. I have informed the deputy president of the ZdI, *Geheimer Finanzrat* Jencke, of this request and he has thought it appropriate, for obvious reasons, not to refuse this rather special call for help. *Geheimrat* Jencke has made available for the above purpose a sum of 5,000 marks on behalf of the firm of F. A. Krupp.[132]

The head of the Bavarian legation in Berlin, Count Lerchenfeld, reported on 26 October,

> I am certain that the publication of the Bueck letter is not an accident. This disclosure forms a link in a series of attacks which have been directed at the State Secretary for the Interior for some time. Count Posadowsky has made himself unpopular with major industrial concerns as a result of his agrarian sympathies . . . Without doubt the publication of the letter was intended to trip him up, and at the same time act as a warning to the new Chancellor not to open the door too much to the agrarians.[133]

It was, in fact, the first crisis which Bülow had to face as successor to Hohenlohe. During the Reichstag debate, on a motion brought in by the SPD and supported by the Centre Party and the Progressives, Bülow described the incident as a blunder and gave an assurance that the mistake would not be repeated again.[134] The Chancellor's handling of criticism in the Reichstag seemed to reflect unfavourably on Posadowsky, and there was considerable speculation as to an imminent resignation. The SPD professed no strong feelings either way; the party was convinced that Posadowsky could only be replaced with someone of the same ilk, and in any case found the prospect of a leading government minister who continued in office and whose nose could therefore be periodically rubbed in scandal, quite attractive.[135]

Despite the outrage felt in ZdI circles that Posadowsky had tried to disown the relationship between government and industry, there was no real possibility of his dismissal, however, since such a step would have been interpreted publicly as a victory for the SPD. In addition, the departure of Posadowsky would have been seen as a serious affront to agrarian circles, on whose support in the Reichstag the government was still dependent, and his qualities as an administrator would have been sorely missed.[136] For his part, Posadowsky was concerned to extricate himself from an unhappy situation and, with the agreement of Bülow, arranged for a statement to be published in the semi-official *Berliner Correspondenz*, which transferred responsibility for the initiative made to the ZdI onto the shoulders of a leading civil servant, *Ministerialdirektor* von Woedtke.[137]

This was a demonstrably uncavalier act and succeeded in fooling none of the accredited heads of legation in Berlin. As Dr Klügmann of the Hanseatic legation made clear,[138] Posadowsky had authorised preliminary discussions to take place between Bueck and Woedtke, with a view to financing a campaign through various pro-government publishing agencies. Although no reference had been made to the Bundesrat, Hohenlohe had given his blessing to the scheme and it was simply the storm following the unfortunate publication which necessitated Posadowsky's public retreat from responsibility. He was certain that he could count on the tactful silence of Woedtke, especially since he had forbidden the latter to appear – as was possible under the rules of procedure – before the Reichstag.[139] Woedtke was removed from his position within the ministry, albeit under protest, and transferred to an unexceptionable post in the provinces, where he died less than a year later.

A great deal of attention was devoted to establishing the source of the leak and the reasons behind it. The general reaction to the affair in the establishment press revealed much about the way in which individual newspapers steadfastly represented the viewpoints of organisations or individual ministers, and the extent to which such journals depended on a steady flow of confidential information and personal briefings from the participants. Thus, the *Münchener Allgemeine Zeitung* acted on behalf of Posadowsky, and Bueck availed himself of the *Berliner Neueste Nachrichten*, which was in any case financed from ZdI funds. A sequence of charges and counter-charges filled the columns over several months, with the SPD reiterating its accusations and Bueck attempting to deny, for example, that his directive had been issued in August 1898, as the *Leipziger Volkszeitung* continued to claim, but rather one year later.[140] It is symptomatic of the fact that there was no accepted forum for making public statements of this kind, and of the failure of the Reichstag to develop any kind of tradition in this respect, that most of the substantive discussion on the '12,000 marks affair' took place in the press. Although no conclusive evidence emerged, it is more than likely that the decision to provide the *Leipziger Volkszeitung* with a copy of the vital Bueck memorandum came from within the ZdI itself.

Compared with the budget of the Reich Office of the Interior, which in 1901 totalled more than seven-and-a-half million marks, the sum of 12,000 marks was a drop in the ocean. As far as the SPD press was concerned, however, the actual sum acquired a deep symbolic importance. As so often, the individual details of a particular affair were subordinated to the practical consequences for the party and to the demands of a thematic, rather than analytical, approach to the question of propaganda.[141] The symbiotic relationship between politics and industry developed still further in the decade after 1900, giving point and substance to the *Hamburger Echo*'s facetious query whether the Reichsamt des Innern (RdI) was really an independent ministry or merely a branch office of the ZdI.[142] Thus, for example, the ZdI made a substantial contribution towards the gratis distribution of some three million copies of an anti-socialist pamphlet during the 1903 Reichstag election campaign.[143] Something of this close financial collaboration with government interests was also evident in the 1907 campaign, when several hundred thousands of marks were made available by the ZdI for distribution amongst the members of the projected 'Block'. When the National Liberals were so unwise as to deny some three years later that they had profited from this arrangement, the *Deutsche Wirtschaftliche Korrespondenz* promptly published full details.[144] The extent to which formal cooperation and collaboration of this kind was being institutionalised at all levels can be gauged from the formation of specialist organisations, such as the Reichsverband in 1904, described by the *Vorwärts*[145] as a 'political praetorian guard', and the Julius-türmer (*Wahlfonds der Industrie*) in 1909.

The house of Krupp

In the changed economic circumstances of the last decades of the nineteenth and first decade of the twentieth centuries, which catapulted imperial Germany to a position of pre-eminence in the world economy, the representatives of organised industrial power sought more and more to influence the course of policy-making at the national level. In order to underpin the traditional basis of its political authority, the German nation-state came to depend increasingly on the economic co-operation of the vast new industrial groupings which had already begun to disfigure the skyline of Wilhelmine society. In particular, the disastrous foundations were laid for that marriage between the state and the heavy armaments industry which was to flourish so successfully in the Third Reich. One relationship especially, that between Berlin and the Essen firm of Friedrich Krupp, seemed particularly blessed, not just in terms of the favourable trade winds which blew in its direction, but also as a direct result of the personal interest which Wilhelm II took in the fate and fortunes of the company.

In 1887, when Fritz Krupp became sole proprietor of the enterprise, the firm already employed 19,000 men, occupied more than 1,000 acres of land and had an annual production in excess of 50 million marks.[146] By April 1901 it had a managerial staff of 3,823 and a labour force of 46,077, of whom 25,925 were employed in Essen alone. The family residence, the Villa Hügel, linked to the national railway network by means of a special station, was itself graced by a permanent domestic staff of 150. The scale of operations was such that the Essen factory had its own gas-works, whose annual output of 18,713,000 cubic metres of gas-light was greater than that required for the whole of the city of Breslau.[147] The firm's interests, however, were truly nation-wide: it bought out its chief rival, the Gruson works at Magdeburg, by a clever system of middleman intrigue,[148] and in 1896 obtained control of a large shipyard at Kiel, the Germania-Werft, which between 1899 and 1914 built no fewer than 57 warships.[149] These contracts alone were worth more than 130 million marks. In the circumstances, it was hardly surprising that Krupp's personal annual income increased threefold between 1895 and 1902.[150]

Krupp was also clearly identified with the aspirations of the new expansionist Germany. In the early 1890s he became proprietor of the *Berliner Politische Nachrichten*, one of many newspapers which was to serve exclusively the interests and personal economic preferences of leading industrialists and whose editor-in-chief, Viktor Schweinburg, was also translated to the position of General Secretary of the Flottenverein in 1898. From 1897 onwards Krupp capital had been involved in financing the *Süddeutsche Reichskorrespondenz*, whose broad intention was to infiltrate those South German editorial concerns which viewed overtly pro-Prussian propaganda with some suspicion, and whose specific aims included the organisation of national support for the Flottenpolitik programme.[151] Krupp was clearly behind the efforts made after 1900 to intensify the navy-building schedule, partly because of the recessionist state of industry, but also because of the temptations of still higher profits. As it was, the *Hamburger Echo*,[152] in a reference to the period covered by the Second Navy Law, pointed out in 1899 that Krupp could look forward to 'seventeen fat years', a procedure by which the ordinary taxpayer was being forced to keep the 'cannon-king' in luxury.

The extent of Hohenzollern financial support for the Krupp industrial empire has always been something of a mystery, but it is known, for instance, that in 1908 the Kaiser bought 50,000 marks of Krupp bonds through the Deutsche Bank.[153] What is not in doubt is the degree of marked imperial approval bestowed on Krupp the man and Krupp the firm. Wilhelm II awarded the man the title of Wirklicher Geheimrat – an offer of ennoblement having been declined – and conferred membership of the Herrenhaus and the Prussian Staatsrat upon him, whilst gracing innumerable official business functions and receptions in Essen with his presence.

The SPD's attitude to the Krupp empire was that its material success rested entirely on the exploitation of the productive capacity of its workers.[154] Despite the fact that Krupp employees in the Ruhr lived in model homes, their existence was scarcely different from a form of *Leibeigenschaft* or feudal tutelage, since this privilege was accorded only in exchange for the undertaking never to associate with trade union organisations or indulge in socialist activities. This kind of patriarchal tyranny was underlined during the 1893 elections, when both Krupp and Stumm led their workers to the ballot-boxes in order to get themselves elected.[155] Understandably, therefore, attacks on the Krupp industrial system filled the columns of the SPD press. Nor was the spiciness of social scandal ever far away; in 1893, for example, the *Essener Volkszeitung* obtained details of personal indiscretions made by Krupp's doctor to his patient in reporting confidential opinions expressed by his former patient Bismarck.[156]

Much more substantial was the sort of polemic which another local SPD paper in the Ruhr, the *Bergische Arbeiterstimme* at Solingen, directed against the operation of the Krupp pension fund, to which every Krupp employee was obliged to belong.[157] In addition to a basic non-recurring membership fee, which was usually the value of a day-and-a-half's wages, a percentage of earnings was subtracted to provide regular contributions. On average this amounted to 34 marks per annum. However, before any worker became entitled to payments from this pension fund, he was required to remain in employment with the firm for a minimum of 15–20 years. The *Arbeiterstimme* quoted instances where some employees, who had each contributed in excess of 1,000 marks to the fund, were dismissed shortly before reaching the retiring age, and since there was a phenomenal annual turnover in staff of between 7,500 and 8,000, it was obvious that this much-vaunted social welfare scheme was actually working to the detriment of the labour-force. In fact, in 1900 the pension fund made a profit of 1,167,216 marks and showed capital assets totalling 10,742,423 marks.

Krupp was therefore not a man on whom the SPD was likely to expend many tears or to whom it might conceivably show much sympathy.

Fritz Krupp's homosexual inclinations had been known to interested circles for some time before his personal scandal became public. It was conspicuous that whenever he and his wife visited Berlin together, they never stayed at the same hotel.[158] The 20-mark pieces, which he used to bestow liberally on court flunkeys and hotel staff, had also become legendary, and by the turn of the century his name was already in the secret register of homosexuals kept by the Berlin police.

During the spring of 1902 the excesses and extravagances on the island of Capri, to which Krupp had become accustomed, reached a new pitch of reckless abandon. Tresckow of the Berlin police department received information that Krupp had begun exceeding even the bounds of tolerability accepted by Italian society, where homosexual practices did not *ipso facto* constitute a criminal offence, to the extent of seducing young boys and allowing himself to be featured in pictorial representations of group orgies. By this time an article had already appeared in the Rome paper of the Italian socialist movement, *Avanti*, but Tresckow's suggestion that the Kaiser should be informed was rejected by Polizeipräsident von Windheim.[159] Such was the level of interest aroused by the affair that even when Krupp suddenly departed from Capri at the end of May, the Neapolitan socialist paper *Propaganda* and gradually the entire Italian press simmered with disclosures of one kind or another. In the circumstances it was only a matter of time before the news began to cross national frontiers. It first reached the German public by means of a veiled article in the leading journal of the Bavarian Centre Party, the *Augsburger Postzeitung*, on 8 November. The real scandal did not come, however, until the *Vorwärts* published its celebrated article exactly a week later.

The subject of homosexuality had appeared before in the columns of the SPD press. In 1894, the *Schwäbische Tagwacht* in Stuttgart had been sued by the Prinzlicher Hofmarschall and Kammerherr Freiherr von Simolin-Bathory, on the basis of charges of homosexual practices which the paper had made against 'a certain aristocratic gentleman'. Because the local state prosecutor declined to bring a charge on behalf of the state, Simolin issued a private writ for libel and the case was heard at the Schöffengericht level. However, the presiding judge refused to permit the editor of the *Tagwacht* to bring forward supporting evidence for his accusations, and the outcome was a prison sentence of two months. This curious refusal to side with the injured party, but simultaneous determination not to permit the SPD any kind of moral triumph, was again evident at the appeal stage, when the court declined to hear fresh evidence from the defendants. By this time details of the affair were making their social rounds in Stuttgart and the scandal became a topic of open conversation. When an anonymous pamphlet appeared (actually Social Democratic in origin), which concerned itself with the injustice of the sentence against the editor of the *Tagwacht,* and a new witness came forward to testify on oath that Simolin had committed a number of indecent acts against him, public pressure for the reopening of the case steadily mounted. In the light of substantial evidence which the courts had previously viewed as inadmissible, the original verdict was reversed at a special hearing in July 1894 and costs were awarded against Simolin.[160]

The *Vorwärts* article of 15 November 1902 was altogether more sensational and, since it resulted in so much personal misery and public scandal, it is perhaps worth considering in detail.[161] It began by referring to the recent spate of rumours in the foreign press, together with its own veiled allusions to the affair. Whilst stressing the unfortunate and constant threat of blackmail or prosecution under §175 of the *Strafgesetzbuch,* to which homosexuals were exposed, and suggesting that this section of the criminal code had outlived its usefulness, the *Vorwärts* nonetheless paid particular attention to the cultural and political implications of the affair. The case of Fritz Krupp, whose function within society as a war-lord given to exploiting the German working class was carefully underlined, was seen by the paper as showing 'a picture of capitalistic culture of the grossest kind'. The scandal was important not merely for its sexual content, but because it revealed the worst financial temptations of bourgeois society:

An unfortunate predisposition of this kind, which in the case of a man of no private means can prey on his mind to the point of absolute despair, can become a terrible source of corruption under the influence of capitalist power, which then transforms the personal fate of such an individual into a matter of public concern.

Indeed, the *Vorwärts* found evidence of such corruption in the reports of the Neapolitan press, which suggested that financial inducements in plenty had all but succeeded in keeping news of Krupp's personal pleasures out of the public eye. So, for example, after the editor of a mainland newspaper, which had referred to events on Capri, returned from a visit to the island, no further mention of the matter was made in the columns of his paper. Similarly, when the Italian Prime Minister arrived on Capri, the local Mayor advised him to send Krupp a telegram of good wishes. The clear inference to be drawn from the *Vorwärts* article was that though homosexuality might simply be 'a fatal weakness of nature', there could be little sympathy for a man who put his millions at the service of abnormal pleasures. It was the supreme irony that a Social Democratic newspaper should take on the task of reminding its readership that as long as Krupp remained resident in Germany, he was bound by the operation of §175, which made homosexual acts a criminal offence, punishable by terms of imprisonment and the deprivation of all civic rights. 'Now that perversion has become the subject of a public scandal', the *Vorwärts* argued, 'it must be the duty of the state prosecutor's office to take action.'

The *Staatsanwaltschaft* did, in fact, take immediate action, but not quite in the way the SPD had expected. On the day the fateful article appeared, telegrams were exchanged between Berlin and Essen on the basis of which the Berlin state prosecutor, acting on behalf of Krupp, issued a writ for libel against the *Vorwärts*. At the same time, the police searched the whole of the *Vorwärts* publishing-house, even breaking open the personal lockers belonging to members of the SPD Reichstag group. All remaining copies of the paper were confiscated and similar writs for libel were served on a number of journals in the provinces, where the local police took the extraordinary step of fetching individual copies of offending SPD newspapers from the homes of subscribers.[162] In short, the whole apparatus of the state was launched against those who had unleashed the scandal, and as the National Liberal *Münchener Neueste Nachrichten* pointed out, such speedy action on the part of the authorities would never have happened if Krupp had been an ordinary citizen.[163] There was, of course, no reason for the 'ordinary' citizen to doubt that the SPD was once more spinning a yarn, since the party's general untruthfulness and willingness to compromise honesty for the sake of political gain had received such widespread official condemnation in the perjury trials of the preceding decade.

Events moved rapidly in the days that followed. Krupp returned to the Villa Hügel on 19 November, after three days in Kiel, and on 22 November came the announcement of his sudden death. Despite the attempts of his personal physicians, friends and a number of contemporary observers to suggest otherwise,[164] the circumstances suggest that Fritz Krupp had taken his own life. This was borne out by the speed with which the coffin was sealed and the funeral service arranged. The mystery which surrounded Krupp's death was further emphasised when the *Münchener Post*[165] published additional sensational reports relating to attempts to secure the legal incapacitation (*Entmündigungs-*

verfahren) of his wife Margarethe. Confronted with a series of anonymous letters and press cuttings, she had sought advice from the Kaiser,
with a view to turning over the management of the family enterprise
to a fiduciary committee. Unfortunately, members of the board in
Essen were alerted to her initiative and, branded by them as a hysterical,
crazed woman in need of urgent psychiatric treatment, Margarethe
was hustled off to a sanatorium in Jena.[166]

The funeral was held on 26 November and the mourners, including
Tirpitz, the Minister of the Interior, von Rheinbaben, and the Minister
of Public Works, von Budde, were led by the Kaiser. Curiously enough,
no representative was present from the Reichspartei, the party to which
Krupp himself had belonged.[167] Although the funeral ceremony itself
passed off without incident, the day was notable for a speech delivered
by the Kaiser to the Krupp directorate and members of the labour-
force.[168] In it emerged not only Wilhelm II's personal emotion at the
loss of a close friend, on whom he bestowed the accolade 'kern-
deutsch', but a quite obvious and deliberate identification between the
house of Hohenzollern and the house of Krupp.

A crime has been committed in German lands, so base and vile . . . which with
its consequences is nothing else than murder; for there is no difference between
someone who mixes a poisoned draught and hands it to his victim and someone
else who, from the safe hiding-place of his editorial office and with the poisoned
arrows of his calumny, succeeds in depriving a fellow human being of his
honourable name and, through the resultant anguish of mind, in killing him.[169]

A similar attack on the responsibility of the socialist 'Staatsfeinde' for
the death of Krupp, was made by the Kaiser in a second speech at
Breslau on 5 December, to an 'officially' organised deputation of
workers.

Such was the manner in which this branding of the SPD with
'editorial murder' captured the public imagination that the poet Ernst
von Wildenbruch, who had received the Schiller Prize in place of
Gerhart Hauptmann in 1896, immediately wrote a letter to the Kaiser,
both warmly appreciative in tone and excessively maudlin in sentiment.[170] Further initiative was shown by the officer corps of a field
artillery regiment in Fulda, who decided to duplicate and distribute the
texts of the 'Kaiserreden' at Essen and Breslau.[171] Such action was
complemented by an officially-inspired campaign in the establishment
press directed at turning public opinion against the SPD. Scherl's
paper *Der Tag* accused the party of having made Fritz Krupp into a
hunted animal, and the process of public vilification of the party continued for several weeks.

The government, for its part, could consider itself pleased at the positive response its campaign had elicited. The Polizeipräsident at Cologne, for example, reported that the texts of both speeches by the Kaiser had been printed in every local paper, with hostile reaction coming only – predictably enough – from the *Rheinische Zeitung*; and that, in addition, the publisher of the *Kölner Tageblatt* had taken it upon himself to organise the distribution of offprints of the Essen speech to all local factories. In some cases the text was displayed in the form of a huge placard inside the premises of leading manufacturers, such as at the important Stollwerck chocolate factory.[172] In Essen, Bochum, Kiel and several other towns, employees in Krupp enterprises and state concerns were ordered to show demonstrations of loyalty and allegiance to the Kaiser by signing an approbatory 'Huldigungstelegramm'.[173] Not all chose to comply with official instructions, however; a lathe-operator in the Krupp–Gruson steel works at Magdeburg was dismissed after 22 years service for refusing to sign, and a fellow-worker with 16 years service to his credit suffered the same fate.[174]

There had, however, been some misgivings within the SPD at the wisdom of publishing what could only be interpreted as a highly scandalous personal attack on a prominent member of the establishment. Friedrich Stampfer was particularly doubtful about the value of such journalism, and when the news of Krupp's death was announced Paul Singer was heard to comment to the *Vorwärts* staff, 'It's just not done.'[175] In the wake of the Kaiser's speech at Essen, the *Vorwärts* actually shifted editorial ground inasmuch as it argued increasingly in favour of a reform of §175, claiming that it wished to prevent a recurrence of such personal tragedies and denying all charges of scandalmongering.[176] No doubt the paper was taken by surprise at the fury of the counter-propagandistic response from the establishment and was anxiously awaiting the outcome of the libel proceedings, especially since its chances of escaping without serious penalty seemed fairly remote.[177] Curiously enough, this tactical retreat was matched on the other side. On 15 December, the Oberstaatsanwalt for Berlin informed the *Vorwärts* that the charges against the paper were being dropped at the express wish of Krupp's widow.[178] Whether or not other factors were involved, such as the possibility that Krupp's reputation might have suffered still further during a court hearing, it was remarkable, as *Die neue Zeit* acidly pointed out,[179] that the prosecuting authorities should suddenly have allowed their conduct of a legal action undertaken in the interests of state to be affected by considerations of sentimentality.

The affair had a sequel. On 20 January 1903, when Georg von Vollmar attempted to raise, on behalf of the SPD, the question of the Kaiser's intervention in the case, he was involved in a lengthy altercation with the President of the Reichstag, Count von Ballestrem, who refused to permit any public discussion.[180] The executive of the parliamentary party thereupon issued a strongly worded statement, and the *Vorwärts* spoke with some justification of 'an assassination of freedom of speech'. From the *Münchener Post*[181] came the suggestion that Ballestrem had been instructed by court circles to resist all attempts by the SPD at raising the Krupp affair in the Reichstag. In the light of the generally unfavourable reaction which Ballestrem's action received in the non-socialist press including, somewhat surprisingly, the *Kreuzzeitung*, he tendered his resignation on 23 January. A few days later he was appointed a hereditary member of the Herrenhaus and re-elected President of the Reichstag by a substantial margin. The charade of the resignation and re-election was concluded without a single personal statement from the chief participants.

What to all intents and purposes had started out as the public humiliation of a private individual had developed into a great affair of state. It was clear from general editorial comment that the SPD hoped to expose the 'double morality' of the ruling classes, and in this respect the case of Krupp's homosexuality was as convenient a stick with which to beat conventional bourgeois morality as Hammerstein's fraud had been seven years earlier. There were, however, several conscious attempts at drawing a parallel between the widespread homosexuality which characterised the moral and political decline of previous civilisations, and the apparent decay and collapse of the bourgeois capitalist state as manifest in the rash of *fin-de-siècle* symptoms, of which the Krupp affair was probably the most spectacular example.[182] The Kaiser's quite explicit public identification with Krupp, together with his astonishing attacks on the SPD, merely drove Social Democracy into a position of further entrenchment, and when a similar constellation of a sexual scandal and the interests of the Hohenzollern state clouded the heavens of public morality some four years later, the party needed no second prompting before making the obvious connections.

The liaison between state and industry had in no way suffered as a result of Fritz Krupp's personal downfall. Indeed, on the occasion of the marriage in October 1906 of his daughter Bertha to Gustav von Bohlen and Halbach (who himself took the name of Krupp), the Kaiser reaffirmed the continuation of the 'special relationship' between the

firm and the state.[183] A significant intermeshing of government bureaucracy and Krupp administration had already been taking place over a
number of years; Bülow's brother was the head of the firm's Berlin
office for a time and a brother of the Minister of Public Works, von
Budde, was employed by them as a senior engineer. The Krupp
directorate was itself staffed by men of wide experience and business
contacts. In 1903 its chairman, G. Hartmann, was simultaneously a
member of the board of directors of the Dresdner Bank, a manufacturing company in Chemnitz, a mining concern in Dortmund and the
Deutsche Waffen- und Munitionsfabrik in Berlin.[184] Other directors
with Krupp were drawn from prominent positions in public life. The
net effect was that the company at Essen had an efficient tier of 'lobby-
ists' in all branches of industry and public administration, who often
paid out money either to receive information or to secure contracts.
What Berlin knew, Essen needed to know also, so that to all intents
and purposes the firm of Friedrich Krupp had become a kind of
'Reichsinstitution'. It was by no means a one-sided relationship either,
since the government received details of every major arms shipment
to foreign destinations.[185]

SPD attacks on the firm of Krupp centred in the main on its responsibility for stoking up the fires of the highly profitable war industry
and for supplying foreign belligerents with war material. In particular,
party newspapers often posed the question whether the much-vaunted
patriotism of the Essen firm was not largely a myth. It was Social
Democracy which pointed to the bizarre state of affairs in the wake
of the Boxer rebellion in 1900, when firearms supplied to the Chinese
by Mauser and cannons and heavy artillery provided by Krupp were
used against German troops.[186] This sort of situation highlighted the
degree to which Krupp was dependent on foreign arms sales as a means
of ensuring its own future prosperity, and right up to 1914 it continued
to market as much as two-thirds of its total output abroad. Nonetheless,
there was a certain pride and material satisfaction in the widespread
use of German weaponry in other European armies, and in January
1913 the head of the legation in Sofia was able to stress the marked
superiority of German artillery material in the Bulgarian army, over
the proportion enjoyed by French armaments suppliers.[187]

It was inevitable that such financially rewarding contracts often
came about as the result of intrigue and skilful arms diplomacy.
Almost at the same time as the *Vorwärts* was painting a lurid picture
of Fritz Krupp's sexual deviancy, the *Hamburger Echo* was reprinting
details of a scandal involving the Essen firm which the Social Demo-

cratic party newspaper in Copenhagen had uncovered.[188] The previous winter a majority coalition of liberals in the Danish parliament had voted a sum of five million crowns for the purchase of military equipment, and a special commission had unanimously proposed the purchase of 128 cannon from Krupp. As a result, the General of the Danish Artillery protested to the Minister of War, on the grounds that valuable arms contracts were being concluded with a traditional enemy. It eventually emerged that the Minister had been a Krupp agent before taking up his appointment, and that his predecessor in office had taken over the Minister's job with Krupp. Since, in addition to receiving a fixed annual salary, such agents were paid a commission according to the contracts they were able to secure for Krupp, the ex-War Minister would have stood to gain a handsome 100,000 crowns on this contract alone.

The considerable experience of Krupp agents in the field of agitatory journalism was put to use in 1913, when an article appeared in *Le Figaro*, revealing the alleged intention of the French Minister of War to double the number of machine-guns. This evidence of increasing war-like preparations on Germany's borders was felt likely to sway influential groups in the Reichstag into agreeing to a much larger military budget.[189] A similar kind of unscrupulousness was in evidence during the celebrations held in 1912 to mark the 100th anniversary of the Essen firm, when the news of the death of 109 miners in a local pit disaster was deliberately suppressed so that the convivial and festive atmosphere should not adversely be affected.[190]

A complete reluctance to accept the fact that there was anything untoward in the unique relationship between Krupp and the state marked official reaction to the disclosures made in the Reichstag on 18 April 1913 by Karl Liebknecht. During the course of a debate on the administration of the army, Liebknecht broke an undertaking of silence which he had given to the Minister of War, von Heeringen, the previous October, when he had passed on details relating to the criminal activities of the Krupp bureau in Berlin. Liebknecht had anonymously received a parcel containing seventeen secret reports or *Kornwalzer*,[191] relating to government arms-procurement intentions. These highly-confidential documents had been obtained by the head of the Krupp bureau, Maximilian Brandt, for transmission to named members of the directorate in Essen. Such was the size of the operation that some 750 secret reports, all stemming from the period 1910–12, were confiscated from Brandt's office and, according to a notebook found on the premises, at least as many documents again had been copied in the period before 1910.[192] A considerable number of such copies was confiscated from the safe of a member of the Krupp directorate in Essen.[193] As the result of this information, von Heeringen had instructed the political police to carry out extensive inquiries, which included the continuous surveillance of the Krupp bureau in the Voß-straße. In February 1913 seven of those responsible, in addition to Brandt, were taken into custody, but it was the patent failure to initiate proceedings against them which caused Liebknecht to bring the matter into the open.

From the Social Democratic point of view, this particular scandal highlighted the growing danger of powerful industrial cartels. The *Vorwärts* had already pointed out, for instance, that a cartel existed amongst navy suppliers, which succeeded in excluding unwelcome competition and enabled steel manufacturers to dictate their own prices.[194] By way of its secret links with appropriate government departments, the firm of Krupp was able to operate, through the special bureau in Berlin, its own supply monopoly. Because it obtained precise details of the tenders for government contracts submitted by its competitors, especially by the Rheinisch-Westfälische Metallwarenfabrik, it was able first to undercut them and then, confident in the knowledge of government dependence on further supplies, to increase the cost of spare parts and other replacements. This whole ingenious scheme was tantamount to a licence to print money.[195] The willingness of government officials in Berlin to cooperate in providing the Krupp bureau with the information it required was ensured by an elaborate system of bribes, interest-free loans and lavish expense accounts.

But whereas the War Minister, if only in private, had been prepared to agree to a thorough investigation of these illicit operations, the refusal of Liebknecht to condone the continuing prevarication of the authorities, together with his subsequent disclosures in the Reichstag, simply drove government officials into minimising the importance of the affair and, moreover, into finding ways of publicly exonerating the firm in Essen. This was also the attitude of the directorate. Although at first he attempted to preserve a studious silence on the matter, the chairman of the board, Geheimrat Alfred Hugenberg, was persuaded by the pressure of events into making a number of statements to the press on 25 April. To the correspondent of the *Kölnische Zeitung*, he spoke of attempts to hypnotise public opinion and claimed not to have read one word of the alleged transcripts sent on from the Berlin bureau; and in an interview with a representative from the *Rheinisch-West-*

fälische Zeitung, he dismissed the affair in terms of 'the socialist need for scandal'.[196]

The SPD had not failed to present charges of corruption in terms of the highest moral outrage it could command, together with the most calculated exploitation of colourful rhetoric. Thus, Liebknecht himself described the activities of military suppliers as 'a vampire at work on the body politic',[197] and the *Leipziger Volkszeitung* began its editorial on the case, 'The matter stinks to high heaven.'[198] In a similar way, the *Rheinische Zeitung*, quoting further evidence of irregularities in military purchasing, which had emerged after Liebknecht's initial disclosures, was able to posit a general formula, *nulla dies sine linea* – no day without a military scandal.[199]

The establishment press, taking its cue from government spokesmen, complained that the SPD was trying to force its own 'proletarian morality' upon Wilhelmine society and spread guilt and complicity by innuendo.[200] Concern at the way in which the SPD was succeeding in knocking away at the pillars of the establishment emerged in a letter which Gustav Krupp wrote to the former Minister of Cults, von Studt, in May 1913.[201] In it he spoke of 'gross distortion and misrepresentation' which had appeared in recent press articles, even as far away as the United States, where a leading industrial journal, *The Iron Age*, had proceeded to charge the firm of Krupp with primary responsibility for increased martial activity in Europe. Far worse in Krupp's view, however, was the feeling that the Reichstag, the government and the establishment press were allowing themselves to be unduly influenced by 'popular' feeling.

That the SPD had clearly brought out the criminal significance of the operations of the Brandt bureau was underlined by the unavoidable necessity of holding some form of trial. At least one contemporary observer even went so far as to suggest that the court hearing which eventually took place in July and August 1913 was only carried out because of an overriding fear of the SPD, although he also complained bitterly that the party's chief concern had simply been to tickle the palate of the public and pander to their lowest instincts.[202]

However, SPD suspicions that as little incriminating detail as possible would be uncovered during the proceedings, were strengthened when Brandt was discovered to be suffering from amnesia and was unable (or unwilling) to expand on statements he had made in custody. Similarly, although seven participants in the affair, all ordnance officers (*Zeugoffiziere*) or employees of the War Ministry, faced charges of corruption and the disclosure of confidential military information,

Brandt was not himself charged. Nor was the public disquiet dispelled when, despite protestations that the affair had no wider political significance, the defence managed to establish that, at least in the period between 1895 and 1897, artillery commands were instructed 'from the highest possible level' to favour the firm of Krupp with major arms contracts.[203] When the verdicts were announced, under which all seven accused received sentences ranging from six weeks to six months, there was little sense that all the washing of dirty linen had taken place. In particular, Liebknecht repeatedly returned to the matter, principally in two major articles for the *Vorwärts*,[204] in which he characterised the action of officialdom as little more than 'hocus-pocus'. Indeed, the news of Brandt's dismissal as head of the Krupp bureau only a few days earlier seemed to suggest that only the surface of the affair had been scratched.

In October a further court-martial took place in Berlin, of an ordnance officer accused of having contributed to the flow of information from the ministry to the bureau. A few weeks later, Brandt was himself brought before the court to face charges – together with an assessor employed by Krupp in Essen – of having conspired to corrupt War Ministry officials into disclosing military secrets. Not one of the thirteen members of the Krupp directorate was prosecuted, although several papers carried statements by a highly-placed employee of the firm to the effect that Brandt had acted with the full knowledge and consent of the whole board.[205] Those directors who were called were forced to admit under cross-examination that they had known of the existence of the 'Kornwalzer', though several used the totally specious argument that the Reich had actually profited from the operation of the Brandt bureau, inasmuch as Krupp prices were reduced below those of their rivals.[206] The fact that the firm had often obtained highly useful information about their competitors through this elaborate system of industrial espionage, and by patently corrupt means at that, was conveniently overlooked by the court. In the event, Brandt and the Krupp assessor were the only two public scapegoats in the affair and escaped comparatively lightly; the former was able to leave the court-room straightaway, since his sentence of four months imprisonment was regarded as having been covered by periods spent in custody, and the latter received a fine of 1,200 marks.[207]

In the light of these recent events, the *Vorwärts*[208] argued that Germans had no right to get upset at the news of Tammany-Hall practices, or express their disgust at the merest mention of Panama. Official capacity for putting a fine gloss on the scandal merely confirmed SPD views that capitalist society was intent on blurring all questions of ethics and public morality. Especially reprehensible in socialist eyes had been the tendency of the bourgeois press to report details of the court hearings quite uncritically, without any attempt to draw more general conclusions from the affair. Where editorial comment was forthcoming, however, it often took the form of open attacks on Social Democratic motives. The anti-semitic *Deutsch–Soziale Blätter*,[209] for example, conjured up a grotesque picture of SPD journalists lurking at keyholes, rummaging in waste-paper baskets, greasing the palms of hotel porters and deliberately fishing in troubled waters, all in the hope of stirring up as much scandal as possible.

The political maelstrom, for which the SPD was almost entirely responsible, did produce one apparently significant government concession. This was the decision to set up a parliamentary committee of inquiry into the armaments industry, on which representatives from all the parties in the Reichstag were invited to serve. However, SPD suspicions that this action was a meaningless charade were confirmed in the light of subsequent political manoeuvring. The committee was not given the full powers the party had expected or asked for, the terms of reference were narrowly defined and the party's nominee, Karl Liebknecht, was declared to be unacceptable to the government. When it was made known to the SPD that Gustav Noske would be an 'appropriate' choice, the party immediately withdrew from participation in the inquiry.[210] It was a sad reflection on the lack of determination of the other parties to subject the armaments industry to the closest political scrutiny, that the committee held only two sessions before the summer recess in 1914.

EPILOGUE

In one sense, the Wilhelmine SPD fits into a continuing pattern of revolutionary Romanticism in recent German history. Its leadership was convinced of the inevitable triumph of its cause and righteously proclaimed this fact to all who would listen. Equally, it made the fatal mistake of underestimating, as its forefathers had done in 1848, the strength of established autocracy and its capacity to endure, survive and regroup, even in moments of severe structural crisis. It would be wrong, however, to see the SPD merely as a glorified protest party, since the revolutionary ideology to which it continued to hold was both a link with the past and a bridgehead into the future. On the other hand, the Social Democrats regarded themselves as the only true heirs of early nineteenth-century 'liberal' and humanitarian traditions. At the same time, because of the nature of Germany's historical development, no strong section of middle-class society had emerged to question the ethics of political orthodoxy. In that respect, the Wilhelmine SPD first gave expression to the idea of organised public protest against the cancer of corruption and the injustices which flowed from an illiberal political tradition. Because of the relative ineffectiveness of middle-class opinion, for whom the uncovering by the SPD of one outrage after another was unlikely to provide a spur to decisive action, the Social Democrats had to labour hard in their struggle towards political re-education.

The Marxist ideology which continued to characterise the outward posture of the party was not only a form of contemporary economic and social analysis, it was also its emotional sustenance. Bebel's strongest strictures were usually directed at those like the Bavarian, Georg von Vollmar, whom he felt were depriving the SPD of the one thing without which a party like theirs could not exist: inspirational enthusiasm. Since all kinds of sacrifices were inevitably demanded of Social Democratic activists, a philosophy which contented itself with a pragmatic analysis of political problems could not hope to capture and hold the public imagination. This partly helps to explain the contribution made by psycho-emotional factors in the formation of political allegiances.

That such 'irrational' influences were also invoked within government circles is indicated by the almost pathological fear of encirclement before 1914, and its exploitation in official propaganda.

Within the SPD, the ready resonance which revolutionary ideology enjoyed reflected the feeling of powerlessness and impotence in the *Klassenstaat*. This in turn strengthened the flights of fancy into a utopian world. Despite the apparent dynamic of a steadily growing Reichstag vote, the Social Democrats had little direct influence on the formulation of government policy. By its emphatic insistence on the validity of its revolutionary rhetoric, especially in the 1890s, the SPD had worked itself into a position of intransigence, from which it was very difficult to depart with much confidence or self-esteem.

By its very nature, the party served as a means of perpetuating the traditional attitudes inherited from the years under the Sozialisten-gesetz. At the same time, by diverting attention from internal disagreements over ideology and tactics towards exposing the hollowness of the Wilhelmine Rechtsstaat, in which the independence of the judiciary was purely theoretical and basic rights were ostentatiously denied to all 'Reichsfeinde', the press went a long way towards maintaining a strong measure of party unity. It acted as a necessary lifeline between activists and sympathisers in the field, as well as providing the whole party with a forum for active political discussion. Above all, until the generation of men like Friedrich Ebert succeeded to the leadership bequeathed by Bebel, Liebknecht and Auer, every Social Democrat of standing had earned his mark as a sharp-tongued journalist, and most had paid for their audacity with long spells of imprisonment.

Despite the differing experience of Social Democrats in many of the southern states, where a measure of collaboration had already pointed the way towards an alternative political course, it remains significant that German Social Democracy was the only force not completely integrated into the Reich. The Catholic Centre Party had been effectively assimilated, antisemitism had already advanced towards respectability by way of the Conservatives' Tivoli programme and the growing attractions of Pan-Germanism, and even the Danes and Poles had been forced to conform by a ruthlessly-pursued policy of 'nationalising'. Similarly, the militarisation of society and the subordination of education to heightened nationalist aims had succeeded in producing a high degree of political homogeneity. The fact that the Reich was able to digest and assimilate potentially opposing forces in this way, to neutralise them politically, accounted for its ability to survive all the domestic crises it faced.

It is partly because this degree of integration did not extend to the SPD, and partly because of its quasi-cosmetic approach to political fighting – using words to improve a political posture, putting the gloss on the weaknesses of a tactical position – that the party faced such huge difficulties after 1918. The very strength of the imperial idea, the *Reichsmythos* of 1871, in the Weimar period showed the solidity of the ideological consensus of the pre-war period. At the same time, the failures of the SPD in the 1920s were clearly compounded of earlier failures – the reluctance, indeed inability, to put forward detailed policies, which in turn reflected the fact that party thinking had not reached the stage of pragmatic policy-making, and the almost complete lack of governmental experience. The status of Social Democrats as pariahs within Wilhelmine society had deprived them of any responsible share in decision-making and of the unqualified recognition of their legitimate political rights within the community. Unlike the Bolsheviks in neighbouring Soviet Russia, the SPD did not have the advantage of imposing itself on a new political and social structure, from which all vestiges of the old order had been eradicated. It had no 'positive' relationship to the state in 1918, and for this reason alone the party was in no sense master of its own destinies in the turbulence of the Weimar Republic.

Worst of all, although the outward trappings of the monarchial order had been swept away, the old elites, nurtured on the social and political intransigence of the Kaiserreich, still remained to block and frustrate any radical changes in the fabric of society. Thus, it was characteristic of German justice in the Weimar republic that no judge thought it appropriate to proceed against a book like Hitler's *Mein Kampf*, which attacked and vilified parliamentary democracy. Equally, Ebert was forced within the space of five months in 1924 to issue no less than 173 writs, as the result of attempts by conservative reactionaries to discredit him as a drunkard and profiteer, and prevent his re-election as President of the Reich. Certainly, the vast majority of the judges, especially those of the Reichsgericht, belonged in the main to those who utterly rejected the republic. Having been hounded in the courts of Wilhelmine Germany, Social Democrats thus suffered further repression at the hands of the passive discrimination practised by the Weimar courts.

The skilfully exploited fears engendered by threats of a 'red peril' and an ingrained institutional hatred of socialism were amongst the chief legacies of the imperial era, thereby providing the fertile ground on which the 'Dolchstoßlegende' could so effectively flourish. From this perspective, it is in no way surprising that Hitler set himself up as the continuation of a tradition which had begun with Bismarck's persecution of the socialists. There is a clear thread of continuity from the Kaiser's '*vaterlandslose Gesellen*' to Hitler's '*November criminals*'.

Above all, the social conflict and class bitterness of Wilhelmine times remained a consistent feature of political life after the 1914–18 war, and the fighting spirit of the party press was reflected in the rancour of public debate between democratic socialists and anti-democratic and fascist forces. A leading election slogan of the German Communist Party (KPD) in 1932 proclaimed, 'Wer noch der SPD vertraut, dem hat man das Gehirn geklaut.' In the SPD's last restatement of its fundamental beliefs before 1933, the Heidelberg programme of 1925, it is instructive to note that in its theoretical context it differs only marginally from that of the Erfurt programme of 1891. When the party emerged after a further twelve years of official proscription, during which time many of its leaders had been imprisoned in concentration camps, the SPD still remained wedded to its revolutionary beliefs. Not until 1959 did the Bad Godesberg programme signify an official recantation of earlier views.

The history of undisguised harassment and repression of German Social Democracy between 1878 and 1945 left a deep mark on public consciousness. Even the first Chancellor of the Federal Republic, Konrad Adenauer, could speak of the prospects of socialist rule in terms of 'the ruin of Germany', and it is arguable whether this powerful historical imprint of discrimination was ever fully expunged until the formation of the 'Grand Coalition' in 1966. At a more general level, the experience of the Wilhelmine SPD confirms the suspicion that 'Freiheit für Andersdenkende' has always been a hard struggle in the German context: Pfarrer Weidig was allowed to die in prison because he had published a leaflet detailing the income from taxation derived by his Grand Duke, and the poet Georg Büchner was chased out of home and country in 1835 because of alleged 'treasonable acts against the state'.

Yet in spite of constant attempts at organised repression, one cannot ignore the fact that Social Democracy was the first movement to emerge in the political development of modern Germany, which based its appeal on capturing the loyalties of the working masses. The period before the outbreak of war in 1914 also saw the growth of a recognisable form of public opinion, which by the time of the *Daily Telegraph* affair was not without its consequences for official policy-making. It was precisely in stirring up popular emotion by means of political agitation, and in organising the masses behind its electoral banner, that the

SPD scored its greatest triumphs. With the exception of 1907, Social Democracy continued to make major advances at the polls, so that by 1912 it was the strongest single party. These undiminished successes tended to intensify the radical outlook of a party for whom events had vindicated the long-term structural analysis of Germany's problems, as well as the validity of its immediate revolutionary propaganda.

The 1890s marked a period when the critical power of the press was perhaps first recognised. Certainly, a common factor in many of the scandals of the Wilhelmine era is that their existence would never have become public, had it not been for journalistic disclosures of one form or another. Indeed, several political affairs of the period owed their origin to the direct influence of the press. It is an indication of the anti-democratic nature of public institutions, however, that very often the only effective way of highlighting abuses within the state was 'to publish and be damned'. In the exploitation of scandal there could, of course, be no question of engineering the resignation of ministers or of per-suading governments to admit their mistakes. That was not how Wil-helmine Germany was organised. The effect, if it can ever be measured quantitatively, was largely to be seen in the electoral advantage and the degree of popular recognition which accrued to the SPD. What is cer-tainly clear is that in addition to the 'historical memory' of the Sozial-istengesetz, the SPD press was the most important reinforcing factor in steering the party along a course of official non-alignment to the state. Indeed, the very existence of highly critical pieces of journalism and an almost unabated stream of damning editorials right up to 1914, suggests that revolutionary radicalism was far from being a meaningless ideological charade.

Especially remarkable was the way in which tendentious journalism, of the kind pursued in the SPD press, was used as a political weapon, as a spearhead of political opposition. German society was subjected to critical review under a journalistic magnifying-glass. In the event, it is perhaps not so surprising if the results appear somewhat larger than life. But the picture which emerges, even allowing for an inevitable de-gree of exaggeration, throws into question the assertion that Wilhel-mine Germany was a state in which political enlightenment had any secure place. Other societies have certainly produced their forms of repression and unspeakable barbarism. The motives of British govern-ments in the nineteenth century, for instance, in fighting the Opium Wars or in setting up concentration camps in southern Africa, or the record of Belgian rule in the Congo under Leopold II, or the incarcera-tion of Ezra Pound in a mental asylum for twelve years and the later political witch-hunts in the United States, all bear eloquent testimony to the fact that other nations have their own skeletons in the cupboard. Yet the nature of that 'golden age' of recent German history is especially significant, precisely because it tells us so much about the linking threads in the problem of historical continuity. The absence of justice for all, irrespective of political views or social station, which disfigured the first attempts at constitutional democracy in the 1920s, was already apparent during the lifetime of the preceding generation. If the Social Democrats attacked the operation of Klassenjustiz, there were immediate complaints about their 'Rechtslosigkeit', about the way in which they regarded themselves as being above the law. It was perfectly all right for the Kaiser to attack the SPD *en masse*, but it was not in order for the party, collectively or individually, to defend itself.

As has already been pointed out, the existence of this depressing state of affairs, the continued manipulation of the processes of the law in order to achieve a built-in ideological and practical advantage against the threat posed by the SPD, was in itself grist to the publications mill. One outrageously biased court judgment after another was thrust forward and dissected editorially, in order to yield the maximum political effect and convey the victims to the pantheon of martyred socialist heroes. The frequent claim of the SPD press that it was 'cleansing' society by its various sensational disclosures reflected the idealistic sense of righteousness which pervaded this kind of journalism. Few could wear their political haloes more proudly and convincingly than party journalists. Indeed, the SPD learned from its exposure of scandal in Wilhelmine times a technique which it proceeded to apply in its practical struggle against National Socialism in the late 1920s, when the foibles and peccadilloes of prominent Nazi politicians were mercilessly exposed.

If the Social Democrats were to some extent the keepers of the public conscience, they were also the 'doomwatchers' of Wilhelmine society. Each example of personal or institutional corruption was interpreted as further evidence of the worm-ridden superstructure of the old order, although the SPD press always disclaimed with boundless indignation that it was concerned in any way with 'Sensationsmacherei'. In the 1890s, Social Democracy was content to sit and watch the house of cards collapse of its own accord. Indeed, its contemporary cultural analysis seemed to be vindicated in the course of public events. Between 1894 and 1897 there took place an almost unceasing account of the moral degeneracy of Wilhelmine society: the *Kladderadatsch*, Kotze and Hammerstein affairs, Fuchsmühl, the Mariaberg disgrace, the

Essen perjury trial, the operation of the *Köllerpolitik* and the Leckert–Lützow–Tausch affair. And yet, once the Reichsleitung had weathered this highly critical phase, it became more or less clear that it could survive practically anything else that the winds of fate might happen to throw up.

This is not to say that little strikes could not fell big oaks. Helmuth Rogge has written of the cumulative effect of these scandals as 'der stete Tropfen, der den anscheinend granitfesten Stein der monarchischen Ordnung höhlte', of the constant drops which hollowed out the apparently firm basis of monarchical authority. Edmund Burke and Alexis de Tocqueville, in their respective analyses of the French Revolution, both refer to the contribution made by journalists to the overthrow of the existing order. Certainly, the Oberpräsident of Brandenburg province, von Conrad, was convinced of the power wielded by the SPD press. Writing to the Minister of the Interior in October 1913, he voiced his fears of giving any hostages to fortune and warned against the introduction of any new repressive measures aimed at socialist publications, unless accompanied by cast-iron justifications. In his opinion, such an opportunity would only arise when war – and not simply mobilisation – became inevitable.

Any prospects of revolution, real or imagined, were forestalled by war in 1914 and frustrated in 1918. It seems to me that the collapse of the Hohenzollern monarchy cannot be ascribed solely to defeat in war or to the revolutionary aftermath of 1918. The seeds were sown much earlier.

NOTES

PROLOGUE

1 F. Fischer, *Griff nach der Weltmacht*, 4th edit. (Düsseldorf, 1971). A review of the academic controversy Fischer's book caused is given by James Joll, 'The 1914 Debate Continues', *Past and Present* (July 1966), pp. 100–13; also useful is the issue on 1914 of *The Journal of Contemporary History*, I, 3 (July 1966), and John A. Moses, *The Politics of Illusion* (London, 1975).

2 Cp. for example *Geschichtsschreibung*, ed. Jürgen Scheschkewitz (Düsseldorf, 1968) and Georg G. Iggers, *The German Conception of History* (Middletown, Conn., 1968).

3 Eckart Kehr, *Der Primat der Innenpolitik*, ed. H.-U. Wehler (Berlin, 1970).

4 Gerhard Ritter, *The Sword and the Sceptre*, vol II (London, 1970), p. 2.

5 Apart from Fischer's sequel, *Krieg der Illusionen* (Düsseldorf, 1969), which directs its attention to internal affairs, there are a number of specialist studies by his pupils, including Dirk Stegmann, *Bismarcks Erben* (Düsseldorf, 1970) and Peter-Christian Witt, *Die Finanzpolitik des Deutschen Reiches* (Hamburg and Lübeck, 1970). Invaluable are also Volker R. Berghahn, *Der Tirpitz Plan* (Düsseldorf, 1971), whose sub-title, 'Genesis und Verfall einer innenpolitischen Krisenstrategie unter Wilhelm II', points especially to the intermeshing of internal and external factors; idem., *Germany and the Approach of War in 1914* (London, 1973) and the editorial contribution of H. W. Koch in *The Origins of the First World War* (London, 1972), which all show clearly to what extent aggressive nationalism abroad resulted from increasingly desperate attempts to preserve the narrow basis of domestic political authority. Werner Conze's essay in *The New Cambridge Modern History*, vol XI (Cambridge, 1962), pp. 274–95 points up the institutional weaknesses in the system, as does Arthur Rosenberg, *Die Entstehung der deutschen Republik 1871–1918* (Berlin, 1928). A valuable source for the domestic political history of the period is *Philipp Eulenburgs politische Korrespondenz*, ed. John C. G. Röhl, 3 vols (Boppard, 1975).

6 K. E. Born, *Staat und Sozialpolitik seit Bismarcks Sturz* (Wiesbaden, 1957), p. 249.

7 Cp. Otto Pflanze, 'Juridical and political responsibility in nineteenth-century Germany', in *The Responsibility of Power*, eds. Leonard Krieger & Fritz Stern (New York, 1967), p. 162ff.

8 Cp. Leonard Krieger, *The German Idea of Freedom* (Boston, Mass., 1957), which includes a useful section on the Rechtsstaat, p. 252ff. According to Otto Hintze, writing in 1911, parties were not political groupings but rather socio-economic or religious formations; Hintze, *Staat und Verfassung*, vol I, 2nd edit. (Göttingen, 1962), p. 378.

9 Cp. Elisabeth Fehrenbach, *Wandlungen des deutschen Kaisergedankens 1871–1918* (Munich, 1969) and Peter Domann, *Sozialdemokratie und Kaisertum unter Wilhelm II* (Wiesbaden, 1974).

10 *Hamburger Echo* (hereafter *Echo*), 11 September 1894.

11 Wilhelm Schröder, *Das persönliche Regiment* (Munich, 1907), p. 14. In March 1894 the semi-official *Norddeutsche Allgemeine Zeitung* wrote 'Monarchie und Christentum sind jene beiden erhaltenden und aufbauenden Kräfte, unter deren Schutz unser der Monarchie erworbener Kulturzustand geborgen erscheint; diese Pfeiler sind es, welche die Sozialdemokrati zunächst erschüttern und dann beseitigen muß, falls sie an das Ziel ihre Wünsche, die Herrschaft der Massen, gelangen will', quoted in *Echo* 22 March 1894.

12 The speech made by the Kaiser on 4 May 1891 was highly characteristic 'There is only one person who is master in this Empire and I am not going to tolerate any other.'

13 Quoted in Isolde Rieger, *Die wilhelminische Presse im Überblick 1888–191* (Munich, 1957), p. 13.

14 The text is given by Emilie Schröder, *Ein Tagebuch Kaiser Wilhelms I. 1888–1902* (Breslau, 1903), p. 109.

15 Cp. Michael Balfour, *The Kaiser and his Times* (London, 1964).

16 Siegfried Schöne, *Von der Reichskanzlei zum Bundeskanzleramt* (Berlin 1968), p. 43.

17 The concept of personal rule received its first major statement in Erich Eyck *Das persönliche Regiment Wilhelms II* (Zürich, 1948), which prompted alternative views from Fritz Hartung, *Das persönliche Regiment Wilhelms I.* (Berlin, 1952) and Wilhelm Schüssler, *Kaiser Wilhelm II* (Göttingen, 1962) John C. G. Röhl, *Germany without Bismarck* (London, 1967), has traced the development of policy in the 1890s to the point where, with the dismissal o three Reich Secretaries of State in 1897, against the wishes of the Chancellor the Kaiser effectively answered the question as to who really ruled in Berlin H.-U. Wehler, *Das deutsche Kaiserreich 1871–1918* (Göttingen, 1973), claims p. 70ff. that the Reich was governed not so much by the Kaiser as by coalition of oligarchical interest-groups.

18 *Stenographische Berichte des Deutschen Reichstags* (hereafter RT), 10 Legislatur Periode, I, Bd 5, p. 3966.

19 Rudolf Morsey, 'Zur Geschichte der obersten Reichsverwaltung im wilhelminischen Deutschland 1890–1900', *Deutsches Verwaltungsblatt*, 86 (1971), p. 14 The Civil Cabinet provided a commentary on all reports, drafts of laws and regulations issued by the Prussian Ministries and Reich Offices. During the many journeys undertaken by Wilhelm II, the three Cabinet heads and a Foreign Office attaché were the only lines of communication between the Kaiser, his ministers and the affairs of state.

20 Cp. K. E. Born, *Preußen und Deutschland im Kaiserreich* (Tübingen, 1967) who argues that there was no dissimilarity or incompatibility between Prussian and Reich objectives.

21 Quoted in Kuno Graf Westarp, *Konservative Politik im letzten Jahrzehnt de. Kaiserreiches* (Berlin, 1935), p. 116.

22 In a diary entry for 15 December 1898, Chancellor Hohenlohe noted his conviction that the South German liberals had no hope at all of winning against the Prussian Junkers, who were too numerous, too powerful and had the monarchy and army on their side, and with whom the Catholic Centre

Party was content to ally itself. An article published by Friedrich Naumann, published in 1904 and quoted by Harry Pross, *Literatur und Politik* (Olten and Freiburg i.B., 1963), p. 205, pointed to the shrinking importance and increasing isolation of the South German states relative to the Reich. In that year they covered one-quarter of the total land area and accounted for a little less than a quarter of the population, whereas a century earlier this proportion had been one-third. In a letter to his friend Philipp Eulenburg at the end of 1895, Wilhelm II argued that *'Preußentum'* must again assert its primacy, for that alone was capable of holding the Reich together; Eberhard von Vietsch, *Bethmann Hollweg* (Boppard, 1969), p. 65.

23 The State Secretaries of the various Reich Offices were admitted to those deliberations of the Ministry of State dealing with their specific portfolios, but had to wait in an ante-room until the respective points on the agenda were reached; Schöne, op. cit., p. 30. The special treatment of the Reich Offices and their development into powerful, all-competent ministries would have led to a reduction in Prussian power and influence, and this was therefore strongly resisted.

24 Just before the 1907 Reichstag elections, Chancellor Bülow organised a coalition of Conservatives, National Liberals and Progressives against the Catholic Centre Party and SPD. This Bülow-Block lasted for some three years before falling apart on the question of financial reform.

25 Westarp, op. cit., p. 18.

26 A different view is put forward by Eberhart Pikart, 'Die Rolle der Parteien im Deutschen Konstitutionellen System vor 1914', *Zeitschrift für Politik*, XI (1962), Nr 1, pp. 12–32, whose arguments that the deputies felt themselves close to the centre of real power are open to question.

27 Klaus Saul, *Staat, Industrie, Arbeiterbewegung im Kaiserreich* (Düsseldorf, 1974), p. 35.

28 Kai Detlev Sievers, *Die Köllerpolitik und ihr Echo in der deutschen Presse 1897–1901* (Neumünster, 1964), p. 24.

29 Theobald von Bethmann Hollweg, *Betrachtungen zum Weltkriege*, 2 vols (Berlin, 1919–21), vol II, p. 176.

30 By 1895 Max Weber was diagnosing the 'economic death agonies' of the Junkers; cp. Wehler, op. cit., p. 54.

31 The enormous increase in population meant that Germany ceased to be a net exporter of grain and was forced to import large quantities. At the same time, the opening up of the North American grain lands caused a steep fall in grain prices, so that only in 1912 was the price level of the 1870s regained. Such was the precariousness of the situation that the agrarians formed a pressure-group, the Bund der Landwirte, early in 1893, and by the end of the year it already had recruited 200,000 members.

32 Cp. Michael Stürmer, 'Machtgefüge und Verbandsentwicklung im wilhelminischen Deutschland', *Neue Politische Literatur* (1969), p. 490. The seizure of Kiaochow in 1897 may be seen as a diversionary tactic against the domestic uproar caused by the Tausch trial and proposed courts-martial bill.

33 Cp. esp. Berghahn, *Tirpitz*, op. cit. The *Marineaeternat* was a deliberate attempt at bypassing the budgetary powers of the Reichstag.

34 J. C. G. Röhl, 'The Disintegration of the Kartell and the Politics of Bismarck's Fall from Power 1887–1890', *Historical Journal*, IX (1966), p. 6ff. shows how Bismarck was even prepared to enter into a political alliance with the Centre Party. On the background to the Bismarckian Reich cp. Michael

Stürmer, *Regierung und Reichstag im Bismarckreich 1871–1880* (Düsseldorf, 1974).

35 Cp. Theodor Schieder, *The State and Society in our Time* (London, 1962), and the contributions in *Moderne deutsche Sozialgeschichte*, ed. H.-U. Wehler, 2nd edit. (Cologne and Berlin, 1968). Also valuable are Klaus Epstein, 'The Socio-Economic History of the Second German Empire', *Review of Politics*, 29 (1967), pp. 100–12, and Kenneth D. Barkin, *The Controversy over German Industrialisation 1890–1902* (Chicago, 1970), as well as Carl Jantke, *Der vierte Stand* (Freiburg i.B., 1955).

36 Cp. Wolfgang Pack, *Das parlamentarische Ringen um das Sozialistengesetz Bismarcks 1878–1890* (Düsseldorf, 1961), p. 8.

37 Hugo Preuss, *Staat, Recht und Freiheit* (Hildesheim, 1964), p. 144.

38 Quoted in Wehler, *Kaiserreich*, op. cit., p. 231.

39 Writing in the edition of *Roter Tag* for 13 May 1914; quoted in Westarp, op. cit., p. 338. Westarp, ibid., describes the struggle against the ideas and doctrines of Social Democracy, 'to whom no bridge of understanding led'.

40 *Max Webers Gesammelte Politische Schriften*, ed. Johannes Winckelmann (Tübingen, 1971), p. 319.

41 Wehler, op. cit., p. 230.

42 Each of the separate Prussian provinces, such as Posen, Brandenburg, Schleswig-Holstein, Rheinprovinz and Saxony, was ruled by a governor or *Oberpräsident*. Within these provinces and subordinate to the governor were the 36 *Regierungsbezirke* or sub-regional administrative areas, centred on towns such as Potsdam, Merseburg, Kassel, Wiesbaden, Cologne, Düsseldorf, Arnsberg and Kiel. Each of these areas was controlled by a *Regierungspräsident*, an administrative director with considerable executive functions. The *Regierungspräsident* often worked in close harmony with the local *Polizeipräsident* (known as the *Polizeidirektor* in Hamburg until 1912) who, though comparable in status with a Chief Constable, was nonetheless not a career policeman, but usually somebody appointed from the ranks of the higher civil service. The pyramidical structure of provincial government was completed at the lower level with the office of area prefect or *Landrat* (also called *Amtsmann* in Bavaria and *Amtshauptmann* in Saxony and Oldenburg), whose position within this network of authority was by no means insignificant, since each *Landrat* received a copy of every item of state business and was expected to contribute regular reports on the local political situation. Cp. Rudolf Morsey, *Die oberste Reichsverwaltung unter Bismarck 1867–1890* (Münster, 1957) and Herbert Jacob, *German Administration since Bismarck* (New Haven, Conn., 1963), pp. 22–66.

43 Wehler, op. cit., p. 76.

44 Ernest Hamburger, *Juden im öffentlichen Leben Deutschlands* (Tübingen, 1968), p. 3. *Deutsche Sozialgeschichte, Dokumente und Skizzen*, vol II, 1870–1914, eds. Gerhard A. Ritter and Jürgen Kocka (Munich, 1974), p. 369, has some interesting figures on the social parentage of civil servants.

45 Cp. Hellmut von Gerlach, *Meine Erlebnisse in der preußischen Verwaltung* (Berlin, 1919), for details of the difficulties involved in being accepted as a Regierungsreferendar. Catholics as well as Jews faced overt discrimination. Between 1888 and 1914, of the 90 leading Prussian and Reich officials, only 7 were Catholics and none was a Jew; Wehler, ibid.

46 *Das kaiserliche Deutschland*, ed. Michael Stürmer (Düsseldorf, 1970), p. 127. In the wake of the 1848 revolutions the conservative reaction had succeeded

in replacing the principle of universal, direct suffrage with an elaborate and complex electoral system, in which voters were categorised according to their income and property qualifications, so that landowners and the monied classes in general had a disproportionately large say in determining the composition of the lower house (*Abgeordnetenhaus*) of the Prussian Landtag.

47 *Deutsche Sozialgeschichte*, op. cit., p. 399ff. By 1907 the boundaries for the Reichstag constituencies were grossly out of date, since each Conservative deputy required an average of only 18,000 votes for election, whereas a socialist deputy needed 70,000.

48 Rudolf Martin, *Jahrbuch des Vermögens und Einkommens der Millionäre Preußen* (Berlin, 1912), p. 7ff.

CHAPTER 1

1 Cp. Vernon T. Lidtke, *The Outlawed Party. Social Democracy in Germany 1878–1890* (Princeton, N.J., 1966), p. 73ff.; Pack, op. cit.

2 Cp. the figures quoted in *Protokoll des Parteitages der Sozialdemokratischen Partei Deutschlands* (hereafter PT), Bremen, 1904, p. 13. A veteran of the period, Paul Kampffmeyer, gives slightly different figures in *Arbeiterbewegung und Sozialdemokratie* (Berlin, 1919), pp. 70–1.

3 Quoted in Lidtke, op. cit., p. 132.

4 On the other hand, the activities of anarcho-radical groups of the extreme Left, and the need to differentiate clearly between such aims and those of the Social Democrats, required the party to accept at least the principle of parliamentarism, op. cit., p. 128.

5 The second section referred to specific short-term objectives, such as votes for women, proportional representation, biennial parliaments, secular education, the 8-hour day, and a national militia.

6 PT Erfurt 1891, p. 171. In other words, the capitalist clockwork was running down according to Marxist laws, and there was no point in trying prematurely to smash it up. Cp. *Revisionism*, ed. Leopold Labedz (London, 1962), p. 104.

7 PT Erfurt 1891, p. 156. This attitude already signalises a modification of Bebel's view, as expressed in a letter to Engels in December 1885, 'Every night I go to sleep with the thought that the last hour of bourgeois society will soon strike', *August Bebels Briefwechsel mit Friedrich Engels*, ed. Werner Blumenberg (The Hague, 1965), p. 249.

8 Karl Kautsky, *Das Erfurter Programm* (Stuttgart, 1892), pp. 106–7.

9 Frederick William Wile, *Men around the Kaiser* (London, 1913), p. 81. Arthur Rosenberg, op. cit., p. 47, describes Bebel as 'eine Art von Gegenkaiser', and Klaus Epstein, 'Three American Studies of German Socialism', *World Politics*, XI (1959), p. 643, analyses the way in which Bebel acted as both the brake and spur of the party.

10 Quoted in Dieter Groh, *Negative Integration und revolutionärer Attentismus* (Frankfurt a.M. and Berlin, 1973), p. 188.

11 Victor Adler, *Briefwechsel mit August Bebel und Karl Kautsky* (Vienna, 1954), p. 608, writing in a letter to Kautsky, dated 1 February 1915. A similar admiration for Bebel's organisational genius led Adler in 1908 to describe the SPD as 'the greatest political machine which exists in the

whole world, a true and unique work of art', Victor Adler, *Aufsätze, Reden und Briefe* (Vienna, 1929), p. 277.

12 PT Erfurt 1891, p. 275, in a retort to Georg von Vollmar.

13 PT Hannover 1899, p. 120. As late as May 1914 Friedrich Ebert declared in a similar spirit, 'We have survived the Sozialistengesetz and saw Bismarck off too. We will deal in time with Bethmann and his backers who stir things up ...', quoted in Saul, op. cit., p. 386.

14 Thus, for example, the work of Emil Gregorovius, *Der Himmel auf Erden in den Jahren 1901 bis 1912* (Leipzig, 1892), to be found in Bundesarchiv (hereafter BA) Koblenz, Sammlung Fehrenbach, Bd 67, also E. Klein, *Das Paradies der Sozialdemokratie, so wie es wirklich sein wird*, 3rd edit. (Freiburg i.B., 1891). Very popular was the German translation of a work first published in the United States as *Looking Backward, 2000–1887* (Boston, Mass., 1888), Edward Bellamy, *Ein Rückblick aus dem Jahre 2000 auf 1887* (Leipzig, n.d.).

15 Leading Social Democratic Jews included Paul Singer, Emanuel Wurm, Hugo Haase, Ludwig Frank, and Eduard Bernstein who in 1921 recalled that in 50 years of membership he had never heard of a single case where a Jew had been the object of internal party discrimination, Hamburger, op. cit., p. 150.

16 B. Uwe Weller, *Maximilian Harden und die 'Zukunft'* (Bremen, 1970), p. 134.

17 D. Schultze, *Was trennt uns von der Sozialdemokratie?* (Leipzig, 1895), p. 5ff. Bismarck, in a conversation with Smalley in November 1895, published in the SPD *Maifeier-Zeitung* for 1898, a copy of which is in Staatsarchiv (hereafter StA) Hamburg, Senat, C1 VII Lit Me No 12 Vol 18 Fasc 7 Inv 11, made his own view clear: 'The fact that the government treats the socialists as a political party, as a power in the land to be treated seriously and to be reckoned with, instead of robbers and thieves who need to be crushed ... has greatly increased their power and importance. I would never have sanctioned that. They are the rats in the land and should be destroyed.'

18 The extent of the parliamentary successes could not be overlooked. At only one of the five elections to the Reichstag between 1893 and 1912 did the SPD lose seats, and its total vote rose dramatically during the period from 1,787,000 to 4,250,000. By 1912 it held 110 seats and was in fact the largest single group in the Reichstag. In a special introduction published in 1895 to Marx's study of French politics in 1848–50, Engels had described the main task of the SPD as 'to keep this growth going without interruption, until it automatically gets beyond the control of the prevailing government system, not to fritter away this daily increasing shock force in vanguard skirmishes, but to keep it intact until the decisive day'; quoted in A. J. Ryder, *The German Revolution of 1918* (Cambridge, 1967), p. 19.

19 When during a break in a Reichstag sitting in 1912 Bethmann Hollweg asked Bebel after the state of his health, the SPD leader later turned to a colleague to say, 'I have been a member of this House since 1868 and that was the first time that a member of the government – apart from during the debates – has said anything to me', Ernst Schraepler, *August Bebel* (Göttingen, 1966), p. 77. Cp. also Waldemar Besson, *Friedrich Ebert* (Göttingen, 1963), p. 37. At the other extreme, it is remarkable that a leading Social Democrat in Hamburg and member of the Reichstag, Karl Frohme,

carried on a highly secret exchange of views on contemporary matters with officials of the Hamburg police department, StA Hamburg, Senat, Ci VII, Lit Me No 12 Vol 18 Fasc 7 Inv 8c.

20 PT Dresden 1903, p. 313.

21 Cp. Wehler, op. cit., p. 139. Middle-class attempts at social reform, represented in the main by the activities of the Gesellschaft für Soziale Reform (whose first chairman was the one time Prussian Minister of Trade, Freiherr von Berlepsch), and the pronouncements of the intellectual 'Kathedersozialisten', met with unbridled opposition from heavy industry and the scorn of the SPD; cp. Saul, op. cit., p. 26ff. Born, *Sozialpolitik*, op. cit., takes a more favourable view of their importance.

22 See pp. 51–64, Social Democracy in Conflict with the Law.

23 Cp. Egmont Zechlin, *Staatsstreichpläne Bismarcks und Wilhelms II 1890–1914* (Stuttgart and Berlin, 1929), Werner Pöls, *Sozialistenfrage und Revolutionsfurcht in ihrem Zusammenhang mit den angeblichen Staatsstreichplänen Bismarcks* (Lübeck and Hamburg, 1960), J. C. G. Röhl, 'Staatsstreichplan oder Staatsstreichbereitschaft? Bismarcks Politik in der Entlassungskrise', *Historische Zeitschrift* (hereafter HZ), 203 (1966), p. 610ff., Michael Stürmer, 'Staatsstreichgedanken im Bismarckreich', HZ, 209 (1969), p. 566ff.

24 Philipp Eulenburg after the Reichstag election of February 1890, as quoted in Röhl, op. cit., p. 613. Cp. also Dieter Groh, 'Je eher, desto besser. Innenpolitische Faktoren für die Präventivkriegsbereitschaft des Deutschen Reiches 1913/14', *Politische Vierteljahresschrift*, 13 (1972), p. 501ff.

25 Cp. Saul, op. cit., p. 15; *Fürst Chlodwig zu Hohenlohe-Schillingsfürst, Denkwürdigkeiten der Reichskanzlerzeit*, ed. K. A. von Müller (Stuttgart, 1931), p. 451ff.; Röhl, *Bismarck*, op. cit., p. 71. The Kaiser told Eulenburg that he 'did not dream of avoiding' a conflict with the Reichstag, op. cit., p. 72.

26 Count Waldersee took up the theme in a memorandum to the Prussian Minister of War, dated 20 February 1897, *Politisches Archiv des Auswärtigen Amts*, Bonn (hereafter PA/AA), Europa Generalia, Nr 82, Nr 1, Nr 1, Bd 6, and in various communications to the Kaiser, *Denkwürdigkeiten des General Feldmarschalls Alfred Grafen von Waldersee*, ed. H. O. Meisner, vol II (Stuttgart, 1922), pp. 386–9. Similarly, the Alldeutscher Verband explored several theoretical possibilities after 1912; cp. Hartmut Pogge von Strandmann and Imanuel Geiß, *Die Erforderlichkeit des Unmöglichen* (Frankfurt a.M. 1965), p. 9ff.

27 Saul, op. cit., pp. 393–4.

28 Cp. esp. Stegmann, op. cit.

29 Miquel, generally regarded as its principal architect, declared as early as September 1890 that the government's aim should be to 'rally all the elements which support the state' around the throne; Röhl, op. cit., p. 62.

30 Cp. Wehler, op. cit., p. 176ff.

31 Cp. Alex Hall, 'The War of Words: Anti-socialist offensives and counter-propaganda in Wilhelmine Germany 1890–1914', in *Journal of Contemporary History*, vol. II, Nos 2 and 3, July 1976.

32 Cp. Dieter Fricke, 'Der Reichsverband gegen die Sozialdemokratie von seiner Gründung bis zu den Reichstagswahlen von 1907', *Zeitschrift für Geschichtswissenschaft* (hereafter ZfGW) 1959, Heft 2, p. 237ff.; Saul, op. cit., p. 115ff.

33 By the spring of 1914, for example, 3,748 employers were arranging for 1,309,000 items to be sent through the post to some 460,000 workers, op. cit.. p. 127. This propaganda struggle was carried on by many other organisations. The *Neue Reichskorrespondenz*, the organ of the federation of industrial employers, Zentralverband deutscher Industrieller, whose subscribers included all the Prussian Oberpräsidenten, Regierungspräsidenten and Landräte, was distributed to several hundred newspapers; Klaus Wernecke, *Der Wille zur Weltgeltung* (Düsseldorf, 1970), p. 25. Saul, op. cit., p. 66ff. documents clearly how pressure by employers to prevent workers from joining trade union organisations was stepped up in the years after 1907.

34 Saul, op. cit., p. 128.

35 Otto Rückert, *Zur Geschichte der Arbeiterbewegung im Reichstagswahlkreis Potsdam–Spandau–Osthavelland 1871–1917* (Potsdam, 1965), p. 183.

36 Cp. Rosalowsky's report, dated 13 April 1898, in StA Hamburg, Senat, Cl VII Lit Me No 12 Vol 18 Fasc 7 Inv 11. To some extent government strategy was succeeding in deterring the party leadership from holding too many meetings, but very often the absence of numerical support was due to boredom and the inevitable lulls in political controversy.

37 Published in *Hamburger General-Anzeiger*, 26 April 1892.

38 A copy is in StA Hamburg, Senat, Cl VII Lit Me No 12 Vol 18 Fasc 7 Inv 6b.

39 This view, initially expressed in an article in *Die neue Zeit* in December 1893, was later published in one of Kautsky's leading contributions to ideological debate within the party, *Der Weg zur Macht* (Hamburg, 1909). Two years later, during a debate in the Reichstag on the Moroccan situation, Bebel pronounced with ironical foresight that 'the *Götterdämmerung* of the capitalist world is approaching fast'.

40 The most persuasive statement of such ideas has come in Groh, op. cit., *passim*, who argues convincingly in socio-psychological terms that the sublimated frustrations which characterised the Wilhelmine SPD emerged in the acerbity of its propaganda. In particular, he shows p. 61, that the lack of clarity in strategical and tactical thinking was positively encouraged from outside the movement: decades of experience had taught the party that the more concrete its contributions to political debate, the more explicit its ideas in print, so the easier it was for governments to act against the movement.

41 Cp. Rosalowsky's report, dated 11 January 1898, StA Hamburg, Senat, Cl VII Lit Me No 12 Vol 18 Fasc 7 Inv 10c Anlage 1.

42 Wile, op. cit., p. 82.

43 Cp. Dieter Fricke, 'Die sozialdemokratische Parteischule 1906–1914', ZfGW 1957, Heft 2, p. 229ff. The two permanent teaching members were Franz Mehring and Heinrich Schulz, responsible directly to the party executive in Berlin. Numerous difficulties faced the organisers, not least the determination of the political police to expel two members of the staff, the Austrian Rudolf Hilferding and the Dutchman Anton Pannekoek, on the grounds of their non-German citizenship. The police refrained from acting during the 1907 election campaign as had been planned, because of the fear of providing the SPD with further material for agitation. It must be stated, however, that the school had only a limited success, since the number of political activists from all over the country, who attended these courses, was fairly small.

44 Carl E. Schorske, *German Social Democracy 1905–17* (Cambridge, Mass., 1955), p. 191.

45 On the impact of the ideological controversy cp. Adolf J. Berlau, *The German Social Democratic Party 1914–21* (New York, 1949); Peter J. Gay, *The Dilemma of Democratic Socialism* (New York, 1952); Schorske, op. cit., and the review of all three works in Epstein, op. cit. Also useful are Guenther Roth, *Social Democrats in Imperial Germany* (Totowa, N.J., 1963) and J. P. Nettl, 'The German Social Democratic Party 1890–1914', *Past and Present*, 30 (April 1965), p. 65ff.

46 Gerhard A. Ritter, *Die Arbeiterbewegung im Wilhelminischen Reich 1890–1900* (Berlin 1959), p. 217 and *passim*, makes the mistake of assuming that the SPD had abandoned its opposition to the state and his account, though containing valuable analysis, exaggerates the importance of the purely eonomic struggle of the trade unions within the working-class movement. Hans-Josef Steinberg, *Sozialismus und deutsche Sozialdemokratie* (Hannover, 1967), stands in the tradition of those West German historians who attempt to relate the Wilhelmine SPD to post-1945 developments in the Federal Republic, although he is quite right in criticising Ralf Dahrendorf for believing that Marxism had never been 'on board' the party. In fact, Marxism was an indispensable part of the SPD's ideological outfit. Others such as Born, op. cit., and Susanne Miller, *Das Problem der Freiheit im Sozialismus* (Frankfurt a.M., 1964), clearly believe that the ideological readjustments which did take place were due to some kind of divine internal revelation, rather than as the result of the influence exerted by the government's 'big stick' policy. There was a limit to the amount of martyrdom the SPD was prepared to suffer, and if the element of caution had a deeper cause, it was due as much to a fear of stiffer government measures as any dawning recognition of the futility of violent action.

47 Quoted in Hamburger, op. cit., p. 456.

48 Cp. Hans J. L. Adolph, *Otto Wels und die Politik der deutschen Sozialdemokratie 1894–1939* (Berlin, 1971), p. 16.

49 Adler, op. cit., p. 63.

50 *Die Zukunft*, 21 October 1899. For a slightly different view of the results of the Hannover party conference cp. Karl Frohme, *Sozialistische Monatshefte*, December 1899, p. 615ff.

51 *Berliner Correspondenz*, Nr 37, 17 April 1899, a copy of which is in StA Wiesbaden, Abt 407, Nr 43, Bd I, Bl 80.

52 Report dated 22 October 1901, in StA Hamburg, Hans. Ges. Berlin, Neuere Reg., AI4, 1901, Acta 17.

53 To some extent the diminished radicalism of the trade unions may be explained by the considerable successes achieved through participatory struggles at the purely local level, whereas at the national level the SPD was given little room for manoeuvre. A consideration of the rôle of the trade unions in the formulation of party policy is beyond the scope of this study; cp. Schorske, op. cit., Saul, op. cit., and Hans Josef Varain, *Freie Gewerkschaften, Sozialdemokratie und Staat* (Düsseldorf, 1956).

54 Cp. Georg Fülberth, 'Zur Genese des Revisionismus in der deutschen Sozialdemokratie vor 1914', *Das Argument*, March 1971, p. 1ff.

55 Hamburger, op. cit., p. 449ff. On the other hand, there were more than enough sharp words about the danger of the SPD simply becoming a 'Posadowsky-Partei'; cp. Ledebour's speech at the 1904 party conference,

PT Bremen 1904, p. 214. The dangers of even the least offensive form of collaboration were underlined by Albert Südekum, when quoting the French saying 'Qui mange du pape, en meurt', PT Essen 1907, p. 229.

56 PT Erfurt 1891, p. 223.

57 Maximilian Harden, writing in *Die Zukunft*, 26 September 1903, was characteristically pointed in his criticism. 'Bebel dominates the strongest party in Germany with the unlimited power of an Asiatic despot. His will reigns supreme. He is censor, judge, general, king, god. He interrupts every speaker who does not please him with coarse words of abuse and perfidious insinuations. In his own party he treats his opponents, educated people who have been working for the socialist cause for decades, like a gang of arrested swindlers.'

58 Saul, op. cit., p. 23, note 120.

59 Kautsky's views were expressed in *Der Weg zur Macht*, described by J. P. Nettl, *Rosa Luxemburg*, 2 vols (London, 1966), p. 408, as combining 'a complete negation of practical revolution with a strict emphasis on revolutionary attitudes'. Cp. also Richard J. Geary, *Karl Kautsky and the development of Marxism*, Unpublished Cambridge PhD Dissertation, 1972, and Schorske, op. cit., p. 112ff. Kautsky's theoretical formulations had the function of illuminating the nearness of the eventual breakdown, of arguing that the period of waiting was for a natural event, which the party could not make happen, but for which it could create favourable conditions.

60 The most important statement of the influence wielded by Kautsky's 'Integrationsideologie' within the party is by Erich Matthias, 'Kautsky und der Kautskyanismus', *Marxismus-Studien*, 2. Folge (Tübingen, 1957), p. 151ff. Cp. also the essay by Volker Ullrich, 'Emanzipation durch Integration?', *Das Argument*, 75 (1972), p. 104ff.

61 West German historiography has in most cases attempted a rationalisation on the basis of the Bad Godesberg programme of 1959; cp. Miller, op. cit., p. 298. Steinberg, op. cit., p. 124, views the history of German Social Democracy between 1890 and 1914 as the increasing emancipation from theory, and p. 145 claims that the SPD was grounded in the Wilhelmine Reich and its institutions. Saul, op. cit., p. 21, argues that the party was one of the most important stabilising factors in the country, and Ritter, op. cit., p. 150, regards the differences between the bourgeois and socialist worlds as minimal. The tendency to define and re-define the dominant 'isms' of the period – *Revisionismus, Reformismus, Kautskyanismus*, the *Praktizismus* of Auer and Molkenbuhr (Steinberg, op. cit., p. 124) – serves merely to categorise what was in fact an organic process, and to cloud the all-important fact that what united the pre-war SPD was much greater than what divided it.

62 This is the predominant view as expressed in DDR historiography. Cp., for example, *Geschichte der deutschen Arbeiterbewegung 1871–1914* (Berlin, 1966–7); Helmut Hesselbarth, *Revolutionäre Sozialdemokraten, Opportunisten und die Bauern am Vorabend des Imperialismus* (Berlin, 1968); Kurt Stenkewitz, *Gegen Bajonett und Dividende* (Berlin, 1960).

63 Social and political unrest was marked by serious street riots in the Moabit part of Berlin in 1910, a miners' strike in 1912 and vigorous repression through the courts. Ullrich, op. cit., p. 136, makes the point that some of the best paid and most highly qualified metalworkers in the First World War – those who had everything to gain from an accommodation with the state

– were precisely those who played a leading part in the revolutionary cadres of 1918–19. At the same time, the party executive reaffirmed in January 1913 that members should ignore all court functions, and the entire party remained seated for the traditional 'Kaiserhoch' in May 1914; Groh, op. cit., p. 543, note 314.

64 Gerhard Masur, *Imperial Berlin* (London, 1971), p. 72, is typical of this dismissive attitude, when he refers to the socialist press of the period as 'lifeless and dogmatic', and he passes over SPD journalism in scarcely more than a sentence. The work of Klausjürgen Miersch, *Die Arbeiterpresse der Jahre 1869 bis 1889 als Kampfmittel der österreichischen Sozialdemokratie* (Vienna, 1969), is practically the only study which attempts to point to the rôle of the press in a purely agitatory context, and which relates the development of the press to the internal history of a socialist party. Regional studies of the Wilhelmine SPD usually take account of the local press and reference will be made to these wherever relevant. The 1920s produced a number of university dissertations in this field, chiefly Anton Dang, *Die sozialdemokratische Presse Deutschlands* (Diss. Frankfurt a.M., 1928) and Elfriede Fischer, *Grundlagen der Interpretation der Politik der deutschen Sozialdemokratie durch die sozialdemokratische Presse* (Diss. Heidelberg, 1928). Also of use, although somewhat negative in its general conclusions, is Ludwig Kantorowicz, *Die sozialdemokratische Presse Deutschlands* (Tübingen, 1922). There are also the valuable studies of Kurt Koszyk, *Anfänge und frühe Entwicklung der sozialdemokratischen Presse im Ruhrgebiet 1875–1908* (Dortmund, 1953); idem, *Deutsche Presse im 19. Jahrhundert* (Berlin, 1966), and the bibliographical survey, *Die Presse der deutschen Sozialdemokratie* (Hannover, 1967). On a more general level, the encyclopaedic work of Otto Groth, *Die Zeitung* (Mannheim and Berlin, 1928) gave rise to the study of journalism as a science (Zeitungswissenschaft). Peter de Mendelssohn, *Zeitungsstadt Berlin* (Berlin, 1959), provides an account of the teeming centre of the German newspaper publishing industry; Curt Erler, *Von der Macht der Presse in Deutschland* (Berlin, 1911) and Wernecke, op. cit., are specialist studies of the influence of the press on contemporary affairs. Rieger, op. cit., includes a useful section on the development of the SPD press. The origins of a repressive government policy against political dissidents are examined in Hans-Wolfgang Wetzel, *Presseinnenpolitik im Bismarkreich 1874–1890* (Bern and Frankfurt a.M., 1975).

65 According to Ferdinand Tönnies, *Der Kampf um das Sozialistengesetz* (Berlin, 1929), p. 60, 'its exaggeration and distortion of the facts to the point of the grotesque was a reality which could not be denied'.

66 Cp. Lidtke, op. cit., p. 8off.

67 Amongst the editorial leadership were Georg von Vollmar and Eduard Bernstein who, interestingly enough in the light of their later development, had to be restrained in some of their radical excesses by Engels; cp. *Eduard Bernsteins Briefwechsel mit Friedrich Engels*, ed. Helmut Hirsch (Assen, 1970), p. 160. The *Sozialdemokrat* had to be smuggled into Germany and relied on an illegal but highly efficient distribution system; cp. Ernst Engelberg, *Revolutionäre Politik und Rote Feldpost 1878–1890* (Berlin, 1959).

68 Cp. the wealth of documentation in StA Marburg, Bestand 165, Nr 3142. On the complexities of the combination laws and local police regulations, see pp. 51–64, Social Democracy in Conflict with the Law. At the 1893 party conference, Auer declared that the 'forcible dissolution of our

meetings and the restrictions placed in our path by the police authorities have done a great deal to cut down our work via the spoken word'; PT Cologne 1893, p. 109. Cp. also the comments of the party executive, PT Frankfurt 1894, p. 25, and Auer's speech in 1903 on the way in which an extensive network of party newspapers at the local level was supplanting the system of peripatetic demagogues and agents the party had used hitherto; PT Dresden 1903, p. 427.

69 Quoted in Rolf Engelsing, *Massenpublikum und Journalistentum im 19. Jahrhundert in Nordwestdeutschland* (Berlin, 1966), p. 88.

70 The party executive was firmly of the opinion that 'the first and most important means of agitation we possess is the press'; PT Erfurt 1891, p. 47. Cp. also PT Halle 1890, p. 231ff., PT Berlin 1892, p. 88, and the speeches of Auer, PT Cologne 1893, p. 109, Schoenlank, p. 115, and Pfannkuch, PT Breslau 1895, p. 36; also the views of Adolf Braun as quoted in Kantorowicz, op. cit., p. 1. On the importance of propaganda through the press in relation to the party's total effectiveness, see especially Kautsky's letter to Victor Adler, dated 27 November 1901, in *Adlers Briefwechsel*, op. cit., p. 384.

71 Quoted in Dang, op. cit., p. 12.

72 PT Erfurt 1891, p. 206. This subordination of the Reichstag to the total impact achieved by means of the party's written propaganda was underlined in a series of articles which Franz Mehring wrote for the *Chemnitzer Volksstimme* in May 1914. Extracts from these articles are printed in *Dokumente der deutschen Arbeiterbewegung zur Journalistik*, Teil II *1900–1945* (Leipzig, 1963); Part I, dealing with the period between the *Vormärz* and 1905 (Leipzig, 1961), includes p. 162ff. extracts from debates and business discussions on the rôle and importance of the party press, taken from the various annual party conferences. In contrast, one of the party's leading journalists, Kurt Eisner, was not convinced of the absolute supremacy of the press; cp. Eisner, *Taggeist* (Berlin, 1901), p. 126ff.

73 Cp. especially the views of Richard Calwer, *Sozialistische Monatshefte*, September 1901, pp. 699–704. The same journal complained in 1907 that party newspapers were too large and bulky, and that a working-man needed several hours to cope with the *Vorwärts* or *Leipziger Volkszeitung*; time which he could ill afford. However, the *Monatshefte* were widely regarded as being far from socialist; cp. Arthur Stadthagen's attack, PT Munich 1902, p. 137.

74 Cp. Scheidemann, PT Jena 1913, p. 226.

75 Cp. the article of the chief editor of the *Volksblatt für Halle*, reprinted in *Echo*, 6 September 1899, with the accompanying marginalia of Hamburg's Polizeidirektor, StA Hamburg, Senat, Cl VII Lit Me No 12 Vol 18 Fasc 7 Inv 12. An article by Julian Borchardt in *Die neue Zeit* (hereafter NZ), 1901–2, II, Nr 3, p. 72, referred to the need for the party press to repair the damage resulting from the educational inadequacies of the elementary schools.

76 Cp. the commentary of Arno Franke in NZ, 1913–14, I, Nr 1, p. 22.

77 PT Erfurt 1891, p. 92.

78 Quoted in *Echo*, 24 February 1892.

79 Report for 1909, p. 21, in StA Bremen, 4, 14–XII, C.2.bb.1; also in StA Münster, Reg. Münster, Abt VII, Nr 44a.

80 StA Münster, Reg. Münster, Abt VII, Nr 62r; report dated 18 December 1913, p. 25.

81 *Die Sozialdemokratie im Urteile ihrer Gegner* (Berlin, 1911), a copy of which is in BA Koblenz, Z Sg 1–90/24(1).
82 Op. cit., p. 104.
83 Op. cit., p. 108.
84 PT Bremen 1904, p. 143. Paul Singer made much the same sort of comment, PT Essen 1907, p. 268.
85 Heinrich Braun, *Die sozialdemokratische Presse* (Berlin, 1896), p. 31.
86 Kurt Baschwitz, *Du und die Masse* (Amsterdam, 1959), p. 66.
87 *Echo*, 7 February 1893; article entitled 'Englands Panama'. 'Scandal is at home in its columns . . . day after day these do service as a court of judgment on capitalism and industrial enterprise'; Braun, op. cit., p. 94.
88 *Adlers Briefwechsel*, op. cit., p. 225.
89 NZ, 1891–2, I, Nr 3, p. 68.
90 NZ, 1891–2, II, Nr 38, p. 353.
91 NZ, 1895–6, II, Nr 44, p. 556.
92 NZ, 1903–4, II, Nr 41, p. 451.
93 NZ, 1907–8, II, Nr 36, p. 316. Cp. also *Leipziger Volkszeitung*, 28 November 1903, reprinted in *Franz Mehring. Politische Publizistik 1891 bis 1904*, ed. Josef Schleifstein (Berlin, 1964), pp. 614–16.
94 Tresckow, *Von Fürsten und anderen Sterblichen* (Berlin, 1922), p. 149. A useful survey of some of the more significant blemishes on the surface of Wilhelmine society is given by Helmuth Rogge, 'Affairen im Kaiserreich', *Die politische Meinung*, February 1963, pp. 58–72.
95 PT Berlin 1892, p. 115.
96 Donald Warren Jnr., *The Red Kingdom of Saxony* (The Hague, 1964), p. 35.
97 Cp. the police report, dated 1 January 1897, in StA Bremen, 4, 14–XII. C.2.bb.1.
98 As a result of these and other disclosures, the *Vorwärts* was frequently referred to as 'der rote *Reichs- und Staatsanzeiger*'.
99 Cp. Otto Hammann, *Der neue Kurs* (Berlin, 1918), pp. 158–9.
100 *Vorwärts*, 18 October 1911.
101 They were often far from being so. Cp. Hall, op. cit.
102 Quoted in *Berliner Volkszeitung*, 3 July 1913.
103 According to *Berliner Volkszeitung*, 14 December 1904, more than 1,500 newspapers and periodicals were being published in Berlin, including some 50 political papers and no less than 28 journals devoted to the arts.
104 Cp. *Ein Leben für das politische Buch*, ed. Gustav Schmidt-Küster (Hannover, 1963), for a survey of Dietz' publishing career. The file kept by the Hamburg political police on Dietz, StA Hamburg, S 6665, includes some useful information.
105 PT Berlin 1892, p. 44.
106 PT Chemnitz 1912, p. 45.
107 Despite the tendency of the authorities to view declining attendances at May Day rallies – often, unless the first of May actually fell on a Sunday, working-people were compelled under threat of dismissal to abstain from celebrating the occasion – as proof of diminishing revolutionary fervour, the 'pull' which such events exercised on the party faithful was still surprisingly strong. In 1900, for example, the Berlin SPD announced over 40 different meetings on May Day, which attracted a total attendance of more than

25,000. By way of contrast, the May Day rally held in London's Crystal Palace was attended by less than 20,000; *Hamburger Fremdenblatt*, 2 May 1900. In 1911 attendances exceeded those for the years 1907–9.

108 *Echo*, 1 May 1900.

109 Cp. the comments of the political police in StA Hamburg, Senat, Cl VII Lit Me No 12 Vol 18 Fasc 7 Inv 8c.

110 For the 1903 Reichstag election campaign, the party in Bremen produced over a period of three weeks a special daily edition of its journal, with an increased circulation, and in 1909 it published a special monthly propaganda paper, *Sozialdemokrat*, which was distributed free, together with numerous other tracts and pamphlets; cp. Engelsing, op. cit., p. 104.

111 This method of operations is described in the report dated 20 May 1899, of the Regierungspräsident at Kassel to the Ministry of the Interior, StA Marburg, Bestand 165, Nr 706, Bd 3, Bl 708ff.

112 Cp. Hall, op. cit.

113 The *Arbeiter-Radfahrer* increased its circulation from 11,000 in 1902, to 152,000 by 1912, and the Arbeitersängerbund, with a membership of over 150,000, published more than 80 pieces of sheet music devoted to political themes (Tendenzlieder); *Hamburger Nachrichten*, 29 October 1912. The *Deutsche Arbeiter-Sängerzeitung* had a circulation of 112,000 in 1913, only 7,000 fewer than that of the *Arbeiter-Turnzeitung*. These and other valuable statistics are quoted in Dieter Fricke, *Zur Organisation und Tätigkeit der deutschen Arbeiterbewegung 1890–1914* (Leipzig, 1962).

114 The choice of title had in some cases been critical. Several papers founded in the late 1880s, amongst them the *Hamburger Echo*, had been able to avoid the possibility of prosecution under the terms of the anti-socialist legislation, only by seeming as respectable and non-socialist as possible, in appearance as well as editorial policy.

115 Kantorowicz, op. cit., p. 53.

116 Dang, op. cit., p. 16.

117 This latter publication encountered considerable disapproval from within the party. Founded in 1895 by the 24-year-old Joseph Bloch, it was widely regarded as being arch-revisionist in its editorial policy. Bebel himself launched an attack on it during the 1902 party conference, because it refused to subject itself to any form of party control. In a letter to Luise Kautsky in September 1910, Bebel referred to it as 'the paper for salon socialists . . . for party stultification'; *August Bebels Briefwechsel mit Karl Kautsky*, ed. Karl Kautsky Jnr. (Amsterdam, 1971), p. 236.

118 Quoted by Friedrich Stampfer, *Erfahrungen und Erkenntnisse* (Cologne, 1957), p. 27.

119 Ebert was one notable exception. Although he had worked for the party newspaper in Bremen, his talent was more for statistics than rhetoric. 'Since he was neither well educated, nor intellectually gifted, nor radical, he was not predestined to make a reputation as a sharp-tongued political journalist', Engelsing, op. cit., p. 254.

120 Cp. Elfriede Fischer, op. cit., p. 44.

121 Cp. the views of the party executive as stated in PT Berlin 1892, p. 42. See also the article by Emil Rabold on the conditions appertaining to the vacancy as editor of a party paper, for which he had applied, in *Mitteilungen des Vereins Arbeiterpresse*, 1913, Nr 122.

122 Karl-Ernst Moring, *Die sozialdemokratische Partei in Bremen 1890–1914*

(Diss. Hamburg, 1968), p. 17; also quoted in *Bremer Bürgerzeitung*, 1 May 1970.

123 PT Berlin 1892, p. 121.

124 *Die Post*, 17 January 1904.

125 Kantorowicz, op. cit., p. 99. The *Jahrbuch des Vereins Arbeiterpresse*, III (Berlin, 1914), produced an interesting statistic, which showed that of the 241 journalists employed by the party in 1914, 20 were members of the Reichstag (8.3%), 22 members of the regional parliaments (9.1%), 58 members of local councils (24.7%), and 47 were chairman or members of the executive of local parties (19.5%).

126 Kantorowicz, op. cit., p. 104.

127 Cp. the report of the Oberstaatsanwalt at Dortmund in November 1894 on the system of the Sitzredakteur; Geheimes StA Berlin–Dahlem, Rep 84a, Nr 8469, Bl 294–95.

128 Thus, for example, the Hamburg police kept running files on all the members of the editorial staff of the *Echo*, often including verbatim accounts of speeches delivered at political gatherings, meetings attended outside the city either as a delegate or observer, and a full list of all previous convictions. Cp. especially the files on Hermann Molkenbuhr and Gustav Stengele, StA Hamburg, S 4687 and S 2169 respectively. The political police even went so far as to send one of its officials to record the details of Stengele's funeral in April 1917.

129 Quoted in Waldemar Besson, op. cit., p. 36.

130 The only biography to have appeared to date, based largely on Schoenlank's own diaries, is Paul Mayer, *Bruno Schoenlank 1859–1901* (Hannover, 1971). Friedrich Stampfer, originally the paper's Austrian correspondent, joined the *Leipziger Volkszeitung* in 1900 and records his impressions of working with Schoenlank in Stampfer, op. cit., p. 57.

131 Quoted in Labedz, op. cit., p. 106. Rosa Luxemburg and Konrad Haenisch also contributed articles to the paper.

132 Philipp Scheidemann, *Memoiren eines Sozialdemokraten* (Dresden, 1928), p. 61.

133 One of the few histories of an individual SPD newspaper is by Gert Rückel, *Die Fränkische Tagespost* (Nuremberg, 1964). Other editors of the paper included Emanuel Wurm, Albert Südekum, Alfred Braun and Kurt Eisner.

134 PT Munich 1902, p. 117.

135 Cp. also Steinberg, op. cit., p. 122.

136 PT Hamburg 1897, p. 67.

137 Op. cit., p. 176.

138 Koszyk, *Presse der Sozialdemokratie*, p. 12.

139 The first steps in this direction had been undertaken by the Erfurt party conference in 1891. Earlier that year the Bremen party had set up a 'Zeitungskommission', one of whose later chairmen was Wilhelm Pieck; Moring, op. cit., p. 15.

140 The report was published in *Echo*, 13 September 1894. The annual reports of the committee were regularly published. Cp. also StA Hamburg, S 1365, Bd 25, for matters affecting the *Echo* in general.

141 Stampfer, op. cit., p. 72.

142 This was a professional organisation of all those employed on behalf of the party press, which in 1904, four years after its formation, numbered more than 150 editors and 1,700 technical and administrative staff.

143 Dang, op. cit., pp. 69–70. The results of the survey were published in *Mitteilungen des Vereins Arbeiterpresse*, 1907, Nr 62.

144 PT Berlin 1892, p. 93. The high salary paid to Liebknecht probably reflected his special position within the party. The report compiled by the Berlin political police for 1904–5, a copy of which is in StA Bremen, 4, 14–XII, C.2.bb.1, showed that the members of the editorial staff of the *Vorwärts* were paid between 2,400 and 5,000 marks, and those on the *Echo* between 2,700 and 3,900 marks. The wage paid in 1893 to Ebert as court reporter for the *Bremer Bürgerzeitung* was not sufficient to enable him to support his wife and family and so he resigned; Engelsing, op. cit., p. 248. A breakdown of the annual running costs of the *Volksblatt für Hessen und Waldeck* (later the *Kasseler Volksblatt*), prepared by the Polizeipräsident in Kassel, is in StA Marburg, Bestand 165, Nr 3142, Bl 567. Here an expenditure of 27,860 marks was matched by an income of less than 24,000 marks. Similar figures for the *Bremer Bürgerzeitung* are given by Engelsing, op. cit., pp. 103–4.

145 PT Jena 1905, p. 42.

146 PT Cologne 1893, p. 109. *Unsere Betriebe von 1890 bis 1925* (Berlin, 1926), a copy of which is in the International Institute for Social History, Amsterdam (hereafter IISH), includes full details of annual financial subsidies. An all-time high was reached in 1907, when a sum of 137,866 marks was made available from central funds.

147 PT Essen 1907, p. 68.

148 PT Hamburg 1897, p. 82.

149 Cp. the report of the Berlin political police for 1911, in StA Münster, Reg. Münster, Abt VII, Nr 62r.

150 Kantorowicz, op. cit., p. 62. In the month of December 1900 most of the larger *General-Anzeiger* publications had an income of between 20,000 and 100,000 marks from advertising alone; Koszyk, *Deutsche Presse*, p. 272.

151 Thus, the Regierungspräsident at Arnsberg complained in November 1896 to the Minister of the Interior, 'It is deplorable that this dangerous weapon [the press] is only kept on a viable footing by the support given to it through advertising by Jewish businesses'; StA Marburg, Bestand 165, Nr 706, Bd 2, Bl 640.

152 Dang, op. cit., p. 31.

153 Jürgen Jensen, *Presse und Politische Polizei* (Hannover, 1966), p. 19.

154 Koszyk, ibid.

155 The first break with this system came with the appearance of *Die B.Z. am Mittag* in 1904, based as it was entirely on the principle of street-pavement selling.

156 The *Hamburger Nachrichten*, 3 October 1912, estimated this to approximate to a readership of 250,000.

157 In the period 1890–1914, the number of trade union papers increased from 41 to 50, and the circulation from 201,000 to 2,665,000. The largest single circulation was held by the paper of the metalworkers union, the *Metallarbeiterzeitung*, which sold almost 600,000 copies by 1913. These and other statistics are in Fricke, op. cit., *passim*. Cp. also Ernst Drahn, *Die deutsche Sozialdemokratie* (Berlin, 1926), p. 30.

158 The *Essener Arbeiterzeitung*, 1 March 1910, reported that it had increased its circulation by 1,600 in the previous five months, of which 600 alone were accounted for after a single week of concerted agitation. House-to-house visits also yielded results; cp. the report of the Regierungspräsident at

Arnsberg, dated 1 November 1912, p. 18, in StA Münster, Reg. Münster, Abt VII, Nr 62r. The *Echo*, 21 November 1906, explicitly stated that every court case against the paper merely resulted in new subscribers. In its edition for 6 April 1910, it proudly reported, for the benefit of merchant sailors, that regular copies of the paper were also available at the Hongkew Club in Shanghai.

159 Cp. especially the views of Heinrich Stubbe, the Hamburg delegate to the 1913 party conference, PT Jena 1913, pp. 251–2.

160 Dang, op. cit., p. 21. This sorry state of affairs continued until well after the end of the First World War.

161 PT Stuttgart 1898, p. 119. The party treasurer Gerisch maintained that if gains made by the SPD in the 1903 election were to be consolidated, the number of subscribers would need to approximate to one-third of the total votes cast; PT Bremen 1904, p. 156. There were, of course, enormous regional variations. In Mannheim, 45.3% of the SPD electorate in 1907 took the *Volksstimme*, and in Magdeburg, a survey conducted by the local party showed that of some 4,000 members in 1912, only 3% did not subscribe to the local paper; Dang, op. cit., p. 40. A survey carried out in 1906 showed that of some 50,000 Social Democrats in Berlin, about 90% claimed to read the party press; Fricke, op. cit., p. 134. In 1907, the *Bremer Bürgerzeitung* had twice as many subscribers as the party had official members, and more than two-thirds of all SPD voters also subscribed to the party press; Engelsing, op. cit., p. 105.

162 Quoted in the report of the Berlin political police for 1904–5, in StA Bremen, 4, 14–XII, C.2.bb.1.

163 Cp. his article in *Leipziger Volkszeitung*, 3 September 1907.

164 As a consequence, those papers which had hitherto published Reichstag debates three or four dates late were only a day behind; Koszyk, *Anfänge*, p. 140.

165 Cp. the proceedings of the 1901 regional party conference for the province, a copy of which is in StA Hamburg, S 2392. By 1914 the Wolff agency had some 40 branch-offices throughout Germany.

166 For details see PT Essen 1907, p. 176 and 341–4; also Koszyk, op. cit., p. 141. The *Vorwärts*, 27 August 1907, devoted a long article to the project.

167 PT Chemnitz 1912, p. 40.

168 Stampfer, op. cit., pp. 73 and 93.

169 Op. cit., p. 94.

170 A valuable source of information on the party's material for propaganda, the *Partei-Correspondenz*, enlisted the help of party workers throughout Germany in sending in information and items of note from the bourgeois press. It regularly had a circulation in excess of 40,000, but required considerable financial support. Between 1910 and 1913, it accounted for more than 110,000 marks from central funds; Koszyk, op. cit., p. 141.

171 An article by Karski on the Zabern affair was reprinted from the *Sozial-demokratische Korrespondenz* by six other SPD papers with a total circulation of 110,000, and earned its author a prison sentence of three months; cp. Groh, op. cit., p. 202ff. and Josef Schleifstein, *Franz Mehring* (Berlin, 1959), p. 298.

172 For the background to this case, see the report of the Polizeipräsident in Essen, dated 26 November 1910, in Hauptstaatsarchiv (hereafter HStA) Düsseldorf, Reg. Düsseldorf 42798.

173 Dated 7 March 1911, ibid. The Regierungspräsident at Düsseldorf described the bureau in December 1911 as 'a significant development towards furthering agitation', HStA Düsseldorf, Reg. Köln, 7690, Bl 41.

174 Cp. p. 15 of the report, dated 18 December 1913, sent to the Ministry of the Interior by the Regierungspräsident in Düsseldorf, StA Münster, Abt VII, Nr 62r.

175 Richard Fischer, writing in December 1905, to an unnamed party colleague, commented that the central executive and the party leadership in Berlin had decided 'to get rid of the so-called revisionist majority in the editorial offices of the paper'; *Bebels Briefwechsel*, op. cit., p. 329. For Stampfer's views on the crisis, see Stampfer, op. cit., p. 109ff. Adolph, op. cit., p. 18ff. emphasises the extent to which the crisis grew out of a determination by the Berlin Presse-Commission to exert more influence.

176 PA/AA, Europa Generalia Nr 82, Nr 14, Bd 7, letter dated 1 November 1905.

177 *Vorwärts*, 24 October 1905.

178 *Vorwärts*, 7 November 1905.

179 *Vorwärts*, 10 November 1905.

180 *Der Vorwärts-Konflikt. Gesammelte Aktenstücke* (Munich, 1905), a copy of which is in BA Koblenz, Z Sg 1–90/45(10).

181 The *Echo*, 2 and 10 November 1905, for instance, although accepting the grounds for dissatisfaction with the *Vorwärts* and condemning the undignified exit of the six, was saddened that the recent expressions of party unity at the Jena conference had been of no avail, and that the crisis had provided the occasion for outbursts of '*Schadenfreude*' from the bourgeois press. Cp. also NZ 1905–6, 1, Nr 9, p. 273ff. Significantly, in terms of the pull of party unity, none of the six failed to secure re-employment within the party press.

182 Already in the winter of 1910–11 extreme radical members of the central organ of the Württemberg socialists, the *Schwäbische Tagwacht*, had been excluded; Groh, op. cit., p. 200.

183 For background to this affair, cp. Otto Ernst Schüddekopf, 'Der Revolution entgegen: Materialien und Dokumente zur Geschichte des linken Flügels der deutschen Sozialdemokratie vor dem 1. Weltkrieg', *Archiv für Sozialgeschichte*, IX (Hannover, 1969), pp. 451–97; Groh, op. cit., p. 200ff.; Hannelore Schlemmer, *Die Rolle der Sozialdemokratie in den Landtagen Badens und Württembergs und ihr Einfluß auf die Entwicklung der Gesamtpartei zwischen 1890 und 1914* (Diss. Freiburg i.B., 1953), p. 119ff. – who tends to exaggerate the importance of personal differences – and the excellent analysis given by Moring, op. cit., pp. 177–86.

184 The *Bremer Bürgerzeitung*, 1 June 1912, which described the affair as 'a party scandal of the first order' and the *Leipziger Volkszeitung*, 4 June 1912, were foremost in criticising the action of the party leadership. Bebel, while agreeing about the scandalous proportions of the row, had characteristically pungent comments to make on the participants, as well as castigating the party executive's 'pussy-footedness'; cp. his letter to Luise Kautsky, dated 10 June 1912, in *Bebels Briefwechsel*, op. cit., p. 302.

CHAPTER 2

1 For a detailed examination of the way in which these bulwarks were expected to, and succeeded in, stemming the ever-increasing tide of socialist agitation, cp. Klaus Saul, 'Der Staat und die "Mächte des Umsturzes"', *Archiv für Sozialgeschichte*, Bd XII (1972), pp. 293-350.

2 Like the administration, the courts operated according to a strictly hierarchical structure. The local Amtsgericht was the smallest judicial unit, equivalent to the petty sessions. Its powers of sentencing were not large, and more substantial cases were invariably referred to the Landesgericht, which also acted as an appellate court for the Amtsgericht. In turn, appeals from the Landgericht were heard by one of 13 different Oberlandesgerichte throughout Prussia. The final appeal stage for the whole Reich was the Reichsgericht, the Imperial Supreme Court in Leipzig, although each of the states also had its own highest judicial authority. In Prussia, for example, this was called the Kammergericht. Other courts which diverged from this normal pattern were the Schöffengerichte, which provided for an element of lay-judge participation, and the Schwurgerichte (jury-courts). To emphasise the close alliance of interests between the state prosecutor's office (Staatsanwaltschaft) and the judicial authorities, I have used the word 'judicature', as distinct from the narrower meaning ascribed to 'judiciary'.

3 Haase's speech to the party conference at Mannheim on 29 September 1906 is quoted in Ernst Haase, *Hugo Haase* (Berlin, 1929), p. 207. Cp. also Otto Kirchheimer, *Political Justice* (Princeton, N.J., 1961), on related aspects of this problem.

4 PA/AA, Europa Generalia Nr 82 secr. Nr 1, Bd 9, memorandum dated 25 June 1890.

5 Herrfurth's recommendations were incorporated in a directive sent out by the Ministry of the Interior on 18 July 1890, a copy of which is in StA Hamburg, Senat, Cl I Lit T Nr 7 Vol 6 Fasc 11b Inv 9. Cp. also Karl Frohme, *Politische Polizei und Justiz im monarchischen Deutschland* (Hamburg, 1926), p. 73. In order to ensure the absolute dependability of all executive forces, Herrfurth also gave instructions that the Regierungspräsidenten were to be responsible for checking the personal particulars of all police employees.

6 Caprivi's submissions to the Ministry of State, dated 4 July 1890, are in GStA Berlin-Dahlem, Rep 84a, Nr 8463, Bl 239-40. At the meeting of the Ministry of State on 13 July, there was broad general agreement for a policy of active discrimination through the courts. The minutes are in op. cit., Bl 243-6.

7 The draft of Schelling's circular is in op. cit., Bl 250-1. The final text, which on Schelling's instructions was not to be cyclostyled but – for reasons of maximum secrecy – to be copied out by hand, is given by Richard Lipinski, *Die Sozialdemokratie von ihren Anfängen bis zur Gegenwart* (Berlin, 1928), Bd II, pp. 136-7.

8 GStA Berlin-Dahlem, op. cit., Bl 268-9.

9 The Eulenburg decree, dated 29 July 1893, is in PA/AA, Europa Generalia Nr 82, Nr 1, Bd 12. Its contents were quickly communicated to all lower administrative echelons; cp. StA Osnabrück, Dep 3bI, Nr 436, Bl 108-11. On the decree itself, cp. Hellmut Hesselbarth, *Revolutionäre Sozialdemokraten, Opportunisten und die Bauern am Vorabend des Imperialismus*

(Berlin, 1968), p. 170ff. Cp. also Eulenburg's views on the continuing legal battle against the SPD, contained in a memorandum to Schelling dated 30 December 1893, in GStA Berlin-Dahlem, Rep 84a, Nr 8464, Bl 21–5.

10 For an analysis of the Arons affair, cp. Dieter Fricke, 'Zur Militarisierung des deutschen Geisteslebens im wilhelminischen Deutschland. Der Fall Leo Arons', ZfGW 1960, Nr 5, p. 1069ff.; also Fritz K. Ringer, *The Decline of the German Mandarins* (Cambridge, Mass., 1969), p. 141ff. and Susanne Miller, op. cit., p. 259. Additional information is contained in *Die Aktenstücke des Disziplinarverfahrens gegen den Privatdozent Dr. Arons* (Berlin, 1900).

11 Cp. Fritz K. Ringer, 'Higher Education in Germany in the 19th Century', *Journal of Contemporary History*, 1967, 3, p. 124.

12 No Social Democrat was appointed to any professorial position in the period before 1918.

13 Fricke, op. cit., p. 1086. The case had occupied the attention of the Ministry of State the previous winter.

14 This was the first attempt since Bismarck's 'Arnimparagraph' to create a piece of legislation tailor-made for a given situation. The 'Arnimparagraph' was §353a of the *Strafgesetzbuch*, and had been introduced in February 1872 as Bismarck's answer to the legal battle he was engaged in pursuing against the former German ambassador in Paris; cp. Rogge, op. cit., pp. 60–1.

15 Cp. Ernst Rudolf Huber, *Nationalstaat und Verfassungsstaat* (Stuttgart, 1965), p. 150. The system of justice, ideally *ratio scripta* thus ended up becoming *res publica scripta*; cp. Ernst Fraenkel, *Zur Soziologie der Klassenjustiz und Aufsätze zur Verfassungskrise 1931–32* (Darmstadt, 1968), p. 7.

16 Huber, op. cit., p. 163. Reports from many different countries flowed into the headquarters of the Berlin police and, via the heads of the various legations of the German states, to individual police departments throughout Germany. In the early 1890s there were always three police spies in London; cp. Dieter Fricke, *Bismarcks Prätorianer. Die Berliner politische Polizei im Kampf gegen die deutsche Arbeiterbewegung 1871–1898* (Berlin, 1962), p. 286. The Berlin police department was also responsible for compiling the annual reports on the state of the Social Democratic movement.

17 Leopold Henning, 'Das Wesen und die Entwicklung der politischen Polizei in Berlin', *Mitteilungen des Vereins für die Geschichte Berlins*, 1925, Nr 7–9, p. 89. Administrators frequently headed major police departments; von Windheim, Polizeipräsident in Berlin 1895–1902, had previously been Oberpräsident in East Prussia and his successor, von Borries, had a record of public service in Westphalia. For an analysis of the functions of the political police, cp. Gustav Roscher, *Großstadtpolizei* (Hamburg, 1912), pp. 154–9.

18 Willy Feigell, *Die Entwicklung des Königlichen Polizei-Präsidiums zu Berlin in der Zeit von 1809 bis 1909* (Berlin, 1909), p. 51. The second largest police authority in the country, at Hamburg, employed 4,300 persons.

19 Cp. J. C. G. Röhl, 'Higher Civil Servants in Germany 1890–1900', *Journal of Contemporary History*, 1967, 3, pp. 101–21. A quarter of all men appointed to public office had taken a doctorate in law.

20 Quoted in *Recht, Verwaltung und Politik im neuen Deutschland*, eds. Alfred Bozi & Hugo Heinemann (Stuttgart, 1916), p. 22. Alfred Apfel, a middle-class Jew who was refused officer entry into the army, gives some colourful impressions of his legal training in *Behind the Scenes of German*

Justice (London, 1935), p. 20. The lectures he found 'positively appalling. They purveyed to us an unintelligible litter of formulae, a completely indigestible muddle of petty details of Roman and Germanic law.'

21 Wolfgang Runge, *Politik und Beamtentum im Parteienstaat* (Stuttgart, 1965), pp. 170–1.

22 Otto Hintze, 'Der Beamtenstand', *Gesammelte Abhandlungen II* (Göttingen, 1962), p. 103.

23 Cp. *Sozialgeschichtliches Arbeitsbuch: Materialien zur Statistik des Kaiserreiches 1870–1914*, eds. Gerd Hohorst, Jürgen Kocka & Gerhard A. Ritter (Munich, 1975), p. 168ff.

24 *Fünfzig Jahre Preußischer Justiz 1851–1901*, ed. Friedrich Holtze (Berlin, 1901), p. 30.

25 If a convicted person signed the written verdict of the first court, as many were deliberately induced to do, there was no possibility of an appeal; the signature was an acceptance of both conviction and sentence. Between 1886 and 1898, the highest annual rate of successful appeals by state prosecutors against judgments in lower courts was 62.6%, and the lowest 52.8%. In the period between 1898 and 1908 the corresponding figures were 70.6% and 62%, and in the decade 1908–18 75.6% and 60.4%. The composition of the Reichsgericht tended to emphasise the enormous shaping influence of Prussian law. In the period 1886–1921 all four supreme state prosecutors (*Oberreichsanwälte*) were Prussians, and of the four presiding chairmen of the court between 1879 and 1920, three were Prussians and the fourth, who came from Württemberg, only held office between 1903 and 1905; Adolf Lobe, *Fünfzig Jahre Reichsgericht* (Leipzig, 1929), p. 184.

26 In the years leading up to 1907, of the 5,070 lay-judges and jurors who had been called upon to assist in the processes of the law in Hamburg, the working class had been represented only once, by a chimney-sweep's apprentice; Saul, *Staat*, p. 210.

27 Erich Kuttner, *Warum versagt die Justiz?* (Berlin, 1921), p. 29ff.

28 *Preußische Jahrbücher*, Bd 81 (1895), quotes the concluding remarks of one such judge: 'I hereby ask you to take note of the fact that you should find the accused guilty.' NZ, 1894–5, II, Nr 41, commented that this particular article needed to be reproduced – as indeed it was to be in a larger number of cases – right through the SPD press.

29 NZ, 1904–5, II, Nr 39.

30 NZ, 1906–7, II, Nr 37. Cp. also the editorial on the absence of Habeas Corpus in Germany, *Echo*, 12 November 1902.

31 His essay, 'Zur Genesis des Königlich Preußischen Reserveoffiziers', in Eckart Kehr, *Der Primat der Innenpolitik*, ed. H.-U. Wehler, 2nd edit. (Berlin, 1970), p. 56ff.

32 Between 1879 and 1889, for example, the total number of judges at a lower level (Amtsgericht and Landgericht) increased by only 65, from 3,385 to 3,450, at a time when the population had increased by almost three million; Holtze, op. cit., p. 40.

33 Kehr, op. cit., p. 76.

34 Quoted in Bozi & Heinemann, op. cit., p. 35.

35 Erich Kuttner, *Klassenjustiz* (Berlin, 1913), p. 18.

36 Cp. Haase, op. cit., p. 6ff.

37 Kuttner, op. cit., p. 16, reckoned that a sum of between 30,000 and 50,000 marks was essential before one could hope for an appointment as a minor

judge. Fraenkel, op. cit., p. 10, claims that not until a qualified man reached the age of at least 35 was he likely to be given a permanent pensionable post. Cp. also Saul, *Staat*, op. cit., p. 194.

38 Fraenkel, ibid., makes the point that only those who had twice learned to obey their superiors – as state prosecutors and as reserve army officers – were accepted into the highest echelons.

39 Bozi & Heinemann, op. cit., p. 48. Similarly, the 15 Catholic chairmen of Landgericht courts compared rather unfavourably with their 81 Protestant colleagues in Prussia. As against the 13 senior state prosecutors (Oberstaatsanwälte) who were Protestant, only 2 were of the Catholic faith.

40 Cp. Hamburger, op. cit., pp. 44, 51 and 65.

41 *Preußische Jahrbücher*, Bd 81 (1895), p. 25, thought it was possible to claim that 'in Prussia the administration of justice is in the hands of the state prosecutor, mitigated only by the right of veto of the courts in cases of extravagant demands by the former'. It was perhaps the final irony that senior judges were appointed without exception from the ranks of prosecuting counsel.

42 Werner Roscher, *Vaterstadt und Elternhaus* (Limited Edition, Hamburg, 1959), p. 12.

43 Quoted in Röhl, *Bismarck*, p. 126.

44 An undated entry in Hohenlohe's diary, most probably from the second week of December 1894, referred in despairing tones to the conflict with the Reichstag and the opportunities presented to the SPD, arising from the government's intention to introduce the anti-subversion bill (*Umsturzvorlage*); Hohenlohe, op. cit., p. 21.

45 Quoted in Saul, *Staat*, p. 202, note 171.

46 The Kaiser, for instance, was furious at the decision of the Prussian constitutional court (Oberverwaltungsgericht) in 1895, which reversed a decision of the Polizeipräsident in Berlin, forbidding performances of Hauptmann's *Die Weber*.

47 Karl Erich Born, op. cit., p. 136, in my view over-stresses the strains within the judiciary, and I can find no justification for his assertion that state prosecutors were afraid of being let down by the judges.

48 Weller, op. cit., p. 109.

49 GStA Berlin-Dahlem, Rep 84a, Nr 8464, Bl 16–17, report dated 25 April 1892.

50 Cp. GStA Berlin-Dahlem, Rep 84a, Nr 8469, esp. Bl 98ff. This did not, of course, prevent the existing law from being rigorously applied. Count Dönhoff reported to Caprivi in July 1894 that the authorities in Dresden continued to work energetically against the SPD. More than 150 members of the local party, who had taken part in a May Day rally banned by the police, were sentenced to severe fines and their leaders to terms of imprisonment. Similarly, the 42 delivery agents of the *Sächsische Arbeiterzeitung*, responsible for distributing an issue which contained an appeal for the boycott of a local brewery, were also fined; PA/AA, Europa Generalia, Nr 82 Nr 1, Nr 1, Bd 4, report dated 8 July 1894.

51 StA Hamburg, Senat, Cl VII Lit Me No 12 Vol 18 Fasc 7 Inv 9, Roscher's report dated 19 October 1896. This document also reveals a great deal about the attitude of at least the Hamburg authorities to the development of the ideological schism within the SPD. Roscher argued that it was the concentrated external pressure on the party which was largely responsible for its

bitter attacks on the state; the lessening of this pressure might well result in the movement becoming increasingly occupied with internal theoretical discussions and personal disagreements. The arrest of continued socialist successes, as Roscher thought likely, did not, however, take place, and his colleague Rosalowsky's view, some 15 months later, points to the impossibility of winning over the loyalty of the SPD electorate, no matter how many 'crumbs of comfort' were offered; StA Hamburg, op. cit., Inv 10c, report dated 11 January 1898.

52 The Minister of Justice had to inform Bülow in October 1906 that there was no way of ensuring a conviction against the *Vorwärts* on the basis of an inflammatory article it had recently published; *Archivalische Forschungen zur Geschichte der deutschen Arbeiterbewegung*, ed. Leo Stern, Bd 2/II (Berlin 1956), p. 244. In much the same way, the Oberstaatsanwalt in Kiel had occasion to complain in 1902 that a recent distribution of propaganda leaflets had provided no grounds for proceeding against the party; GStA Berlin-Dahlem, Rep 84a, Nr 8465, Bl 322.

53 Lidtke, op. cit., p. 253.

54 Gert Rückel, *Die Fränkische Tagespost* (Nuremberg, 1964), p. 54.

55 Cp. Frohme, op. cit., p. 108ff. and Ernst Drahn, *Die deutsche Sozialdemokratie* (Munich, 1926), p. 32. The considerable fear of repercussions for the nationalities problem – those put on trial were also accused of distributing Latvian pamphlets – is shown by internal government reactions; cp. the file on the Königsberg case in GStA Berlin-Dahlem, Rep 84a, Nr 11751.

56 Bebel had pointed to such practices in a Reichstag speech in March 1902, but had failed to elicit a comment from the government. Cp. Frohme, op. cit., p. 109, and Lipinski, op. cit., p. 199.

57 By some curious slip in translation, reciprocity had not been guaranteed; Lipinski, op. cit., p. 200.

58 The trial revealed to a large extent the nature of political repression and social misery under the imperial régime in Russia, and contributed in no small measure to the strength of anti-Russian feeling in the SPD in 1914. The party took advantage of the propaganda opportunities to produce a cheap edition of the stenographic proceedings of the trial, edited by Kurt Eisner. For comment on the implications of the trial cp. NZ, 1903–4, II, Nr 44, and 1904–5, I, Nr 23.

59 PT Bremen 1904, p. 144.

60 A circular from the Ministry of the Interior in November 1894, referred to the way in which the Arbeiter-Turnvereine were being used as a subterfuge for political activity; StA Marburg, Bestand 165, Nr 706, Bd 2, Bl 113–14. The party papers at Elberfeld-Barmen and Solingen published in November 1895 the text of a government circular calling for increased vigilance and regular confidential reports on the state of these associated party activities.

61 Cp. the evident satisfaction as expressed by the Regierungspräsident at Arnsberg, in StA Marburg, op. cit., Bl 556.

62 For measures taken against the socialist youth movement, cp. Walter Sieger, *Das erste Jahrzehnt der deutschen Arbeiterbewegung* (Berlin, 1958). In July 1909, the *Vorwärts* published a series of secret documents relating to the control of socialist influence in schools; cp. *Bremer Bürgerzeitung*, 20 July 1909.

63 The case was first brought to light by the *Frankfurter Volksstimme*. In its edition for 2 September 1894, the paper quoted the judgment of the

Amtsgericht – confirmed at a higher level – that the father was content to see his child become 'vaterlandslos, religionsfeindlich und sittenlos'. The *Landrat* at Hanau expressed his pleasure at the outcome of the case; StA Marburg, Bestand 165, Nr 3142, Bl 623, whilst the unfortunate editor of the *Volksstimme* was sentenced to a fine of 200 marks for libelling the *Amtsgericht* judge; *Volksstimme*, 23 November 1894.

64 Cp. the pamphlet by Parvus, *Wohin führt die politische Maßregelung der Sozialdemokratie?* (Dresden, 1897), p. 14ff. and Lipinski, op. cit., p. 133ff.

65 *Breslauer Volkswacht*, 6 November 1910, which also quoted the state prosecutor's official reply; also printed in *Sozialdemokratische Partei-Correspondenz*, 7 January 1911. On the cooperation of the courts in enforcing local bye-laws, cp. the comments of the Regierungspräsident at Kassel, in StA Marburg, Bestand 165, Nr 706, Bd 4, Bl 119.

66 *Vorwärts*, 13 April 1907.

67 Since military patronage was economically rewarding, landlords often did everything they could to rescind such bans, even when they entertained strong socialist sympathies. Cp. the report of the Polizeipräsident at Kassel, dated 14 September 1892, in StA Marburg, Bestand 165, Nr 3142, Bl 150. Martin Kitchen, *The German Officer Corps 1890–1914* (Oxford, 1968), p. 152ff., refers to the efforts of military commanders to arrest the spread of Social Democratic propaganda.

68 *Vorwärts*, 16 February 1911.

69 In the first full year after the Sozialistengesetz, the city witnessed 42 separate confiscations, 76 house-searches and 133 summonses and charges, affecting 91 different members of the party, which all resulted in five years of imprisonment and fines exceeding 16,000 marks. Cp. the speech of the Magdeburg delegate, PT Erfurt 1891, p. 225.

70 Cp. the 10th anniversary copy (Festnummer) of the *Magdeburger Volksstimme*, 1 July 1900, a copy of which is in IISH Amsterdam. For an editorial analysis of the sharp measures against the SPD in Breslau, cp. *Echo*, 19 January 1911.

71 The judge who presided over what came to be known as the 'Gummischlauchprozeß' in May 1894, was committed to a lunatic asylum a few years later. Bebel, writing to Engels, saw nothing but positive gain for the party arising from the case; *Bebels Briefwechsel*, op. cit., p. 764. Indeed, the SPD made a handsome profit out of selling the stenographic proceedings of the trial in pamphlet form. All the nine editors involved were given varying terms of imprisonment; cp. Eugen Ernst, *Polizeispitzeleien und Ausnahmegesetze 1878–1910* (Berlin, 1911), p. 106ff.

72 Cp. Reinhard Höhn, *Die Armee als Erziehungsschule der Nation* (Bad Harzburg, 1963), p. 160. In 1895 Engels commented, 'We the "revolutionaries", the "rebels" – we are thriving far better on legal methods than on illegal ones and rebellion. The parties of order, as they call themselves, are perishing under the legal conditions created by themselves'; quoted in Ryder, op. cit., p. 20.

73 Quoted in Dieter Schuster, *Das preußische Dreiklassenwahlrecht, der politische Streik und die deutsche Sozialdemokratie bis zum Jahr 1914* (Diss. Bonn, 1958), p. 91. In a similar way Wolfgang Heine warned in *Sozialistische Monatshefte*, September 1905, p. 754ff., of the dangers of provoking a government backlash by pressing ahead with demands for a mass strike.

74 In February 1910 the party had been forbidden to hold an open-air meeting in Treptow Park in Berlin, but made it known that it intended to carry out its plans. As a result, almost the entire police force was ordered to Treptow to deal with the demonstration, whilst the party leadership had secretly arranged for the meeting to take place in the Tiergarten. The conservative *Reichsbote*, 8 March 1910, was highly alarmed at the ability of the SPD to defy the authorities in this clandestine manner; and the fury of the Kaiser at the size of the anti-war demonstrations held in the city on 28 July 1914, led him to consider proclaiming a state of emergency and imprisoning the SPD leadership 'tutti quanti', Cp. Egmont Zechlin, 'Bethmann Hollweg, Kriegsrisiko und SPD 1914', *Der Monat*, January 1966, p. 24.

75 Cp. the speech of the Minister for Railways, von Budde, in the Prussian Landtag on 22 February 1903, quoted in *Sozialdemokratische Partei-Correspondenz*, Nr 4, 25 January 1908.

76 Cp. Moring, op. cit., p. 120. Amongst those deprived of their living was Christian Döring, who shortly afterwards joined the editorial staff of the *Echo*. The SPD press, naturally enough, had a field day.

77 Fricke, *Materialien*, p. 272.

78 Röhl, op. cit., p. 112. The uncompromising attitude of Wilhelm II and the monarchs of Saxony and Württemberg emerges clearly in a telegram from the Kaiser to Caprivi, dated 9 September 1894, Zechlin, *Staatsstreichpläne*, pp. 191–2; cp. also p. 193ff. for details of the discussions in the Ministry of State the following month.

79 Hohenlohe, op. cit., p. 47, letter to Grand Duke Friedrich of Baden, dated 5 March 1895.

80 Röhl, op. cit., p. 223.

81 Hohenlohe, op. cit., p. 21. 'It is necessary to proceed against Social Democracy, but only when it gives us reason to do so. Laws against Social Democracy do not help. They lead to a conflict with the Reichstag, to a dissolution and a partial Staatsstreich, and merely increase the power and influence of Social Democracy'.

82 Op. cit., p. 47.

83 GStA Berlin-Dahlem, Rep 84a, Nr 8469, Bl 202–3.

84 StA Hamburg, Hans. Gesandtschaft Berlin, Neuere Reg. PI6b, Bl 11.

85 *Bebels Briefwechsel*, op. cit., p. 793.

86 Lipinski, op. cit., p. 157.

87 *Preußische Jahrbücher*, Bd 82 (1895), p. 138.

88 Cp. *Akten zur Staatlichen Sozialpolitik in Deutschland 1890–1914*, eds. Peter Rassow & Karl Erich Born (Wiesbaden, 1959), p. 63ff.; also Hohenlohe, p. 135 and Ernst, p. 113ff.

89 Röhl, p. 225.

90 PA/AA, Europa Generalia, Nr 82 Nr 1, Nr 1, Bd 5. All the copies of the *Vorwärts* for 2 September 1895 were 'eagerly swept up by sensation-minded people'; Fedor von Zobeltitz, *Chronik der Gesellschaft unter dem letzten Kaiserreich*, 2 vols. (Hamburg, 1922), p. 95.

91 Hohenlohe, p. 92.

92 PA/AA, ibid. With reference to SPD attacks on Wilhelm I, the Kaiser declared that the least disparagement of his grandfather's memory or criticism of his actions had to be regarded as an insult to the whole nation. The course of the official reaction was closely observed by the party press; cp. the editorial 'Der Septemberkurs', in NZ, 1895–6, 1, Nr 6 and *Echo*,

12 September 1895. Such comment merely provoked a harsh response from the courts: the editor of the *Magdeburger Volksstimme*, for example, received a year's imprisonment for his pains. A young middle-class academic, who had dared to criticise the nature of the official campaign against the SPD, was himself convicted under §95, and was forced to abandon his university career in Germany; cp. Friedrich Wilhelm Foerster, *Erlebte Weltgeschichte 1869–1953* (Nuremberg, 1953), p. 120.

93 Cp. Philipp Eulenburg's letter to Hohenlohe, in Hohenlohe, op. cit., p. 97.

94 Op. cit., p. 98.

95 Op. cit., p. 99. A day later, in a letter to Graf zu Solms-Laubach, op. cit., p. 385, Hohenlohe argued that a renewed attempt at combating subversive tendencies through laws of proscription was entirely without prospects. The implication underlying Hohenlohe's considerable personal vacillation was that he was not against such measures *in principle*, but that they stood no chance of success.

96 Cp. *Stenographische Berichte über die Verhandlungen des Preußischen Landtages*, Bd 4, 1896–7, p. 2767ff. On the considerations affecting the contents of the bill, see the comments of the Kaiser on the report from the Prussian legation in Munich to Hohenlohe, dated 19 September 1895, in PA/AA, ibid.

97 *Vorwärts*, 14 May 1897.

98 *Stenographische Berichte*, op. cit., p. 2775.

99 Op. cit., p. 2820.

100 Op. cit., p. 3016.

101 *Vorwärts*, 15 January 1898. Cp. also the commentary in NZ, II, 1897–8, Nr 18.

102 Cp. StA Hamburg, Senatskommission für die Reichs- und Auswärtigen Angelegenheiten, Ältere Reg. CI b 10.

103 Rassow & Born, op. cit., p. 107ff. Cp. the detailed legal discussion by Arthur Stadthagen in NZ, 1898–9, II, Nr 39.

104 Cp. Hohenlohe, op. cit., p. 472 and Röhl, op. cit., p. 262.

105 Hohenlohe, op. cit., p. 508. The background to this bill reveals Hohenlohe as the perfect servant of his political master, attempting wherever possible to persuade the Kaiser of the folly of certain policies, but nonetheless carrying them out to the best of his abilities.

106 Op. cit., p. 532.

107 This section, which remained in force until May 1918, made any attempt at forcing people to join a trade union a criminal offence, which meant that the strike as a weapon was diminished in its potential effectiveness. Agricultural workers, household servants, railway workers and sailors were in any case excluded from the guaranteed right to join a trade union. Cp. NZ 1898–9, I, Nr 1.

108 Cp. Saul, *Staat*, op. cit., p. 193 and p. 211ff. on the combination laws.

109 Quoted in Frohme, op. cit., p. 171.

110 Quoted in Lidtke, op. cit., p. 247.

111 Saul, op. cit., p. 283. The Bund der Landwirte, the Zentralverband deutscher Industrieller and the conservative parties demanded a complete ban on all strike pickets, but the government saw no possibility of securing parliamentary support for this proposal.

112 *Vorwärts*, 15 December 1904.

113 Axel Schnorbus, *Arbeit und Sozialordnung in Bayern vor dem Ersten Weltkrieg* (Munich, 1969), p. 207.
114 Unlike Britain, France and the United States, where real wages in the period 1890–1914 increased by 4%, the comparable figures for Germany are a mere 1%; Wehler, op. cit., p. 53.
115 For background to this affair cp. Helmut Bleiber, 'Die Moabiter Unruhen 1910', ZfGW 1955, Nr 2, p. 173ff.; Frohme, op. cit., p. 164ff.; Saul, op. cit., p. 306ff.
116 *Echo*, 12 January 1911.
117 *Echo*, 6 December 1910. In the following March, the conservative *Reichsbote* demanded that the whole SPD executive be imprisoned, by way of retribution.
118 Saul, op. cit., p. 308.
119 Frohme, op. cit., pp. 164–5.
120 According to the *Echo*, 12 January 1911, the prosecution had lamentably failed to bring evidence for its claim that the Moabit riots were 'a dress-rehearsal for revolution'.
121 Saul, op. cit., p. 201.
122 No information was forthcoming; cp. PT Jena 1911, p. 58 and *Echo*, 8 March 1911
123 Cp. *Archivalische Forschungen*, op. cit., p. 191.
124 Of those cases heard, there were 885 convictions and 372 acquittals; 199 men and 84 women were sentenced to terms of imprisonment totalling 31 years, and 274 men and 148 women were fined more than 16,000 marks; Frohme, op. cit., p. 172. Cp. also NZ, 1911–12, II, Nr 29 and Saul, op. cit., p. 269ff.
125 Friedrich Grimm, *Politische Justiz. Die Krankheit unserer Zeit* (Bonn, 1953), p. 17.
126 Cp. Lipinski, op. cit., p. 160ff.
127 Johannes Schult, *Geschichte der Hamburger Arbeiter 1890–1919* (Hannover, 1967), p. 69.
128 Cp. Ursula Herrmann, 'Der Kampf der Sozialdemokratie gegen das Dreiklassenwahlrecht in Sachsen in den Jahren 1905/6', ZfGW 1955, Nr 6, p. 856ff. Because of the ferocity of the action undertaken by the authorities, the *Sächsische Arbeiterzeitung*, 20 January 1906, advised its readers not to participate in any further demonstrations.
129 Cp. *Archivalische Forschungen*, op. cit., and Dieter Fricke, 'Der Aufschwung der Massenkämpfe der deutschen Arbeiterklasse unter dem Einfluß der russischen Revolution von 1905', ZfGW 1957, Nr 4, p. 770ff.
130 Cp. *Echo*, 11 July 1905.
131 The chief beneficiaries of this law were really the trade unions, who were for the first time enabled to sue in the courts. Perhaps, to pursue a line of argument adopted by Schorske, op. cit., p. 51ff., this is not altogether surprising, since trade unionists were in general somewhat less belligerent than their colleagues in the SPD.
132 Kurt Stenkewitz, *Gegen Bajonett und Dividende* (Berlin, 1960), p. 24. Cp. NZ 1907–8, II, Nr 29, for a critical analysis of the new law.
133 Cp. the furious correspondence arising from the mistaken decision of the *Polizeipräsident* at Kassel to authorise a local meeting; StA Marburg, Bestand 165, Nr 706, Bd 4, Bl 547ff.
134 *Vorwärts*, 21 October 1910.
135 *Hamburger Echo*, 11 May 1912. §105 of the *Strafgesetzbuch* threatened

with a sentence of Zuchthaus anyone who attempted to remove by force a member of a representative assembly.

136 *Echo*, 4 June 1912; see also NZ, 1911–12, II, Nr 33.

137 When their appeals were eventually rejected by the Reichsgericht in May 1913, the *Vorwärts* devoted a stinging editorial to the arbitrary use of such police power.

138 *Magdeburger Volksstimme-Festnummer*, op. cit. The works of the poet Freiligrath were similarly banned in local schools, because of their allegedly socialist contents.

139 *Echo*, 19 July 1892.

140 *Hamburger General-Anzeiger*, 2 October 1900. A copy of the *Reichspresse-gesetz* is in StA Hamburg, S 2170 Bd 20, and Bd 21 contains useful material on the application of this law.

141 According to Erich Schosser, *Presse und Landtag in Bayern von 1850 bis 1918* (Munich, 1968), p. 117, the Bavarian government would have been quite happy, if at all possible, to eliminate the press altogether. For an examination of the relationships between the press and society, see Gerd Heinrich Kemper, *Pressefreiheit und Polizei* (Berlin, 1964); E. P. Oberholtzer, *Die Beziehungen zwischen dem Staat und der Zeitungspresse im Deutschen Reich* (Berlin, 1895); and Peter J. Fliess, *Freedom of the Press in the German Republic 1918–1933* (Baton Rouge, La, 1955), p. 18ff.

142 Only in isolated cases did members of the technical staff face charges arising from the publication of material which contravened the law. A notable instance, however, was the sentence of 18 months passed on a printer with the staff of the anarchist paper *Der Sozialist*; cp. NZ 1893–4, I, Nr 34. Max von Brauchitsch, in *Verwaltungsgesetze für Preußen*, vol IIa, 22nd edit., (Berlin, 1932), p. 474ff., offers a commentary on the 1874 Press Law.

143 Two laws of 1893 and 1914 threatened with severe penalties those responsible for the disclosure of any military information prejudicial to the interests of the state.

144 Cp. Oberholtzer, op. cit., p. 116.

145 Op. cit., p. 119, and Rudolf von Busch, *Die Beschlagnahme von Druckschriften unter besonderer Berücksichtigung der Presse* (Diss. Kiel, 1929).

146 GStA Berlin-Dahlem, Rep 84a, Nr 3932, Bl 131–32: 'Die Aufgabe der Verfolgung ist in erster Linie die möglichst rasche Herbeiführung der Aburteilung.' To ensure the practical success of this principle, Schelling ordered a number of internal administrative measures to speed up the judicial process. It is evident, however, that the courts were beginning to creak under the heavy load of litigation in the early 1890s.

147 Cp. his circular to the *Oberstaatsanwalt* at Osnabrück, dated 9 October 1894, in StA Osnabrück, Rep 335, Nr 13562.

148 Thus, in April 1895, some 51,000 Maifestzeitungen were confiscated from the party bookshop in Berlin – as were similar issues in Dresden, Breslau and many other cities – and only released well after May Day itself, when the point had already been lost; cp. *Echo*, 29 April 1895. There were, however, certain exceptions: police raids on the offices of the *Echo* at the end of August 1913 involved the confiscation of all remaining copies of a particularly acerbic editorial 'Deutschlands Schande', which had appeared in the edition for 27 June. Cp. *Echo*, 31 August 1913.

149 A copy of this register, which included a ban on the stenographic proceed-

ings of the treason trial against Liebknecht, Bebel and Hepner in 1872, is in GStA Berlin-Dahlem, Rep 180, Nr 14441.

150 Cp. Solveig-Maria Braig, *Die Presse um 1900 im Spiegel der Satire* (Diss. Munich, 1954), p. 200ff.

151 Quoted by Wolfgang Heine, in Bozi & Heinemann, op. cit., p. 68. Since all press offences in Bavaria were heard by the Schwurgerichte, that state was spared the epidemic of cases of *lèse-majesté* such as existed in Prussia and Saxony. In Oldenburg, *lèse-majesté* fell under the jurisdiction of the jury-courts, but cases of libel on public servants were heard by the Landgericht. As a result Oldenburg had little of one, but a surfeit of the other.

152 Between 1874 and 1903 there were 14 such cases, and the editors of SPD papers in Kiel and Bochum faced proceedings in 1908 and 1912; cp. Hans Badewitz, *Der Zeugniszwang gegen die Presse* (Munich, 1952), p. 23.

153 Variations on this theme included the offence of 'üble Nachrede' – §183 of the *Strafgesetzbuch* – which related to the use of factual assertions likely to malign the integrity of an individual; cp. Oberholtzer, op. cit., p. 50. Moritz Liepmann, *Die Beleidigung* (Berlin, 1909), offers a reasonably intelligible path through this aspect of the legal undergrowth.

154 GStA Berlin-Dahlem, Rep 84a, Nr 8464, Bl 2.

155 Writing to the Regierungspräsident at Kassel in March 1897, in StA Marburg, Bestand 165, Nr 706, Bd 3, Bl 57.

156 RT, Bd 150, p. 5879.

157 For an analysis of this problem, see Alex Hall, 'The Kaiser, the Wilhelmine State and Lèse-Majesté', *German Life & Letters*, January 1974. Cp. also B. Doehn, 'Der Begriff der Majestätsbeleidigung und ihr Verhältnis zur gewöhnlichen Beleidigung nach dem Reichsstrafgesetzbuch', *Zeitschrift für die gesamte Strafrechtswissenschaft*, Bd 21 (Berlin, 1901), pp. 468–538; the article of Prof. von Calker in *Deutsche Juristenzeitung*, Nr 10, 15 May 1907, and Kirchheimer, op. cit., p. 27.

158 Section 166 (*Gotteslästerung*) was invoked against the apparently blaspheming Social Democrats on a number of occasions, although in 1904 the Staatsanwalt in Hannover had a difficult task in finding two priests whose sense of piety had been sufficiently outraged by the remarks of the local party editor for them to act as witnesses; cp. Friedrich Feldmann, *Geschichte des Ortsvereins Hannover der SPD vom Gründungsjahr 1864 bis 1933* (Hannover, 1952), p. 66.

159 *Echo*, 27 July 1894.

160 *Altona Nachrichten*, 23 August 1905. This article and a wealth of additional material are contained in StA Hamburg, S 7300, Bd 2 and 3.

161 For a legal commentary on these sections, see Justus Olshausen, *Kommentar zum Strafgesetzbuch für das Deutsche Reich*, 8th edit. (Berlin, 1909), p. 399ff.

162 GStA Berlin-Dahlem, Rep 84a, Nr 8213, Bl 100. The text concluded 'Quousque tandem?'.

163 For the circumstances surrounding this extraordinary case, cp. Hall, op. cit.

164 The *Vorwärts*, in its edition for 23 November 1895, for example, specifically requested individuals, as well as editorial offices, to cooperate in sending details of cases of *lèse-majesté* to Ignaz Auer in Berlin. Scarcely a day passed without further additions to this unhappy saga.

165 Rights of full citizenship – 'bürgerliche Ehrenrechte' – were restricted to Reich Germans, and their loss – following conviction under certain sections

of the *Strafgestzbuch* – entailed being struck off the franchise list and being deprived of any publicly elected office.

166 The *Reichsgericht* rejected the second appeal; *Echo*, 22 December 1892.

167 *Bebels Briefwechsel*, op. cit., p. 508ff.

168 Cp. the figures prepared by the *Sächsische Arbeiterzeitung* and published in the *Echo*, 22 December 1897.

169 Quoted in the *Eisenbahn-Zeitung* (Lübeck), 11 August 1900.

170 Cp. Stadthagen's strictures on the 'dolus' in a speech to the Reichstag in November 1896, RT, Bd 147, p. 3346.

171 The editor of the *Leipziger Volkszeitung* was himself sentenced to three months imprisonment for criticising Liebknecht's sentence. The *Vorwärts*, 15 October 1897, devoted a stinging editorial to the verdicts in the Liebknecht and Stenzel (*Echo*) cases, and concluded that recent events had left the German press muzzled as never before. StA Hamburg, S 6699, Bd 1, contains a large number of press cuttings on the Liebknecht trial.

172 *Caligula. Eine Studie über Cäsarenwahnsinn*, which first appeared in *Die Gesellschaft*, April 1894. It occasioned a reply by a Prof. Gustav Dannehl, *Cäsarenwahnsinn oder Professorenwahn. Biographisch-historische Studie über Quiddes Caligula*. Cp. also Utz-Friedebert Taube, *Ludwig Quidde* (Kallmünz Opf., 1963).

173 Schönstedt, writing to senior state prosecutors in February 1900, had referred to increases in the number of acquittals, which were tending to make the courts look silly; GStA Berlin-Dahlem, Rep 84a, Nr 8213, Bl 161–2. The same file contains letters from members of the general public pointing to the disturbing effect produced by the hounding of cases of *lèse-majesté*. Cp. Schönstedt's circular of 19 January 1905, in GStA Berlin-Dahlem, Rep 84a, Nr 8214, Bl 13.

174 The State Secretary in the Reich Office of Justice, Nieberding, was responsible for introducing the bill into the Reichstag in November 1907, and piloting it through its various stages; cp. RT, Bd 229, p. 1729ff. The SPD parliamentary group had tried on a number of occasions to introduce a measure abolishing the offence of *lèse-majesté*.

175 *Vorwärts*, 29 April 1907. The *Bremer Bürgerzeitung*, 25 November 1907, had found it not without significance that the decree coincided with the Reichstag elections, and had obviously been intended to aid the electoral chances of the anti-socialist 'Block'.

176 GStA Berlin-Dahlem, op. cit., Bl 56.

177 In January 1908, for example, the editor of the *Königsberger Volkszeitung* was sentenced to 15 months' imprisonment for *lèse-majesté*, contained in an article criticising the erection of a national monument in Memel; and in the first half of 1911, four Social Democrats were sentenced to a total of 23 months imprisonment for contravening §95. At the same time, the right-wing press insisted that the existing laws against the party were totally insufficient; Scheidemann, op. cit., p. 99. In July 1913, the Minister of the Interior, von Dallwitz, inquired of his colleagues in the Ministry of Justice whether it was not possible to proceed against the *Vorwärts* on the basis of an article which had appeared the previous month and, in the negative case, whether a change in the law might not therefore be considered necessary; GStA Berlin-Dahlem, Rep 84a, Nr 3932, Bl 153.

178 *Weserzeitung*, 23 August 1894.

179 Cp. the judgment of the *Oberlandesgericht* at Naumburg, dated 30 October

1890, in StA Marburg, Bestand 165, Nr 1262. The editor of the *Bremer Bürgerzeitung*, who in 1904 called upon his readers to avoid patronising those firms which declined to advertise in the party paper, was convicted of blackmail and sent to prison for three months; quoted by Koszyk, *Deutsche Presse*, op. cit., p. 203. Conversely, the Staatsanwalt at Görlitz called in September 1908 for a boycott against all those who advertised in the local SPD paper; *Sozialdemokratische Partei-Correspondenz*, Nr 34, 17 October 1908.

180 Cp. Wolfgang Heine in Bozi & Heinemann, op. cit., p. 69.

181 Feldmann, op. cit., p. 65.

182 The 1874 Press Law was not introduced into Alsace-Lorraine until August 1898. On more general background cp. D. P. Silverman, *Reluctant Union. Alsace-Lorraine and Imperial Germany 1871–1918* (University Park, Pa., 1972).

183 Quoted in *Echo*, 8 January 1892. These measures were supplemented by official boycotts of the businesses of socialist shopkeepers.

184 The National Liberal *Hannoverscher Courier*, which reported this campaign in September 1892, concluded that the effects of this sort of propaganda were 'a hundred times more likely to stir the passions of the ordinary worker than the sweetest popularisation of current socialist problems'; quoted in Hartmut Soell, *Die sozialdemokratische Arbeiterbewegung im Reichsland Elsaß-Lothringen 1871–1918* (Diss. Heidelberg, 1963), p. 67.

185 This section of the administrative law of 30 December 1879 enabled the Statthalter to set aside the basic rights under the constitution. It was allowed to lapse in 1902, and its removal, together with the introduction of the Reichspressegesetz, were constantly bemoaned by the Statthalter Count Wedel. On two occasions, in 1911 and 1913, he had proposed new restrictive press laws for the Reichsland, but Bethmann Hollweg had replied that he was unable to guarantee a Reichstag majority. When the Kaiser visited Straßburg in May 1912 he declared that, if necessary, he would rip the constitution into pieces. Wedel opined that once the initial hullabaloo had died down, the effect of this speech might be quite beneficial: it would show the inhabitants that, besides the parliament, there were other power factors in Germany with which they had to reckon; cp. Hans-Günter Zmarzlik, *Bethmann Hollweg als Reichskanzler 1909–1914* (Düsseldorf, 1957), p. 112.

186 Soell, op. cit., p. 95.

187 Haase, op. cit., p. 9.

188 *Rheinische Zeitung*, 15 February 1906.

189 *Vorwärts*, 10 and 13 February 1906; cp. also PT Essen 1907, p. 60.

190 *Vorwärts*, 5 May 1913. The three years 1894–6 accounted for 227 years of imprisonment and 112,852 marks in fines; NZ, 1896–7, I, Nr 17.

191 NZ, 1909–10, I, Nr 20.

192 *Echo*, 7 March 1913 and 12 July 1913. Of the five editors-in-chief of the *Breslauer Volkswacht* in the four years before 1911, the first received 13 months, the second 14 months and a fine of 1,200 marks, the third 7 months and 1,500 marks, the fourth 3 months and a fine of 400 marks, and the fifth 4 months and a fine of 2,000 marks. At the time of the 1911 party conference, nine cases were still pending; PT Jena 1911, p. 105.

193 There was a corresponding increase in the number of cases referred to higher courts by prosecutors who were dissatisfied with the original verdict;

Bozi & Heinemann, op. cit., p. 77. In 1901, of the 627,592 persons against whom charges were brought, about a fifth were acquitted; *Echo*, 15 September 1903.

194 Bozi & Heinemann, op. cit., p. 92.

195 Cp. *Preußische Jahrbücher*, Bd 82 (1895), pp. 380 and 558. The first issue of the *Deutsche Richterzeitung*, founded in 1909 as the organ of the Deutscher Richterbund, noted that complaints were being voiced in all quarters about the standing of the courts. See also *Justiz und Öffentlichkeit*, ed. Heinrich Reynold (Cologne and Berlin, 1966), p. 7.

196 Cp. NZ, 1892–3, 1, Nr 15 and 1896–7, 1, Nr 8.

197 During the inter-ministerial discussions in 1905–6, it was argued that the 1874 Press Law should be strengthened by making newspaper owners liable to be fined according to the size of the paper's circulation; and that all domestic publications, which had twice been convicted within a year, should be suppressed – a ruling which already applied to material published outside the Reich. Cp. *Archivalische Forschungen*, op. cit., pp. 193 and 220.

198 NZ, 1904–5, 11, Nr 39. As Ludwig Frank pointed out, this might well have had the effect of making those convicted by a lower court think twice before lodging an appeal. Proposals published by a group of university lawyers – Professors Liszt, Lilienthal, Goldschmidt and Kahl – indicated that sentences for libel and slander should actually be increased; cp. NZ, 1911–12, 1, Nr 12.

199 *Preußische Jahrbücher*, Bd 113 (1903), p. 377.

200 On the extent of popular feeling on this issue, cp. A. Berthold, *Volksjustiz oder Klassenjustiz?* (Hamburg, 1895), a copy of which is in StA Hamburg, Senat, Cl VIII Lit Me No 12 Vol 18 Fasc 7 Inv 8e. The *Echo*, 17 January 1914, transformed the dictum in Lessing's *Nathan*, 'Der Jude wird verbrannt' into 'Der Sozialdemokrat wird verurteilt.' On the differing kinds of prison treatment, see the weekly SPD paper *Der Landbote*, 1 March 1891, a copy of which is in StA Hannover, Hann Des 80, Hild II, I, Nr 547, vol IV.

201 Cp. Heinrich Hannover and Elisabeth Hannover-Drück, *Politische Justiz 1918–1933* (Frankfurt a.M., 1966), p. 23.

202 *Kreuzzeitung*, 1 September 1891.

203 Cp. Liebknecht's speech to the 1905 party conference, PT Jena 1905, p. 362.

204 *Archivalische Forschungen*, op. cit., p. 190.

205 *Vorwärts*, 18 January 1906.

206 Cp. for instance the *Hannoverscher Volkswille*, 16 June 1895.

207 Thus, for example, Dieter Brüggemann, *Die rechtsprechende Gewalt* (Berlin, 1962). On the other hand, Ulrich Scheuner, 'Die neuere Entwicklung des Rechtsstaats in Deutschland', *Hundert Jahre Deutsches Rechtsleben*, 2 vols (Karlsruhe, 1960), vol 11, p. 229ff. places its origin much earlier.

208 Cp. Leonard Krieger, op. cit., p. 175, also p. 252ff.

209 Hannover and Hannover-Drück, op. cit., p. 24.

210 Otto Hintze, 'Regierung und Verwaltung', in *Gesammelte Abhandlungen* 111, 2nd edit. (Göttingen, 1967), pp. 97–163.

211 Cp. p. 68 and note 169.

212 Quoted in Haase, op. cit., p. 209.

213 Cp. Fraenkel, op. cit., p. 30. He attempts, p. 36, a distinction between 'politische Justiz' and 'Klassenjustiz'; a separation which I am not convinced holds much validity for the Wilhelmine period, and whose pedantry would have been of little comfort to the SPD.

214 Freiherr von Friesen, *Gesichtspunkte für ein revidiertes konservatives Programm* (n.p., 1891).
215 Section 161 of the *Strafgesetzbuch* was applicable in all cases of conviction for perjury or incitement to perjure. The suspension of civic rights always began *after* the sentence had been served and could last between one and five years in cases of imprisonment or between two and ten years in cases of penal servitude. For a technical commentary on the perjury laws, cp. Olshausen, op. cit., pp. 588–621.
216 As the *Berliner Börsen-Courier*, 30 August 1895, pointed out, without its religious character the oath lost all its significance.
217 Cp. *Vorwärts*, 6 November 1892.
218 See especially Hans Blum, *Die Lügen unserer Sozialdemokratie* (Wismar, 1891).
219 Cp. *Sozialdemokratische Partei-Correspondenz*, Nr 4, 18 February 1911. Between the summer of 1891 and the summer of 1892, the state prosecutor's office at Magdeburg succeeded in sending some twelve Social Democrats to hard labour, for contravention of the perjury laws; Frohme, op. cit., p. 127.
220 For further details of the Romen affair and the operation of the perjury laws, see Alex Hall, 'By Other Means: The Legal Struggle against the SPD in Wilhelmine Germany 1890–1900', *Historical Journal*, June 1974.
221 *Echo*, 15 July 1892.
222 On the details of the interplay between the *Echo* and the local authorities, cp. Frohme, op. cit., p. 131ff.
223 Cp. the editorial in the *Echo*, 7 August 1892.
224 *Frankfurter Zeitung*, 8 August 1892. The National Liberal *National Zeitung*, 11 August, and *Münchener Allgemeine Zeitung*, 12 August, both regarded Romen's accusations as judicially indefensible.
225 Cp. Hall, op. cit., and StA Hamburg, S 1365, Bd 1. Both here and in GStA Berlin-Dahlem, Rep 84a, Nr 10771, Bl 547–77 and the continuation in Nr 10772, there are useful digests of wide-ranging press comment on the affair.
226 Frohme, Molkenbuhr and Metzger had originally pleaded pressure of parliamentary business. Molkenbuhr had refused to comply with 'Zeugniszwang' proceedings initiated against him, with the intention of compelling him to reveal the authorship of certain leading articles in the *Echo*, and he was fined for contempt of court; cp. *Vorwärts*, 4 May 1893.
227 Frohme, op. cit., p. 135.
228 *Vorwärts*, 12 July 1893.
229 Cp. for example *Echo*, 17 February 1912, in which Romen's arguments in favour of corporal punishment – 'he who behaves like a beast must be treated like one' – were given short shrift.
230 *Vorwärts*, 11 July 1893.
231 *Echo*, 8 July 1911.
232 *Münchener Post*, 8 September 1892.
233 A report of the meeting was carried by the *Vorwärts*, 15 September 1892.
234 *Echo*, 22 December 1892. The prosecutor at the trial of Thiel in January 1893, on the charge of libelling a local policeman, announced that since animosity against public servants had become second nature to Social Democrats, no credibility could be placed in the evidence of defence witnesses. Thiel was duly convicted and sentenced to an additional term of imprisonment; *Berliner Zeitung*, 8 January 1893.
235 *Vorwärts*, 23 August 1895; cp. also the edition for 23 April 1899.

236 The stream of officially-inspired litigation against the party, which in the period between the summer of 1890 and the summer of 1895 alone had resulted in sentences of 78 years hard labour, 355 years imprisonment and fines of 150,000 marks, had virtually become accepted as the necessary price of daily political martyrdom. It required something out of the ordinary, a court hearing in which the interaction of social, political and judicial factors was clearly manifested, to give fresh impetus to the press campaign against 'Klassenjustiz'.

237 In 1889, Schröder had been one of three men, the 'Kaiserdelegierte', summoned before the Kaiser during the miners' strike of that year. On that occasion the Kaiser had declared, 'Denn für mich ist jeder Sozialdemokrat gleichbedeutend mit Reichs- oder Vaterlandsfeind'; cp. *Sozialdemokratische Partei-Correspondenz*, Nr 3, 4 February 1911. In January 1893, a strike of 22,000 miners had resulted in mass arrests and convictions for serious breaches of the peace; cp. Dieter Fricke, 'Der Essener Meineidsprozeß von 1895 – ein Beispiel preußischer Klassenjustiz', *Geschichte in der Schule*, 1957, Nr 4, p. 186.

238 The chairman was apparently furious at the number of members he had been losing to the miners' union, as a result of the skilled interventions of Schröder and others in the free discussion that followed a meeting; Fricke, op. cit., p. 187.

239 Cp. Frohme, op. cit., p. 148.

240 Frohme, op. cit., p. 150. An account of the trial proceedings is given by Friedrich Karl Kaul, *So wahr mir Gott helfe*, 2nd edit. (Berlin, 1969), pp. 7–60. StA Hamburg, S 5150 Bd 1 and Bd 2, contain numerous press cuttings on the case.

241 *Hannoverscher Volkswille*, 23 August 1895

242 NZ, 1894–5, II, Nr 49.

243 *Vorwärts*, 23 August 1895, which also carried full details of the censure motion passed in Frankfurt, together with the text of the statement issued by the staff of the *Volksstimme*.

244 *Echo*, 28 September 1895.

245 *Hamburger Nachrichten*, 22 November 1895.

246 Cp. the tenor of an article by an Amtsgericht judge in *Der Reichsbote*, 15 December 1895.

247 *Die Post*, 22 October 1895.

248 The Gesellschaft für ethische Kultur claimed to have the names of 2,100 prominent people in public life on its petition. As the *Vorwärts*, 9 August 1896, commented, it was not clemency that the Social Democrats were seeking, but justice.

249 Cp. *Echo*, 18 September 1896.

250 Cp. Kaul, op. cit., p. 53.

251 Cp. Fricke, op. cit., p. 189.

252 Frohme, op. cit., p. 155.

253 Op. cit., p. 157.

254 *Bremer Bürgerzeitung*, 4 February 1911.

255 Quoted in *Berliner Lokal-Anzeiger*, 8 February 1911.

256 Cp. *Vorwärts*, 24 May 1911. On the occasion of Schröder's funeral in May 1914, the police in Essen refused permission for the cortège to pass through the town, and banned the use of red ribbons on the funeral wreaths; *Echo*, 23 May 1914.

257 *Echo*, 20 December 1898.

258 *Rheinische Zeitung*, 9 July 1913, which referred to the way in which the ultra-conservative *Die Post* had taken a lead in stirring up the issue of Social Democratic involvement in perjury cases. Cp. also the editorial in the edition for 12 July 1913.

259 Cp. *Echo*, 20 October 1892.

260 See the article by Wolfgang Heine in the *Bremer Bürgerzeitung*, 14 March 1901. Information on other perjury trials is contained in StA Hamburg, S 1365, Bd 27 Teil 2. The *Rheinische Zeitung*, 7 July and 6 August 1913, unearthed a case at Waldenburg in which the editor of the local conservative paper, egged on by colliery owners incensed at the success of propaganda in the SPD *Schlesische Bergwacht*, succeeded in bribing a former employer of the paper to denounce the *Bergwacht's* general manager on a charge of perjury.

261 Cp. *Echo*, 11 and 25 March 1900. The same paper, 29 March, complained that this case, which in any other country would have occasioned a storm of protest, had been all but totally ignored by the bourgeois press. The editors of the *Vorwärts* and *Mecklenburger Volkszeitung* were amongst those convicted of libelling the court at Güstrow in their commentary on the trial.

262 *Echo*, 17 February 1911.

263 Ibid.

264 *Frankfurter Zeitung*, 27 October 1911. Unfortunately, there is no accurate record of all known convictions for perjury; the *Echo*, 22 February 1899, put the annual average in the period 1882–1896 at 1,520 cases and recorded a total of 1,747 convictions for 1895.

265 *Hamburger Fremdenblatt*, 2 April 1905.

266 Cp. *Echo*, 27 August 1895.

267 Despite the evidence of several independent witnesses that a local landowner at Unter-Lindow had grossly slandered the SPD, two separate courts acquitted him of any criminal intent; cp. *Vorwärts*, 18 March 1911 and *Sozialdemokratische Partei-Correspondenz*, Nr 8, 19 April 1911.

268 *Vorwärts*, 7 February 1899.

269 Six weeks later, the fund stood at 90,000 marks; *Echo*, 21 March 1899. StA Hamburg, S 7410, contains a large number of press cuttings on what came to be known as the 'Löbtauer Krawallprozeß'.

270 Edition for 15 February 1899. As the Polizeipräsident at Kassel commented to the Regierungspräsident, both in the spoken and written word the SPD was finding the affair extremely rewarding from the propaganda point of view; StA Marburg, Bestand 165, Nr 706, Bd 3, Bl 646.

271 NZ, 1898–9, I, Nr 21. Cp. also Nr 22 and Nr 23.

272 Quoted in *Echo*, 8 February 1899. The *Kreuzzeitung* was credited with having described the judgment as 'very draconian'.

273 Quoted with much approval by the *Vorwärts*, 25 February 1899, which regretted that because of restrictions under the 1874 Press Law it was unable to print in translation any critical editorial comment from abroad. There was considerable interest in the case in Holland, where an SPD speaker addressed a well-attended meeting in Amsterdam and collections were made on behalf of the dependants; *Echo*, 14 March 1899.

274 *Vorwärts*, 15 February 1899. Cp. also *Echo*, 7 February 1899, which referred to a case heard by the same court in Dresden, when a landowner who had killed an employee after an argument over wages, escaped with a mere two years imprisonment.

275 Quoted in *Vorwärts*, 4 March 1899. The paper's editor, Georg Ledebour, was prohibited from speaking in Leipzig, because of the radical tone of his editorials; *Echo*, 18 February 1899.

276 Those in Hamburg were attended by several thousand people; cp. *Echo*, 24 February 1899. Most of those scheduled for Saxony were banned by the authorities.

277 *Vorwärts*, 22 February 1899.

278 Cp. *Echo*, 23 February 1899. Since there were no trial proceedings to publish in pamphlet form, the SPD issued instead a digest of the debates in the Reichstag, *Das Dresdener Zuchthausurteil vor dem Reichstag*, a copy of which is in BA Koblenz, Z Sg 1–90/5 (8).

279 NZ, 1898–9, II, Nr 28. The implication in the statement of the executive was that, since not all of those involved in the brawl were members of the SPD, the party should not be seen to be taking up cudgels on behalf of general lawlessness. *Die neue Zeit* thought this an impossibly parochial attitude.

280 *Bremer Bürgerzeitung*, 4 January 1901.

281 Cp. *Frankfurter Zeitung*, 4 June 1905. Press cuttings on the 'Blankeneser Notzuchtsprozeß' are to be found in StA Hamburg, S 1365, Bd 27 Teil 1.

282 *Echo*, 15 January 1905.

283 As a result of this article, ibid., ten of the twelve jurors issued writs on the paper for libel, and the police carried out raids on the editorial offices. Cp. *Echo*, 19 January 1905 and 10 February 1905.

284 *Echo*, 30 March 1905.

285 *Echo*, 7 October 1905.

286 She herself was charged with slandering the presiding judge at the trial; cp. *Hamburger Nachrichten*, 12 and 13 May 1905.

287 This was reduced to two months after a successful appeal had been made to the *Reichsgericht*; cp. *Echo*, 7 June and 6 December 1905. The *Hamburger Nachrichten*, 22 September 1905, complained that the fine imposed on the editor of the party paper in Kiel was quite inappropriate and should have been replaced with a prison sentence.

288 *Magdeburger Volksstimme*, Festnummer, 1 July 1900.

289 Cp. PT Jena 1911, p. 57.

290 *Echo*, 19 August 1909, whose editorial quoted a large number of similar cases.

291 NZ, 1905–6, I, Nr 17.

292 *Echo*, 23 August 1912.

293 *Vorwärts*, 18 June 1897.

294 PT Mannheim 1906, p. 89.

295 Saul, *Staat*, op. cit., p. 266.

296 Section 8 of the Erfurt programme called for abolition of the death penalty, compensation for wrongful arrest and conviction, and a system of legal aid. See NZ, 1908–9, II, Nr 35. Cp. also the article in the *Hessischer Volkskalender für 1898*, a copy of which is in StA Marburg, Bestand 165, Nr 706, Bd 3, Bl 283–300.

297 NZ, 1905–6, I, Nr 16.

CHAPTER 3

1 On this fascinating aspect of Russian history see Sidney Monas, *The Third Section* (Cambridge, Mass., 1961) and the more detailed and instructive account by P. S. Squire, *The Third Department* (Cambridge, 1968).

2 Feigell, op. cit., p. 6.

3 Bleiber, op. cit., p. 192, footnote 102.

4 These departments drew on the tradition of the 'Hohe Polizei', which had existed as a tool of Metternich's repression after the Carlsbad Decrees, and which had carried out a systematic surveillance of all political affairs in Prussia during the period of the 1848 revolutions; cp. Jensen, op. cit., p. 26.

5 Quoted in Ernst, op. cit., p. 24.

6 NZ, 1896–7, II, Nr 38.

7 Cp. Werner Pöls, 'Staat und Sozialdemokratie im Bismarckreich', *Jahrbuch für die Geschichte Mittel- und Ostdeutschlands*, Bd 13–14 (1965), pp. 200–21.

8 Hohenlohe, op. cit., p. 12.

9 *Echo*, 24 October 1909.

10 StA Hamburg, S 5800, Bd 1.

11 Cp. StA Hamburg, Polizeibehörde I, Arb. Sig. 255, Dienstvorschrift für die Abteilung IV. See also 'Dienstanweisung für die Kgl. Polizei-Bezirkskommissare im niederrheinisch-westfälischen Industriegebiet', GStA Berlin-Dahlem, Rep 84a, Nr 10772, Bl 109–10.

12 The significance of the choice of Aegir lies in the absorbing fascination which this name and its Nordic associations had for the Kaiser.

13 *Bremer Bürgerzeitung*, 29 July 1907. There was a small but growing problem posed by foreign nationals working in the country. In July 1903 there was a minor riot of Italian labourers in Fulda; cp. StA Marburg, Bestand 150, Nr 1928, Bl 9.

14 Cp. Hall, in *Journal of Contemporary History*, op. cit.

15 *Leipziger Volkszeitung*, 16 March 1912.

16 *Echo*, 16 January 1903.

17 Walter Wittwer, *Streit um Schicksalsfragen. Die deutsche Sozialdemokratie zu Krieg und Vaterlandsverteidigung 1907–1914* (Berlin, 1964), p. 131.

18 Op. cit., p. 133, footnote 335.

19 StA Marburg, Bestand 150, Nr 2220, Bl 230ff. In a memorandum to Hohenlohe and Schönstedt, dated 4 July 1895, Köller expressed the view that the manpower resources of police authorities in the Ruhr were not equal to the task of providing adequate surveillance; GStA Berlin-Dahlem, Rep 84a, Nr 10772, Bl 57ff.

20 Op. cit., Bl 234.

21 *Echo*, 14 January 1903.

22 Cp. the press cuttings in StA Hamburg, S 5160, Bd 4.

23 *Altona Nachrichten*, 28 July 1903.

24 StA Marburg, Bestand 165, Nr 3142, Bl 570.

25 Memo dated 9 May 1897, in StA Hamburg, S 2170, Bd 20.

26 *Echo*, 12 September 1906.

27 Cp. *Berliner Volkszeitung*, 9 October 1898.

28 *Freie Presse*, 30 November 1895.

29 Cp. StA Koblenz, Abt 403, Nr 6841, Bl 675–8.

30 *Schlesische Zeitung*, 7 December 1895.

31 Cp. *Korrespondenz des Reichsverbands*, 22 July 1906, in StA Marburg, Bestand 150, Nr 633, Bl 184ff.

32 StA Münster, Reg. Arnsberg, Nr 1447.

33 StA Münster, Kreis Bochum, 1. Landratsamt, Nr 177, letter dated 21 February 1902.

34 StA Münster, Reg. Arnsberg, Nr 1447.
35 Details of the course of events can be traced from the correspondence in the above file.
36 StA Marburg, Nr 706, Bl 475–6.
37 *Altona Nachrichten*, 7 December 1911. The appeal to the *Reichsgericht* was, of course, rejected; *Leipziger Volkszeitung*, 10 February 1912.
38 *Der Stukkateur*, 13 July 1907, in StA Hamburg, S 5160, Bd 5.
39 HStA Düsseldorf 42798, von Dallwitz' directive of 9 November 1910.
40 *Echo*, 26 September 1912.
41 *Echo*, 8 October 1898.
42 *Vorwärts*, 11 March 1910.
43 *Vorwärts*, 1, 3 and 4 January 1899.
44 StA Marburg, Bestand 150, Nr 2220, Bl 226ff. Cp. also the report of the *Regierungspräsident* in Wiesbaden, dated 21 December 1900; op. cit., Bl 242–6.
45 See the extensive list of press cuttings in StA Hamburg, S 5160, Bd 1.
46 Cp. StA Hamburg, S 4127, Bl 144–6, and also the report dated 3 April 1896, in Senat, Cl VII, Lit Me, No 12, Vol 18, Fasc 7, Inv 9.
47 Cp. the departmental report, dated 20 March 1896, in StA Hamburg, S 5160, Bd 1. Karl Frohme's views on the 'Rechtsschutzverein' in secret conversations with a member of the department, are in Senat, Cl VII, Lit Me, No 12, Vol 18, Fasc 7, Inv 8c.
48 Cp. for instance *Echo*, 20 May 1897. See also the press cuttings on the Schow affair in StA Hamburg, S 3165, Bd 26.
49 As quoted in the *Hamburger Zeitung*, 13 May 1897.
50 *Hamburger Correspondent*, 26 November 1898.
51 The *Echo*'s comment on the affair, 6 November 1907, was characteristic: 'Pfui Teufel!'.
52 Cp. Wolfgang Heine in NZ, 1913/14, I, Nr 17. The unravelling of different strands of the scandal took place over several weeks; see *Rheinische Zeitung*, 29 November 1913, and the cuttings in StA Hamburg, S 5160, Bd 7.
53 *Vorwärts*, 18 January 1914.
54 *Echo*, 17 January 1914.
55 As reported in the *Vorwärts*, 29 December 1913.
56 *Berliner Volkszeitung*, 18 January 1914.
57 *Vorwärts*, 1 February 1914. The scandal was debated by the Prussian parliament on 12 February.
58 *Vorwärts*, 4 March 1914.
59 *Echo*, 19 April 1914.
60 Gudrun Jilg, *Der neue Kurs in der deutschen Presspolitik 1890–1914* (Diss. Vienna, 1959), p. 12.
61 Fricke, *Bismarcks Prätorianer*, p. 291.
62 Cp. *Bismarcks großes Spiel. Die geheimen Tagebücher Ludwig Bambergers*, ed. Ernst Feder (Frankfurt a.M., 1932), p. 463; also Hammann, *Der neue Kurs*, p. 114.
63 Cp. Hans von Tresckow, *Von Fürsten und anderen Sterblichen* (Berlin, 1922), p. 56. Such methods of intelligence were quite common practice. Hohenlohe's son records that his father was regularly spied upon by the political police; Alexander Hohenlohe, *Aus meinem Leben* (Frankfurt a.M., 1925), p. 305.
64 Cp. *Echo*, 5 June 1897.

65 PA/AA, Deutschland Nr 122, Nr 3a secr., Bd 1, letter dated 18 January 1895.
66 Op. cit., report dated 9 February 1895.
67 Fricke, op. cit., p. 297. Cp. *Vorwärts*, 22 and 25 April 1893.
68 Dieter Fricke, 'Die Affäre Leckert–Lützow–Tausch und die Regierungskrise von 1897 in Deutschland', ZfGW 1960, Heft 7, p. 1587. There is considerable material, including numerous contemporary newspaper sources in StA Hamburg, S 5135, Bd 2–4, and PA/AA, Deutschland Nr 122, Nr 3b, Bd 1–3.
69 Frohme, op. cit., p. 96, recalls that the SPD had received information on Lützow, who appeared regularly on the press benches in the Reichstag, to the effect that he was an agent of the political police, long before the scandal actually broke.
70 Hohenlohe, op. cit., p. 269.
71 Fricke, *Bismarcks Prätorianer*, p. 290.
72 *Das kleine Journal*, 20 October 1895.
73 Cp. NZ, 1896–7, 1, Nr 14.
74 Eisner, *Taggeist*, p. 130. Cp. also pp. 130–7 on the ramifications of the affair.
75 Fricke, op. cit., p. 295.
76 PA/AA, Deutschland Nr 122, Nr 3b, Bd 1.
77 Ibid.
78 Quoted by Fricke, in ZfGW 1960, p. 1590.
79 PA/AA, op. cit., report dated 9 December 1896.
80 *Adlers Briefwechsel*, p. 224.
81 Op. cit., p. 226.
82 *Vorwärts*, 8 December 1896.
83 NZ, 1896–7, 1, Nr 12.
84 Cp. PA/AA, Hamburg 2 secr. Cp. also Fricke, op. cit., p. 1595. An interesting sideline is provided by Tresckow's recollection of a trip to Cherbourg on official business in 1895, during which he only just managed to prevent a fellow police official and confidant of Tausch from carrying out a private spying operation for the German Admiralty; Tresckow, op. cit., p. 91.
85 Waldersee, *Denkwürdigkeiten*, Bd II, p. 388.
86 *Vorwärts*, 22 March 1904. Waldersee had been responsible for providing Normann-Schumann with funds to enable him to live abroad; Hammann, op. cit., p. 124.
87 Paul Mayer, op. cit., p. 112.
88 Friedländer, op. cit., Bd 4, p. 146. The Leckert–Lützow–Tausch trials are discussed p. 72ff.
89 *Rheinisch-Westfälische Zeitung*, 9 March 1897, in BA Koblenz, Z Sg 113, Sammlung Fechenbach, Bd 162, which contains considerable press material, as does Bd 163.
90 Waldersee, op. cit., p. 396. Cp. also Fricke, *Bismarcks Prätorianer*, p. 300.
91 Waldersee, op. cit., p. 398.
92 See Hohenlohe's diary entry for 29 April 1897, in Hohenlohe, op. cit., p. 333, in which he contemplated a *quid pro quo* with the Kaiser. According to Fricke, op. cit., p. 300, the *Oberstaatsanwalt* and presiding judge were both subjected to pressure from above.
93 *Das Tagebuch der Baronin Spitzemberg*, ed. Rudolf Vierhaus (Göttingen, 1960), p. 350.
94 Fricke, op. cit., p. 296. Marschall had been privileged to see confidential material which had been accumulated during the course of the preliminary hearings up to the trial against Leckert and Lützow.

95 Fricke, in ZfGW 1960, p. 1592.
96 In July 1896, a pamphlet by Fritz Friedemann, *Wilhelm II und die Revolution von oben. Der Fall Kotze, des Rätsels Lösung* (Zürich, 1896), as well as its French version, were confiscated by a court in Berlin. The following year an anonymous pamphlet, *Herr von Tausch und die Verfasser der anonymen Briefe der Hofgesellschaft* (Zürich, 1897), was similarly banned. These court rulings were immediately communicated to lower echelons in the Prussian administration; cp. StA Osnabrück, Rep 450, Mel XI, Nr 325. The Kotze scandal is described by Helmuth Rogge in *Die politische Meinung*, 1963, p. 65.
97 Cp. Frohme, op. cit., p. 98.
98 Cp. *Vorwärts*, 5 June 1897, also the edition for 9 June.
99 Fricke, op. cit., p. 1599.
100 *Echo*, 9 June 1897.
101 NZ, 1896–7, II, Nr 38.
102 *Adlers Briefwechsel*, p. 232.
103 Cp. Röhl, *Bismarck*, p. 132ff. on the Marschall crisis.
104 Fricke, op. cit., p. 1589.
105 Fricke, *Bismarcks Prätorianer*, p. 302; Marschall later became ambassador to Britain.
106 The *Vorwärts*, 20 November 1897, uncovered a series of different *noms de plume* used by Normann-Schumann.
107 Cp. *Echo*, 25 November 1897.
108 *Hamburger Fremdenblatt*, 19 January 1899. Tausch died in 1912.
109 Thus, in 1904 he was sentenced to a year's imprisonment for theft; *Vorwärts*, 19 July 1904.
110 Amongst a plethora of articles, see esp. the editorial in the *Vorwärts*, 26 May 1897.
111 *Bremer Bürgerzeitung*, 21 March 1901.
112 Bernhard Weiß, *Polizei und Politik* (Berlin, 1928), p. 60.
113 Speech to the Reichstag, 23 May 1906, quoted by Weiß, op. cit., p. 57.
114 *Echo*, 13 October 1899.
115 *Vorwärts*, 1 October 1911
116 *Frankfurter Volksstimme*, 14 August 1894; cp. StA Wiesbaden, Abt 425, Nr 421, Bl 10.
117 See for instance *Volksstimme*, 10 May 1898.
118 *Volksstimme*, 21 April 1900. StA Wiesbaden, Abt 425, Nr 422, contains a large number of relevant press cuttings.
119 This pamphlet, which appeared in September 1894, was entitled '39 Monate bei gesundem Geiste als irrsinnig eingekerkert! Erlebnisse des katholischen Geistlichen Mr. Forbes aus Schottland im Alexianerkloster Mariaberg in Aachen während der Zeit vom 18.2.1891 bis 30.5.1894'.
120 Cp. for example *Echo*, 9 June 1895.
121 *Echo*, 7 June 1895.
122 NZ, 1894–5, II, Nr 38.
123 *Echo*, 27 June 1895. The SPD press attacked the proposed budget of 8,000 marks, which would only take effect from the following year, as being woefully inadequate for the task in hand.
124 NZ, 1894–5, II, Nr 38 and Nr 40.
125 Karl Kautsky, *Die Vernichtung der Sozialdemokratie durch den Gelehrten des Zentralverbandes deutscher Industrieller* (Berlin, 1911), p. 40.

126 Cp. *Echo*, 19 September 1895. The *Aachener Volksfreund* unearthed a particularly disturbing affair in Eschweiler; cp. *Echo*, 16 July 1897.

127 *Echo*, 27 June 1895.

128 StA Koblenz, Abt 403, Nr 6841, Bl 629.

129 *Echo*, 15 December 1895.

130 *Echo*, 24 December 1895. Cp. also *Echo*, 5 July 1896.

131 Cp. *Echo*, 8 December 1898.

132 Gerhard Ritter, *The Sword and the Sceptre: the Problem of Militarism in Germany*, 4 vols (London, 1967–74). Cp. also Gordon A. Craig, *The Politics of the Prussian Army 1640–1945* (Oxford, 1964); Martin Kitchen, *The German Officer Corps 1890–1914* (Oxford, 1968) and Karl Demeter, *The German Officer Corps in Society and State 1650–1945* (London, 1965).

133 Emilie Schröder, *Ein Tagebuch Kaiser Wilhelms II 1888–1902* (Breslau, 1903), p. 86. An important bibliographical contribution to this problem-complex is Manfred Messerschmidt, *Zum Verhältnis von Militär und Politik in der Bismarckzeit und in der Wilhelminischen Ära* (Darmstadt, 1975).

134 See Dieter Fricke, 'Zur Rolle des Militarismus nach innen in Deutschland vor dem 1. Weltkrieg', ZfGW 1958, Heft 6, p. 1309, as well as the party comment in PT Magdeburg 1910, p. 112.

135 Morsey, *Deutsches Verwaltungsblatt*, p. 13.

136 Cp. Gordon A. Craig, 'Relations between Civil and Military Authorities in the Second German Empire. Chancellor and Chief of Staff 1871–1918', in *War, Politics and Diplomacy* (London, 1966), p. 121ff.

137 The ceremony was held on 13 November 1893; cp. *Echo*, 4 January 1902.

138 Wilhelm Schröder, *Das persönliche Regiment* (Munich, 1907), p. 13.

139 *Der Militarismus im Deutschen Reich. Eine Anklageschrift von einem deutschen Historiker* (Stuttgart, 1893). A précis of the work, together with extensive editorial comment, appeared in *Echo*, 13 June 1893.

140 Hartmann Goertz, *Preußens Gloria* (Munich, 1962), pp. 257–8.

141 Röhl, *Bismarck*, p. 21. As a result of the extension of Prussian ideology into southern Germany, there was an increasing disinclination in Bavaria to appoint Jews to the army reserves; Demeter, op. cit., p. 217.

142 Cp. Otto Hintze, op. cit., p. 103.

143 See *Echo*, 20 January 1893, which commented, 'Nicht mehr der Schulmeister macht die Soldaten, sondern die Soldaten den Schulmeister.'

144 *Echo*, 16 March 1894.

145 Cp. Friedrich Wendel, *Wilhelm II in der Karikatur* (Dresden, 1928), p. 43. An entry in the column of classified advertisements read, 'Heirat. Prinz aus altem Hause – zur Zeit in ca. 70 Orten bedenkmalt – wünscht sich eben-bürtig zu vermählen. Offerten unter Beifügung von Auto-Skulpturen nebst Entwürfen der zu erwartenden Nachkommenschaft unter "Blauestes Blut" an die Expedition von *Hau-Mich-Aus*'; quoted op. cit., p. 46.

146 Cp. Kitchen, op. cit., p. 49ff. and Demeter, op. cit., p. 116ff.

147 The duel featured regularly in editorial comment; cp. for example *Echo*, 3 August 1893 and 14 July and 20 January 1901.

148 SPD newspapers were forever pointing up the differences between immediate police and legal action against the party organisation, and the failure of the authorities to intervene in cases of previously announced duelling en-counters. There was a considerable delay before action was taken against Kotze and the sentence – two years *custodia honesta* – was typical of the

absurd degree of official leniency in such matters; *Echo* 14 and 22 April 1896.

149 *Echo*, 8 January 1908.

150 Emilie Schröder, op. cit., p. 263.

151 Kitchen, op. cit., p. 154 and Fricke, op. cit., p. 1300. Bebel referred to a directive which threatened army reserve officers with loss of their uniforms, if they published anything which ran contrary to accepted establishment doctrines; RT, Bd 200, p. 2853. In July 1911 the Prussian Minister of War warned all army reserve officers that those involved in supporting the election campaigns of Social Democrats would be dismissed; E. O. Volkmann, *Der Marxismus und das deutsche Heer im Weltkriege* (Berlin, 1925), p. 49. This had already been underlined in the Reichstag by von Einem in March 1909.

152 Frohme, op. cit., p. 80.

153 Kitchen, op. cit., p. 161.

154 *Bebels Briefwechsel*, op. cit., p. 668.

155 *Rheinische Zeitung*, 17 December 1913.

156 Groh, op. cit., p. 38.

157 Despite the fact that the use of the army in civil disturbances was confined to relatively few industrial 'flashpoints' – the murder of a striker by a blackleg in Nuremberg in 1906, or the Mansfeld miners strike in 1909, during which cavalry and machine-guns were used for the first time – there existed precise arrangements for cooperation between military and civil authorities in suppressing political activity; cp. Schnorbus, op. cit., p. 208, and Fricke, op. cit., p. 1308.

158 Waldersee, op. cit., pp. 106 and 388.

159 Stürmer, in *Historische Zeitschrift*, op cit., p. 567, argues that the bill was intended to produce a head-on collision with the Reichstag.

160 Cp. Röhl, op. cit., p. 71, who emphasises the rôle of the Kaiser, and Silvermann, op. cit., p. 116ff. The increased numbers, of the order of 84,000 men, were intended to compensate militarily for growing evidence of a Franco-Russian rapprochement.

161 Cp. Morsey, *Deutsches Verwaltungsblatt*, p. 15.

162 *Fränkische Tagespost*, 28 October 1892.

163 The *Vorwärts*, 28 September 1910, published long extracts; cp. also *Sozialdemokratische Partei-Correspondenz*, 15 October 1910. The full text is given by Fricke, op. cit., p. 1302ff.; cp. also Lipinski, op. cit., p. 269.

164 'Abwarten bringt auch den Geist der Truppen ins Wanken, während Angriff und Kampf ihre Gesinnung befestigt.'

165 StA Marburg, Bestand 150, Nr 1927, Bl 69ff.

166 Op. cit., Bl 130ff.

167 *Vorwärts*, 2 October 1898; the document was dated 22 June 1898. A similar 'Schießerlaß' for Saxony was published by the *Leipziger Volkszeitung*, 3 April 1906.

168 StA Marburg, Bestand 165, Nr 706, Bd 4, Bl 373.

169 Wilhelm Schröder, op. cit., pp. 12–13; the comment was made at a ceremony on 23 November 1891.

170 Cp. the letter sent in March 1906 by the GHQ of the 9th Army Corps to the local police in Altona, quoted by Frohme, op. cit., p. 81.

171 Cp. the circular of 7 August 1913 from the GOC of the 7th Army Corps, in StA Münster, Kreis Bochum, 1. Landratsamt, Nr 177.

172 Kitchen, op. cit., p. 156. On the need for the military to monitor socialist activities, cp. the directive from the War Minister quoted by Saul, *Archiv für Sozialgeschichte*, p. 295.

173 The full text was given by *Echo*, 4 October 1906. A similar document was discovered in the street by a group of workers, who immediately sent it to the *Karlsruher Volksfreund*; PA/AA, Europa Generalia, Nr 82, Nr 1 secr., Bd 20.

174 Cp. *Echo*, 16 October 1906.

175 On the *Kriegervereine*, see Klaus Saul, 'Der "Deutsche Kriegerbund". Zur innenpolitischen Funktion eines "nationalen" Verbandes im kaiserlichen Deutschland', *Militärgeschichtliche Mitteilungen*, 2/1969, pp. 95–159, and the more questionable contribution of Hansjoachim Henning, 'Kriegervereine in den preußischen Westprovinzen', *Rheinische Vierteljahresblätter*, vol. 32, 1968, pp. 430–75; also Kitchen, op. cit., p. 129ff.

176 This circular, dated 24 January 1891, and quoted by Saul, op. cit., pp. 133–4, was also published in the *Breslauer Volkswacht* and *Schwäbische Tagwacht* for 7 July 1892.

177 Details of this directive were published in *Echo*, 9 January 1904.

178 A wealth of material on the *Kriegervereine* is contained in StA Marburg, Bestand 150, Nr 1968.

179 The *Regierungspräsident* at Osnabrück commended to all area prefects A. Westphal's *Kriegervereine gegen Sozialdemokratie. Ein Mahnwort an die gebildeten Stände* (Berlin, 1891); cp. StA Osnabrück, Dep. 3b I, Nr 436, Bl 102.

180 Höhn, op. cit., p. 336.

181 Bebel's speech of 7 March 1904 to the Reichstag was typical of this attitude. At the 1907 party conference, Bebel said that if it came to it Social Democrats would defend Germany from external attack, 'because it is our Fatherland too'; PT Essen 1907, p. 255. Cp. also the editorial in *Echo*, 21 April 1912.

182 RT, 11. Legislatur Periode, 1, Sess. Bd 2, p. 1588. Two days later he proclaimed that between Social Democracy and capitalism there could be no real understanding or agreement – 'we face each other like water and fire'; p. 1662.

183 Helga Grebing, *Geschichte der deutschen Arbeiterbewegung* (Munich, 1966), p. 141.

184 This is precisely the gist of an article by Max Victor, 'Die Stellung der deutschen Sozialdemokratie zu den Fragen der auswärtigen Politik 1896–1914', *Archiv für Sozialwissenschaft und Sozialpolitik*, Vol 60, 1928', pp. 147–79, who cites amongst his evidence an editorial from the *Vorwärts*, 8 April 1907.

185 Cp. Zechlin, *Der Monat*, op. cit., p. 29. Carl Severing, *Mein Lebensweg*, Bd 1 (Cologne, 1950), p. 147, quotes a speech he made in the 1903 election campaign in which he said, 'Vaterland ist der Ackerboden, der uns *alle* nähren soll . . . Und dieses Vaterland ist auch unser, der Arbeiter Vaterland.'

186 PT Berlin 1892, pp. 131–2. Cp. also G. Hennig, *August Bebel – Todfeind des preußisch-deutschen Militärstaates* (Berlin, 1963). In March 1893, the *Echo* devoted five major editorials to 'Eine Kritik der Militärherrschaft'.

187 *Geschichte der deutschen Arbeiterbewegung*, vol iii (Berlin, 1966), p. 144. Cp. also *Echo*, 21 January 1893.

188 *Echo*, 4 May 1895, which spoke contemptuously of the 'höfisch-militärische Prunk'.

189 PT Jena 1913, p. 364.

190 Walter Bartel, *Die Linken in der deutschen Sozialdemokratie im Kampf gegen Militarismus und Krieg* (Berlin, 1958), p. 70; cp. also Lipinski, op. cit., p. 267.

191 Quoted in Volkmann, op. cit., p. 34.

192 'Militarismus und Antimilitarismus', which was reviewed in NZ, 1906–7, II, Nr 34.

193 Cp. NZ, 1907–8, I, Nr 3.

194 *Archivalische Forschungen*, p. 259. After his release in June 1909, for which the local party had organised a special reception, attended by over 5,000 workers, Liebknecht described his sentence in a speech to the Prussian Landtag as 'the greatest honour which has been done to me . . . better to be in a penitentiary convicted of rape than to sit here as a victim of rape'; cp. Rückert, *Zur Geschichte*, op. cit., pp. 132–4.

195 Klaus Saul, 'Der Kampf um die Jugend zwischen Volksschule und Kaserne', *Militärgeschichtliche Mitteilungen*, 1/1971, p. 125.

196 J. M. Griesser, *In der Ferienkolonie* (Stuttgart, 1896), p. 11, a copy of which is in StA Hamburg, S 1365, Bd 24. Cp. also Edmund Miller, *Ein Aufschrei mißhandelter Soldaten, deutscher Landeskinder*, 4th edit. (Stuttgart, 1892), pp. 67–74.

197 *Echo*, 27 March 1914.

198 Dieter Fricke, 'Zum Bündnis des preußisch-deutschen Militarismus mit dem Klerus gegen die sozialistische Arbeiterbewegung am Ende des 19. Jahrhunderts', ZfGW 1960, Nr 6, p. 1380. Cp. also NZ, 1911–12, II, Nr 31, and Hermann Schöler, *Militärische Schreckensbilder in Friedenszeiten* (Stuttgart, 1895).

199 No fewer than 2,855 convictions were secured annually for desertions and a further 2,984 for contravening military discipline; *Geschichte der deutschen Arbeiterbewegung*, vol IV (Berlin, 1967), p. 200.

200 Griesser, op. cit., p. 13, who recalls that during his period of service in a battalion of 600 men, only two or three men in the whole regiment dared to lodge formal complaints.

201 Kitchen, op. cit., p. 184.

202 Fricke, ibid.

203 *Echo*, 8 September 1901.

204 The text of the circular is given by Miller, op. cit., pp. 85–92. On party reaction, see NZ, 1891–2, I, Nr 20.

205 Fricke, ZfGW 1958, p. 1306.

206 PA/AA, Europa Generalia, Nr 82, Nr 14, Bd 5, report dated 12 February 1892.

207 *Echo*, 24 September and 18 December 1903.

208 Quoted in *Echo*, 24 September 1903. Similar sentiments were expressed by the *Nationalliberale Korrespondenz*, 'Die Sozialdemokratie gewinnt durch diese betrübenden Erscheinungen immer neues Wasser auf ihre Wahlmühle'.

209 RT, 1894–5, Bd 3, p. 2150.

210 Miller, op. cit., p. 53. Cp. also Hans Rau, *Der Sadismus in der Armee* (Berlin, 1904) and the experiences related by Otto Buchwitz, *50 Jahre Funktionär der deutschen Arbeiterbewegung* (Berlin, 1949), p. 40.

211 Wilhelm Schröder, op. cit., p. 18. The Kaiser acted in similar fashion in

many other cases of 'brave action' by his soldiers against the civilian population; op. cit., p. 19.

212 *Die Rundschau* (Hannover), December 1896, Nr 23.

213 *Echo*, 28 January 1897. The Karlsruher Hoftheater also banned Sudermann's *Fritzchen* in September of the same year.

214 *Preußischer Kommiß. Soldatengeschichten von August Winnig* (Berlin, 1910). The Polizeipräsident at Hamburg regarded it as the lowest form of anti-military trash, intended to stir up popular feelings against the army; StA Hamburg, S 13339, memorandum dated 9 November 1912.

215 *Echo*, 27 June 1913; cp. also the editorial for 31 July 1909.

216 Kurt Stenkewitz, *Immer feste druff* (Berlin, 1962), p. 71, and *Echo*, 30 June 1914. Cp. also Groh, op. cit., p. 539ff. and also *Rosa Luxemburg im Kampf gegen den deutschen Militarismus. Prozeßberichte und Materialien aus den Jahren 1913 bis 1915* (Berlin, 1960), pp. 223–61. Luxemburg's own view was that 'giving up the struggle against the militarist system is virtually the same as giving up the struggle against the present order of society'; quoted in Kitchen, op. cit., p. 143.

217 *Echo*, 14 November 1903 and *Leipziger Volkszeitung*, 28 November 1903.

218 *Vorwärts*, 18 December 1897.

219 Berthold, op. cit., p. 36ff.

220 *Sozialdemokratische Partei-Correspondenz*, Nr 25, 20 June 1908.

221 The text of the circular is given by Demeter, op. cit., pp. 346–7.

222 Cp. for example, PT (Stenographische Aufzeichnungen) 1899, p. 109.

223 PA/AA, Europa Generalia, Nr 82, Nr 1 secr., Bd 13, report dated 13 November 1893.

224 Albrecht Lothholz, *Die Haltung der Sozialdemokratie in den Heeres-Flotten- und Weltmachtsfragen 1890–1914* (Diss. Freiburg i.B., 1958), p. 36.

225 The composition of the military courts was not itself unrepresentative of rank structure. The full court-martial (*Kriegsgericht*), for example, was presided over by a panel of judges consisting of 3 soldiers, 3 NCOs, 3 sub-alterns, 3 captains and one senior officer as chairman. Members of the drum-head court-martial (*Standgericht*) were similarly drawn from both senior and junior ranks. Nevertheless, military rank and seniority carried con-siderable weight in the deliberations which preceded a judgement; Griesser, op. cit., p. 45. Cp. also the somewhat superficial account of military law given by Oskar Ehrl, 'The Development of the German Military Criminal Procedure during the 19th Century', *Revue de Droit Penal Militaire et de Droit de la Guerre*, VII, 2 (1968), pp. 241–61.

226 Cp. Rauh, op. cit., p. 158ff.

227 Röhl, op. cit., p. 139.

228 Rauh, op. cit., p. 162.

229 Hohenlohe, op. cit., p. 116.

230 This was one of the clearest indications of the attitude which viewed the army as a state within the state.

231 Rauh, op. cit., pp. 164–5.

232 Cp. Röhl, op. cit., p. 142ff.

233 Röhl, op. cit., p. 224.

234 Cp. StA Hamburg, Hans. Gesandtschaft Berlin, Neuere Reg. M I b 6.

235 Morsey, *Deutsches Verwaltungsblatt*, p. 12.

236 *Vorwärts*, 31 July 1907. The sections referred to in the new code were §106 and §107.

237 Quoted and discussed by NZ, 1906–7, ΙΙ, Nr 45.

238 *Bremer Bürgerzeitung*, 20 August 1907.

239 The literature on this episode is extremely sparse and I have drawn heavily on Adolf Müller, *Fuchsmühl. Eine Skizze aus dem Rechtsstaat der Gegenwart* (Munich, 1895) and Willy Albrecht, 'Die Fuchsmühler Ereignisse vom Oktober 1894 und ihre Folgen für die innere Entwicklung Bayerns im letzten Jahrzehnt des 19. Jahrhunderts', *Zeitschrift für bayerische Landesgeschichte*, Bd 33, Heft 8 (1970), pp. 307–54.

240 Cp. the article by Adolf Müller in NZ, 1894–5, ΙΙ, Nr 35.

241 Fricke, in ZfGW 1958, p. 1299.

242 *Münchener Post*, 3 November 1894.

243 Albrecht, op. cit., p. 322.

244 Op. cit., p. 346.

245 *Münchener Post*, 3 January 1896. The incident actually occasioned a debate in the Bavarian Landtag on 9 January.

246 Stampfer, op. cit., p. 61. The correspondent of the *Frankfurter Zeitung* was prevented, on the orders of Bülow, from telegraphing a verbatim account of the speech to his paper's office; *Echo*, 1 August 1900. On the great power involvement in China, see esp. William L. Langer, *The Diplomacy of Imperialism 1890–1902* (New York, 1956), p. 694ff.

247 This letter was published by the *Magdeburger Volksstimme* and quoted by *Echo*, 27 October 1900.

248 Quoted by *Echo*, 24 January 1901.

249 Cp. *Bremer Bürgerzeitung*, 11 January 1901.

250 This letter, originally published by the *Bremer Bürgerzeitung*, was quoted by *Echo*, 2 November 1900.

251 *Echo*, 4 December 1901.

252 StA Hamburg, S 1365, Bd 22. Reference to the award of 1,700 'Hunnenmedaillen' or what the popular tongue dubbed 'Apfelsinenorden', also resulted in charges of *lèse-majesté*; cp. the speech of Wolfgang Heine in RT, 12. L.P. 1. Sess. Bd 229, p. 1740.

253 StA Hamburg, S 3423, vol VI, contains considerable press material on the affair.

254 *Vorwärts*, 18 October 1906; cp. also the editorial for 28 October.

255 *Die Hilfe*, 1906, vol 12, Nr 44.

256 *Leipziger Volkszeitung*, 6 February 1913.

257 On the Zabern affair, cp. esp. H.-U. Wehler, *Krisenherde des Kaiserreichs 1871–1918* (Göttingen, 1970), pp. 65–83; Kitchen, op. cit., p. 187ff.; Kurt Stenkewitz, op. cit., Hermann Wendel, *Zabern! Militäranarchie und Militärjustiz* (Frankfurt a.M., 1914); Erwin Schenk, *Der Fall Zabern* (Stuttgart, 1927).

258 Stenkewitz, op. cit., p. 13.

259 op. cit., p. 35. Count Karl von Wedel had held various posts as military attaché and ambassador, before becoming governor of Alsace-Lorraine in 1907. Balfour, *The Kaiser and his Times*, op. cit., p. 300, claims that Wedel actually refused the Reich Chancellorship in 1909, the offer of which was an indication of the trust the Kaiser put in him. Cp. also Count Bogdan Hutten-Czapski, *Sechzig Jahre Politik und Gesellschaft*, 2 vols (Berlin, 1936), ΙΙ, pp. 127–9.

260 Wendel, op. cit., p. 5.

261 Wehler, op. cit., p. 71.

262 Cp. *Rheinische Zeitung*, 3 December 1913 and NZ, 1913–14, I, Nr 18.

263 On the protest meeting held at Offenbach in January 1914, at which the main speaker was Hermann Wendel of the SPD Reichstag group, see PA/AA, Europa Generalia, Nr 82, Nr 1 secr., Bd 23. Julian Marchlewski's comment, in the *Sozialdemokratische Korrespondez*, 17 January 1914, that the troops had behaved like 'the Cossacks on the streets of St Petersburg', resulted in his imprisonment for several months.

264 *Echo*, 4 December 1913.

265 Wendel, op. cit., p. 7.

266 Stenkewitz, op. cit., p. 100.

267 *Rheinische Zeitung*, 29 December 1913; cp. also *Echo*, 24 December 1913.

268 Wendel, ibid.

269 Wendel, p. 11.

270 Quoted in Vietsch, op. cit., p. 169.

271 *Vorwärts*, 3 December 1913.

272 Cp. Groh, op. cit., p 517. The bourgeois parties for their part showed little willingness to assert themselves vis-à-vis the military, as the rejection of the SPD amendments to the Army Bill of 1913 showed. These were directed towards ensuring the political neutrality of the army in domestic conflicts, and preventing its use in disturbances or strikes; cp. Domann, op. cit., p. 192ff.

CHAPTER 4

1 Freiherr Lucius von Ballhausen, *Bismarck-Erinnerungen* (Stuttgart and Berlin, 1920), p. 22.

2 Barbara Tuchman, *The Proud Tower* (London, 1966), p. 291ff., conveys this sense of impending collapse better than most. Cp. also Gerhard Masur, *Prophets of Yesterday* (London, 1963); H. Stuart Hughes, *Consciousness and Society* (New York, 1961); Fritz Stern, *The Politics of Cultural Despair* (New York, 1965) and Bernhard Guttmann, *Schattenriß einer Generation 1888–1919* (Stuttgart, 1950).

3 *Echo*, 23 October 1900.

4 Cp. J. Alden Nichols, *Germany after Bismarck* (Cambridge, Mass., 1958), p. 218. In April 1892 Ahlwardt alleged that a Jewish munitions firm was indulging in sabotage against the state, by supplying the army with defective rifles.

5 *Vorwärts*, 3 August 1894.

6 *Die Post*, 8 May and 4 December 1904.

7 Wile, op. cit., p. 88.

8 *Vorwärts*, 15 February 1907.

9 A copy is in StA Hamburg, S 11792, Bd 2. Another leaflet, addressed to parents, declared that Social Democrats were all set to brainwash the new generation into a total revaluation of all values.

10 Cp. Klaus Epstein, 'Erzberger and the German Colonial Scandals 1905–1910', *English Historical Review*, 1959, pp. 637–63, and idem., *Matthias Erzberger and the Dilemma of German Democracy* (Princeton, N.J., 1959), p. 52ff. External affairs played only a minor rôle in SPD propaganda; on the relationship of the party to colonialism, cp. Gerda Weinberger, 'Die deutsche

Sozialdemokratie und die Kolonialpolitik', ZfGW 1967, Nr 3, pp. 402-23. To *Die neue Zeit*, 1906-7, II, Nr 41, Carl Peters was but a symbol of a decaying and corrupted capitalist society.

11 Cp. Hans Jaeger, *Unternehmer in der deutschen Politik 1890-1918* (Bonn, 1967), p. 166ff. and Richard Lewinsohn, *Das Geld in der Politik* (Berlin, 1931), pp. 37-9.

12 Cp. NZ, 1895-6, I, Nr 2. There were often widely differing views on what constituted proletarian morality. Vernon T. Lidtke, 'Naturalism and Socialism', in *The American Historical Review*, February 1974, pp. 14-37, has some pertinent points to make on the extent of prudery within the leadership of the party.

13 *Echo*, 26 May 1892.

14 *Echo*, 10 October 1905.

15 *Echo*, 16 November 1902. The implication in the formation of organisations bearing the name 'Sittlichkeitsvereine zur Hebung der Moral in den unteren Volksschichten' was that immorality was the preserve of the lower classes. As the *Echo* pointed out in a neat analogy, no sensible charwoman would dream of starting to scrub the bottom step before working her way up a flight of stairs. Cp. also Goertz, op. cit., p. 225.

16 *Echo*, 6 October 1904.

17 *Echo*, 21 February 1897.

18 Cp. Robin J. V. Lenman, 'Art, Society and the Law in Wilhelmine Germany: the Lex Heinze', *Oxford German Studies*, No 8 (Oxford, 1973), pp. 86-113.

19 NZ, 1891-2, I, Nr 3.

20 Emilie Schröder, op. cit., p. 97.

21 Cp. Friedländer, op. cit., Bd 2, p. 221ff. Similar trials, involving the seedier aspects of criminal vice, are dealt with by Friedrich Karl Kaul, *So wahr mir Gott helfe* (Berlin, 1969).

22 *Echo*, 20 and 23 December 1900.

23 NZ, 1900-1, I, Nr 13.

24 NZ, 1904-5, II, Nr 50.

25 There is only one biography of Hammerstein, and a very much hagiographical one at that, by Hans Leuß, *Wilhelm Freiherr von Hammerstein* (Berlin, 1905), and the reviews are rather more instructive; cp. for example *Echo*, 11 May 1905, and NZ, 1904-5, II, Nr 33. On piecing together details of this affair, I have therefore relied heavily on contemporary newspaper sources.

26 Leuß, op. cit., p. 108.

27 Op. cit., pp. 116-17. After Leuß's book appeared, Eulenburg published a statement in the *Kreuzzeitung*, denying this version of the facts, but it is clear that he and Hammerstein were involved in a joint initiative of sorts; cp. *Echo*, 16 May 1905.

28 *Echo*, 4 April 1895.

29 *Echo*, 9 July 1895.

30 *Echo*, 16 and 24 July 1895.

31 It took its title from a passage in the letter. 'Man muß rings um das Kartell Scheiterhaufen anzünden und sie hell auflodern lassen, den herrschenden Optimismus in die Flammen werfen und dadurch die Lage beleuchten.' The letter, which Stoecker later conveniently claimed not to remember writing, was dated 14 August 1888; cp. *Echo*, 7 September 1895.

32 Cp. Hammann, *Der neue Kurs*, op. cit., p. 218. On the cartel see Röhl, in *Historical Journal*, March 1966, op. cit.

33 Cp. *Echo*, 29 July 1896.

34 *Echo*, 8 January 1896.

35 NZ, 1895–6, I, Nr 1.

36 NZ, 1895–6, II, Nr 42.

37 *Echo*, 7 December 1895.

38 *Echo*, 29 January and 6 February 1896.

39 Cp. Waldersee, *Denkwürdigkeiten*, p. 358, and Alson J. Smith, op. cit., p. 200.

40 Cp. the report of the trial proceedings in *Echo*, 23 April 1896.

41 Solveig-Maria Braig, *Die Presse um 1900 im Spiegel der Satire* (Diss. Munich, 1954), p. 72.

42 *Echo*, 23 April 1897.

43 Jeremiah 7, 23 and John 15, 5.

44 Wilhelm Schröder, op. cit., p. 51.

45 Stampfer, op. cit., p. 57, describes Schoenlank's campaign against 'das persönliche Regiment', and recalls his colleague's intriguing explanation for the 'syphilitischer Schnarrton' of the Prussian Junkers. However, his view that Germans underestimated the 'dangerousness' of Wilhelm II, as they did thirty years later with Hitler, is rather open to question.

46 On the Kaiser's 'Sedanrede' of September 1895, see esp. NZ, 1894–5, II, Nr 50, and on the 'Kaiserreden' in general cp. Karl Frohme, *Monarchie oder Republik?* (Hamburg, 1904), p. 295ff. The nature of these speeches was raised in the Reichstag by Bebel and Vollmar in 1903 and gave rise to a propaganda pamphlet, *Die Kaiser-Reden im Reichstag und die Sozialdemokratie* (Berlin, 1903), a copy of which is in BA Koblenz, Z Sg 1–90/6 (3).

47 Cp. Gerhard A. Ritter, *Arbeiterbewegung*, op. cit., p. 27.

48 NZ, 1894–5, II, Nr 51.

49 Quoted in Friedrich Zipfel, *Kritik der deutschen Öffentlichkeit an der Person und an der Monarchie Wilhelms II bis zum Ausbruch des Weltkrieges* (Diss. FU Berlin, 1952), p. 102.

50 StA Hamburg, Senatskommission für die Reichs- und Auswärtige Angelegenheiten, P II 3/1908, letter to the governing mayor of Hamburg, dated 2 November 1908.

51 In the report for 1898, p. 13, a copy of which is in StA Bremen, 4, 14–XII, C.2.bb.1.

52 PT Stuttgart 1898, p. 160. Cp. also Wilhelm Liebknecht's speech, PT Hamburg 1897, p. 131, and Kautsky's letter to Adler, 20 June 1907, in *Adlers Briefwechsel*, op. cit., p. 480.

53 Report for 1904–5, p. 5, in StA Bremen, op. cit. NZ, 1907–8, I, Nr 2, declared that the party would have to deny itself, if it were to give up its fundamental opposition to the monarchy.

54 Frohme, op. cit.

55 Cp. *Echo*, 18 September 1904.

56 Quoted by Frohme, op. cit., p. 300.

57 Cp. the correspondence between the *Reichsverband* and the Minister of Justice, in GStA Berlin-Dahlem, Rep 84a, Nr 10773, Bl 65.

58 Lewinsohn, op. cit., pp. 25–7.

59 Tresckow, op. cit., p. 132.

60 Op. cit., p. 173.

61 Op. cit., p. 174.
62 Kurt Heinig, *Die Finanzskandale des Kaiserreichs* (Berlin, 1925), p. 32.
63 Lewinsohn, op. cit., p. 30.
64 *Hannoverscher Volkswille*, 29 September 1895.
65 Heinig, op. cit., p. 30.
66 NZ, 1895–6, I, Nr 6.
67 Werner Roscher, op. cit., p. 26ff.
68 This incident is recalled by Stampfer, op. cit., p. 100ff.
69 PA/AA, Deutschand Nr 126, Nr 6 secr.
70 Ibid.
71 NZ, 1903–4, I, Nr 5.
72 For details of the proceedings, see Friedländer, op. cit., Bd 6, p. 82ff.
73 Stampfer, op. cit., p. 102.
74 On this episode, see Bülow's own account in his *Memoirs* (London, 1931), vol II, p. 134ff.; Friedrich Thimme (ed.), *Front wider Bülow* (Munich, 1931); Friedrich Freiherr Hiller von Gaertringen, *Fürst Bülows Denkwürdigkeiten* (Tübingen, 1956), p. 119ff.; Maximilian Harden, *Von Versailles nach Versailles* (Hellerau, Dresden, 1927), p. 489ff.; Hellmut Teschner, *Die Daily-Telegraph-Affäre vom November 1908 in der Beurteilung der öffentlichen Meinung* (Diss. Breslau, 1931); and Wilhelm Schüssler, *Die Daily Telegraph Affäre* (Göttingen, 1952).
75 Only a few days after the appearance of the *Daily Telegraph* article, the New York *World* magazine published an interview with the Kaiser granted to its correspondent during the annual Kiel regatta, the essence of which was a proposal that the United States should join an international alliance to oppose British naval strength.
76 Spectator, *Prince Bülow and the Kaiser* (London, 1931), which deals with the *Daily Telegraph* affair, p. 65ff., seems to me to make the mistake of assuming that Bülow's strategy was to remove all possible rivals to his own personal position – Holstein, Philipp Eulenburg and the Kaiser himself. Similarly, I find Johannes Haller, *Aus dem Leben des Fürsten Philipp zu Eulenburg-Hertefeld* (Leipzig and Berlin, 1924), who refers p. 40 to 'eine gehässige Entstellung der Wahrheit', is concerned more with protecting a personal reputation than with establishing a course of events.
77 The absence of Hammann was crucial and involves a further diversion into the social scandal of the period. After the sudden loss of his first wife, around whose demise Holstein – with whom Hammann had quarrelled – chose to weave grizzly suggestions of murder, Hammann fell in love with a married woman. He drove her husband into agreeing to a divorce, but broke a court undertaking not to meet his prospective second wife until her decree became absolute. It was in the midst of this personal entanglement, with the threat of a perjury charge hanging over him, that Hammann took extended leave and was therefore not on hand when the fateful *Daily Telegraph* manuscript passed through his office; Jilg, op. cit., p. 41ff.
78 Gaertringen, op. cit., p. 140.
79 However, it soon became clear that the Reichstag lacked a clear vision of the necessary constitutional objectives, and was unable to act with any decisiveness; Schüssler, op. cit., p. 78.
80 Jilg, op. cit., p. 174, and Thimme, op. cit., p. 19. Cp. also the report of the head of the Hanseatic legation in Berlin, 2 November 1908, in StA Hamburg, Hans. Gesandtschaft, Neuere Reg., 1908, Acta 4.

81 StA Hamburg, Senatskommission für die Reichs- und Auswärtige Angelegenheiten, P II 3/1908. The *Rheinische Zeitung*, 11 November 1908, described
   the treatment of the Kaiser in the Reichstag debate as 'the darkest day for
   the Prusso-German monarchy since 1848'.
82 StA Hamburg, op. cit.
83 Berlin police report for 1908, in StA Bremen, 4, 14–XII, C.2.bb.1.
84 Stenkewitz, *Gegen Bajonett und Dividende*, p. 48. Cp. Westarp, op. cit.,
   p. 37ff.
85 *Echo*, 2 July 1909.
86 Quoted in *Echo*, 4 June 1907.
87 Cp. *Philipp Eulenburgs politische Korrespondenz*, ed. John C. G. Röhl
   (Boppard, 1975), vol I, pp. 9–53.
88 The word itself is Spanish in origin and derives from the chamber party's
   attempts at political manipulation during the reign of Ferdinand VII.
89 Cp. *Echo*, 7 June 1907, 20 November 1908 and 14 December 1912; also
   NZ., 1907–8, I, Nr 5 and II, Nr 40. The SPD press was full of articles devoted
   to the inner mysteries of the operations of the camarilla.
90 Cp. Helmuth Rogge, 'Die Kladderadatsch-Affäre', *Historische Zeitschrift*,
   Bd 195 (1962), p. 90ff.; idem., *Die politische Meinung*, op. cit., pp. 63–4;
   Otto Hammann, *Bilder aus der letzten Kaiserzeit* (Berlin, 1922); Röhl,
   Bismarck, op. cit., p. 108ff.
91 For example, Kiderlen, who was anxious to retrieve his honour, and the
   editor of the *Kladderadatsch* fought a duel; Guttmann op. cit., p. 83.
92 NZ, 1893–4, II, Nr 29.
93 Cp. Weller, op. cit., p. 167, and Röhl, *Eulenburg*, op. cit., pp. 35–53.
94 Helmuth Rogge, *Holstein und Harden* (Munich, 1959), p. 9.
95 Bernhard Menne, *Krupp. Deutschlands Kanonenkönige* (Zürich, 1937),
   p. 216.
96 The head of the criminal police had left instructions that on his death the
   secret register was to be forwarded to the Kaiser for his 'enlightenment'.
   When he received it, Wilhelm II did not open it, assuming the contents to
   be an internal police matter, and sent it back to the Berlin Polizeipräsident;
   op. cit., p. 217.
97 The relationships between the two men are discussed in Rogge, op. cit.,
   Cp. also the review of the same work by Dieter Fricke, in ZfGW 1960, Nr 6,
   p. 149ff. On Holstein's rôle in the events after his dismissal cp. Norman Rich,
   Friedrich von Holstein, 2 vols (Cambridge, 1965), p. 757ff., and Günter
   Richter, *Friedrich von Holstein* (Göttingen, 1969).
98 The clearest and most detailed account is given by Weller, op. cit., p. 188ff.
99 The charges were contained in a leaflet pleading for a reform of the laws on
   homosexuality, which appeared in September 1907. Its author received a
   sentence of 18 months for his audacity; cp. Rogge, op. cit., p. 211.
100 Quoted in *Echo*, 22 May 1908.
101 StA Hamburg, Hans. Gesandtschaft, Neuere Reg. 1907, Acta 4, report dated
   5 December 1907. In May 1907, Bethmann Hollweg had talked with
   Tresckow and had asked him if it might not prove possible to 'arrange
   matters', in order to prevent too much of a scandal; Tresckow, op. cit.,
   p. 165.
102 *Echo*, 27 October 1907.
103 Cp. the editorial in *Hamburger Landbote*, 10 November 1907. Thus, Moltke
   was alleged to have described marriage as 'eine Schweinerei', the conjugal

bedroom as 'eine Notzuchtsanstalt' and a wife as no more than 'das Klosett ihres Mannes'.

104 *Rheinische Zeitung*, 23 April 1908.
105 *Bremer Bürgerzeitung*, 30 October 1907.
106 Cp. the speech of Ludwig Frank, given in Karlsruhe in November 1907, which was published as a pamphlet, *Die Prozesse gegen Liebknecht und Harden*, a copy of which is in BA Koblenz, Z Sg 1–90/46 (9); also NZ, 1907–8, I, Nr 15. A large number of meetings organised by the SPD in the Frankfurt area dealt with the implications of the Moltke–Harden trial; cp. StA Wiesbaden, Abt 407, Nr 43, Bd 4.
107 *Echo*, 20 September 1908.
108 *Rheinische Zeitung*, 23 April 1908.
109 Rogge, op. cit., p. 465.
110 *Rheinische Zeitung*, 31 October 1908.
111 NZ, 1907–8, I, Nr 5. Rich, op. cit., p. 796, makes the valid comment that 'though the pederasts might be removed, the sycophants remained'.
112 Fritz Fischer, *Krieg der Illusionen* (Düsseldorf, 1969), p. 42. On Stumm, see esp. Fritz Hellwig, *Carl Ferdinand Freiherr von Stumm-Halberg 1826–1901* (Heidelberg, 1936).
113 Cp. for instance PT Jena 1905, p. 293.
114 *Echo*, 25 January 1901.
115 Quoted by Ritter, *Arbeiterbewegung*, p. 29.
116 Quoted by Schraepler, op. cit., p. 29.
117 Karl Buchheim, *Das Deutsche Kaiserreich 1871–1918* (Munich, 1969), p. 194.
118 Reichstag debate, 12 February 1892, quoted in the *Maifeier Zeitung* for 1892, in StA Hannover, Hann Des 80, Hild II, I, Nr 547, vol VI. A similar view was echoed by Kardorff.
119 *Echo*, 4 January 1905.
120 *Bremer Bürgerzeitung*, 12 March 1901.
121 Cp. the wealth of press cuttings in StA Hamburg, S 2362, also Saul, *Staat*, passim.
122 *Vorwärts*, 28 March 1907. Cp. also details of the long list issued by the *Gesamtverband deutscher Metallindustrieller*, as published in the edition for 29 November 1908.
123 *Echo*, 10 September 1907.
124 *Echo*, 26 June 1908.
125 *Echo*, 5 December 1901.
126 This evidence was published by the SPD press in 1891 and recalled by the *Echo*, 3 November 1900.
127 Details as quoted by *Echo*, 31 October and 3 November 1900.
128 Hartmut Kaelble, *Industrielle Interessenpolitik in der Wilhelminischen Gesellschaft, ZdI 1895–1914* (Berlin, 1967), p. 17.
129 As quoted in the *Echo*, 22 January 1901.
130 Diary entry dated 10 January 1896, *Denkwürdigkeiten des Fürsten Chlodwig zu Hohenlohe-Schillingsfürst*, ed. Friedrich Curtius, Bd II (Stuttgart and Leipzig, 1906), p. 523.
131 The circular, dated 11 December 1897, was published by the *Vorwärts*, 15 January 1898. Cp. also PT Stuttgart 1898, pp. 15 and 46.
132 Auer quoted the letter in a debate in the Reichstag on 24 November; RT, 10 L.P. 2 Sess., p. 132. The text of the memorandum is also given by Menne,

op. cit., p. 207. According to Stampfer, op. cit., p 67, a copy of the letter was sent to the office of the *Leipziger Volkszeitung* by some of his friends in Southern Germany.

133 Quoted in Rassow & Born, op. cit., p. 131.

134 Op. cit., p. 130.

135 *Echo*, 28 November 1900.

136 StA Hamburg, Hans. Gesandtschaft, Neuere Reg., 1901, Acta 14, dated 22 June 1901.

137 Bülow, *Memoirs*, vol I, p. 464.

138 StA Hamburg, ibid., and A I 4, 1900, Acta 14, dated 9 November 1900.

139 *Echo*, 28 June 1901.

140 Cp. *Echo*, 1 and 2 November 1900.

141 Cp. NZ, 1900–1, I, Nr 5 and 17.

142 *Echo*, 15 January 1901.

143 Kautsky, *Vernichtung*, op. cit., p. 6. The pamphlet was by H. Bürger (itself a pseudonym for a leading demagogue of the Freisinnige Volkspartei, Heinrich Fraenkel), *Soziale Tatsachen und sozialdemokratische Lehren. Ein Büchlein für denkende Menschen und besonders für denkende Arbeiter*.

144 *Echo*, 10 December 1909. Cp. also details of the secret ZdI protocol referred to by Stampfer, op. cit., p. 130.

145 *Vorwärts*, 3 May 1911.

146 Jonathan Steinberg, 'The Case of Herr Fritz Krupp', *Midstream* (New York), November 1967, pp. 10–19.

147 *Bergische Arbeiterstimme* (Solingen), 18 November 1901.

148 Menne, op. cit., p. 174.

149 Walter Bartel, *Karl Liebknecht gegen Krupp* (Berlin, 1951), p. 6.

150 In 1902 it stood at 21 million marks; Menne, op. cit., p. 188.

151 Willi A. Boelcke (ed.), *Krupp und die Hohenzollern in Dokumenten* (Frankfurt a.M., 1970), p. 112. Even the *Süddeutsche Monatshefte*, for which Friedrich Naumann wrote, received Krupp subsidies.

152 *Echo*, 8 November 1899.

153 Boelcke, op. cit., p. 113, footnote 33.

154 Cp. for example *Vorwärts*, 6 October 1906.

155 William Manchester, *Krupp. Zwölf Generationen* (Munich, 1968), p. 219.

156 *Essener Volkszeitung*, 16 May and 1 June 1893; as quoted in Manchester, op. cit., p. 220.

157 *Bergische Arbeiterstimme*, 18 November 1901.

158 Menne, op. cit., p. 218.

159 Op. cit., p. 221. Cp. also Tresckow, op. cit., p. 126.

160 *Echo*, 7 July 1894 and 2 November 1898.

161 The article is also quoted in full by Boelcke, op. cit., pp. 164–5.

162 Menne, op. cit., p. 222.

163 Quoted in *Echo*, 26 November 1902.

164 Tresckow, op. cit., p. 129, is of the opinion that Krupp inadvertently took an excessive sleeping-draught to cope with his notorious insomnia; the memoirs of Finanzrat Faux, as quoted by Bernt Engelmann, *Krupp* (Munich, 1969), p. 567, suggests that Krupp suffered a stroke, while four doctors who signed the official death certificate concocted a curious scenario, in which their patient spent some nine hours in a semi-coma before eventually expiring.

165 *Münchener Post*, 1 December 1902.

166 Menne, op. cit., p. 225; Manchester, op. cit., p. 230.

167 This caused some surprise at the time; cp. *Der Fall Krupp. Sein Verlauf und seine Folgen* (Munich, 1903), a copy of which is in BA Koblenz, Z Sg 1–90/6 (6).

168 On the other hand, stirred up no doubt by the contents of the latest *Kaiserrede*, wild mobs had to be restrained by the works police from desecrating the grave; *Essener Volkszeitung*, 27 November 1902 and Manchester, op. cit., p. 188.

169 The text is given by Wilhelm Schröder, op. cit., p. 66. Cp. also Engelmann, pp. 568–9.

170 Engelmann, op. cit., p. 570. On 16 December, when the Crown Prince received a working-men's deputation at Castle Oels, he referred to SPD workers as 'jene Elenden'.

171 *Echo*, 17 December 1902.

172 Report dated 10 December 1902, to the *Regierungspräsident*, in HStA Düsseldorf, Reg. Köln 7572. The editor of the *Mainzer Volkszeitung*, who received three months, was one of several SPD journalists who found themselves in prison as a result of critical editorial comment on the speeches.

173 Cp. Manchester, op. cit., p. 236.

174 *Magdeburger Volksstimme*, 7 December 1902.

175 Stampfer, op. cit., p. 99. Cp. also Hedwig Wachenheim, *Die deutsche Arbeiterbewegung 1844 bis 1914* (Cologne and Opladen, 1967), p. 371.

176 *Vorwärts*, 28 November 1902.

177 Krupp's friends readily assumed that the Kaiser would be willing to put pressure on the Italian government to provide no evidence favourable to the defence at a resultant court hearing, without which the charges made by the *Vorwärts* were doomed to remain unsubstantiated; cp. Manchester, op. cit., p. 232. In the very last article which Maximilian Harden wrote for *Die Zukunft*, he claimed that Eisner and other members of the editorial staff had expressed their concern at the impending prosecution, and had asked Harden to intercede with the authorities on their behalf; quoted in Harry F. Young, *Maximilian Harden* (Münster, 1971), p. 86. I think that in this respect Harden overestimated the importance of his own position.

178 Boelcke, op. cit., p. 571, quotes the letter of Margarethe Krupp, dated 10 December 1902, in which this request was made. This explanation actually seemed the least plausible at the time; according to Menne, op. cit., p. 230, the Krupp directorate issued a statement to the effect that the final decision had been left to the Oberstaatsanwalt, and the *Münchener Post*, 10 January 1903, suggested that the courts had bowed once again to internal governmental pressure.

179 NZ 1902–3, i, Nr 12.

180 Cp. Zipfel, op. cit., p. 101, and Menne, op. cit., p. 231ff.

181 *Münchener Post*, 21 January 1903.

182 This was the argument underlying the propaganda pamphlet produced by the SPD (and cited above in note 167), whose first edition, incidentally, sold out within three days.

183 Menne, op. cit., p. 245.

184 Boelcke, op. cit., p. 185. Liebknecht quoted in May 1914 the names of seven members of the Krupp directorate who had previously been high-ranking army or naval officers; Lothholz, op. cit., p. 85.

185 Op. cit., p. 18.

186 *Echo*, 9 October 1900.
187 StA Hamburg, Senatskommission für die Reichs- und Auswärtige Angelegenheiten, 1913, P II 6/1908, vol 7. Krupp supplied 75% of the heavy artillery ammunition and 90% of the shells.
188 *Echo*, 25 October 1902.
189 Bartel, op. cit., p. 10. Cp. also Manchester, op. cit., p .269.
190 Cp. *Echo*, 22 April 1913.
191 This was the codename used for the transcripts sent to Essen. Since they were too bulky and their contents too confidential to be entrusted to normal postal traffic, they were specially sealed and sent as freight under the description of 'grain rollers' (*Kornwalzer*); cp. *Vorwärts*, 30 July 1913. There is a wealth of press material on Liebknecht's disclosures in StA Hamburg, S 19250, Bd 2 and Bd 3. Liebknecht made the Krupp affair the subject of a major speech to several thousand workers on 25 April 1913. Since the hall was crammed full of interested spectators, hundreds had to stand in the street outside; Rückert, *Zur Geschichte*, op. cit., p. 191.
192 Lothholz, op. cit., p. 82.
193 Cp. *Prozeß Brandt und Genossen. Der sogenannte Krupp–Prozeß*, ed. Adolf Zimmermann (Berlin, 1914), p. 385.
194 *Vorwärts*, 13 April 1913, which published a letter of the Deutsche Waffen- und Munitionsfabriken Aktiengesellschaft. Cp. also the edition for 28 April 1913.
195 Cp. *Vorwärts*, 16 December 1913.
196 Quoted in Zimmermann, op. cit., p. 385.
197 Quoted in *Vorwärts*, 19 April 1913.
198 *Leipziger Volkszeitung*, 21 April 1913. The Berlin paper *Der Pionier*, 7 May 1913, 'Waffenspekulation und Kriegsfreude gehören also zusammen, wie die Farbe zum Pinsel und zum Soldatenschinder die Gemeinheit.'
199 *Rheinische Zeitung*, 23 April 1914.
200 The semi-official *Norddeutsche Allgemeine Zeitung* spoke of the participants in the affair as 'untergeordnete Persönlichkeiten'; quoted in *Echo*, 20 July 1913. Staatsanwalt Romen argued in *Der Tag* that the case was simply 'eine Schmiergeldgeschichte gewöhnlicher Art'; *Echo*, 12 November 1913.
201 Quoted in Boelcke, op. cit., pp. 219–19.
202 Zimmermann, op. cit., pp. viii and xii.
203 Menne, op. cit., p. 209.
204 *Vorwärts*, 27 and 28 August 1913.
205 Cp. *Echo*, 22 October 1913.
206 Cp. *Vorwärts*, 25 October and 2 November 1913.
207 Brandt was actually charged under a section of the criminal code which could have led to a maximum sentence of five years imprisonment.
208 *Vorwärts*, 9 November 1913.
209 *Deutsch–Soziale Blätter*, 19 November 1913. The establishment press was especially incensed at evidence of what it assumed to be socialist 'Schadenfreude', and felt that the affair could only rebound to the advantage of Germany's enemies abroad.
210 Stenkewitz, op. cit., p. 32; Westarp, op. cit., p. 327. Cp. also *Echo*, 1 May 1914.

SOURCES

A. Newspapers and archives

(Newspapers are for the period 1890–1914, except where otherwise stated.)
Hamburger Echo (1892ff.) (StA Hamburg.)
Bremer Bürgerzeitung (1895ff.) (StA Bremen.)
Vorwärts (IISH Amsterdam.)
Leipziger Volkszeitung (1894ff., selected years.) (IISH Amsterdam.)
Rheinische Zeitung (1908ff.) (IISH Amsterdam.)
Die neue Zeit (1890ff.) (Forschungsstelle für die Geschichte des Nationalsozialismus in Hamburg, FGNS.)
Sozialistische Monatshefte (1900ff.) (FGNS.)
Sozialdemokratische Partei-Correspondenz (1906–13) (IISH Amsterdam.)
Protokolle der Parteitage der Sozialdemokratischen Partei Deutschlands (1891–1913) (FGNS.)
Stenographische Berichte des Deutschen Reichstags (FGNS.)

A useful additional source is the

Internationale Wissenschaftliche Korrespondenz zur Geschichte der deutschen Arbeiterbewegung, ed. Henryk Skrzypczak (Berlin, 1965ff.)

Extensive press cuttings are also contained within the files of the political police.

StA Hamburg

Bestand Politische Polizei
S 1365 Bd 24, S 1365 Bd 26, S 1365 Bd 27 Teil 1 and 3, S 1365 Bd 28 Teil 1–8, S 1861, S 2169, S 2267, S 3698, S 3918, S 4127, S 4456, S 4687, S 5283, S 5930, S 6520, S 12074, S 13339, S 14894, S 16969, S 17702 (newspaper editors and party journalists).

S 2170 Bd 20–22 (press controls), S 1365 Bd 12 and Bd 22 (*Hamburger Echo*), S 1365 Bd 25 (Presse-Commission), S 4275 (Bérard).

S 733 Bd 1 (Frohme), S 1768 (Legien), S 3871 (Pfannkuch), S 6430 (Arons), S 6506 (Scheidemann), S 6538 (Lütgenau), S 6619 (Wurm), S 6665 (Dietz), S 6677 (Auer), S 6694 (Bebel), S 6699 Bd 1 and 2 (W. Liebknecht), S 6704 (Schoenlank), S 6705 (Singer), S 6724 (Blos), S 9340 (Kautsky).

S 1809, vol I–III (May Day 1890), S 4475 (1895), S 7690 (1900), S 12460 (1905), S 17300 (1910), S 5800 Bd 1 (1897 party conference), S 2392 (1903 Schleswig-Holstein party conference), S 2362 (industrial blacklists), S 3423 vol VI (army and navy), S 5135 Bd 2–4 (Leckert–Lützow–Tausch affair), S 5160 Bd 1 and 2

(Rechtsschutzverein), S 5160 Bd 3–7 (police affairs), S 6381 (Chr. Zeitschriften-verein), S 11792 Bd 1 and 2 (Reichsverband), S 14980 Bd 1 and 2 (Reichsverband, Hamburg), S 19250 Bd 1–3 (Krupp).

S 1365 Bd 1, S 1365 Bd 15 Teil 2, S 1365 Bd 27 Teil 2 (perjury cases), S 5150 Bd 1 and 2 (Essen perjury trial), S 2170 Bd 11 UA 1, S 7300 Bd 2 and 3 (*lèse-majesté*), S 2505 Bd 16 UA 2 (judicial proceedings), S 7410 (Löbtau case).

Polizeibehörde I, Arb. Sig. 255 (Dienstvorschrift für die Abteilung IV, Politische Polizei).

Senat
Cl I, Lit T, Nr 18b, Vol 4–7 (political associations); Cl VII, Lit Me, No 12, Vol 18, Fasc 7, Inv 4b, 5a, 5e, 6a, 6b, 7d, 8a–e, 9, 10c, 11–13 (political reports on the SPD).

Senatskommission für die Reichs- und Auswärtigen Angelegenheiten
C I b 10, P II 16/1894, P IV 1/1897, P II 4/1907, P II 3/1908, P II 6/ 1908 vols 6 and 7.

Archiv der Hanseatischen Gesandtschaft Berlin, Neuere Registratur
A I 4 (political reports 1897–1912), VII P I (police affairs 1897–1919), M I b 6 (military legal code), P I 6 b and c (Zuchthausvorlage).

StA Bremen
4, 14–XII A.2.bh (SPD)
4, 14–XII C.2.ba (SPD press)
4, 14–XII C.2.bb.1 (political reports)
3 – S.30, Nr 27 (anti-socialist measures)

StA Marburg
Bestand 150, Nr 630, 632, 633, 639, 640, 1596, 2055 (anti-socialist measures), 1843 (government influencing of the press), 1927 and 1928 (breaches of the peace), 1968 (Kriegervereine)

Bestand 165, Nr 706 Bd 2–5 (SPD), 707 (Chr. Zeitschriftenverein), 709 Bd 1–3 (socialist press agitation), 1241 (SPD), 1245 (Reichsverband), 1262 (judicial matters), 3142 (anti-socialist measures)

StA Hannover
Ha 80, Ha II, Nr 702 (SPD press)
Hann Des 80, Hild II, I, Nr 547, vols IV and V (SPD agitation)

StA Münster
Oberpräsidium Nr 2670 (press affairs), Nr 2694 Bd 2 (political reports), Regierung Arnsberg, Nr 1447 (SPD disclosures), Regierung Arnsberg I, Nr 100a, Regierung Münster, Abt VII, Nr 62r, Kreis Bochum, 1. Landratsamt and Nr 44a (political reports)

StA Osnabrück
Dep 3b I, Nr 436 (anti-socialist strategy)
Rep 335, Nr 13562 (judicial affairs)

Rep 430, Nr 840 (government influencing of the press)
Rep 450, Bent I, Nr 48 (anti-socialist strategy)

HStA Düsseldorf
Reg. Düsseldorf 42798 and 42806 (anti-socialist strategy)
Reg. Aachen, Präsidialbüro Nr 919 (Chr. Zeitschriftenverein)

StA Koblenz
Abt 403, Nr 6826 and 6827 (legal restrictions), 6841 (SPD), 6857 and 6862 (anti-socialist measures)

StA Wiesbaden
Abt 407, Nr 43, Bd 1–5 (SPD)
Abt 425, Nr 421 and 422 (Frankfurter Volksstimme)

StA Speyer
Bestand H1, Nr 2030–2032 (May Day)

BA Koblenz
Z Sg 1 (SPD pamphlets)
Z Sg 113, Bd 67, 162 and 163 (Sammlung Fechenbach)

GStA Berlin–Dahlem
Rep 84a, Nr 3932 (press affairs), Nr 3986 (press law), Nr 8213 and 8214 (*lèse-majesté*), Nr 8221–3 (statistics), Nr 8255 (perjury cases), Nr 8418 and 8419 (revision of Strafgesetzbuch), Nr 8463–5 and 8469 (anti-socialist strategy), Nr 8471 (Umsturzvorlage), Nr 10771–3 (SPD).

Rep 90, Nr 2412 (government influencing of the press), Nr 2414 (press affairs)
Rep 180, Nr 13400 (press affairs, Danzig), Nr 13998 (SPD)

Politisches Archiv des Auswärtigen Amts, Bonn
Europa Generalia, Nr 82, Nr 1, Nr 1, Bd 4–8 (anti-socialist strategy)
Europa Generalia, Nr 82 secr., Nr 1, Bd 9–23 (SPD)
Europa Generalia, Nr 82, Nr 14, Bd 4–8 (SPD)
Deutschland Nr 122, Nr 3a secr., Bd 1–3 (Normann–Schumann)
Deutschland Nr 122, Nr 36, Bd 1–3 (Leckert–Lützow–Tausch affair)
Deutschland Nr 126, Nr 6 secr. (*lèse-majesté*)
Deutschland Nr 126, Nr 8 and Nr 10 secr. (government influencing of the press)

IISH Amsterdam
NL Wolfgang Heine

B. Published source material

Akten zur staatlichen Sozialpolitik in Deutschland 1890–1914, eds. Peter Rassow and Karl Erich Born (Wiesbaden, 1959).
Archivalische Forschungen zur Geschichte der deutschen Arbeiterbewegung, ed. Leo Stern (Berlin, 1956ff.).
Deutsche Sozialgeschichte, Dokumente und Skizzen, vol II 1870–1914, eds. Gerhard A. Ritter and Jürgen Kocka (Munich, 1974).

Dokumente der deutschen Arbeiterbewegung zur Journalistik, Teil I 1848–1905 (Leipzig, 1961); Teil II 1900–1945 (Leipzig, 1963).

Dokumente und Materialien zu den sozialen und politischen Verhältnissen in der Provinz Brandenburg von 1871 bis 1917, eds. Rudolf Knaack and Otto Rückert (Potsdam, 1968).

Geschichte der deutschen Arbeiterbewegung 1871–1914 (Berlin, 1966–7).

Jahrbuch des Vereins Arbeiterpresse, I–III (Berlin, 1912–14).

Rudolf Martin, *Jahrbuch des Vermögens und Einkommens der Millionäre Preußen* (Berlin, 1912).

Krupp und die Hohenzollern in Dokumenten, ed. Willi A. Boelcke (Frankfurt a.M., 1970).

Rosa Luxemburg im Kampf gegen den deutschen Militarismus. Prozeßberichte und Materialien aus den Jahren 1913 bis 1915 (Berlin, 1960).

Franz Mehring. Politische Publizistik 1891 bis 1904, ed. Josef Schleifstein (Berlin, 1964).

Quellensammlung zur Geschichte der deutschen Sozialpolitik 1867–1914 (Wiesbaden, 1966).

Sozialgeschichtliches Arbeitsbuch : Materialien zur Statistik des Kaiserreiches 1870–1914, eds. Gerd Hohorst, Jürgen Kocka and Gerhard A. Ritter (Munich, 1975).

Unsere Betriebe von 1890 bis 1925 (Berlin, 1926).

Vierzig Jahre Volkswacht 1890–1930 (Bielefeld, 1930).

Otto Rückert, *Zur Geschichte der Arbeiterbewegung im Reichstagswahlkreis Potsdam–Spandau–Osthavelland 1871–1917* (Potsdam, 1965).

C. Correspondence, diaries, memoirs, recollections

Adler, Victor *Briefwechsel mit August Bebel und Karl Kautsky* (Vienna, 1954).

Ballhausen, Freiherr Lucius von *Bismarck–Erinnerungen* (Stuttgart and Berlin 1920).

Bismarcks großes Spiel. Die geheimen Tagebücher Ludwig Bambergers, ed. Ernst Feder (Frankfurt a.M, 1932).

August Bebels Briefwechsel mit Friedrich Engels, ed. Werner Blumenberg (The Hague, 1965).

August Bebels Briefwechsel mit Karl Kautsky, ed. Karl Kautsky, Jnr. (Amsterdam, 1971).

Eduard Bernsteins Briefwechsel mit Friedrich Engels, ed. Helmut Hirsch (Assen, 1970).

Bethmann Hollweg, Theobald von *Betrachtungen zum Weltkriege*, 2 vols, (Berlin, 1919–21).

Bülow, Prince *Memoirs* (London, 1931).

Eisner, Kurt *Taggeist* (Berlin, 1901).

Philipp Eulenburgs politische Korrespondenz, ed. John C. G. Röhl, 3 vols., (Boppard, 1975).

Gerlach, Hellmut von *Meine Erlebnisse in der preußischen Verwaltung* (Berlin, 1919).

Denkwürdigkeiten des Fürsten Chlodwig zu Hohenlohe–Schillingsfürst, ed. Friedrich Curtius, Bd II (Stuttgart and Leipzig, 1906).

Fürst Chlodwig zu Hohenlohe–Schillingsfürst, Denkwürdigkeiten der Reichskanzlerzeit, ed. K. A. von Müller (Stuttgart, 1931).

Hohenlohe, Alexander *Aus meinem Leben* (Frankfurt a.M., 1925).
Mayer, Gustav *Erinnerungen. Vom Journalisten zum Historiker der deutschen Arbeiterbewegung* (Munich, 1951).
Aufzeichnungen des Chefs des Marinekabinetts Admiral Georg Alexander von Müller über die Ära Wilhelms II, ed. Walter Görlitz (Göttingen, 1965).
Scheidemann, Philipp *Memoiren eines Sozialdemokraten* (Dresden, 1928).
Das Tagebuch der Baronin Spitzemberg, ed. Rudolf Vierhaus (Göttingen, 1960).
Denkwürdigkeiten des General Feldmarschalls Alfred Grafen von Waldersee, ed. H. O. Meisner (Stuttgart, 1922).
Zedlitz-Trützschler, Graf Robert *Zwölf Jahre am deutschen Kaiserhof* (Stuttgart, 1925).

D. Secondary works

Adler, Victor *Aufsätze, Reden und Briefe* (Vienna, 1929).
Adolph, Hans J. L. *Otto Wels und die Politik der deutschen Sozialdemokratie 1894–1939* (Berlin, 1971).
Albrecht, Willy *Die Fuchsmühler Ereignisse vom Oktober 1894 und ihre Folgen für die innere Entwicklung Bayerns im letzten Jahrzehnt des 19. Jahrhunderts* (*Zeitschrift für bayerische Landesgeschichte*, Bd 33, Heft 8, 1970).
Apfel Alfred *Behind the Scenes of German Justice* (London, 1935).
Baasch, Ernst *Geschichte des Hamburgischen Zeitungswesens von den Anfängen bis 1914* (Hamburg, 1930).
Badewitz, Hans *Der Zeugniszwang gegen die Presse* (Munich, 1952).
Balfour, Michael *The Kaiser and his Times* (London, 1964).
Barkin, Kenneth *The Controversy over German Industrialisation 1890–1902* (Chicago, 1970).
Bartel, Walter *Karl Liebknecht gegen Krupp* (Berlin, 1951).
  Die Linke in der deutschen Sozialdemokratie im Kampf gegen Militarismus und Krieg (Berlin, 1958).
Baschwitz, Kurt *Du und die Masse* (Amsterdam, 1959).
Berghahn, Volker R. *Der Tirpitz Plan* (Düsseldorf, 1971).
  Germany and the Approach of War in 1914 (London, 1973).
Berlau, Adolf J. *The German Social Democratic Party 1914–21* (New York, 1949).
Bertheau, Franz R. *Das Zeitungswesen in Hamburg 1616 bis 1913* (Hamburg, 1914).
Bertram, Jürgen *Die Wahlen zum Deutschen Reichstag vom Jahre 1912* (Düsseldorf, 1964).
Besson, Waldemar *Friedrich Ebert* (Göttingen, 1963).
Bleiber, Helmut *Die Moabiter Unruhen 1910* (*Zeitschrift für Geschichtswissenschaft*, 1955, Heft 2).
Blum, Hans *Die Lügen unserer Sozialdemokratie* (Wismar, 1891).
Born, Karl Erich *Staat und Sozialpolitik seit Bismarcks Sturz* (Wiesbaden, 1957).
  Preußen und Deutschland im Kaiserreich (Tübingen, 1967).
Bozi, Alfred and Hugo Heinmann (eds.), *Recht, Verwaltung und Politik im neuen Deutschland* (Stuttgart, 1916).

Bracher, K. D. *Das deutsche Dilemma* (Munich, 1971).

Braig, Solveig-Maria *Die Presse um 1900 im Spiegel der Satire* (Diss. Munich, 1954).

Brauchitsch, Max von *Verwaltungsgesetze für Preußen*, vol IIa, 22nd edit. (Berlin, 1932).

Braun, Heinrich *Die sozialdemokratische Presse* (Berlin, 1896).

Brüggemann, Dieter *Die rechtsprechende Gewalt* (Berlin, 1962).

Buchheim, Karl *Das Deutsche Kaiserreich 1871–1918* (Munich, 1969).

Buchwitz, Otto *50 Jahre Funktionär der deutschen Arbeiterbewegung* (Berlin, 1949).

Busch, Rudolf von *Die Beschlagnahme von Druckschriften unter besonderer Berücksichtigung der Presse* (Diss. Kiel, 1929).

Conring, Franz *Das deutsche Militär in der Karikatur* (Stuttgart, 1907).

Conze, Werner in *The New Cambridge Modern History*, vol XI (Cambridge, 1962), pp. 274–95.

Die Zeit Wilhelms II und die Weimarer Republik (Stuttgart, 1964).

Craig, Gordon A. *The Politics of the Prussian Army 1640–1945* (Oxford, 1964).

War, Politics and Diplomacy (London, 1966).

Dahrendorf, Ralf *Gesellschaft und Demokratie in Deutschland* (Munich, 1965).

Dang, Anton *Die sozialdemokratische Presse Deutschlands* (Diss. Frankfurt a.M., 1928).

Demeter, Karl *The German Officer Corps in Society and State 1650–1945* (London, 1965).

Doehn, B. *Der Begriff der Majestätsbeleidigung und ihr Verhältnis zur gewöhnlichen Beleidigung nach dem Reichsstrafgesetzbuch*, (*Zeitschrift für die gesamte Strafrechtswissenschaft, Bd 21*) (Berlin, 1901).

Domann, Peter *Sozialdemokratie und Kaisertum unter Wilhelm II* (Wiesbaden, 1974).

Drahn, Ernst *Die deutsche Sozialdemokratie* (Berlin, 1926).

Dunger, Ingrid *Wilhelmshaven 1870–1914* (Wiesbaden, 1962).

Ehrl, Oskar *The Development of the German Military Criminal Procedure during the 19th Century* (*Revue de Droit Penal Militaire et de Droit de la Guerre*, VII, 2, 1968).

Engelberg, Ernst *Revolutionäre Politik und Rote Feldpost 1878–1890* (Berlin, 1959).

Engelmann, Bernt *Krupp* (Munich, 1969).

Engelsing, Rolf *Massenpublikum und Journalistentum im 19. Jahrhundert in Nordwestdeutschland* (Berlin, 1966).

Epstein, Klaus 'Three American Studies of German Socialism,' *World Politics*, XI (1959).

'Erzberger and the German Colonial Scandals 1905–1910', *English Historical Review*, 1959, pp. 637–63.

Matthias Erzberger and the Dilemma of German Democracy (Princeton, N.J., 1959).

'The Socio-Economic History of the Second German Empire', *Review of Politics*, 29 (1967).

Erler, Curt *Von der Macht der Presse in Deutschland* (Berlin, 1911).

Ernst, Eugen *Polizeispitzeleien und Ausnahmegesetze 1878–1910* (Berlin, 1911).

Eyck, Erich *Das persönliche Regiment Wilhelms II* (Zürich, 1948).

Fehrenbach, Elisabeth *Wandlungen des deutschen Kaisergedankens 1871–1918* (Munich, 1969).

Feigell, Willy *Die Entwicklung des Königlichen Polizei–Präsidiums zu Berlin in der Zeit von 1809 bis 1909* (Berlin, 1909).

Feldmann, Friedrich *Geschichte des Ortsvereins Hannover der SPD vom Gründungsjahr 1864 bis 1933* (Hannover, 1952).

Fischer, Elfriede *Grundlagen der Interpretation der Politik der deutschen Sozialdemokratie durch die sozialdemokratische Presse* (Diss. Heidelberg, 1928).

Fischer, Fritz *Griff nach der Weltmacht*, 4th edit. (Düsseldorf, 1971).

    Krieg der Illusionen (Düsseldorf, 1969).

Fliess, Peter J. *Freedom of the Press in the German Republic 1918–1933* (Baton Rouge, La, 1955).

Foerster, Friedrich Wilhelm *Erlebte Weltgeschichte 1869–1953* (Nuremberg, 1953).

Fraenkel, Ernst *Zur Soziologie der Klassenjustiz und Aufsätze zur Verfassungskrise 1931–32* (Darmstadt, 1968).

Freudenberg, Anne Marie *Das Jahr 1913 im Spiegel der deutschen Öffentlichkeit.* (Diss. Göttingen, 1948).

Fricke, Dieter 'Die sozialdemokratische Parteischule 1906–1914', *Zeitschrift für Geschichtswissenschaft*, 1957, Heft 2.

    'Der Aufschwung der Massenkämpfe der deutschen Arbeiterklasse unter dem Einfluß der russischen Revolution von 1905', *Zeitschrift für Geschichtswissenschaft*, 1957, Heft 4.

    'Der Essener Meineidsprozeß von 1895 – ein Beispiel preußischer Klassenjustiz', *Geschichte in der Schule*, 1957, Nr 4.

    'Zur Rolle des Militarismus nach innen in Deutschland vor dem 1. Weltkrieg', *Zeitschrift für Geschichtswissenschaft*, 1958, Heft 6.

    'Der Reichsverband gegen die Sozialdemokratie von seiner Gründung bis zu den Reichstagswahlen von 1907', *Zeitschrift für Geschichtswissenschaft*, 1959, Heft 2.

    'Zur Militarisierung des deutschen Geisteslebens im wilhelminischen Deutschland. Der Fall Leo Arons', *Zeitschrift für Geschichtswissenschaft*, 1960, Heft 5.

    'Zum Bündnis des preußisch-deutschen Militarismus mit dem Klerus gegen die sozialistische Arbeiterbewegung am Ende des 19. Jahrhunderts', *Zeitschrift für Geschichtswissenschaft*, 1960, Heft 6.

    'Die Affäre Leckert–Lützow–Tausch und die Regierungskrise von 1897 in Deutschland', *Zeitschrift für Gesichtswissenschaft*, 1960, Heft 7.

    Bismarcks Prätorianer. Die Berliner politische Polizei im Kampf gegen die deutsche Arbeiterbewegung 1871–1898 (Berlin, 1962).

    Zur Organisation und Tätigkeit der deutschen Arbeiterbewegung 1890–1914 (Leipzig, 1962).

Friedländer, Hugo *Interessante Kriminal-Prozesse von kulturhistorischer Bedeutung* (Berlin, 1922).

Frohme, Karl *Monarchie oder Republik?* (Hamburg, 1904).

    Politische Polizei und Justiz im monarchischen Deutschland (Hamburg, 1926).

Fülberth, Georg 'Zur Genese des Revisionismus in der deutschen Sozialdemokratie vor 1914', *Das Argument*, March 1971.

Gay, Peter J. *The Dilemma of Democratic Socialism* (New York, 1952).

Geary, Richard J. *Karl Kautsky and the Development of Marxism* (Diss. Cambridge, 1972).

Gemkow, Heinrich *Paul Singer* (Berlin, 1957).

Gilg, Peter *Die Erneuerung des demokratischen Denkens im wilhelminischen Deutschland* (Wiesbaden, 1965).

Gisevius, Hans Bernd *Der Anfang vom Ende* (Zürich, 1971).

Glaser, Fritz *Das Verhältnis der Presse zur Justiz* (Berlin, 1914).

Göhring, Martin *Bismarcks Erben 1890–1945* (Wiesbaden, 1958).

Goertz, Hartmann *Preußens Gloria* (Munich, 1962).

Grebing, Helga *Geschichte der deutschen Arbeiterbewegung* (Munich, 1966).

Grimm, Friedrich *Politische Justiz. Die Krankheit unserer Zeit* (Bonn, 1953).

Groh, Dieter 'Hundert Jahre deutsche Arbeiterbewegung?', *Der Staat* (1963).

' "The Unpatriotic Socialists" and the State', *Journal of Contemporary History*, October 1966.

'Je eher, desto besser. Innenpolitische Faktoren für die Präventivkriegsbereitschaft des Deutschen Reiches 1913/14', *Politische Vierteljahresschrift*, 13 (1972).

Negative Integration und revolutionärer Attentismus (Frankfurt a.M. and Berlin, 1973).

Groth, Otto *Die Zeitung* (Mannheim and Berlin, 1928).

Die unerkannte Kulturmacht (Berlin, 1960).

Guttmann, Bernhard *Schattenriß einer Generation 1888–1918* (Stuttgart, 1950).

Haase, Ernst *Hugo Haase* (Berlin, 1929).

Halbe, Max *Jahrhundertwende* (Danzig, 1935).

Hall, Alex 'The Kaiser, the Wilhelmine State and Lèse-Majesté', *German Life & Letters*, January 1974.

'By Other Means: The Legal Struggle against the SPD in Wilhelmine Germany 1890–1900', *Historical Journal*, June, 1974.

'The War of Words: Anti-socialist offensives and counter-propaganda in Wilhelmine Germany 1890–1914', *Journal of Contemporary History*, vol. 11, Nos 2 and 3, July 1976.

'Youth in Rebellion. The Beginnings of the Socialist Youth Movement 1904–1914', in *Society and Politics in Wilhelmine Germany 1889–1918*, ed. Richard J. Evans (Croom Helm, London, 1977).

Haller, Johannes *Aus dem Leben des Fürsten Philipp zu Eulenburg-Hertefeld* (Leipzig and Berlin, 1924).

Hammann, Otto *Der neue Kurs* (Berlin, 1918).

Hamburger, Ernest *Juden im öffentlichen Leben Deutschlands* (Tübingen, 1968).

Bilder aus der letzen Kaiserzeit (Berlin, 1922).

Hannover, Heinrich and Elisabeth Hannover-Drück, *Politische Justiz 1918–1933* (Frankfurt a.M., 1966).

Harden, Maximilian *Von Versailles nach Versailles* (Hellerau, Dresden, 1927).

Hartung, Fritz *Das persönliche Regiment Wilhelms II* (Berlin, 1952).

Heidegger, Hermann *Die deutsche Sozialdemokratie und der nationale Staat 1870–1920* (Göttingen, 1956).

Heinig, Kurt *Die Finanzskandale des Kaiserreichs* (Berlin, 1925).

Helfritz, Hans *Wilhelm II als Kaiser und König* (Zürich, 1954).

Hellwig, Fritz *Carl Ferdinand Freiherr von Stumm-Halberg 1836–1901* (Heidelberg, 1936).

Hennig, G. *August Bebel – Todfeind des preußisch-deutschen Militärstaates* (Berlin, 1963).

Henning, Hansjoachim 'Kriegervereine in den preußischen Westprovinzen', *Rheinische Vierteljahresblätter*, vol 32 (1968).

Henning, Leopold 'Das Wesen und die Entwicklung der politischen Polizei in Berlin', *Mitteilungen des Vereins für die Geschichte Berlins*, 1925, Nr 7–9.

Herrmann, Ursula 'Der Kampf der Sozialdemokratie gegen das Dreiklassen-wahlrecht in Sachsen in den Jahren 1905/06', *Zeitschrift für die Geschichts-wissenschaft*, 1955, Heft 6.

Hesselbarth, Helmut *Revolutionäre Sozialdemokraten, Opportunisten und die Bauern am Vorabend des Imperialismus* (Berlin, 1968).

Hiller von Gaertringen, Friedrich Freiherr *Fürst Bülows Denkwürdigkeiten* (Tübingen, 1956).

Hintze, Otto *Gesammelte Abhandlungen*, ed. Gerhard Oestreich, 2nd edit., Bd 1–3:

Staat und Verfassung (Göttingen, 1962).

Soziologie und Geschichte (Göttingen, 1964).

Regierung und Verwaltung (Göttingen, 1967).

Hirsch, Paul *Der Weg der Sozialdemokratie zur Macht in Preußen* (Berlin, 1929).

Höhn, Reinhard *Die Armee als Erziehungsschule der Nation* (Bad Harzburg, 1963).

Die vaterlandslosen Gesellen (Cologne and Opladen, 1964).

Holtze Friedrich (ed.), *Fünfzig Jahre Preußischer Justiz 1851–1901* (Berlin, 1901).

Huber, Ernst Rudolf *Nationalstaat und Verfassungsstaat* (Stuttgart, 1965).

Deutsche Verfassungsgeschichte seit 1789, Bd iv (Stuttgart, 1969).

Hughes, H. S. *Consciousness and Society* (New York, 1961).

Hundert Jahre Deutsches Rechtsleben, 2 vols (Karlsruhe, 1960).

Hutten-Czapski, Count Bogdan *Sechzig Jahre Politik und Gesellschaft*, 2 vols (Berlin, 1936).

Iggers, Georg G. *The German Conception of History* (Middletown, Conn., 1968).

Jacob, Herbert *German Administration since Bismarck* (New Haven, Conn., 1963).

Jaeger, Hans *Unternehmer in der deutschen Politik 1890–1918* (Bonn, 1967).

Jantke, Carl *Der vierte Stand* (Freiburg i.B., 1955).

Jarausch, K. *The Enigmatic Chancellor: Bethmann-Hollweg* (New Haven, Conn., 1972).

Jensen, Jürgen *Presse und Politische Polizei* (Hannover, 1966).

Jilg, Gudrun *Der neue Kurs in der deutschen Presspolitik 1890–1914* (Diss. Vienna, 1959).

Johannsen, Harro *Der Revisionismus in der deutschen Sozialdemokratie 1890 bis 1914* (Diss. Hamburg, 1954).

Joll, James 'The 1914 Debate Continues', *Past and Present*, July 1966.

Journal of Contemporary History, 1, 3 (July 1966). [Issue on 1914.]

Kaelble, Hartmut *Industrielle Interessenpolitik in der Wilhelminischen Gesells-chaft, ZdI 1895–1914* (Berlin, 1967).

Kampffmeyer, Paul *Arbeiterbewegung und Sozialdemokratie* (Berlin, 1919).

Kanghi-Tschu, *Deutschland, der Kaiser und der Simplicissimus* (Munich, 1911).

Kantorowicz, Ludwig *Die sozialdemokratische Presse Deutschlands* (Tübingen, 1922).

Kaul, Friedrich Karl *So wahr mir Gott helfe*, 2nd edit., (Berlin, 1969).

Kautsky, Karl *Das Erfurter Programm* (Stuttgart, 1892).

Der Weg zur Macht (Hamburg, 1909).

Die Vernichtung der Sozialdemokratie durch den Gelehrten des Zentral-verbandes deutscher Industrieller (Berlin, 1911).

Kehr, Eckart *Der Primat der Innenpolitik*, ed. H.-U. Wehler (Berlin, 1970).

Keim, August *Erlestes und Erstrestes* (Hannover, 1925).

Kemper, Gerd Heinrich *Pressefreiheit und Polizei* (Berlin, 1964).

Kirchheimer, Otto *Political Justice* (Princeton, N.J., 1961).

Kitchen, Martin *The German Officer Corps 1890–1914* (Oxford, 1968).

Klein, Ernst 'Funktion und Bedeutung des Preußischen Staatsministeriums', *Jahrbuch für die Geschichte Mittel- und Ostdeutschlands*, Bd 9/10 (Tübingen, 1961).

Klein, Fritz 'Das Heranreifen einer politischen Krise in Deutschland am Vorabend des 1. Weltkrieges', *Zeitschrift für Geschichtswissenschaft*, 1955. Heft 4.

Koch, H. W. (ed.), *The Origins of the First World War* (London, 1972).

Koch, Max Jürgen *Die Bergarbeiterbewegung im Ruhrgebiet zur Zeit Wilhelms II 1889–1914* (Düsseldorf, 1957).

Kocka, Jürgen *Klassengesellschaft im Krieg. Deutsche Sozialgeschichte 1914–1918* (Göttingen, 1973).

Kolb, E. (ed.), *Vom Kaiserreich zur Weimarer Republik* (Cologne, 1972).

Koszyk, Kurt *Anfänge und frühe Entwicklung der sozialdemokratischen Presse im Ruhrgebiet 1875–1908* (Dortmund, 1953).

Deutsche Presse im 19. Jahrhundert (Berlin, 1966).

Die Presse der deutschen Sozialdemokratie (Hannover, 1967).

Deutsche Pressepolitik im Ersten Weltkrieg (Düsseldorf, 1968).

Kotowski, Georg, Werner Pöls, Gerhard A. Ritter (eds.), *Das wilhelminische Deutschland, Stimmen der Zeitgenossen* (Frankfurt a.M., 1965).

Kracke, Friedrich *Prinz und Kaiser. Wilhelm II im Urteil seiner Zeit* (Munich, 1960).

Krafft, Rudolf *Kasernen-Elend*, 4th edit., (Stuttgart, 1895).

Krieger, Leonard *The German Idea of Freedom* (Boston, 1957).

Krieger, Leonard and Fritz Stern (eds.), *The Responsibility of Power* (New York, 1967).

Kuczynski, Jürgen *Studien zur Geschichte des deutschen Imperialismus*, Bd 1/11 (Berlin, 1948/50).

Kuttner, Erich *Klassenjustiz* (Berlin, 1913).

Warum versagt die Justiz? (Berlin, 1921).

Labedz, Leopold (ed.), *Revisionism* (London, 1962).

Labusch, Lothar Franz *Die Entwicklung der deutschen Sozialdemokratie zur "konstitutionellen Oppositionspartei" 1890–1914* (Diss. Göttingen, 1956).

Lenman, Robin J. V. 'Art, Society and the Law in Wilhelmine Germany: the Lex Heinze', *Oxford German Studies*, No. 8 (Oxford, 1973).

Leuß, Hans *Wilhelm Freiherr von Hammerstein* (Berlin, 1905).

Lewinsohn, Richard *Das Geld in der Politik* (Berlin, 1931).

Lidtke, Vernon T. *The Outlawed Party. Social Democracy in Germany 1878–1890* (Princeton, N.J., 1966).

'Naturalism and Socialism', *The American Historical Review*, February 1974.

Liepmann, Moritz *Die Beleidigung* (Berlin, 1909).

Lipinski, Richard *Die Sozialdemokratie von ihren Anfängen bis zur Gegenwart* (Berlin, 1928).

Lobe, Adolf *Fünfzig Jahre Reichsgericht* (Leipzig, 1929).

Lothholz, Albrecht *Die Haltung der Sozialdemokratie in den Heeres- Flotten- und Weltmachtsfragen 1890–1914* (Diss. Freiburg i.B., 1958).

Manchester, William *Krupp. Zwölf Generationen* (Munich, 1968).

Masur, Gerhard *Prophets of Yesterday* (London, 1963).

Imperial Berlin (London, 1971).

Matthias, Erich 'Kautsky und der Kautskyanismus', *Marxismus-Studien*, 2. Folge (Tübingen, 1957).

Mayer, Paul *Bruno Schoenlank 1859–1901* (Hannover, 1971).

de Mendelssohn, Peter *Zeitungsstadt Berlin* (Berlin, 1959).

Menne, Bernhard *Krupp. Deutschlands Kanonenkönige* (Zürich, 1937).

Messerschmidt, Manfred *Zum Verhältnis von Militär und Politik in der Bismarckzeit und in der Wilhelminischen Ära* (Darmstadt, 1975).

Miersch, Hansjürgen *Die Arbeiterpresse der Jahre 1869 bis 1889 als Kampfmittel der österreichischen Sozialdemokratie* (Vienna, 1969).

Miller, Edmund *Ein Aufschrei mißhandelter Soldaten, deutscher Landeskinder*, 4th edit., (Stuttgart, 1892).

Miller, Susanne *Das Problem der Freiheit im Sozialismus* (Frankfurt a.M., 1964).

Molt, Peter *Der Reichstag vor der improvisierten Revolution* (Cologne and Opladen, 1963).

Mommsen, Wolfgang, J. *Max Weber und die deutsche Politik 1890–1920* (Tübingen, 1959).

Moring, Karl-Ernst *Die sozialdemokratische Partei in Bremen 1890–1914* (Diss. Hamburg, 1968).

Morsey, Rudolf *Die oberste Reichsverwaltung unter Bismarck 1867–1890* (Münster, 1957).

Zur Geschichte der obersten Reichsverwaltung im wilhelminischen Deutschland 1890–1900', *Deutsches Verwaltungsblatt*, 86 (1971).

Moses, John A. *The Politics of Illusion* (London, 1975).

Müller, Adolf *Fuchsmühl. Eine Skizze aus dem Rechtsstaat der Gegenwart* (Munich, 1895).

Nettl, J. P. 'The German Social Democratic Party 1890–1914', *Past and Present*, 30 (April 1965).

Rosa Luxemburg, 2 vols (London, 1966).

Nichols, J. Alden *Germany after Bismarck* (Cambridge, Mass., 1958).

Oberholtzer, E. P. *Die Beziehungen zwischen dem Staat und der Zeitungspresse im Deutschen Reich* (Berlin, 1895).

Olshausen, Justus *Kommentar zum Strafgesetzbuch für das Deutsche Reich*, 8th edit., (Berlin, 1909).

Pack, Wolfgang *Das parlamentarische Ringen um das Sozialistengesetz Bismarcks 1878–1890* (Düsseldorf, 1961).

Pikart, Eberhart 'Die Rolle der Parteien im Deutschen Konstitutionellen System vor 1914', *Zeitschrift für Politik*, XI (1962), Nr 1.

Pöls, Werner *Sozialistenfrage und Revolutionsfurcht in ihrem Zusammenhang mit den angeblichen Staatsstreichplänen Bismarcks* (Lübeck and Hamburg, 1960).

'Staat und Sozialdemokratie im Bismarckreich', *Jahrbuch für die Geschichte Mittel- und Ostdeutschlands*, Bd 13/14 (1965).

Pogge von Strandmann, Hartmut and Imanuel Geiß, *Die Erforderlichkeit des Unmöglichen* (Frankfurt a.M., 1965).

Preuss, Hugo *Staat, Recht und Freiheit* (Hildesheim, 1964).

Pross, Harry *Literatur und Politik* (Olten and Freiburg i.B., 1963).

Puhle, Hans-Jürgen *Agrarische Interessenpolitik und preußischer Konservatismus im wilhelminischen Reich 1893–1914* (Hannover, 1967).

Ratz, Ursula *Georg Ledebour 1850–1947* (Berlin, 1969).

Rau, Johannes *Der Sadismus in der Armee* (Berlin, 1904).

Reulecke, Jürgen (ed.), *Arbeiterbewegung an Rhein und Ruhr* (Wuppertal, 1974).

Reynold, Heinrich (ed.), *Justiz und Öffentlichkeit* (Cologne and Berlin, 1966).

Rich, Norman *Friedrich von Holstein*, 2 vols (Cambridge, 1965).

Richter, Günter *Friedrich von Holstein* (Göttingen, 1969).

Rieger, Isolde *Die wilhelminische Presse im Überblick 1888–1918* (Munich, 1957).

Ringer, Fritz K. 'Higher Education in Germany in the 19th Century', *Journal of Contemporary History*, 1967, 3.

The Decline of the German Mandarins (Cambridge, Mass., 1969).

Ritter, Gerhard A. *Die Arbeiterbewegung im Wilhelminischen Reich 1890–1900* (Berlin, 1959).

Ritter, Gerhard *The Sword and the Sceptre: The Problem of Militarism in Germany*, 4 vols (London, 1967–74).

Röhl, John C. G. 'The Disintegration of the Kartell and the Politics of Bismarck's Fall from Power 1887–1890', *Historical Journal*, XI (1966).

'Staatsstreichplan oder Staatsstreichbereitschaft? Bismarcks Politik in der Entlassungskrise', *Historische Zeitschrift*, 203 (1966).

'Higher Civil Servants in Germany 1890–1900', *Journal of Contemporary History*, 1967, 3.

Germany without Bismarck (London, 1967).

Rogge, Helmuth *Holstein und Harden* (Munich, 1959).

'Die Kladderadatsch-Affäre', *Historische Zeitschrift*, 195 (1962).

'Affairen im Kaiserreich', *Die politische Meinung* (February, 1963).

Roscher, Gustav *Großstadtpolizei* (Hamburg, 1912).

Roscher, Werner *Vaterstadt und Elternhaus* (Limited Edition, Hamburg, 1959).

Rosenberg, Arthur *Die Entstehung der deutschen Republik 1871–1918* (Berlin, 1928).

Geschichte der deutschen Republik (Karlsbad, 1935).

Demokratie und Sozialismus (Frankfurt a.M., 1962).

Roth, Eugen (ed.), *Simplicissimus* (Hannover, 1954).

Roth, Guenther *The Social Democrats in Imperial Germany* (Totowa, N.J., 1963).

Rückel, Gert *Die Fränkische Tagespost* (Nuremberg, 1964).

Runge, Wolfgang *Politik und Beamtentum im Parteienstaat* (Stuttgart, 1965).

Ryder, A. J. *The German Revolution of 1918* (Cambridge, 1967).

Saul, Klaus 'Der "Deutsche Kriegerbund". Zur Innenpolitischen Funktion eines "nationalen" Verbandes im kaiserlichen Deutschland', *Militärgeschichtliche Mitteilungen*, 2/1969.

'Der Kampf um die Jugend zwischen Volksschule und Kaserne', *Militärgeschichtliche Mitteilungen*, 1/1971.

'Der Staat und die "Mächte des Umsturzes"', *Archiv für Sozialgeschichte*, Bd XII (Hannover, 1972).

Staat, Industrie, Arbeiterbewegung im Kaiserreich (Düsseldorf, 1974).

Schadt, Jörg *Die Sozialdemokratische Partei in Baden von den Anfängen bis zur Jahrhundertwende 1868–1900* (Diss. Heidelberg, 1966).

Schaefer, Jürgen W. *Kanzlerbild und Kanzlermythos in der Zeit des "Neuen Curses"* (Paderborn, 1973).

Schenk, Erwin *Der Fall Zabern* (Stuttgart, 1927).

Scheschkewitz, Jürgen (ed.), *Geschichtsschreibung* (Düsseldorf, 1968).

Schieder, Theodor *The State and Society in our Time* (London, 1962).

Schleifstein, Josef *Franz Mehring* (Berlin, 1959).

Schlemmer, Hannelore *Die Rolle der Sozialdemokratie in den Landtagen Badens und Württembergs und ihr Einfluß auf die Entwicklung der Gesamtpartei zwischen 1890 und 1914* (Diss. Freiburg i.B., 1953).

Schmidt-Küster, Gustav (ed.), *Ein Leben für das politische Buch* (Hannover, 1963).

Schneidt, Karl *Die Magdeburger Majestätsbeleidigungsprozesse* (Berlin, 1899).
Schnorbus, Axel *Arbeit und Sozialordnung in Bayern vor dem Ersten Weltkrieg* (Munich, 1969).
Schöler, Hermann *Militärische Schreckensbilder in Friedenszeiten* (Stuttgart, 1895).
Schöne, Siegfried *Von der Reichskanzlei zum Bundeskanzleramt* (Berlin, 1968).
Schorske, Carl E. *German Social Democracy 1905–17* (Cambridge, Mass., 1955).
Schosser, Erich *Presse und Landtag in Bayern von 1850 bis 1918* (Munich, 1968).
Schraepler, Ernst *August Bebel* (Göttingen, 1966).
Schröder, Emilie *Ein Tagebuch Kaiser Wilhelms II* (Breslau, 1903).
Schröder, Wilhelm *Das persönliche Regiment* (Munich, 1907).
Schüddekopf, Otto Ernst 'Der Revolution entgegen: Materialien und Dokumente zur Geschichte des linken Flügels der deutschen Sozialdemokratie vor dem 1. Weltkrieg', *Archiv für Sozialgeschichte*, Bd IX (Hannover, 1969).
Schüssler, Wilhelm *Die Daily Telegraph Affäre* (Göttingen, 1952).
Kaiser Wilhelm II, 2nd edit., (Göttingen, 1962).
Schult, Johannes *Geschichte der Hamburger Arbeiter 1890–1919* (Hannover, 1967).
Schultze, D. *Was trennt uns von der Sozialdemokratie?* (Leipzig, 1895).
Schulz, Ursula *Friedrich Ebert in Bremen* (Bremen, 1963).
Schuster, Dieter *Das preußische Dreiklassenwahlrecht, der politische Streik und die deutsche Sozialdemokratie bis zum Jahr 1914* (Diss. Bonn, 1958).
Severing, Carl *Mein Lebensweg* (Cologne, 1950).
Sheehan, James H. (ed.), *Imperial Germany* (New Viewpoints, 1976).
Sievers, Kai Detlev *Die Köllerpolitik und ihr Echo in der deutschen Presse 1897–1901* (Neumünster, 1964).
Sieger, Walter *Das erste Jahrzehnt der deutschen Arbeiterjugendbewegung* (Berlin, 1958).
Silverman, D. P. *Reluctant Union. Alsace-Lorraine and Imperial Germany 1871–1918* (University Park, Pa., 1972).
Skriver, Ansgar *Gotteslästerung* (Hamburg, 1962).
Smith, Alson Jesse *In Preußen keine Pompadour* (Stuttgart, 1965).
Soell, Hartmut *Die sozialdemokratische Arbeiterbewegung im Reichsland Elsaß-Lothringen 1872–1918* (Diss. Heidelberg, 1963).
'Spectator', *Prince Bülow and the Kaiser* (London, 1931).
Stampfer, Friedrich *Erfahrungen und Erkenntnisse* (Cologne, 1957).
Stegmann, Dirk *Bismarcks Erben. Parteien und Verbände in der Spätphase des wilhelminischen Deutschlands. Sammlungspolitik 1897–1918* (Düsseldorf, 1970).
Steinberg, Jonathan 'The Case of Herr Fritz Krupp', *Midstream* (New York), November 1967.
Stenkewitz, Kurt *Gegen Bajonett und Dividende* (Berlin, 1960).
Immer feste druff (Berlin, 1962).
Stern, Fritz *The Politics of Cultural Despair* (New York, 1965).
Stern-Rubarth, Edgar *Die Propaganda als politisches Instrument*, 2nd edit., (Berlin, 1921).
Stümke, Bruno *Die Entstehung der deutschen Republik* (Frankfurt a.M., 1923).
Stürmer, Michael 'Staatsstreichgedanken im Bismarckreich', *Historische Zeitschrift*, 209 (1969).
'Machtgefüge und Verbandsentwicklung im wilhelminischen Deutschland', *Neue Politische Literatur*, 1969.

(ed.), *Das kaiserliche Deutschland* (Düsseldorf, 1970).
Regierung und Reichstag im Bismarckreich 1871–1880 (Düsseldorf, 1974).
Taube, Utz-Friedebert *Ludwig Quidde* (Kallmünz, Opf., 1963).
Teschner, Hellmut *Die Daily-Telegraph-Affäre von November 1908 in der Beurteilung der öffentlichen Meinung* (Diss. Breslau, 1931).
Thimme, Annelise *Hans Delbrück als Kritiker der wilhelminischen Epoche* (Düsseldorf, 1955).
Thimme, Friedrich (ed.), *Front wider Bülow* (Munich, 1931).
Tönnies, Ferdinand *Der Kampf um das Sozialistengesetz* (Berlin, 1929).
Tresckow, Hans von *Von Fürsten und anderen Sterblichen* (Berlin, 1922).
Tuchman, Barbara *The Proud Tower* (London, 1966).
Ullrich, Volker 'Emanzipation durch Integration?', *Das Argument*, 75 (1972).
Varain, Hans Josef *Freie Gewerkschaften, Sozialdemokratie und Staat* (Düsseldorf, 1956).
Victor, Max 'Die Stellung der deutschen Sozialdemokratie zu den Fragen der auswärtigen Politik 1869–1914', *Archiv für Sozialwissenschaft und Sozialpolitik*, Vol 60 (1928).
Vietsch, Eberhard von *Bethmann Hollweg* (Boppard, 1969).
Vogel, Walter 'Die Organisation der amtlichen Presse- und Propagandapolitik des Deutschen Reiches', *Zeitungswissenschaft*, 8/9 (1941), Sonderheft.
Volkmann, E. O. *Der Marxismus und das deutsche Heer im Weltkriege* (Berlin, 1925).
Wachenheim, Hedwig *Die deutsche Arbeiterbewegung 1844 bis 1914* (Cologne and Opladen, 1967).
Warren, Donald Jnr. *The Red Kingdom of Saxony* (The Hague, 1964).
Wehler, Hans-Ulrich (ed.), *Moderne deutsche Sozialgeschichte*, 2nd edit. (Cologne and Berlin, 1968).
Krisenherde des Kaiserreichs 1871–1918 (Göttingen, 1970).
Sozialdemokratie und Nationalstaat 1840–1914, 2nd edit. (Göttingen, 1971).
Das deutsche Kaiserreich 1871–1918 (Göttingen, 1973).
Weinberger, Gerda 'Die deutsche Sozialdemokratie und die Kolonialpolitik', *Zeitschrift für Geschichtswissenschaft*, 1967, Heft 3.
Weiss, Andreas von *Die Diskussion über den historischen Materialismus in der Sozialdemokratie 1891–1918* (Wiesbaden, 1965).
Weiß, Bernhard *Polizei und Politik* (Berlin, 1928).
Weller, B. Uwe *Maximilian Harden und die "Zukunft"* (Bremen, 1970).
Wendel, Friedrich *Wilhelm II in der Karikatur* (Dresden, 1928).
Wendel, Hermann *Zabern! Militäranarchie und Militärjustiz* (Frankfurt a.M., 1914).
Wernecke, Klaus *Der Wille zur Weltgeltung* (Düsseldorf, 1970).
Westarp, Kuno Graf *Konservative Politik im letzten Jahrzehnt des Kaiserreiches* (Berlin, 1935).
Wetzel, Hans-Wolfgang. *Presseinnenpolitik im Bismarckreich 1874–1890* (Bern and Frankfurt a.M., 1975).
Wile, Frederick William *Men around the Kaiser* (London, 1913).
Wilke, Ekkehard-Teja P. W. *Political Decadence in Imperial Germany. Personnel-Political Aspects of the German Government Crisis 1894–97* (Illinois, 1976).
Winckelmann, Johannes (ed.) *Max Webers Gesammelte Politische Schriften* (Tübingen, 1971).
Witt, Peter-Christian *Die Finanzpolitik des Deutschen Reiches* (Hamburg and Lübeck, 1970).

Wittwer, Walter *Streit um Schicksalsfragen. Die deutsche Sozialdemokratie zu Krieg und Vaterlandsverteidigung 1907–1914* (Berlin, 1964).

Young, Harry F. *Maximilian Harden* (Münster, 1971).

Zechlin, Egmont *Staatsstreichpläne Bismarcks und Wilhelms II 1890–1911* (Stuttgart and Berlin, 1929).

'Bethmann Hollweg, Kriegsrisiko und SPD 1914', *Der Monat*, January 1966.

Zimmermann, Adolf (ed.) *Prozeß Brandt und Genossen* (Berlin, 1914).

Zippel, Friedrich *Kritik der deutschen Öffentlichkeit an der Person und an der Monarchie Wilhelms II bis zum Ausbruch des Weltkrieges* (Diss. F.U. Berlin, 1952).

Zmarzlik, Hans-Günter *Bethmann Hollweg als Reichskanzler 1909–1914* (Düsseldorf, 1957).

Zobeltitz, Fedor von *Chronik der Gesellschaft unter dem letzten Kaiserreich*, 2 vols (Hamburg, 1922).

INDEX